A Message from Lockport

Lockport Savings Bank was founded, in the newly designated city of Lockport, NY, in 1870. Fifteen citizens, seeing a need for a bank for the people, established the Farmers and Mechanics Savings Bank. Our incorporation by the New York State Legislature stated our purpose to be the promotion of thrift; and to help secure financial stability for community members.

Lockport Savings Bank has always been proud of its roots in Lockport, and the fact that our origin can be traced specifically to the Erie Canal. Our founding philosophy was reflective of the needs that were created from the tremendous growth the Lockport community experienced over 120 years ago because of the canal. The canal provided the area with inexpensive transportation and water power, attracting many industries and creating a population explosion. Our formation closely followed the birth of the City of Lockport and throughout the bank's history there have been deep ties to the people we serve.

We understand the people of Western New York. Our customers tell us that our strength and stability is comforting to them. The tradition we have set, was a standard that was shared by many financial institutions. Unfortunately very few remain today. Keeping pace with new regulations, lifestyles and business opportunities hasn't been easy. We have tried hard to balance the dynamics of change while staying true to our traditions and founding philosophy. Our growth has been earned a customer at a time -- all Western New Yorkers -- the people we know best. We have stuck to the basics, contained our growth to Western New York, and have tried not to lose sight of what has made us successful.

Corporate citizenship, through community enrichment, is an element of Lockport Savings Bank's mission statement we feel a strong commitment to. Providing financial support to Canisius College and the Western New York Heritage Institute for this new edition of CANAL WATER AND WHISKEY demonstrates our continued commitment to the communities we serve. Revenues derived from the sale of this book will enable the Western New York Heritage Institute to develop additional curricula and resource materials that are desperately needed by educators. The funding of this project helps show our appreciation to the Western New York community for helping us prosper. Educating and recording the rich heritage of the Erie Canal and its role in helping to build what Western New York is today, is something we take pride in being a part of.

The Erie Canal's relevance to our area is obvious but our story as a successful, enduring savings bank, based and founded in Lockport, is historical in itself. This cooperative publishing project will serve as a visible reminder to all of Western New York that the Lockport Savings Bank is committed to education and enhancing the image of our Western New York community.

William E. Swan
President and Chief Executive Officer
Lockport Savings Bank

CANAL WATER AND WHISKEY
Tall Tales from the Erie Canal Country

by

MARVIN A. RAPP

* Fogelsanger Award Recipient for
outstanding contributions to the
Fields of Education and History
-- Shippensburg, PA 1965

* Friends of Reading Society -- Author Award
Recognition for best seller book, Canal Water and Whiskey
 -- Syracuse, NY 1968

* New York Author's League -- Certificate of Award
For contributions as "Author, Poet, Educator, Lecturer and
Historian"
-- Syracuse, NY 1969

Illustrated by:

Fred Johnson, Canandaigua, NY (cover)
Peggy J. Fisher-Pajak, Buffalo, NY
Norman Truesdale, Buffalo, NY

Western New York Heritage Institute
Canisius College, Buffalo, NY

The Heritage Press
Western New York Heritage Insititute
Canisius College
2001 Main Street
Buffalo, New York 14208

Rapp, Marvin A., 1914-
  Canal water and whiskey; tall tales of the Erie Canal country
    by Marvin A. Rapp

ISBN: 1-878097-07-5

Printed in the United States of America

This book is dedicated to the Irish of South Buffalo (and wherever) who brought joy to my life and to lovers of laughter who, like myself, were not lucky enough to be born Irish.

May the road rise up to meet you and may the wind be always at your back. May the Lord hold you in the hollow of His hand and may you be in Heaven a half hour before the Devil knows you're dead.

CANAL WATER AND WHISKEY

Tall Tales from the Erie Canal Country

TABLE OF CONTENTS

IV. WHORES, WASTRELS AND WATERFRONT GUERRILLAS 99

V. CANAL ENTERTAINMENT 135

FORWARD

A traveler along the route from the Hudson to Lake Erie can still visit, here and there, the choice remains of New York's once incomparable canals. Few who come upon these aging stone locks and tumbled aqueducts actually view them for what they really are -- our Nation's pyramids.

From its very beginnings, the Erie Canal, a project of tremendous imagination and ingenuity, had the makings of myth and folklore. This canal proved bigger than life. Its dimensions staggered the imagination. It vibrated with the gusto and exuberance of a young and confident nation. Certainly to the people of the nineteenth century, the Canal was a catalyst for heroic actions. It encouraged renewed visions of an empire.

There are many different ways to relate the old Canal's story. Some scholars focus on the political struggle that preceded it. Some proudly proclaim it a technological triumph -- a prime example of Yankee ingenuity. Some enumerate its profound economic consequences. Marvin A. Rapp is more concerned with the lives and the lore of the people the Erie touched and shaped.

Many times in his distinguished career as an educator and scholar, Dr. Rapp has received recognition for his contributions to New York State and American History. Canal Water and Whiskey, however, is not written as a tightly drawn historical tome. It is, instead, the prized collection of a proud connoisseur.

Rapp pursued stories on the Old Erie and the Buffalo waterfront like others sought rare prints, porcelain figurines or period furniture. His treasures of historical vignettes, tall tales, poems, songs and other materials has much in common with a box of old glass-plate photographs. It provides evidence of a world now all but vanished. As we thumb through it, that world springs back to life.

And what a life this was! We meet the people of the Erie -- warts and all. Rapp is not interested only in their experience. He recaptures their vision. He records for us their song.

The first publication of this material in a single volume came out in 1965. In this new compilation, published by the Western New York Heritage Institute at Canisius College, he rearranges and expands his earlier effort. Here we see the imprisoned debtor, Jesse Hawley, setting down on paper wild ideas for a water route across the State. Here we see local farmers along with crews of immigrant workers "diggin" their ditch through "gravel, mud and slime." Here, too, are their ghosts and their leprechauns, their miraculous frogs and their collicky mules.

Who can forget the brutalized little orphan boys, commandeered to drive the canal-boat teams; and who can forget the incomparable Kitty and her cohorts who entertained rambunctious "Canawlers" in the promised land at the end of the line.

The great Canal brought on massive problems of growth and change -- but is also inspired creativity in almost every form of human endeavor. If there are only a few tangible remains of the Erie today, Rapp's effort to seek out and record the stories has helped us understand their special meaning. Bold dreams are still well worth pursuing.

Orrin Lehman, Commissioner
New York State Office of Parks,
Recreation and Historic Preservation

INTRODUCTION

Canal Water and Whiskey is the fourth publication of The Western New York Heritage Institute of Canisius College. Preparing and publishing our three earlier books gave us pride and satisfaction, but nothing to date can compare to the pleasures and rewards all of us have experienced in bringing this book to press.

First, there was the realization that this was a most important book because the Erie Canal was not only important in the history of Buffalo -- it was very important in the history of New York State, and it was of vital importance to the growth of this entire nation. This was a story that had to be told, and told again.

Of course, the history of the Canal has been told over and over again. No textbook in American History would be complete without one version or another of "Clinton's Folly," but no historian has ever regaled us with such informative and charming essays, or tales, as Dr. Marvin Rapp.

This was the second reason for our satisfaction. Marvin Rapp is a most distinguished historian and educator. More importantly he is a delightful gentleman without peer: no person has so many wonderful tales to tell; no person tells them so well.

Canisius College and The Western New York Heritage Institute are indebted to Dr. Rapp for permitting us to publish this revised and expanded classic. To those of you who will read this book, we wish you the boundless pleasure we enjoyed in preparing it, and we implore you to share these historical gems with friends and loved ones of all ages.

The Canal, as we knew it, is long gone. Almost all the men and women who worked it or lived on it are also gone now. However, in the pages of Canal Water and Whiskey they spring to life almost magically. Enjoy.

J. David Valaik, Ph.D.
Professor of History
Director, Western New York Heritage Institute
Canisius College

TO TELL THE TALE
(circa 1880)

I've travelled all around this world and Tonawanda too.
Was cast on desert islands and beaten black and blue.
I fought and bled at Bull's Run and wandered since a boy
But I'll never forget the trip I took from Buffalo to Troy.
For it was tramp, tramp, tramp, and tighten in your lines.
And watch the playful flies, as o'er the mules they climb.
Whoa, back! Get up! Forget it I never shall,
When I drove a team of spavined mules on the Erie Canal.

The cook we had on board the deck stood six feet in her
socks,
Her hand was like an elephant's ear, and her breath would
open the locks.
A maid of sixty summers was she, who slept upon the floor,
And when at night she'd get to sleep, oh sufferin', how
she'd snore!

One night on the Erie, I couldn't sleep a wink,
The crew were all bored down on me, because I refused to
drink.
Fearful storms and heavy fogs, forget it I never shall,
But I'm every inch a sailor there, on the Erie Canal.

When we arrived in Buffalo, Sally, Jack and Hank,
We greased ourselves in tallow fat, and slid right off the
plank.
Sally's in the poorhouse, and the rest of the crew's in jail,
And I'm the only son of the ditch that's left to tell the tale.

Sung by:

Henry "Kip" Conway
Morrisburg, Ontario

Johnny Bartley
Alhambra Varieties
Commercial Street
Buffalo, N.Y.

BOTTOMING OUT
(The Original)

Sounds strange, doesn't it? "Bottoming out?" For congenial drinkers, it probably should be "bottoms up," "down the hatch," or "drain the glasses, boy!" But to all Canawlers (as the Irish called those who worked the Erie Canal) "bottoming out" meant draining the Canal in autumn, followed by an annual ritual of spring -- cleaning the Erie Canal for the start of a new season. Dried to the bottom mud was the accumulated debris dumped into the canal during the year: bottles and jugs, garbage and junk, dead mules and horses, dogs and crayfish, cats and catfish -- and bodies, in whole or in part -- the assorted refuse of canal life and death. It was all fair game for the canal scroungers. What they left behind became the "kitchen middens" of canal archeology -- probably the most worthless part of canal remains.

The stories that follow are a kind of "bottoming out" of New York State life along the Erie Canal -- a collection of folklore stories, tall tales, anecdotes, newspaper squibs and folk songs, the flotsam and jetsam of the canal era that belonged not to New York State alone but to the whole country, and indeed to the whole world. These tales are probably not the best. The best have probably long since been forgotten -- dying with the dead. They are certainly not the worst, for the worst probably couldn't be told. These are the mild "left-overs" that came from Canawlers who were over 90 in my boyhood and whose fathers remembered the early canal. What the real stories must have been will probably never be known. One thing was certain, life was hard on the canal; so was the stuff some of them drank. But there was tradition with it.

Long before the Erie Canal -- in the 18th century days of the French and Indians and even before New York was a State -- Lake Champlain, the St. Lawrence River, Lake Ontario, the Niagara River and the upper Great Lakes formed the water lifeline of the fur trade, basic to the economy of America and the world. Its life blood was whiskey, rum and brandy. The spirits flowed abundantly but not freely. As a wag once said, "A belt was worth a pelt." Perhaps this was the way of the wilderness world.

Scientists claim water is older than man and largely responsible for his being; tipplers assert "whiskey is as old as sin and largely responsible for its being." They believed that if water made life possible, whiskey and other spirits made it tolerable. When, in 1825, the Erie Canal joined the lakes and the oceans, the addition of canal water to lake, river and ocean water created a revolution in the internal commerce of the United States.

These waters met at the Niagara Frontier. So did the men who sailed them. To watermen and their women, these canal waters were their daily bread. To not a few, whiskey was their daily spice; and life was a day to day combination of both. The water floated

3

their boats; the whiskey their spirits. So from the shores of the canal, and especially from the Niagara country, washed by the water of the river, the lake and the canal came many of these lusty stories. Probably, many of the watermen and their families led ordinary sober, even pious, lives. But they never made the stories that were told.

The flavor of most of these stories is Irish. It is a rich flavor, too. A richness that comes from people of deep feeling, of laughter and sadness, of wit and wisdom, of affection and hard work, of religion and politics. Wherever the Irish have gone in the world, the leprechauns, hobgoblins and all their spirits have followed them faithfully. They have touched each spot in the world with the magic of their stories. The Irish are natural storymakers and storytellers. The joy of my youth was listening to my Irish neighbors spin these tales as I sat near the stoves in their kitchens or on the wharves of the waterfront. In fact, it was not until I was ten that I learned, to my disappointment, that I was not Irish. I had assumed that my name had lost its O' and my church some of its statuary and furniture. I do not think I ever quite forgave my parents for not being Irish. But then, in this world, you can't have everything.

But I did have a wonderful Grampa. What a man he was. To me, he ran the waterfront. Actually, I guess, he ran the Buffalo Creek Railroad. And it kept the waterfront running. I shall never forget the day the Buffalo "Crick" and the waterfront shut down for 17 minutes, all because of me, age 11, and my Grampa full of years.

I had come down to his shanty and freight office with my father to pick him up at the day's end. As soon as we appeared in the door, things exploded. He shouted orders out the open window behind his back, grabbed several telephones all at once and sent several men in the office flying out of the door with orders. I stood there completely awed, for Grandfather at home was the gentlest of souls. Soon all of the engineers, firemen, brakemen, conductors, dock wallopers and laborers of the railroad filed into the shanty and freight shed. In strong words, Gramps told them to be quiet, grabbed me under the arms, swung me up on top of the desk and said: "Son, tell them that story you spoke at school."

Grandfather was referring to a homework assignment which called for me to write a story, memorize it and deliver it to the class. As soon as I started to talk, I got over my fright. When I had finished they clapped and yelled, "More." So as a last full measure of devotion I threw in the "Gettysburg Address." They liked that also. I shall never forget how proud my Gramps was of me that day. My sixth grade was big, very big, to him for he had no education. When I jumped down from the desk, the men crowded about me and started telling me their stories. What stories they were. They told them in rich dialect and expression even taking the

4

part of the various characters of the story. Perhaps this is the reason why story-telling of this kind has been a hobby and not a vocation with me.

While I continued my education through Colgate and Duke Universities, the waterfront and Canal always drew me back. In my college days I worked on the docks. I wrote my master's and doctorate on the Port of Buffalo. After World War II, on vacations and weekends, over more than a decade, I walked the entire length of the Canal from Buffalo to Albany.

In the middle fifties I took a leave of absence from my teaching duties at the State University College at Buffalo to head the Port Division for the City. Now, like Grampa, I "ran" the waterfront. To meet the challenge of the St. Lawrence Seaway, I helped to develop the Niagara Frontier Port Authority. Later in Albany, as Consultant to the Joint Legislative Committee on the Preservation and Restoration of Historic Sites and the Erie Canal, I sailed the full length of the Canal. Out of that Committee came the recommendation of recreating Canal Town at Fort Hunter.

From all these sources, up and down the Canal, I heard many stories. These are but a few.

When you read these stories, read them aloud -- catch the cadence -- for they were in the beginning "told" stories, not written stories. I never intended to publish them. I wrote them down because they were fun and told them because people seemed to enjoy hearing them.

Then one day a great man and dear friend found out about my stories. His name is Harold Thompson. More than anyone else he is the father of folklore in New York State -- author of <u>Body, Boots and Britches</u>. At the time he was editor of the "New York State Folklore Quarterly." He asked me to send some of these stories to him and I did. Soon I was sending more and more. Most of these have appeared in his and other folklore journals.

For me these stories have been fun. But the most fun has been working with the truly great storytellers and folk singers of New York State: Carl Carmer, Louis Jones, Frank Warner, Harold Thompson, Walter Edmonds, Moritz Jagendorf, Bill Tyrrell, Dave Ennis, Al Gayer, Ben Botkin, Helen Fraser, Lionel Wyld, Grace Hudowalski, Barbara and Warren Walker, John Sprague, Bill Fenton, Charlie Gosnell, Charlie Snyder, Harvey Chalmers, Jared van Wagenen, Eric Faigle, Dick Wright, DeWitt Clinton (that's right), Cliff Lord, Margaret Fess, Aggie Underwood, I. Frank Mogavero, Walter Dunn, Les Smith, Walter McCauland, Blake McKelvey, Bob Rose, Bill Cleary, Arnold Barben, Jeanne Schwartz, Ruth Rubin, Millie Taylor, Dan Button, Bob Rayback, Hugh Flick, Jim Frost, Bill Fink, Emily Madden, Eric Brunger, Arch Merrill, Edith Cutting, Harry Douglas, Jeannette Edwards Rattray, Herb Wisbey, Chuck Wallis, all my waterfront workers and all the Canal Society Canawlers. Special acknowledgment and

thanks go to Sam Sesskin. I am also grateful to my good friend
Helen A. Fraser, Secretary of the New York Folklore Society and
one of the best folklorists in the country, for doing the index. The
wonderful illustrations are by Dr. Norman Truesdale, a professor of
art (and a damned good one) at the State University College at
Buffalo.

To all of them, but most especially to Samuel Hopkins
Adams, these stories are dedicated. Sam Adams was a great man
and a close friend. He loved the Canal as I do. He served as one of
my lecturers at the Canal Seminars, Cooperstown, in the summer of
1957. His book, The Erie Canal, was a joy to children; his
Grandfather Stories to all, young and old. Sam has gone now but
he will never really leave us.

On the last day of the Cooperstown seminars, I wrote some
doggerel to Sam Adams which Dave Ennis, Al Gayer and I gave to
him. Here it is:

"CAPTAIN SAM"

Here's a toast to Captain Sam
Of Adam's Basin where bullheads jam;
A boater from the Old Canal
Sam Adams knew its good old Sal.

With pen and ink and paper stock
He wrote its story, lock by lock;
So none who read would ere forget
To Erie's water, our endless debt.

We who traveled on this way
Will n'er forget his wit so gay;
His kindness, patience without end
Sam Adams-our Canawler friend.

He was pleased, and I was glad. Some time later I asked
him if his grandfather had really told him all of those stories in his
book. With a twinkle in his eye, he just smiled and sipped his
bourbon -- that was a picture that will never fade.

These stories are, of course, not history. They're probably
not folklore because I am not exactly sure what folklore is, although
there are many who think they know. They're just stories. I hope
you enjoy reading them as much as I enjoyed finding them, hearing
them and then writing them down. Now read on -- and please --
aloud.

MORE BOTTOMING OUT

Since the original preface, "Bottoming Out," was written in the middle of the 1960s, much water has gently flowed under the low bridges and much whiskey joyfully over the bars, of the Erie Canal. Since then, "More Bottoming Out" of Erie Canal remembrances and records has uncovered many more of its storied treasures.

Despite the fact that this world has spun around many times since I first heard and read some of these stories spoken and written by people who, a century before, had lived them, the fascination with the Erie still remains with me more strongly than ever. As I wrote in the first preface, I hope these stories from the Erie Canal Country of America will interest, enlighten and amuse you as much as they have me.

I debated a long time with myself about writing this second preface. One ought to be enough. Most people ignore prefaces. They find them dull and boring, because they often are dull and boring; not unlike the endless film Oscar "thank yous" and the breathless non-explanations by the winners as to why they won. But that's movie-land and this is canal-land.

I thought, however, it might be worthwhile before you read these stories and sang these songs, if I had a kind of "off the record" chat with you; a kind of get acquainted moment, so that you'll know a little bit more about me (not that that's so important) and some more of how this book came to be. In what follows, I have tried to set the scene for these stories. I have also interwoven the Canal within the context of my own life.

Since the first publication of <u>Canal Water and Whiskey</u> in the "screaming sixties," a lot more drainin' and diggin' and a little more drinkin' has "bottomed out" more "Canal-a-bilia" from the Erie Canal Country -- a land by its impact not restricted to the small prism of the canal. This new book contains all of the stories from the first book plus a third more material.

Throughout all the many changes in my life and the tumultuous changes in America and the world during the 20th Century, the Canal has flowed steadily and irresistibly like a stream of consciousness through my life.

From the very beginning these canal waters have seemed to hold me in an almost hypnotic spell. I think I understand why. Perhaps, this second preface will help to explain a little more clearly the critical influence of the Canal on my life, and indeed, my life on the canal.

What follows here are separate jigsaw pieces which, when fitted together, form a mosaic of my life as it relates to history and the Canal. So this preface might even be called the making of a book as well as the making of an historian -- the making of a book. It will, I hope, show you where I'm coming from or better still,

7

where I came from so that you will have some idea of the matrix out of which these stories emerged.

To me you really can't separate the writer from the person and his life. All of us, writer or whatever, seem to be the sum total of experiences and stimuli playing inter-actionally on our being (or, for the academically inclined) on our DNA programming. This impacts on all of us, but most especially on teachers and writers.

Looking back from almost four score years, there seems to have been a destiny and design to what evolved in my life. If indeed there was, it has taken almost those 80 years for me to realize it.

I was born in a rented upstairs flat on Abbott Road in South Buffalo. The house almost overlooked Cazenovia Creek, a tributary of Buffalo Creek (later dignified after dredging and straightening as Buffalo River.) In its serpentine course, it finally emptied into Lake Erie. There it formed itself with the help of men, into the Buffalo harbor which became the western terminus of the Grand Canal.

In a sense, here on the Buffalo waterfront, the American West began. For at least 50 years after the opening of the Canal, thousands of immigrants and emigrants travelled west on the Canal from New England, Old England and Europe, transferring at Canal and Commercial Streets in Buffalo to sloops, schooners and steamers for a 1000-mile trip westward through the Great Lakes. Here was America on the move and here was America in the making. In those years, these waterways became the most important link in the westward movement; an historic force that helped to define America and Americans. Here I grew up, surrounded by history on all sides with a feeling that this is where it all happened.

Cazenovia Creek was only a small part of that vast waterway system. As a kid, I swam in that "crick" (polluted as it was) at "Ashman's," "The Trestle" and the "Log," which were names for our favorite swimming holes. These "Huckleberry" days were a fun reality for me, long before I fully sensed the significance of the "crick" or its relationship to the Buffalo River, the City of Buffalo, the Great Lakes, the Erie Canal, "York" State and America.

Little did I realize in those carefree and halcyon days how much these waters would influence my whole life. To get philosophical, or perhaps psychological, humans have an unconscious affinity for water because of the chemical composition of the body. (That's really beyond me.) Over the years no matter where life has taken me, these waters have always seemed to draw me back and nourish my "inner" self. If that sounds mystical, perhaps it is. But I apologize not . Isn't folklore kind of mystical?

Born on the Abbott Road side of Cazenovia "Crick," I grew up across the creek on the Seneca Street side. We lived in many houses on as many streets within a less than ten block area: Seneca Parkside, Dismonda, Indian Church Road, Duerstein Street,

8

Hillside Avenue and Buffum Street. This whole area abutted the old Buffalo Seneca Indian Reservation where the Seneca Nation (Keepers of the Western Gate) had settled after being militarily forced out by the Sullivan-Clinton campaign of the American Revolution from their chosen birthplace on and around Canandaigua Lake.

The Buffalo Reservation was probably the only place on the flat Lake Erie plain which had enough of a rise to be called a hill. For the Seneca, I'm sure, this was only slightly reminiscent of the robust hills around Canandaigua Lake, where their nation had been born. By their Iroquois brethren they were called "People of the Hill."

Much of my boyhood was spent playing in Seneca Indian Park which was originally a Native-American burial ground before the remains were moved elsewhere. In the park near homeplate of our makeshift baseball diamond was a large boulder with a bronze plaque memorializing the burial of Red Jacket, a great leader of the Seneca and Mary Jemison, the "White Woman of the Genesee" and many other Native Americans. The huge stone has since been placed on a knoll that slopes up from our former baseball field. Originally, many of the Seneca had been buried along that slight ridge beneath the "spreading" chestnut trees.

Diagonally across Buffum Street from the park, and directly across the street from where I lived for a number of years at #111, the Seneca had their Mission House. There, they held their meetings. There, treaties were made. And there, missionaries first translated the Bible into Seneca.

One day, while School 70 (now the Indian Park Academy) was being built next to the Mission House, a spark from one of the steam engines set fire to it. Sadly I watched it burn to the ground. Young as I was, I sensed that a precious treasure and symbol of a noble civilization had been destroyed. I vowed then and there that, as much as I could, I would try to preserve and gather the facts and artifacts as well as the stories of all the peoples who have lived on these lands.

By the years of my growing up, at least, almost all of the Native Americans were long gone, save one -- a lovely Indian princess named Twyla Hurd. She became one of my very good friends and she still is. Her beautiful writings have captured the soul of her people and mine.

But in those days, South Buffalo was mainly Irish; descendants of their forefathers who built the Erie Canal. As I wrote in the first preface, it was not until I was ten years old that I realized I was not Irish. By then it was too late to do anything about it. I have always wondered why I, of German heritage, found the Irish so intriguing. Perhaps people of the same blood lineage cannot always truly appreciate their own kind because they are too much alike. Whatever the reason, I grew to love the Irish, their brogue and their stories. I determined to write about them.

The title of these books, <u>Canal Water and Whiskey</u>, comes from a story a 90-year-old Irishman told me in the 1920s. He worked on the Canal in the 1830s as a young lad just a bit older than I was at the telling. I was totally absorbed by the story and even more by the telling of it. I dashed home as fast as my legs would carry me to write it down before I forgot it.

So possessed was I in writing that I did not hear my mother open the door. She startled me with a question: "What are you doing Marvin?" Now let it be known that no boy had more loving parents than I. Since I knew both of them had little schooling, I was afraid Mother would not understand if I told her I was writing a story. Of course she would have.

Not wanting to upset her, I answered quickly, covering my paper at the same time. "Practicing my penmanship, Mother," I lied. Perhaps there are still some readers in this age of computers who remember that invention of the Devil, "The Palmer Method" of penmanship. It consists of finger exercise drills, circles and oblique "up and down" lines. One had to curve one's fingers while clutching the pencil and move the whole hand smoothly and uniformly. No "finger wiggle" was allowed. Many's the time, the patrolling penmanship teacher cracked my knuckles with a thick ruler for "finger wiggle." I'm certain this form of torture must have come out of the Spanish Inquisition. At any rate, my answer seemed to satisfy my mother and I returned to writing my story. For what it's been worth, that began my writing career. I still blame that ruler wielding teacher for the arthritis in my fingers.

At the end of my sixth grade, my father accepted a position with a new company: Monsanto Chemical Works. We moved west to East St. Louis on the mighty Mississippi River. This was Mark Twain country, much different than South Buffalo. Before we arrived in East St. Louis, Illinois, I had already discovered and devoured Tom Sawyer and Huckleberry Finn. They were my buddies. No boy should grow up without these two companions. Often my dad took me up to Hannibal, Missouri where Twain and his characters had grown up. Needless to say, my young friends and I imitated many of the adventures of Mark Twain's boys on the Mississippi River. To me he will always be one of the greatest, if not the greatest, of American writers. He influenced me greatly.

Strange it is that my life should center on three places that also meant much to Twain: Hannibal on the Mississippi, Buffalo on the Erie Canal and Lake, and Elmira, New York, where he wrote much of his work. At Buffalo State Teachers College, I also had the privilege of working with my good friend and colleague, Martin Fried, a professor of English who had written his doctoral dissertation on Mark Twain. Marty's talks with me added enormously to my knowledge and appreciation of the author. Both of us regretted that he did not do for the Lakes and Canal what he had done for the Mississippi River.

Once again, Buffalo beckoned my family. We returned to South Buffalo in time for me to enter South Park High School at the beginning of the second semester. Three and a half years later our class graduated. That year, 1932, marked the centennial of Buffalo's becoming a city. Thus, that was the theme for our senior year and graduation. Our yearbook had drawings and essays on the history of Buffalo. I wrote the one in Latin: "De Urbe Nostra." In the Fall, I went on to college.

At Colgate University, I majored in history and political science. During the summers I worked on the Buffalo docks. Here I learned how the Buffalo waterfront worked. At lunch hour, when I was not swimming out to the breakwater, I explored the harbor and waterfront. What an exciting place!

After two years of teaching high school history at Canisteo, New York, I received an Angier Biddle Duke Fellowship for graduate work in history at Duke University in Durham, North Carolina. The previous summer I had taken a course from a young graduate instructor, Bayrd Still, on the history of the westward movement. Suddenly all of the pieces of my life's jigsaw puzzle fell quickly into place. Dr. Still had been a student of Frederic Logan Paxson who had studied under Frederick Jackson Turner, author of the "Frontier Thesis of American History."

In a short paper delivered to the American Historical Society, Turner, using the 1890 census, stated that by definition, the American Frontier no longer existed. During its time, it influenced more than any other force, the making of America and Americans. As the Frontier moved west across the American continent , it became the cutting edge of European-American civilization. Each new settlement had to establish villages, farms and its own local government. In a sense, each new settlement roughly re-created its former self, modified by frontier conditions. Often beyond the reach of the established law they had to make their own law and governmental arrangements. Each time democracy was reinforced. The Frontier took the Easterners and Europeans and forged them into something American. History, according to Turner, should not be interpreted simply as an extension of European history.

While Turner seemed to emphasize the agricultural frontier, Bayrd Still and his colleagues advanced the theory that the urban frontier was at least equally significant. The Frontier Thesis, therefore, demonstrates the importance of local history. Still had just finished writing the history of Milwaukee, Wisconsin, attesting to the importance of urban history.

At the end of my summer course with him, he called me into the office and asked if I would like to study under him and develop a dissertation on the Port of Buffalo. Steeped as I had been in stories of Native-Americans, canawlers, dock workers and the history of

Buffalo, I accepted enthusiastically. I became Professor Still's first graduate student. I not only completed my masters thesis, The Rise of the Port of Buffalo, but also expanded it into a doctoral dissertation. In the course of that research, which was published in a number of professional journals, I collected many stories not included in those publications. Many of these stories now appear in Canal Water and Whiskey.

After serving in the Air Force, I accepted a position at Buffalo State where I taught American History and the History of New York State and the Niagara Frontier. To these prospective teachers I developed an extension of the Turner-Still thesis: "History begins with you, in your own backyard." History, like politics, is local.

Harold Thompson, author of Body, Boots and Britches, and the father of folklore in New York State, heard that I had written a number of Canal stories and asked if I would consider having them published in the New York State Folklore Journal of which he was the editor. Many of these stories were first published in that journal. Later I became president of the Folklore Society.

Long before Clinton dug his ditch this was the "Land of the Long House," home of the five nations of the Iroquois. At their full flower, these Native Americans fashioned the most powerful military force east of the Mississippi River and a culture of comparable quality. Their many myths and legends, born out of this land, described in lyrical language man's relationship to man, to animals, to nature, to the supernatural and to their past, present and future. For the Seneca and the Iroquois, this was truly a land of enchantment. Their literature ranks with the finest.

The Sullivan-Clinton campaign of the American Revolution defeated the Seneca Nation and forced them out of their Canandaigua-Finger Lakes homeland to Buffalo; into what, more than a century later, virtually became my own backyard.

Since then, Seneca culture has for me become a matter of respect, research, reading, writing and teaching. Strange that my retirement years should now find me living atop a cliff across from Bare and South Hills on Canandaigua Lake, where the Seneca Nation, the "People of the Hill," had been born.

The end of the American Revolution opened up this land, bringing a steady migration of Yankee settlers. They founded communities west from Geneva on Seneca Lake to Lake Erie and the Niagara River, modeled after their New England villages. They also brought with them a Yankee mind-set and their own brand of civilization to the New West. They opened it to settlement and to new ways of looking at life. Yankee money and men helped finance the new settlements.

The New Englanders quickly realized that better transportation was needed to get the people in, and the products out, of western New York. Yankee ingenuity soon made itself evident.

It may, therefore, not be all that strange that Canandaigua, their first urban center in Western New York, became the birthplace of the Erie Canal. What is unusual is that the conception occurred in a jail.

Jesse Hawley, a bankrupt freight forwarder, was serving time in debtor's prison of Ontario County. In 1807, while still in jail, he wrote a series of articles describing in great detail a proposed canal connecting Buffalo and Albany. When reality caught up with his knowledge and imagination, the accuracy of his account proved most remarkable.

This series appeared in the local newspaper, the antecedent of the present Daily Messenger of Canandaigua. It was almost immediately picked up by the press across the country. Eventually, it came to the attention of DeWitt Clinton, for whom it became an all-consuming political commitment. The start of the canal had to wait for the end of the War of 1812.

So it was that on the Fourth of July, 1817, near Rome, New York, that officials broke ground. With its completion, new people flooded into upstate New York, bringing lifestyles foreign to the transplanted Yankee puritanism. This clash of cultures among Yankees, Yorkers and immigrants, especially the Irish "canawlers," sparked a rich "people-lore." I have tried to catch a bit of that flash and fire in these stories.

One canawler, in the folk tradition of making fun of its four-foot depth, described the canal as not much more than a damp cloth stretching from Buffalo to Albany. Although the canal was only belly-button deep and two canal boat bottoms wide, its ripple effect extended well beyond its berms into the hinterland, and of course down the Hudson River into the New York Harbor. That wide swath was canal country.

From this land of the mainline canals and its laterals has come a treasure trove of folklore and history. Some writers have wondered somewhat mystically, if it might not have something to do with the interactive chemistry of the people and this particular land. Carl Carmer, a York State writer and folklorist with a national reputation, came from the banks of the old Erie. He called this strip of land and water a "psychic highway," certainly it's true that amazing things have happened here.

Even as the canal itself was developing a culture all its own, it was bringing in settlers from distant lands headed for York State and beyond. York State and the nation were in flux.

Out of the stimuli of the canal and the emotional mix of Yankee and non-Yankee were born new religions, such as the Mormons, Adventists, Shakers, Perfectionists, Spiritualists and others; and new reforms, such as abolitionism, women's rights, temperance and others. The land flamed with intellectual and religious passions. Historians described this land nourished by the canal as the "burned over" region. The metaphor referred to the farmers burning the stubble in the fields after harvest. This practice refertilized the soil. Just so, evangelism swept over this canal country like a prairie fire of passion, revitalizing the people into different ways of looking at life both here and hereafter.

Why did this happen where it happened? What was there about this time and land and people that gave rise to the mythology of the Iroquois, the legends of the early York State settlers, the folklore of the Erie Canal and the new religions and reforms of a new America? Could Carl Carmer have been right? Was there something psychic, mythic and magical about this land of the man-made river? One can wonder! Psychics probably know. Folklorists probably don't know. They just enjoy the stories of the land and the people.

In the beginning, the canal was only a dream, demanding a faith that only true believers had. There were not too many who had that kind of faith. But with DeWitt Clinton leading them, the canal would be built. In seven years it was completed. Man, almost God-like, had made a river -- truly a man-made miracle.

Time has made us realize that what the diggers and engineers wrought helped shape the destiny of America. As a canawler once said, "now you can see what God could have done with a little money and a lot of Irish manpower." Despite all of the changes since then, the Erie Canal still flows. What's more, more boats today navigate the Erie than in its "hay day." Today, however, they are recreational rather than commercial vessels. Their crews are vacationers and weekend canawlers sailing for pleasure, not profit.

Traditional historians divide time into B.C. and A.D. To some canal buffs, this means "before canal" and "after digging." The arteries of commerce in York State had become too clogged to accommodate the growing economy of the young nation. It needed by-pass surgery. That is what set Jesse Hawley thinking about the canal. He had spent many frustrating years trying to forward freight down the shallow, unpredictable, rock-strewn Mohawk River in pike-poling Durham boats. The proposed canal would not use natural waterways (as it does now), but would follow the shoreline inland to make use of the natural fall of the land and avoid the uncontrollable rise and fall of rivers and streams.

The Erie Canal operated successfully even before it was completely finished. When completed, it opened up a flow of commerce that brought vigor to the economy of the heartland of New York and the vast country of the inland seas. Some say it was New York State's greatest single public work of the 19th Century. Others think this is too timid a statement and would not restrict it to such limited time and space. Consider that the Erie Canal fathered an economic revolution (commercial, industrial and agricultural), powered the westward movement of peoples and products, turned the transportation flow of America from a North-South orientation to an East-West one, made New York City the greatest port in the world as well as the largest immigrant port, crowned Buffalo the Queen City of the Great Lakes and the largest inland immigrant port in the world, helped develop Great Lakes traffic into the greatest inland waterways commerce in the world, and earned for New York State the title George Washington had earlier bestowed upon it: "The Empire State."

Beyond all that, it produced in York State a political and cultural revolution. It brought a different way of life to York State with its own language, literature, songs, symbols, customs, folklore and history.

In many ways, my continuing interest in the canal has been a life journey. I have boated it end to end, flown over it, swam in it, and, over a period of years and short distances at a time, walked its entire length. I also covered on foot much of the laterals.

At about this time, in my excursions on the canal, I learned of two other canal buffs crazier than I about the canal: Dave Ennis, of Lyons, and Al Gayer, of Schenectady. By profession Dave was a physician and a naval reserve officer and Al worked for General Electric. On weekends we explored the canal by foot, by car and by boat. At night we would "look for a post" (canalese for seeking a safe haven for the night.) Then aboard or ashore, we would swap stories, sing new verses to old canal songs and try to tell the tallest tales that tongues could tell.

Louis C. Jones, then Director of the New York State Historical Association and the Farmers Museum in Cooperstown, invited us to join the famous Cooperstown seminars in 1957 for a folk presentation of the Erie Canal. Reference has been made to this in the first preface. If memory serves right, it was Louis Jones, as a result of these canal seminars, who came up with the idea of forming a canal society. So it came to be that on the mezzanine floor of the then Hotel Statler in Buffalo, that the Canal Society was founded. John Sprague and I suggested that we knew the best person to head the society: DeWitt Clinton, of Buffalo, and a direct descendant of the Father of the Erie Canal. The Board agreed.

In his hometown, Dr. Ennis interested his friend, Assemblywoman Mildred Taylor, in sponsoring legislation to preserve historic canal sites. Mildred Taylor was a great legislator. She often called herself a "petticoat politican" at a time when there were few women in elected offices. She persuaded the Legislature to appoint a joint legislative committee to study and make appropriate recommendations not just for canal sites, but for historic sites throughout the state. I was appointed historian for the committee. Gayer and Ennis served as experts for their various regions.

To assist in the work, Assemblywoman Taylor obtained permission to use the state yacht, INSPECTOR II, for a study cruise of the historic Erie Canal. The trip drew lots of newspaper attention. INSPECTOR II stopped at all the important ports along

15

the way. Historic sites and areas were studied and evaluated. I have told the exciting story of that trip in the official reports of the committee. I assume they are still in the state legislative archives.

The study committee recommended that municipalities along the canal cooperate with the state in preserving canal sites, establishing strip parks for jogging and cycling, marking and tidying up the Port Byron Lock (which is visible from the Thruway,) converting the old Syracuse weighlock building into the Canal Museum, encouraging commercial and canal tours and developing with the state historian (Dr. Albert Corey at the time) a comprehensive plan for the preservation and proper presentation of historic sites throughout the state. Most of these recommendations were eventually implemented. Others are still being carried out. The only one that failed, unfortunately, was the establishment of an historic landmark village to be called "Canal Town" at Fort Hunter, the only place where all three Erie Canals exist within sight of each other. This was a stinging disappointment to all of us. Perhaps some wise government -- state, federal or local -- or a combination there-of in the future will finish this worthy but project.

In the critical eyes of the public, many government study committees have the unfortunate reputation of achieving little. This one achieved much.

For me, great as was the satisfaction of visiting the sites, planning their preservation and plotting linear parks along the tow path, nothing compared with sailing aboard the INSPECTOR II. This was Franklin Delano Roosevelt's state yacht. As governor, he sailed on her many times. To share his quarters, sleep in his bunk and use his facilities was important to me, for I deeply admired the man.

On another canal trip I was aboard MACK'S SHACK, a "twin dolphin" powered house boat, skippered by Captain Jack MacAllister. We were shooting a two-hour film about the canal for P.B.S. and WCNY of Syracuse entitled "The Ditch that Helped Build America." After getting our footage on the canal itself, we took to the air in a helicopter, flying from Albany to Buffalo. Never shall I forget sitting at the open door, the wind hitting me hard in the face, my feet dangling loosely over the edge, without belt or parachute, trying to spot the various sites along the canal for the cameraman who crouched above my head shooting.

Before the film went on national television, it was premiered at Lowe's State Theater in Syracuse to a standing-room only audience. Proceeds went to WCNY and the Canal Museum.

As I mentioned before, Canal Water and Whiskey is an "illegitimate" offshoot of my Ph.D. thesis on the Port of Buffalo and of material that did not seem to fit appropriately in that type of work. Stories that make you smile or even laugh deserve some kind of life. So, if they could not go into a thesis, perhaps they might go into a book.

My thesis and the papers published thereafter led to my appointment as Director-Consultant to the Port of Buffalo. This port position gave me official access to the Buffalo Harbor and the waterfront world. Often, in the history of Buffalo, the waterfront has been a world apart. To me it was a world I had always wanted to become a part of. I now headed the Port of Buffalo, where once as a college student I had worked on its docks.

While serving as head of the port I continued my interest in the Canal Society. One day, Canal Society business brought me to Albany with the president of the society, DeWitt Clinton. During the late 1950s in Albany the DeWitt Clinton Hotel stood off to the south of the foot of the giant staircase of the capitol building. In the years I worked across from the governor's office on the second floor of the capitol I never saw anyone use those magnificent stairs.

DeWitt and I decided to stay at the hotel that night because it was so convenient to the capitol. It was also a favorite rendevous for legislators, especially the cocktail lounge on the mezzanine overlooking the lobby. It was called "The Shelf."

We entered the side door, as almost everyone did, and crossed the lobby to the registration desk. I signed in and DeWitt followed. The clerk turned the register around to examine the names. Slowly he lifted his head. He was not smiling. He was frowning. Like a judge or perhaps more like a a college Dean about to pronounce a sentence, he spoke in an even and acerbic voice, "Sir, we expect this nonsense from local college students but not from older, I hope, more mature, adults." DeWitt and I were taken aback. Until that moment we had been innocently unconsious of how ridiculous it might look to a clerk for a person named DeWitt Clinton to be registering at the DeWitt Clinton Hotel.

I am not sure we ever convinced him that this indeed was DeWitt Clinton, a direct descendent of Gov. DeWitt Clinton, Father of the Erie Canal.

I could imagine that that night when he returned home and was eating dinner with his wife he might, nonchalantly, have said, "Guess what, dear, DeWitt Clinton registered at the hotel today." Knowing some wives, she probably would have said, "I told you not to have your whiskey and water on The Shelf before you come home."

It's been many years since the founding of the Canal Society, but it still continues to flourish. Today, through its fun and informative field trips and meetings, it keeps alive the great history of the Grand Canal. The present (1992) leadership of the Society, headed by Tom Grasso, his fellow officers and the Board of Directors, deserves high credit. They all are in the spirit of true canawlers.

My professional work in college teaching and administration has made it possible for me to live in almost all of the key places along the canal, from Buffalo to New York City. Living in a given area, instead of just visiting it, made it possible for me to absorb, at least in part, the psyche of the place.

A final word of deep appreciation to the group who saved my work from the archival dust bin -- The Western New York Heritage Institute of Canisius College in Buffalo. This group of creative historians and educators has taken as their mission the collection, preservation, presentation and publication of materials on the local history of Western New York and New York State. Hopefully, as a result, the present generation of multi-cultured people and its posterity will appreciate and understand its rich heritage. I hope the muses are kind to the Institute as it instills an understanding of and an enthusiasm for local history, emphasizing what I used to tell my students: "History begins in your own backyard."

I therefore acknowledge the leadership of the Institute, especially Edward J. Patton, Paul F. Redding and their technical assistants, Elizabeth Foy, Jack Messmer, Janice Messmer, John Percy, Mary Dow, Sandra Wardour, Edwin J. Williams, Harvey Holzworth, Nancy Bereck, Joan Felstead and Joseph Rennie, in the achievement of this mission and, most especially, J. David Valaik, Ph.D. and Joseph F. Bieron, Ph.D., co-directors of the Institute, for their great help in making this book possible. A special thanks goes to J. Patrick Greenwald, Vice President of College Relations, for his special role in helping the Institute achieve its goals. Lastly, I thank the Rev. James M. Demske, S.J., President of Canisius College, for his vision and encouragement of the study of local history.

From my balcony on a cliffside overlooking Canandaigua Lake, I often watch the sun rise from behind Bare and South Hills, birthplace of the Seneca Nation. In memory they had been my friends in my boyhood backyard in Buffalo.

As I watch these beautiful Canandaigua Lake waters flow northward, I know they will eventually empty into the Erie Canal. These hills and these waters once again help me to recapture their past and mine.

January, 1992
Canandaigua, New York
Ga'-Nun-Da-Gwa
"A Place Selected for Settlement"
"The Chosen Place"
(Lewis Morgan, League of the Iroquois, p.469)

18

I

THE DREAM

Republic Steam Presses, Buffalo.

"VISION OF COLUMBUS"
Joel Barlow

He saw, as widely spreads the unchannel'd plain
Where inland realms for ages blom'd in vain
Canals, long winding, ope a watery flight,
And distant streams, and seas and lakes unite.
From fair Albania, tow'rd the falling sun,
Back through the midland lengthening channels run;
Meet the far lake, the beauteous towns that lave,
And Hudson joined to broad Ohio's wave.

B.C.-A.D.

For Canawlers, history was divided into B.C. and A.D.:
Before Canal and After Digging.

HENO AND THE BUFFALO CRICK
(Based on Seneca Indian Legend)

Before the Erie Canal, there was the Buffalo Crick. The Senecas knew why it was so crooked.

Captain Sam lifted his fishing pole just a mite, considered the water expertly for a moment and then dropped his line a smidge to the left of his original spot. Sitting on the next snubbing post, watching his Grampa's every move, was Jerry. He knew whatever his grandfather did was the right thing to do whether it was just plain livin' or just plain fishin'. In fact, if there was anything about fishing Captain Sam didn't know, Jerry was certain the fish didn't know about the Great Lakes. "Yes, boy, and all about all the rivers and the cricks that run into them. I should know all about them. I've sailed these inland seas for fifty years as man and boy." Always the ideas and words remained the same. The number of years, however, had a way of growing larger with each telling

Mimicking his Gramp, Jerry himself now lifted his pole, scanned the water momentarily and then placed it back a little bit to his left. Two water circles grew out from the spot where the lines had been reset. They soon overlapped. As Gramp watched them intertwine, they seem to be a sort of symbol of the bond which linked him to his grandson.

For awhile both sat quietly in fishermen's contentment, completely and perfectly in tune with the universe. Then, just as Gramp had cut the satin smoothness of the water when he changed fishing positions, Jerry now decided it was about time to reset the conversation line. He broke into the silence abruptly. "Seems to me, Gramp, that if you outsmarted those blacklegged gamblers who used to fleece the people in the Canal Street saloons on the Buffalo waterfront, they couldn't have been very crooked." A little smile pushed up the edges of Jerry's mouth and he added, "Unless, of course, you were as crooked as they were."

"Now see here, young fellow, your hull is getting a mite too big for the size of your sail. I'm telling you and I know. Those blacklegged gamblers along Canal Street were the crookedest crooks on the lake. I know, 'cause I sailed up them all and, though I never scratched a keel board in any of 'em, I came closest to staving in my port belly right here on this misshapen crick. Believe me, Jerry, many a pilot did just that. No doubt of it, lad, Buffalo Crick is as crooked as a snake."

Captain Sam paused a moment so the comparison would register on Jerry. Then looking directly at him and measuring each word as if he expected opposition, he said, "Fact is, son, it's as crooked as a snake because an oversized snake made it that way." Jerry had heard many of Gramp's stories and had trained himself not to show too much surprise at what he said. This, however, seemed to be going a bit too far, even for Gramp. "Now wait a minute, Gramp, " said Jerry. "That's not what they tell us at school."

"Can't help what they tell you at school," snapped Gramp. "The Indians told me why Buffalo Crick is so crooked and what's good enough for the Indians ought to be good enough for the likes of you and those old maid schoolmarms. I reckon my Indian friends stretch back a lot more years than those book readin', chalk scratchin' teachers of yours. You know, Jerry, I believe you're catchin' too much wind in your canvas. Boy, my advice to you is to trim your sails sharply when those schoolmarms start blowing."

Jerry started to smile but then quickly checked himself because he didn't want his Gramp to see him.

"Okay, son, now do you want to go on believing what those landlubbing teachers tell you or do you really want to find out how Buffalo Crick came to be the crookedest crick on the lakes?"

Jerry knew he didn't have to say anything because Gramp would spin his tale anyhow. So he only smiled at Gramp, settled back into a comfortable position on the snubbing post and wondered whether he had heard this one.

"Well, sir," Gramp began, "a long time ago, long before the white man came to this crick, in fact long before the white man had discovered America, yes, even before the Indians had lived on this bank, Buffalo Crick flowed straight as an arrow and clear as moonlight. Came out of the hills southeast of here and made a plumb line for the mouth over yonder, the way any sensibly minded crick ought to do.

"At that time an Indian tribe lived on the banks of Cayuga Crick which empties into the Niagara River just above the Falls. Today the settlement is called LaSalle. In those days, the Indians called it Ca-U-Cwa, which the white man translated into Cayuga. In that village lived the prettiest young Indian maiden for miles around. Her whole life had been filled with happiness until one day she learned that her mother and father had promised her in marriage to a miserable old man. 'Cordin' to the customs of her people, only death could save her from such a marriage. In this case she preferred death.

"So at sun-up one morning, she pushed her bark canoe out of Cayuga Crick and into the Niagara River. Pointing the bow northward, the current soon caught hold of the canoe and carried it swiftly into the upper rapids above the Falls. Quietly she dropped her paddles, calmly folded her hands and with serene contentment waited to be swept over the cataract to her death. In a few moments the canoe shot over the brink and plunged toward the bottom of the gorge where the waters boiled up from the huge jagged rocks. In these few moments, a miracle occurred.

"When the canoe crashed on the rocks, the Indian girl was not in it. The great God of Thunder, who lived in the Cave of the Winds behind the Falls, had watched the girl floating in her canoe toward the edge of the cataract. Such had been the godlike serenity on her beautiful face and her calm acceptance of fate that Heno, the God of Thunder, had been moved to save her. Quickly, as her canoe caromed through the turbulent waters of the upper rapids and over the Horseshoe Falls, he reached out a blanket of silver mist and caught her in it. He then carried her, uninjured, behind the wall of falling water. There he laid her on a bed of soft mist and told one of his assistants to care for her. No sooner did Heno's helper see her than he fell deeply in love with her. When she awakened, she looked up into his face and knew that this was the Prince she had always dreamed about. He gathered her up into his arms and kissed her. Soon after, Heno married the happy pair.

"Now it so happened that for several years before this happened, the people of Ca-U-Cwa suffered each year from a dreadful pestilence which took a great toll of lives. Nothing they did seemed to prevent or lessen the disease. In the course of time, Heno grew quite fond of the Indian girl he had saved and resolved to tell her the cause and cure of the plague which brought wholesale death to her people. At the year's end, he told her the cause of the pestilence. He then gave her permission to return to her people and save them.

"After she had been safely delivered back to her people, the Indian girl told them the story of her rescue by Heno, the God of

24

Thunder. She also told them that a monster serpent dwelt in the ground beneath the village. Each year he feasted on the dead bodies buried conveniently by the side of the village. To make sure he had enough to eat at his annual feast, the serpent poisoned the waters of the Cayuga Crick and Niagara River. Since the Indians at this time did not know how to get water out of the ground, they depended entirely on the crick and the river for their drinking water. So the Indian girl told her people they would have to leave the village and live on the banks of Buffalo Crick.

"Not long after, the serpent, unable to find enough bodies for his feast, pushed his head above the ground and discovered the village deserted. Enraged, he immediately picked up the scent, plunged madly into the Niagara River and swam southward toward the Lake. At Buffalo Crick, he spotted the new village and prepared to devour the people. Heno, who was watching everything from a mist cloud above the Falls, opened the heavens and discharged his most terrible thunderbolts, one of which wounded the snake severely. In his agony, the snake thrashed madly from one side of the crick to the other. Each desperate lunge pushed back the bank and twisted the crick all out of shape. At one point the monster almost broke through into the open water of the lake. Meanwhile, Heno kept hurling one thunderbolt after another at the huge writhing body. As the lightning bolts took effect, the thrashing and turning became less and less strenuous. Eventually, the body of the serpent lay still, cradled in the new bed of the crick. The serpent was dead. The people were free. But the crick would never be the same. To reach the lake, the crick now took five miles to cover what it had formerly covered in two. In those last five miles, the crick now flowed north, south, east and points between before it finally decided to flow west into the lake.

"Yes, Jerry, my boy, Buffalo Crick is the crookedest crick on the lakes -- crooked as a snake." Jerry smiled back at his Gramp and reset his fishing line. This was one he hadn't heard.

25

HOW THE CANAL WAS BORN

Would you believe the first practical proposal for an Erie Canal was born in jail in the small village of Canandaigua, New York?

In Canandaigua there is a park, postage stamp in size, on the west side of Main Street at the corner of Coach. In spring and summer this oasis of green pleasantly breaks the solid row of brick buildings that step down from the tracks southward to the beginnings of lower Main Street. Except for that, the mini-park, with its plantings, seems relatively undistinguished. It does not seem to have a name.

Over the years, shoppers and vacationers by the thousand have hurried past this spot on foot or wheels with scarcely a glance. Occasionally, when the bench and sun are in their proper place, a tired shopper or weary transient has been known to "sit for a spell" and watch the world of Canandaigua go by. Such a passive present for a mini-park belies its active past.

Despite its being virtually unnoticed, unknown and unmarked, it may well be one of the most historic sites, not just in Canandaigua, but in the whole country. Some writers, more rash than others, might even say "the world."

Many historians believe it was here -- under circumstances most unusual -- that the greatest single public engineering work of the 19th and the 20th centuries was first conceived. Its creation and continuing influence have been described by writers mostly in superlatives. To say it simply, but boldly, its impact revolutionized America.

What happened here in 1807 made headlines in The Ontario Messenger (now called The Daily Messenger.) The story begins in Canandaigua's sister city, Geneva. The year was 1805. Both places had already moved out of the frontier phase and into the village period of development. The farms of their hinterlands were beginning to produce a modest grain surplus. Looking beyond the local markets, some enterprising merchants found the lucrative New York City market more attractive. Two such businessmen, Jesse Hawley and Henry Corl of Geneva, had formed a partnership for forwarding flour and wheat from local farmers to Col. Wilhemus Mynderse, who had a mill at the falls of the Seneca River. Mynderse had founded the village and named it, appropriately, Seneca Falls.

Forwarders shipped their flour by long, shallow draft Durham boats through locks hardly "large enough to swing a cat in," then into the rock strewn Mohawk River, the majestic Hudson and on to the markets of New York City. This primitive land and water system was slow, rough-going, dangerous and -- what was worse for farmers, millers and forwarders -- prohibitively expensive, especially in the low water period of summer.

Beset by this and other economic problems, the two merchants began to feel the fiscal pinch. This caused Hawley to default on the payment of mortgaged Geneva property located at the intersection of Main and Seneca Streets, in what is today downtown Geneva. His partner, Corl, took the easy way out, declared bankruptcy and absconded with $10,000 of partnership assets. This left Hawley holding little more than a ledger full of debts. Pressing for collection, creditors brought suit against Hawley. In those days, the courts could throw a debtor into jail. All they had to do was catch him.

Hawley now found himself in such financial straits that he had to ask a friend to post bail for him. Free on bail and seeing no way to avoid jail, Hawley panicked. In December, 1806, he fled to Pittsburgh, forfeiting the bail money of his friend.

Almost overnight, Hawley had been changed from a respected businessman of the Geneva community to a fugitive from justice. Hiding out in Pittsburgh, although ostensibly safe there, he soon realized he could easily escape the Ontario authorities, but not his conscience. Finally, he could no longer stand it. He resolved to return to Canandaigua and give himself up to his creditors, the courts and jail.

After observing proper legal procedures, the court ruled confinement of Jesse Hawley to the jail limits. This meant the extent of the paved sidewalks and incarceration in Sheriff Elijah Tillotson's hotel, which served as the jail. The turnpike coaches used the alley alongside the building. Gradually people referred to it as Coach Street. The second floor of the hotel was the jail. Since the windows were not too high above the street level, inmates could easily converse with friends as they strolled down Main Street. It was not an uncivilized arrangement.

This is where, on August 7, 1807, the "Sheriff's" men brought Hawley to serve his 20-month sentence for his debts. That first night in jail plunged Hawley into dark despair. In his own words, he confessed, "There I was! -- in a debtor's prison for the relief of my bail; betrayed by my partner; broken down and almost destitute in despondency at the thought that hitherto I had lived to no useful purpose of my own; accompanied with many pensive reflections, that I never want to recall."

Fortunately, a business acquaintance, the Honorable William Peacock, Esq., of Mayville, Chautauqua County, happened to visit Canandaigua and was surprised to see his friend, Hawley, reduced from a position of affluence to jail confinement for his debt. Seeking to encourage him, he said, "(you) are as yet young and healthy. It is a long road which has no turn, and brighter days may come. Keep good courage, and do not give way to despondency nor indulge in improper habits in order to forget trouble. Let your mind, which is necessarily active, have constant employment in reading and study, so that time may not pass without its uses."

Hawley needed this advice, for he now faced the crisis of his life. Painfully, life must have flashed before his eyes. He recalled another day in April, 1805, when he had looked out of the window of Mynderse's mill at Seneca Falls. Both had been worrying aloud about the inefficient and expensive transportation system that penalized miller and forwarder alike. As Hawley had continued to gaze out of the mill window, both men had been silent in their thoughts of what could be done to improve the water system transportation. "(I) sat in a fit of abstraction for some minutes, then took down (Simeon) DeWitt's map of the state, spread it on the table and sat over it with my head reclined in my hands and my elbows on the table, ruminating over it, for -- I cannot tell how long -- muttering 'a head of water;' at length my eye lit on the Falls of Niagara which instantly presented the idea that Lake Erie was that head of water," he recalled. Could this be the missing piece for the completion of the unfinished work of nature -- a man-made river connecting the natural waterways from Lake Erie to the Hudson River ?

While in Pittsburgh, his dream began to take shape. He wrote a letter to the editor of the Pittsburgh paper. Published, it brought no response. After all, when Pittsburgh turned its eyes westward, it watched the Allegheny and Monongahela form the Ohio and flow on to the mighty Mississippi. It had no interest in New York's transportation problems.

Now, as he looked out onto Main Street of Canandaigua, he knew he could give in to despondency or turn misfortune into good fortune. Thankfully for America, he chose the latter. He resolved to write and publish to the world his "fanciful" project.

By lamp-light and sunlight, he started writing. What he wrote in that jail cell at the corner of Main and Coach in Canandaigua described in detail the idea of the Erie Canal. Perhaps others may have vaguely suggested in conversation or correspondence the possibility of a canal from Buffalo to Albany, but it was Hawley who developed the idea of the Erie Canal and gave it to the world publicly in the pages of The Ontario Messenger.

Starting in August, Hawley began writing his fourteen articles on the Erie Canal under the nom de plume "Hercules" and The Ontario Messenger continued publishing the articles over the next six months. The introductory paper repeated the article published originally in Pittsburgh's Commonwealth newspaper on January 14, 1807.

In subsequent issues, Hawley traced the route of the Canal with uncanny accuracy, although he had never travelled the route by foot or by horse. He developed the route by maps in the Canandaigua jail. Notwithstanding the fact that the route would take the canal through an uncharted wilderness using machinery not yet

28

invented, he prophetically estimated the cost of the entire canal to be six million dollars. Under the conditions, it was an unbelievable prognostication.

Hawley described in detail the beneficent effect the canal would have on New York State, the United States and, indeed, the world. He said it all, however, in his introductory theme: "I entertain with ideas of the destiny of these United States: -- A Giant in its infancy, to what point may we not aspire in our maturity. . . . I intend to point out that improvement which I conceive to be of the greatest importance of any which can be undertaken in the United States; and for the proposition of which these numbers were principally written -- a canal from the foot of Lake Erie into (the) Mohawk."

Although many mocked Hawley and his canal with ridicule as "the effusions of a maniac," those who understood the possibility of a canal treated the articles like a Bible. In 1809 General Micah Brooks, a member of the State Legislature from Ontario County, took Hawley's essays to Albany and turned them over to Simeon DeWitt, Esq., their Surveyor General, for investigation.

In 1810 the Legislature appointed the first Board of Canal Commissioners, which included the surveyor general and DeWitt Clinton, later governor of New York State. Two years later, Clinton himself borrowed the Hawley articles. They changed Clinton's life. The canal became his political passion. Clinton, whom history has called the "Father of the Erie Canal," said, "the first hint... (of the Erie Canal) which I have seen in print, was suggested by Jesse Hawley, Esq., of Ontario County -- a gentleman of an ingenious and reflective mind."

Ten years after Jesse Hawley publicly proposed the canal, ground was broken near Rome on July 4, 1817. Eight years later, on October 26, 1825, the Grand Canal opened in Buffalo. The honor of delivering the opening address went to Hawley. Did Hawley, even with his keen perception, believe that his canal, over the years, would:

* Create the greatest inland waterway system in the world by joining the Great Lakes and the Atlantic Ocean?

* Establish the canal era throughout the United States in which hundreds of miles of canals would be built?

* Make New York City the greatest port in the world?

* Earn for New York the title of Empire State?

* Stimulate a ribbon of urban growth along its banks from Buffalo to Albany?

* Cause a farming revolution that made New York the leading agricultural state during the 19th century?

* Found, in its very building, America's first schools of engineering formalized into Rensselaer Polytechnic Institute and the Rochester Institute of Technology, out of which America's great engineering achievements of the 19th and 20th centuries would spring?

* Open the American West to the greatest movement of European immigrants the world has ever seen?

* Affect profoundly the sociological, governmental, financial, literary and religious development of the state?

History supports these impacts on national development, yet it remained for Hawley himself to summarize it best. As the boat, *Seneca Chief*, prepared to leave for New York City on the man-made waterway, Hawley, according to many historians, intoned the most succinctly superlative tribute ever uttered in praise of a public achievement. He said, in part, "New York has made the longest canal -- in the least time -- with the least experience -- for the least money -- and of the greatest public utility as any other in the world."

CANAL PASSED BY ONE VOTE

After the Erie Canal bill had passed the New York State Legislature, it still had to pass the Council of Revision which in those days had veto power. The swing vote was held by Chancellor Kent who seemed to be leaning toward veto; two favored, two opposed.

DeWitt Clinton, the former Governor, and now Vice President of the United States, dropped into the Council of Revision meeting at the last minute. At first he opposed the Canal and contrary to the rules, expressed himself strongly on the subject.

"This peace with Great Britain, gentlemen, is a mere truce. There is no doubt whatever that we shall soon be again at war with that country," he said. "Instead of wasting the credit and resources of this State in the chimerical project, we ought to employ all our revenue and all our credit in preparation of war."

"Do you really think so, sir?" asked Chancellor Kent, who was much more strongly opposed to war than he was to the Erie Canal.

"I do," replied the Vice-President. "Depend on it. England will never forgive us our victories. Take my word for it, we shall have another war within two years."

Chancellor Kent rose to his feet, a determined set to his jaw.

"Gentlemen," he said, "if we must choose between the canal and war, I am in favor of the canal!"

So it happened on April 15, 1817, after a decade of dreaming and years of planning, the building of the Erie Canal was approved.

FEDERAL SON OF A BITCH

It passed, but many, and perhaps most, people opposed it. They put their feelings in a popular chant:

> "Clinton, the federal son-of-a-bitch,
> Taxes our dollars to build him a ditch!"

"WHY GRIN ?"

Others scoffed, "You can't make boats run uphill." Tammany Hall, blind in its hatred of DeWitt Clinton, derided his "Ditch" in vitriolic doggerel:

"Why grin? It will do to bury its mad author in."

II

THE DIGGING

Republic Steam Presses, Buffalo.

"FREE AS AIR"

They all seemed free -- as free as air
To gamble, fight and drink and swear.

IRISH DIGGERS AND WHISKEY JIGGERS

For the most part, the Irish bogtrotters dug the Erie Canal. For their ditch-digging chores they received ten dollars a month and board plus a number of jiggers of whiskey. The jigger was a small measure about one-third the size of an ordinary tumbler. When inquiring of a foreman for work a laborer never asked, "what wages do you pay?" He simply asked, "How many jiggers do ye give?"

"PADDY'S SONG"

"When the Irish began to pick up the pickaxes and shovels most of the Americans were glad to put down, the singing started," wrote Codman Hislop in The Mohawk. "Before the towpath songs there were the diggers' songs, full of nostalgia for an Ireland few of the singers ever saw again. Paddy's song came early. A Paddy who arrived in Philadelphia but couldn't stand the place and moved on to New York wrote:

When I came to this wonderful empire,
It filled me with the greatest surprise
To see such a great undertaking,
On the like I ne'r opened my eyes.

To see a full thousand brave fellows
At work among mountains so tall
To dig through the valleys so level,
Through rocks for to cut a canal.

So fare you well, father and mother,
Likewise to old Ireland too.
So fare you well, sister and brother,
So kindly I'll bid you adieu.

"DIGGIN' A DITCH"

We're diggin' a ditch through the gravel
Through the gravel and mud and slime, B'gawd
So the people and freight can travel
And the packets can move on time, B'gawd.

"MONTEZUMA MUD"

We are Digging the Ditch through the mire
Through the mud and the slime and the mire, by heck
And the mud is our principal hire,
Up our pants, in our shirt, down our neck, by heck
We are digging through gravel, and mud and slime
So people and products can travel on time.

CANAL FEEDERS

By this time, canal building had progressed to a point where its problems were concerned mostly with the matter of water. It had been known from the moment when the first cannon signaled the breaking of sod at Rome, that one of the Old Erie's chief puzzlers was going to be how to keep her channel flooded throughout the boating season, especially on the western two-thirds, after she had cut away from the Mohawk River. From this need had sprung up an additional system of channels, called feeders, which brought water in from the neighboring lakes and creeks and from reservoirs built in the hills for this purpose. To increase the usefulness of these feeders, each was made wide enough to serve also as a branch canal, separated from the main channel by sluice gates so that an attendant could maintain the proper water level. In time this practice would produce hundreds of additional miles of channel, making the entire Erie Canal system into a thousand-mile waterway which would include the entire Finger Lakes district.

Soon it was evident that even so extensive a feeder system would not always be adequate to the task of supplying sufficient water. For it had already been discovered that in times of prolonged dry spells or extensive leakage, even the feeders went dry, making large sections of the Big Ditch useless. So now the spotlight of canal endeavor must be turned to the matter of water economy.

DIG A COMPLETE CANAL

I've always liked the logic used by a member of the Legislature at the time it was debating to dig a complete canal or just segments:

"Might just as well dig a complete canal -- same way if you're going to get married. You might just as well marry a pretty girl as an ugly one, especially if you're going to be home much."

CANAWL WATER AND WHISKEY

It was 1825. The canal was coming. Along the right of way from the Hudson River to Lake Erie, hopes were high and real estate values were going higher. Yankees and Yorkers, sharp for a bargain, counted their future blessings in the currency of the day: coonskins, produce and Spanish quarters. To the pot-stove philosophers of the small wilderness settlement of Buffalo, the canal and little else mattered. Soon the guess-and-gamble travel over the rutted Genesee Road and the portage-broken Ontario Niagara waterway would give way to the smooth green waters of the Grand Canal.

Buried in the newspaper files and in some memories, were the unpleasant recollections of the burning of Buffalo during the War of 1812 and the death struggle with Black Rock over the western terminus of the canal. All that was yesterday. The future belonged to the little village perched atop a low bluff overlooking Buffalo Creek and "Erie's Waters." The dreamers let their imaginations follow their gaze out over the harbor and across the lake to the distant horizon. They dotted the "sweet waters" with the sails of hundreds of vessels and counted the freight from the far and still unpeopled West. These Buffalo pioneers had a right to dream. It was 1825. The canal was coming. So were the Irish.

With pick and shovel and bone-muscle born of the peat bogs and green sod of the counties of Cork and Clare, the Irish inched their way through the rich York soil. Across fields and creeks, through swamps, sand and rock, they moved the canal westward. Little wonder the hard-working, hard-living Irish claimed that they had clawed out the canal with their bare fingers and then filled it with their honest sweat. They were proud of their canawl, as they called it, and prouder still of the name, canawler. Those who shouted, "Folly, Clinton's folly!" were answered by digging. To those who laughed and said that neither Governor DeWitt Clinton nor the Irish could make water run uphill, they replied by building the locks. The canal was coming. The Irish would see to that. Soon the Tonawanda-Buffalo leg was under construction. A part of a day's travel would take the people to the diggings where Irish chanteys filled the Niagara air with an Erin brogue. After days which must have seemed years to those who waited in Buffalo, the ditch left the river's edge and headed straight inland for the Little Buffalo Creek, which emptied into the harbor. In a future day, that last section would become a part of the Niagara section of the Governor Dewey Thruway. But now its future as a canal lay ahead.

Villagers gathered to watch the canawlers lean-to on their picks against the sandy loam. Whatever official celebration might follow the formal completion of the work, they meant to witness the real finish. With the goal so close at hand, the diggers lost no time.

For the impatient pioneers, however, the work moved much too slowly. They watched and waited anxiously. Finally, to someone with American frontier resourcefulness, a "Yankee" idea occurred, or so the legend has it.

The next morning, when the Irish took their places in the ditch, they noticed barrels carefully placed at measured intervals along the route of the canal. They were not ordinary barrels, but whiskey barrels. What was more, they were full. The game was soon out. As the Irish dug their way to a barrel, they drained it and moved on to the next and the next until they reached the Little Buffalo Creek. Old-timers had no trouble boasting that this was the fastest diggin' an' drinkin' the canawl had ever seen. For the people of Buffalo the waiting was over. The canal, their canal, had come. Tomorrow was here. When the formal completion was celebrated, Governor Clinton, from aboard the canal boat *Seneca Chief,* dumped a cask of pure Lake Erie water into the briny waters of the Atlantic Ocean. The official state representatives and other dignitaries toasted the "wedding of the waters" with imported champagne. At least the pioneers on the western frontier heard it rumored that way. It was all right, they thought, for the civilized dandies of the East to toast their canal with imported champagne if they wanted to. But for them, for those who did the diggin', no one would ever make them believe that on that occasion champagne was as fittin' as canawl water and a whiskey chaser.

This was a great day for Buffalo, celebrated on August 9, 1825, with a huge sod-breaking ceremony, there in the wilderness, attended by the entire countryside including a few of the more curious from Black Rock. Let one who was there tell what it was like. "All people with oxen were invited to bring them. All met on a boggy flat and hitched the ten or twelve yoke of oxen to the largest plough in the world, then 'Go lang, Buck!' and the blade bit into the black mold and sod between the stakes that marked the new canal. Along the proposed route were placed barrels of rye whiskey at convenient spots, with part of the head cut off and a tin dipper lying by for all to help themselves free. . . . Everybody worked that day."

And yet, so crude was this outpost village, not a single wheelbarrow nor scraper existed within her borders, although for three years she had been fighting to prove her readiness and desirability as a canal terminus. Now, faced with this lack, a few clever citizens turned their axes to the surrounding forests and fashioned something of their own invention, a contraption they called a "soul cart" because it was so difficult to manage. It consisted of two parallel poles, six to eight feet long, connected at their middles by a crude platform upon which great quantities of sod could be piled and hauled away, requiring the services of only two men. After the first example had been demonstrated, dozens more of these soul carts were immediately hewn from the forest and put

40

into service. And according to the press, "Everyone from judges to urchins pitched in, that day."

* I first heard this story in the 1920's from an Irishman whose work on and memory of the canal went back to the 1840's.

"'TIS DONE"

The fact that broadsides were being printed on the run and simultaneously being distributed to readers was hailed by the wonder-struck celebrators as a most appropriate illustration of the new era that was being ushered into being by the Grand Canal, an era of speed, progress and mechanization that promised a fuller, more satisfying life. Certainly, a different life.

From time to time, as the procession moved toward City Hall, spectators took up the sing-song chant from Woodworth's epic:

> 'Tis done! 'Tis done! The mighty chain
> Which joins bright Erie to the Main,
> For ages shall perpetuate
> The glory of our native state!

"MEETING OF THE WATERS IN NEW YORK HARBOR"

This was the song sung in New York City on November 4, 1825 for the dedication of the opening of the Erie Canal. The words are set to an Irish song, "Meeting of the Waters." The tune is derived from an older Irish song called, "Old Head of Dennis."

Let the day be forever remembered with pride.
That beheld the proud Hudson to Erie allied,
Oh, the last sand of time from his glass shall descend,
E'er a union so fruitful of glory shall end.
E'er a union so fruitful of glory shall end.

Yet it's not that wealth now enriches the scene,
Where the treasures of art, and of nature, convene;
'Tis not that this union our coffers may fill,
Oh! no -- it is something more exquisite still,
Oh! no -- it is something more exquisite still.

'Tis that genius has triumphed, and Science prevailed,
Tho' prejudice flouted and envy assailed,
It is that the vassals of Europe may see,
The progress of mind in a land that is free,
The progress of mind in a land that is free.

All hail to a project so vast and sublime.
A bond that can never be severed by time,
Now unites us still closer -- all jealousies cease,
And our hearts, like our waters, are mingled in peace,
And our hearts, like our waters, are mingled in peace.

"MASTER DIXON"
Author Unknown

Ye brethren dear, who now unite
In this grand scene of pure delight,
We now have reached the glorious height,
        The level of Lake Erie.

The waters of the east and west,
The Hudson, Mohawk and the rest,
In sweet communion now are blest;
        They mingle with Lake Erie.

This day we all rejoice to meet;
The glorious work is now complete,
The mountain's levelled at your feet
        Is levelled with Lake Erie.

Accomplished is the grand design,
The work of Level, Square and Line;
Of Masonry, the art was thine,
        To triumph o'er Lake Erie.

Where is the nation that can show
Such streams as through our mountains flow
To the Atlantic, far below
        The level of Lake Erie?

The work of many a freeman's hand,
A brave, a bold, a noble band --
The guardians of this happy land,
        The conquerors of Lake Erie?

Buffalo -- O! who can ever view
These works so grand, these scenes so new,
And not admire, and love thee, too,
        Thou child of ancient Erie?

Around thy paths I love to roam,
For every house is here a home;
I bless the hour when first I come
        To meet with thee and Erie.

O! who will not this day rejoice,
And lift on high his grateful voice?
Come -- men and women, girls and boys,
        Shout for Buffalo and Lake Erie!

This happy day shall ever be
Remembered as a jubilee;
The Lakes, the Rivers, join the Sea,
The Ocean weds Lake Erie.

THE ERIE CANAL: HOW MAN MADE A MIRACLE

The cheering celebrants gathered along the newly dug Erie
Canal where the freshly turned earth formed the towpath and berm.
The overflow crowd stood on the terrace above where the canal
wedded Lake Erie at Buffalo Harbor. As the ceremonies began, a
calm fell over the crowd and the chattering trickled off. The city, the
state and the nation had held its collective breath for this triumphant
moment -- the opening of the Erie Canal, October 26, 1825. More
than just another event, it symbolized the exploding nationalism of
an America embarking on its manifest destiny.

From the group of designated dignitaries, topside on the
canal boat *Seneca Chief*, Jesse Hawley rose to speak. Eighteen
years before, while serving time for debt in the Ontario County Jail
in Canandaigua, he had described, in a series of articles published
by the Western Repository, his dream of a canal across New York
State. Governor DeWitt Clinton, Father of the Canal, listened
intently to Hawley, the man he justly credited with developing,
writing and publishing the first practical concept of the Erie Canal.

On this occasion, Hawley outlined the work that had made
possible the opening of the canal that very day. Then with what
must be the ultimate tribute of all times for any engineering feat or
other accomplishment he proclaimed, not just to the citizens of
Buffalo but, to the nation, the world and posterity: "America can
never forget to acknowledge that they have built the longest canal in
the world, in the least time, with the least experience, for the least
money, and to the greatest public benefit."

Waiting for the signal, 1812 cannons lined the towpath
within sounding of each other, all the way from Buffalo to New
York City. When the ceremonies ended, the first cannon boomed
forth. On hearing the sound, the cannoneers of the second and then
the third and on and on fired in turn until the bombastic message
reached New York Harbor and returned. Never before and perhaps
never since had such a cannon telegraph been used. This innovation
served to exemplify the frontier ingenuity that had helped the
builders solve the many technical problems of this vast enterprise.

Most historians agree that the Erie Canal was America's
greatest single public work of the 19th century; some might say -- of
any century; and a few buffs, too rash to mention, might include --
the whole world.

How could a people, untutored in engineering, without tools, machinery, proper materials or enough money, build a man-made river through stone mountains and bottomless swamps, through Roman arched aqueducts over Indian streams, channel around hills and hummocks, 360 miles across a state much of which was still wilderness? How Yorkers, Yankees and the Irish did it, is an epic story for all times.

The Erie Canal has had its biography written many times but the phrase in the Hawley peroration quoted above that still needs more attention is "with the least experience." In 1817 when the digging began at Rome, N.Y., Americans had no engineers nor engineering schools. For the little engineering work previously carried out in America, engineers had to be imported from the British Isles.

William Weston had come over from England to connect the Schuylkill and Susquehanna Rivers with a short canal. He also helped engineer the ill-fated Western Inland Navigation Company Canal at Little Falls in 1795 to improve Mohawk River transportation. When New York State invited him to be Chief Engineer of the Erie at the relatively exorbitant salary of $7,000 a year, he acknowledged the honor but declined the offer.

As it turned out, nothing could have been better for New York State and America. Weston's refusal resulted in the development of American engineers and engineering. Few creations could have had greater impact on American history. The Erie Canal itself became in fact the first American "school of engineering." The canal project drew men of talent, but without previous professional engineering experience, education or training. The Canal planning and building turned them, (through "on-the-job" experience) into America's first engineers. Now instead of importing European engineers, American engineers became the envy of the engineering fraternity throughout the world.

With the Canal, American technology had gained its first world-wide attention. The Erie Canal experience led to the establishment of Rensselaer Polytechnic Institute in Troy, the Civil Engineering Department of Union College and the Rochester Institute of Technology. American frontier ingenuity became the hallmark of America and the cynosure of the world.

Yet, in the beginning, many State legislators at Albany did not share the Clinton-Hawley optimistic dream. They didn't think anyone could build such a canal and they didn't think the Canal Commission could find anyone who could make an accurate test survey of a given section of the proposed canal. Undaunted, the Commissioner proposed two judges, James Geddes and Benjamin Wright, as surveyors. On the New York State Assembly floor in Albany, the anti-canallers inquired derisively, "Who is this Geddes, and Wright? What canals have they ever constructed?"

With a public display of confidence which hid their private fears, the commissioners accepted the politicians' challenge. They divided the proposed canal into three parts. They chose the middle section between Rome and Syracuse as the one which would present the fewest topographical and technical difficulties while yielding the greatest commercial results on completion. It would tap a network of natural waterways: the Mohawk, Seneca and Oswego rivers; Oneida and Onondaga Lakes; the Finger Lakes and their potentially productive farmland.

Even Canal Commissioner Samuel Young had little confidence in his amateur engineers. At the moment they were practicing lawyers and judges. As they set out to survey the summit level of the middle section near Rome, Young wrote to DeWitt Clinton that this was "a delicate, important and difficult task." "The whole project hangs," he said, "upon an attenuated thread which could break and cause our destruction if we do not exercise the utmost care, caution and vigilance. A mistake in the summit level would bring irrevocable damnation of this world."

Geddes had used a leveling instrument only once before and then for only a few hours in the determining of some deeds and leases. Nevertheless, he ran a test level line between Rome and Syracuse around Oneida and Onondaga Lakes for nearly a hundred miles. Wright laid off the canal line west of Rome. When the Geddes' survey returned to the canal line laid off by Wright, the levels at the junction differed less than 1 1/2 inches.

In their report to the Legislature, the commissioners noted the "degree of care, skill and precision in the delicate art of levelling" which they believed "had never been exceeded." The test ended much of the deprecating talk of the Legislators' "pretended scientific knowledge." Joshua Forman, also a judge and legislator, believed that "a combination of the occasion and the men produced a high yield of technical innovation that simplified the more difficult tasks that lay ahead."

The canal commissioners wisely adopted the farmer-contractor systems of construction. It had never before been used so extensively. It yielded many benefits. The canal commissioners invited sealed bids for constructing sections as short as a quarter of a mile. Many bid. Each contractor with an award furnished his own tools, hired laborers, and if needed, used funds advanced by the Canal Commissioner to purchase teams of horses or oxen and auxiliary equipment. Such a system made use of available farmer equipment, labor and know-how. It also plowed money back into the communities through which the canal passed. Everyone seemed to profit.

As construction moved along, canal planners came to expect and depend on Yankee-Yorker inventiveness to solve difficult technical problems. With Canvass White supervising the first summer of 1817, the building contractors tested methods and tools on the middle section between Rome and Syracuse. They grappled with mechanical problems by improvisation and common sense.

Even before they could dig, they had to clear the land. This proved no easy task. Huge virgin trees towered into the air and blotted out the sun in places. The Niles Register tells of a walnut tree in the New York wilderness that fell to the ground during a storm. A local entrepreneur hollowed the trunk and converted it into a grocery store. Another bought it from him, shipped it to New York City and turned it into a confectionery store. The tree measured thirty feet in girth.

After soil-boring crews had completed their work, the farmer contractors and their hired hands moved in to clear a sixty-foot path of the giant trees. With no Paul Bunyan to uproot the trees, Yankee ingenuity again came to the rescue. Contractors rigged a relatively small and simple machine that did the job. Applying principles of lever and screw, the men fastened a cable to the top of the tree. Then with an endless screw connected to a roller and crane, pulled by horses or oxen, they toppled the tree much more easily than the back-breaking method farmers had traditionally used.

After pulling down the trees came the onerous task of uprooting the stumps. For this, they invented a stump-pulling contraption. It was a huge machine with two sixteen foot wheels connected by an axle twenty inches in diameter and thirty feet long. The stump pullers then fastened a cable around a wheel drum mounted midway on the axle between the wheels. They then wrapped a cable around the stump. The cable tightened and pulled out the stump more easily than pulling a tooth. Samuel Hopkins Adams' grandfather claimed that a work gang of seven laborers and four horses with this machine could yank out stumps and roots of forty large trees a day. This Yankee contraption cost $250.00. The Canal Museum in Syracuse has a model of the stump-puller.

Clearing out the underbrush by the old method proved not so difficult as it did time consuming and tiring. Fortunately, Jethro Wood, of Montville in the Owasco Valley south of the canal, had invented and patented a cast iron plow in 1819. The farmer-builders simply attached cutting blades to their plows which sheared through the shrubs and brushroots in half the time it had ordinarily taken.

Six months of experimentation in the middle section of the canal proved Wood's cast iron plow and scraper superior to the old European spade and wheelbarrow, and had the added advantage of using the horses as a means of compacting the plowed and excavated ground.

Horses, however, could not be used in wet ground such as the Montezuma marshes. There the diggers employed the old spade and wheelbarrow. By bending a single board to a semi-circular shape, Jeremiah Brainard, of Rome, made a wheelbarrow "lighter, more durable, and easier to unload than any used before."

In the Montezuma swamps, many of the Irish often dug in water up to their waists while the sun burned their heads. At the same time millions of mosquitoes carrying ague, malaria and all manners of swamp fever attacked the diggers unremittingly. Quickly, men would be seized by the shakes. Oftentimes they dropped dead in the ditch. There was not even dry land for a decent burial.

With the basic ditch digging problems solved, the engineers turned next to the even more difficult technical construction questions. One of the most vexing: how is waterproof hydraulic cement made? Young Canvass White, who began as an assistant and protege of Benjamin Wright, set out to find the answer.

At his own expense he went to England and Europe to inspect, on foot, 2,000 miles of canals. White meticulously observed and sketched the mechanical structures of the canals. He paid particular attention to hydraulic (under water) cement without which they could not build stone locks. Expense and logistics prevented the importation of the huge quantities of English waterproof cement required for construction.

Upon his return, the young engineer-in-training carried out a number of experiments with varieties of limestone. Fortuitously, he found the answer to water-proofing almost in the path of the canal near Chittenango in Madison County. There, in Elisha Carey's barroom, with the help of a "Scientific" gentleman from Herkimer, a Dr. Barto, White made his great discovery. They burned, pulverized and mixed the limestone with sand. They rolled it into a ball and set it outside Elisha Carey's barroom in a bucket of water.

In the morning to their amazement they found that the mass "had set into a ball of stone." The future engineer generously permitted the contractors to use his cement on the promise that the state would eventually compensate him. As it turned out the state never remembered its promise. Perhaps an even greater loss was that he received not one cent in royalties from the contractors for the 400,000 bushels of cement used in constructing the locks.

With the waterproofing solved, the engineers next sought a canal "lining" which would prevent water seepage. European canals recorded a loss of two cubic feet per mile per minute through absorption and seepage. In America, because of the nature of the soil, the rate averaged alarmingly higher. Water in a 23-mile stretch of completed canal dropped 2 1/4 inches a day; 16 inches in a week! Since the canal depth was only four feet; such a loss amounted to disaster. Once again the diggers found the answer along the canal, a blue-gray clay called "Blue Mud of the Meadows." This lining cut the water loss in half.

While the farmer-contractors concentrated on the digging, the craftsmen and engineers struggled with the construction problems of the locks. Using White's notes and sketches of English lock construction and their mechanical system, the Americans started building the locks. The magnitude of engineering a lockage system, that stepped down almost 600 feet from Lake Erie to the Hudson, must have discouraged even the strongest-hearted dreamers and doers. Still they pushed on.

The first canals in America constructed by European engineers had wooden locks. They rotted quickly. Next they tried brick. Perhaps due to common lime mortar, the brick lock held together only about six years. The American engineers wisely chose stone blocks mortared with Canvass White's hydraulic cement for the Erie Canal. In all those locks, the builders used iron and stone. The locks measured 90 x 15 feet and cost $1,000 per foot of rise.

The 1819 Report of the Canal Commissioners shows the detailed specifications and care of construction:

> The lock walls are to be sustained by several massive buttress (sic) to be laid in water cement, and thoroughly grouted -- to have all the faces end and bed of each stone laid in front of the wall, together with the hollow quoins, the lock culverts and the ventilators well cut and the whole to be sufficiently clamped together with iron, and the best construction, and properly fitted, secured and hung.

Very soon the Americans understood the technology of ordinary lock construction. The overcoming of the sixty-foot rise of the Niagara Escarpment at Lockport, however, presented an extraordinary lock engineering problem. Even non-engineers realized the usual single lock would not work. For all the so-called Erie engineers, the solution became a challenge.

Nathan S. Roberts, with no advice from anyone and only a few books to guide him, designed a series of five "double combined locks of 12-feet lift working side by side." Although Roberts later became a recognized master of the engineering profession, he always acknowledged that the acceptance of his plans and the subsequent construction of his "Combine" marked the triumphant moment of his entire engineering career. One set of his five locks remain at Lockport today as a monument to him and to this early American miracle of engineering science and technology.

With these combined locks, Roberts succeeded in solving the seemingly impossible: floating boats up and down the same escarpment that carries the plunging waters of the Great Lakes over Niagara Falls seventeen miles west of Lockport. To some, this flight of locks gives the appearance of a cataract standing at the head of a natural basin flanked by steep banks a hundred feet on either side. The long herring-bone arms of the lock gate at each step emphasized the suggestion of waterfall. The overall lock system of the Erie Canal required great quantities of timber, cement, coping iron and 50,000 feet of facing stone. Excellent remnants still remain.

Above the locks at Lockport to the southwest, the engineers had to channel through the limestone of the mountain ridge. This became the most difficult and expensive section of the canal. No spade or plow could do this kind of digging. They had to blast.

DuPont had recently developed a black powder. While still not dynamite nor nitroglycerine, it nonetheless proved effective. Unfortunately, every time they tried to bore a hole in the hard dolomite to insert the powder, the drill-bit broke. Neither New York nor Philadelphia suppliers could produce a drill-bit hard enough to penetrate the rock.

According to a Lockport legend, when the work finally came to a stop, someone suggested looking up "a jack-of-all-trades" from Niagara Falls named Botsford. Reputedly he had a talent for such problems. They found him. He agreed to look at the so-called impenetrable stone. After momentarily checking the rock, he asked for the use of a blacksmith shop and went to work.

A few hours later, he reappeared. In his hand, he held a bit. "Try this," he said to an Irish laborer. "Be Jabers! Won't last a minute," said the Irishman after examining it closely. Of course, he was wrong. The bit of properly tempered steel worked well. The men drilled the holes, packed them with powder, ignited the charge and succeeded in blasting the channel through the 'stone mountain.'

Some stories claim the blasters used plain gunpowder. That, however, does not seem to have had the explosive power of the newly invented DuPont special blasting powder, which they probably used. Some canal writers have even suggested the diggers bored holes and filled them with water. Low temperatures froze them quickly. The expansion of the ice cracked the rock. Perhaps this was done on occasion but it took real blasting to loosen, dislodge and break the rock. Sometimes the blasting hurtled stones 18-20 lbs. They crashed into houses near the Canal. Once, a 20 lb. rock smashed into the small office of Judge Elias Ransom. It landed just within the door, rolled all the way in, hit the legs of the Judge's chair and unseated him in a most "undignified manner." For protection, townspeople devised a kind of air-raid shelter by leaning cut trees against the houses with the lower part ten feet from the house. Apparently this also solved the living quarters problem for the Irish laborers, whom the Lockport natives wished to keep segregated.

Possessing little knowledge for holding the blasting powder, many Irish lost their lives checking on fuses that burned too slowly or, presumably, had gone out. Sometimes they even blew on the fuses to rekindle the flame, occasionally with disastrous results. According to one observer, the list of killed and wounded on some days looked like a battlefield body count.

The rock rubble piled up high as the blasting and digging progressed. Wheelbarrows, even the improved type, proved inefficient and inadequate to remove the debris. Again frontier ingenuity found a solution. Orange H. Dibble constructed a horse-operated-boom, a kind of derrick-crane device. Placed above the cut, approximately every 70 feet, the derrick lowered wooden buckets to the channel. After the laborers had loaded them, the horses pulled the rope, raising the buckets in a relatively effortless operation. The rock debris mounds in some places reached 70 feet in height. Remnants of the pile still remain. When finished, the channel measured 27 feet wide varying from 13-30 feet in depth. The men chiseled a towpath along the cut.

While natives along the canal made up most of the labor force, contractors imported many additional Irish for the digging. They made their presence felt well out of proportion to their numbers. Excellent workmen, these bog-trotters apparently took to their tasks better than other workers. Yet they seemed alien to the Yankees and Yorkers. Townspeople tended to segregate them. Many Irish came to Lockport because the rock digging there seemed to have a special appeal to them. They worked hard, played hard, and enjoyed "the spirits." In later years they continued to give color to the operation of the canal.

Spectacular as many found the Five-Tier-Double Combines, and the rock cut at Lockport, others found the aqueducts even more exciting and beautiful. From Albany to Buffalo the canal had to cross a number of rivers. It needed water bridges called aqueducts. Herman Melville, one of America's first novelists, picturesquely described the aqueducts as "Roman arches over Indian rivers." Today, modern technology has the capability of controlling the waterflow of rivers and streams, thus eliminating the need of aqueducts. Not so in the days of Clinton's Ditch.

One of the most beautiful of all was the Rochester-Genesee Aqueduct. It was 804 feet long with nine massive fifty-foot span support arches and smaller ones attached at the ends. The engineers sank piers six inches into the rock of the river bottom. From this foundation the "parapets of the aqueducts" were fastened securely with "bolts and bars of iron." When it was built, this aqueduct was the longest stone bridge in America. It served as a model for subsequent aqueducts on the canal. Today in Rochester, the graceful arches can still be seen carrying traffic, but now it is land and not water traffic.

Twelve miles east of Schenectady, the longest aqueduct of the Erie stretched 1,188 feet across the Mohawk River Valley on 26 stone piers. The Richmond aqueduct, located at the junction of the Cayuga-Seneca and the Divisions of the New York State Barge Canal, was 894 1/2 feet long and 50 feet wide inside. Thirty piers and two abutments of stone masonry supported the trough of heavy timbers which carried the canal over the river. Thirty-one stone arches supported the towpath. A smaller water bridge 748 feet long spanned the Mohawk, four miles east of Schenectady.

The Rochester area created another canal construction problem. The canal contractors and engineers found Irondequoit Creek valley almost as challenging as the locks and rock cut at Lockport. At first they thought the soil would make an embankment impossible. So they planned to build a wooden aqueduct 60 feet high across the valley. More mature thought made them realize that such a structure could not possibly withstand the winds that blow off Lake Ontario. They chose the embankment model.

The builders sank 900 piles deep into the quicksand of the valley bottom to support a semicircular culvert that permitted the Irondequoit Creek to flow 245 feet through the embankment. The contractors hauled in enough cohesive fill to build a mound 70 feet high. In October of 1822, the completion of the Irondequoit embankment permitted the State to open 180 miles of canal from Little Falls to Rochester. Rochester's boisterous celebration marked the completion. The city, which had previously been not much more than a tiny wilderness settlement, boomed with business. It became the first boom city of America.

With the completion of the embankment and aqueduct at Rochester, the combines and rock cut at Lockport, 84 locks and the 360 miles of ditch, self-taught American engineers had done the job in record time at the lowest cost.

Now, all they had to do was wed the waters and celebrate. And celebrate, they did. New York would not see a party like it until the United States' Bicentennial of 1976.

Fittingly, Phillip Freneau wrote these words:

> For behold it done
> A work from nature's chaos won
> By hearts of oak and hands of toil,
> The spade inverts the rugged soil,
> A work that may remain secure
> While sun exists and moons endure.

"OH! ROCK!"

In 1843, as a panegyric to the rise of the village of Lockport could as well have been written in any canal community west of the Mohawk which had watched this miracle of growth come to pass:

Oh! rock enthroned! fair daughter of the West,
The wilderness is gone and thou are here;
So full of commerce, busy, bustling, gay;
The splashing of a hundred water wheels;
The hum of industry, of a thousand hammers;
The sharp clink, and all the varied forms
Of manly, wealth producing industry --that one
May almost turn the ear incredulous
At the great changes. Thy fathers even, they
Who cut the proud old forest down, are here,
Stand proudly up, almost unbent with years;
See! through thy streets, how Erie's waters come,
Wafting the golden wealth of the great west,
And dashing down thy mountain, bear away
A tide of plenty on to Hudson's tide.

Fair daughter of the West,
Thy circumjacent forest still retires,
And o'er the golden fields which mark the toil
Of husbandmen, rings merrily the harvest home;
Increasing plenty pours along thy streets;
The wilderness is gone, and thou are here.

CANALER VS. LAKER

On the Buffalo waterfront, where Erie Canalers and Great Lakes sailors met, their antagonism for each other often resulted in fisticuffs.

But the rivalry did not end there. Among captains and masters of Lake vessels and canal boats, rivalry was expressed in a more gentlemanly manner.

About 1846, Capt. Henry Randall sold the steamboat WISCONSIN to William Chard, a gentleman largely engaged in canal transportation. Mr. Chard was an expert in canal navigation, but in no sense a lake navigator. Mr. Chard, firstly, changed the orthography of the name of the boat to WISKONSAN, and then, as a business proposition, assumed the command. That's when the trouble commenced.

A "Canaler" as master of a lake steamboat was an absurdity, intolerable, and war was declared against Mr. Chard and his steamboat WISKONSAN. An emblematic war -- a war of ridicule -- was diligently waged. In addition to the blowing of horns and shouting "low bridge," canal harness and wiffletrees were run aloft on the other boats when meeting the WISKONSAN. Steamboat agents were diligent in advising travelers that the master of the WISKONSAN was a landsman, a factor most potent in diverting patronage and Mr. Chard concluded that business demanded a lake navigator for the master of his steamboat and the demand being supplied, hostilities ended and peace was restored. Mr. Chard was energetic in business and social intercourse with all whom he met and, subsequently, was popular in navigation circles.

FISH STORY

Soon after the completion of the Canal, boats from all over the world crowded into New York Harbor. Thanks to the Erie Canal, New York City was becoming the greatest port in the world. With seafaring men from around the world, stories abounded. Here's one:

No doubt the mayor, DeWitt Clinton, received a lot of unsolicited advice on how to deal with the French and British commanders who had been misbehaving in the harbor. Clinton had many friends among the seafarers and shipping tycoons of the city. One of the men who was close to him was a testy mariner with a standout name -- Captain Preserved Fish.

To be absolutely accurate, the old salt's full name was Captain Preserved Fish, Jr. His father had enjoyed the same name, if that is not overstating the fact, and thoughtfully had passed it along to his son when the young'un appeared on the scene in the family's home port of Portsmouth, Rhode Island.

Captain Fish, junior, was a highly successful seaman who, in time, became New York's harbor master and a senior partner in the firm of Fish & Grinnel, shipping merchants. He also had been in partnership briefly with a man named Saul Alley. The way in which the fledgling firm of Fish & Alley foundered provides an insight to the personality of the sea captain.

Alley entered the firm's office one morning and cheerily greeted his partner, who already was at work at his desk.

"Hope you are well this morning, Captain Fish," said Alley cordially, preparing to take off his greatcoat.

The captain turned a fishy eye on Alley.

"This," he said heavily, "is the place for business, sir, not for compliments!"

From that point on the conversation deteriorated and the firm went out of business.

The probability is that Mayor Clinton, like most New Yorkers, savored to the fullest another popular Fish story. This tale alleged that one time, upon his return from a long voyage, Captain Fish's ship was hailed by a revenue cutter in New York Harbor. The official aboard the cutter called out to the ship, demanding identification.

"What's the name of that brig?" he yelled.

"FLYING FISH, sir!"

"Who's your captain?"

"Preserved Fish, sir!"

At that point, it was said, the revenue officer became quite upset over the japery of the ship's officer and boarded the brig with the angry intent of flattening the smart aleck. It took a number of men to convince him that all the replies were straightforward, factual and honest.

III

WORKING ON THE
TOWPATH

Republic Steam Presses, Buffalo.

"CANAWLER, CANAWLER"

Canawler, canawler, you'll never get rich
You work on Sunday
You'll die on the towpath
You'll be buried in the ditch,
(you son of a bitch.)

CONVERSATION WITH A TEAM DRIVER

"Canalling" was (and is) a way of life. Some idea of the old times may be obtained from this conversation in 1883 between J. L. Rigwalt and a team driver on the old Erie. It is quoted from Old Towpaths.

"How do drivers work? By the trip or by the day?"

"Both ways. A man can get a dollar a day or he can hire out by the trip and get about $20 a month!"

"How long does a trip take from Buffalo to Albany and return?"

"Depends on the load -- about 3 weeks on the average. It's easier going to Albany than coming back."

"How many trips can a boat make in a season?"

"About 9 or 10."

"How many months of a year does a driver work?"

"Oh, 8 or 9 months is fair -- sometimes 9 or 10 when the weather is good."

"What do you do winters?"

"Haul up at either end and git what you kin. Sometimes on the railroad and sometimes nothin' at all."

"How many men are there on a boat?"

"Five men generally to a boat -- 2 drivers, 2 steersmen and the captain. A steersman gits about $40 a month."

"HOGGIE ON THE TOWPATH"

Hoggee on the towpath 5 cents a day,
picking up mule balls to eat along the way,

Hoggee on the towpath don't know what to say
walk behind a mule's behind, all the live-long day.

59

MULE DRIVER

Raymond Crean, an Irishman from the Syracuse area, was a mule driver. The following is an interview he gave to the Syracuse Sunday Herald American, June 13, 1976:

"Oh, we were just kids then," Ray tells visitors. "We used to go swimming in the canal up by Allen Street locks, see, and that's how I happened to get the job. They were running short of help and the fellow was looking for someone to drive his mules."

"We young kids got a kick out of it more than anything else." Ray recalls the summer job he held more than half a century ago. "They paid us 50 cents a day, can y' imagine?"

"My job was to drive the mules and keep them a-going. They'd go awful slow, you know. It was just a steady pull, slow, pull," he said, stretching out his arms to show how taut the towline would become.

"They'd work four hours and then they were off four hours," Ray said. "Going down, we get in our shorts - we never did have bathing suits in those days -- we were too poor to have 'em. When the boat would go along, and when you weren't driving why, you'd take a dive in the canal," Ray remembered.

If the weather was good and traffic along the canal wasn't heavy, the group of five or six boats would reach Utica by nightfall.

"See, a certain fellow owned all the boats. He'd have his name on the side of the boat," Ray explained.

"Sometime we wouldn't make Utica that night, and we'd tie up down around Oriskany or Whitesboro," he said.

Once the boats reached the night's destination, the mules would be bedded down for the night.

"We'd take our mules and hay'm up and put'm in the straw where they'd sleep at night. See, out of the five or six boats there'd be one boat where the mules slept," Ray explained.

"We slept with the mules," Ray said. "It was a nice clean straw bed. We had horseblankets we could throw over us if it was cold. Course, it was the summer time and we didn't need much."

Breakfast came early for those who worked on the Erie Canal.

"You'd get up at 5:30 in the morning. Daybreak and you was up. They'd come in and out you'd go! They said, 'Out, Out' and that was it," Ray recalled.

And what breakfasts!

"Oh, there was home fries and eggs and sausages -- all the sausages you could eat. And pancakes and maple syrup -- you could get it cheap then."

Once the crew reached Utica the boats would be turned over to another man. ("I suppose they were working in cahoots together." Ray said) and then the crew would meet up with another group of boats coming from the west.

"As long as you done your work, you was o.k.," Ray said sternly. "If you didn't they'd kick you off at Utica and make you walk home."

Did Ray ever see anyone kicked off a boat?

"Oh sure, there was some of them would get to drinking and then they wouldn't show up next day. But it didn't happen often," he said.

Did Ray remember these older men who worked on the boats?

"Well, let's see, there was Temple Moore and Andy McMullen and. . .," Ray remembered.

"They didn't have much time for us kids. They were good to us and everything but they minded their business and let us alone," he said.

"They were mostly widowers or people who never got married and never made a home for themselves. They worked at whatever they could get. In the summertime, they worked on the canals; in the winter they'd go on other jobs. Just something to survive," Ray said.

The men were between 40 and 65 and "were in good shape for their age, some of these fellas. They were good and tough."

"They smoked old corn cob pipes. Some of them would spit tobacco," Ray recalled.

Ray still has the muledrivers' respect for mules. His voice grew reverent as he described the strength of creatures who pulled the big boats filled with lumber.

"Some of those boats, I don't know what kept them from sinking. The lumber was piled eight or nine feet high. You could feel the boat scraping the bottom of the canal." Ray said.

"Those mules couldn't go any slower because, boy, they were pulling a lot," Ray said

Passing through the locks took 45 minutes or so, and the mules often became a little nervous as they waited.

"They'd get hungry, too," Ray said, pausing to ask the visitor if she'd ever heard a mule haw.

"They'd get a five-pound scoop of oats and corn morning and night. In between time, they'd be a-nibbling on the hay," Ray said.

HOGGIES AND THE SWAMP GHOSTS

Young Hoggies often played tricks on new boys when they tied up near the Rome Swamp. A group would build a fire and sit around it telling ghost stories. Then, someone would speak about the terrible ghost that haunted the swamp, a ghost so horrible that if anyone saw it his hair would turn white as new fallen snow and he never again would be able to speak, and so on. Then gradually they would leave, leaving the new boy alone by the dying fire. As he sat there, nervously looking over his shoulder, a moan would be heard and a white shape rise out of the swamp. With a yell, the boy would run for the boat, convinced that he had seen the dread ghost of the swamp.

THE ERIE'S PAUL BUNYAN

McCarthy, a canalboat mule driver, was supposed to have been the strongest man on the canal in the 1840's. One night, just after his team picked up the tow rope for his six-hour trick, the line broke. McCarthy picked up the rope, put it over his shoulder, and hauled away for five hours, without anyone aboard knowing what was happening to the boat. Meanwhile, the boat, a leaky tub filled with crushed stone, had her bottom ripped out on a sunken rock, and though she sank, McCarthy never stopped pulling. He hauled that barge along the channel for seven miles, its keel sinking deeper into the mud. The state legislature later voted him $500.00 for scooping the canal four feet deeper all along the way from Pittsford to Rochester.

AGNES THE MULE

I'll bet if you took a mule census around the country, you'd find that most of the old canal mules are still alive. A mule don't grow old. And where did you get the idea that a mule is slow? Let me tell you about my mule, Agnes. She had a US brand on her flank, so she was probably a veteran of the Civil War, and she's hauled guns through Georgia for Sherman. I drove Agnes from Buffalo to Albany, and back again, for I don't remember how many years, until she had tuggalls on her backside bigger'n soup-plates, and then I sold her to a farmer up the Genesee Valley. He paid me five dollars for her. He figured maybe she could do a little light work for a few months, maybe.

Some of the rich farmers (most of them named Wadsworth -- well-named too 'cause they were worth wads of greenstuff and I don't mean corn) up the Valley used to have foxhunts, and one day the hounds came right by Agnes' pasture. Well, sir, Agnes just laid back her ears and took after those hounds and, when the fox was cornered, Agnes was there first. After that you just couldn't hold Agnes back when she heard the dogs yip. The farmers' kids took to riding her and they got so many fox tails for getting there first that the hunters began to complain about it. But the farmers told 'em that, if they wanted to hunt over his land, they'd just have to put up with Agnes, sailing over fences like a kangaroo and with a kid in ragged overalls hanging on her back.

"MY OLD CANAL MULE"

Captain Nye describes the canaler's "best friend:" his mule.
The tune is the "Irish Washerwoman."

This world it is great you may get what you want,
There is trouble and fun all depends on your jaunt,
But I love the Latter with laughter and song,
And if you don't like it move peacefully on.
I have an old friend and we get along fine,
He works on the towpath helps keep up the line,
Oh, how he would bray if he could hoist his tail,
But he'll not do for he can't raise his tail.

He was in the army and there you obey,
But he was like others, got smart by the day,
He sure would act stubborn would balk, kick and reel,
And want to kick you at most every meal.
So all became tired at last of his pranks,
For when he felt like it, would run, break the ranks,
He'd bray like a wild ass on mountain, in vale,
'Til a surgeon got wise and cut a nerve in his tail.

Oh, when he's off duty you bet he can run,
He's proud of his record, Old Son-of-a-gun,
Has good traits abundant, a friendly old guy,
But he's an old rounder keep open your eyes.
Can squeal, winnow, prance, kick the bucket, you know,
For grain he is there, naught about him is slow,
What things he would do, you could cry, laugh or wail,
But he says, "I am helpless, I can't raise my tail."

Whatever his failures, I like the old guy,
He is a fun mare, my heart fills with joy.
He's wise as a serpent, I'm sure he's no dove,
Sometimes when I laugh he would send me above.
If he hears firecrackers or gunshot -- look out,
A gray powder lover and may wheel about,
He often gets mad and on me would he sail,
For I snicker and smile when he can't raise his tail.

He has a sharp eye and at me will he stare,
I answered, "Lookout" -- I will not take a dare,
It is then that he acts as though I were to blame,
For all of his troubles, whatever the name.

Oft is playful and pleasant, so pert, like a calf,
He stares like a monkey and then I will laugh,
Oh, yes we are cronies till I he-haw hail,
And he does get mad when he can't raise his tail.

He would kick o'er the traces, spreaders, break the tugs,
Entangle the line, act like he had bugs,
He would go for the brush, straighten up on the run,
And many times, yes, it was more than just fun,
One day did he plaster me, where I'll not say,
But over the bank for awhile I did lay,
The boat stopped to search, I said, groaning, "Some Pal,"
He can sure lift his heels, if he can't lift that tail.

HORACE THE MULE

This story is adapted slightly from a letter to the editor with the name Ed Black and the place Zephyrhills affixed. Search has not revealed who the author is or was beyond the name. I have adaptations of this story from people on the Buffalo waterfront which I collected when I served as Director of the Port of Buffalo.

Mules were hardy. Stronger than horses, they worked harder and longer. They were less prone to accidents.

But on occasion, they became sick. Horace was such a mule. Came down with colic. Don't know if he was related to Agnes, but he did belong to Flennie Ethel.

Concerned, she called the vet, Dr. Squatterfield. "Doctor, Horace is sick -- his stomach is all swollen up, I wish you would come out and look at him."

Dr. Squatterfield said, "Oh, Flennie Ethel, it's after six o'clock and I'm fixing to eat supper. He's just blown up probably with gas and has the colic. Give him an enema of mineral oil and if he isn't better in the morning I"ll come by."

"But, how'll I give it to him?" she asked.

"Ah, Flennie Ethel, you are a farm woman, and know all about those things, get a piece of tube or a piece of hose, put a funnel on one end, and insert the other end and pour in the mineral oil.

"Then make Horace take some exercise; that sometimes unblocks gas."

So Flennie Ethel went out to the barn and there stood Horace with his head down; he was moaning and groaning, and his stomach was so swollen it looked like it was going to burst.

She looked around the barn for a funnel, but the nearest thing she could find was her brother's fox hunting horn hanging on the wall; a beautiful gold-plated instrument with gold tassels hanging from it. She took the horn, lubricated it with axle grease and affixed it -- properly.

Horace didn't pay much attention.

Then she reached up on the shelf where medicines for farm animals were kept. . . . But, instead of picking up a bottle of mineral oil, she picked up a bottle of mineral spirits, otherwise known as turpentine, and poured a right liberal dose into the horn.

Horace raised his head with a sudden jerk. He let out a yell that could have been heard a mile away. He reared up on his hind legs, brought his front legs down, knocked down the barn gate, jumped a five-foot fence and started down the road at a mad gallop.

Now Horace's backside was on fire and all this exercise commenced freeing the trapped gas, so that every so often the horn would give a long drawn out blast.

All the dogs in the neighborhood knew that when that horn was blowing, it meant that Flennie Ethel's brother, Bill, was going fox hunting, and out they dashed, following Horace. It was a marvelous sight: Horace running at full speed with the hunting horn in a most unusual position, the mellow notes issuing therefrom, the tassels waving and the dogs barking joyously as they followed along.

They passed the home of old man Harvey Morgan, who was sitting on his front porch. He hadn't drawn a sober breath in fifteen years, and he gazed in fascinated amazement at the sight that unfolded before his eyes. He couldn't believe what he was seeing. (Incidentally, he became head of Alcoholics Anonymous immediately afterwards).

By this time it was getting dark. Horace and the dogs were approaching the canal. The lock tender heard the horn blowing, figured that a boat was approaching, so he hurried out and started cranking up the bridge.

Horace went overboard and many of the dogs followed him but they all managed to swim out.

Now, it happened that the lock tender was running for the office of sheriff in the county, but he managed only seven votes. The people figured that any man who didn't know the difference between a mule coming down the canal and a boat wasn't fit to hold public office in the county anyway.

"SIMON SLICK"

William Hullfish, in his book, The Canawlers' Songbook, introduces this tune as follows:
"Most Delaware and Hudson Canal songs were adapted from Erie Canal material. However, this song appears to be unique to the area. It was collected in Sullivan County, New York by John Price."

I know an old canaller,
His name is Simon Slick.
He had a mule with dreamy eyes,
Lord how that mule could kick.
He'd wink his eyes,
He'd wag his tail,
And greet you with a smile.
Then gently telegraph his legs,
And send you half a mile.

Chorus:
Whoa! Mule, Whoa! I'm done with you forever.
You ain't no good, you never was and you never will be neither.
You're gonna die and take a trip to the hot place down below.
Old Satan sees you coming, He'll shout Whoa there mule, Whoa.

Now this mule he's a daisy,
He pulverized the hog.
Dissected seven Chinamen
And he kicked a yellar dog.
He kicked as quick as lightin'
And he had an iron jaw.
He's just the mule to have around
to tame your mother-in-law.

Chorus:
Whoa! Mule, Whoa! Why don't you hear them hollar.
Tie a knot right in his tail so he don't slip through his collar.
Why don't they put him on a track, why don't they let him go?
And everytime he comes around shout, "Whoa! there mule, Whoa."

MAKIN' MULES

From <u>The Rochester Democrat & Chronicle</u>
(1985)

Mules are back, and Lloyd Clark's got 'em. And if you want 'em, you can have 'em.

That's because Clark not only keeps mules but, on demand, he also makes mules.

Big mules.

In fact, the <u>biggest</u> mules.

Clark, who's 42 and lives near East Bethany, Genesee County, makes the most of his living as a mobile blacksmith. But he makes an ever-increasing part of his living as something even rarer: a breeder of mules.

People bring mares -- female horses -- to Clark's horse farm on Linden Road. And they leave with mares that, 11 months later, will produce some of the biggest mules in the East.

And just how does Clark know their mules will be big?

Say hello to King Don Juan Carlos.

King Don Juan Carlos -- Carlos for short -- is the ass that, with the mares, produces the mules. But Carlos is no ordinary ass. He's a breed known as the mammoth jack -- and that's the biggest kind of all.

He stands a full 15.3 hands at the withers, which is horse talk for 63 inches at the shoulders. He weighs between 900 and 1,000 pounds, which is twice as much as your average donkey. And his ears measure about 14 inches apiece, creating an earspan of close to three feet.

We won't even discuss his legs.

Indeed, Carlos may be the biggest jack in the state, and he's certainly among the biggest in the upper Northeast. And that's the main reason that Clark chose to buy him.

With mules, bigger is better.

Looks don't count.

Actually, Carlos looks great -- for a mammoth jack. But he doesn't look too good for much of anything else. He has big bulgy eyes and a funny cow rump and a tail with short hair except for a bush at the end.

And he makes a sound reminiscent of an engine with no muffler, suggesting that he wishes he'd been born a Harley-Davidson.

"He's such a homely devil," Clark says, "you feel sorry for the poor slug."

Not too sorry, though. He has a pretty good job.

Last year, Clark fixed Carlos up with three nice mares. This year, he got him dates with 10. And if word of his service continues to travel, the mules, he believes, will continue to multiply.

People, he says, just have to learn that mules can be better buys than horses. "They're a third stronger than a horse of equal size," he says, "and they eat a third less than a horse of equal size. They're also a lot more hardy than a horse. That's why they're used in hot climates; their stamina is unbelievable. The Amish down in Lancaster, Pennsylvania, use mules more than horses; if you talk to them, they'll say a mule's as good as a tractor."

Clark, to be sure, has nothing against horses; as a matter of fact, he raises them, too. But mules just happen to have some advantages. And among them, ironically, is a lot more horse sense.

"You can feed 'em like cattle," Clark says. "Just dump the grain out, and they'll never overeat. Horse'll stick his head in a grain box and eat himself to death.

"Mule paces himself," he continues. "People say they're stubborn; they're not stubborn, they just watch out for themselves. Horse'll work 'til he drops; mule will stop and rest. But he'll go on a lot farther than a horse.

"There are problems, too, of course. They're not as easy to handle. You've got to be patient; you can't be rough on 'em. But once they're trained, they stay trained. You just have to be a partner with a mule; you can't be his boss."

And who would want to be?

Not Clark's customers, who seem to be as satisfied as customers get.

"We're definitely very, very pleased with our mule," says Kay Leslie of Alexander, also in Genesee County.

Kay and her husband, Dave, brought Gretchen, their gray mare, to visit with Carlos in May 1985. Last April, they were happily rewarded with Halley, a mare mule (called a "molly") that they named after the comet.

"She's real beautiful boned," Kay says, "and her personality's so much sweeter than a horse. In fact, we had the same mare bred back to Lloyd's jack. We're going to try to get a driving team."

Does this mean that mules will someday replace horses?

Well, probably not all horses. But maybe quite a few of them.

At least, that's what Betsy Hutchins says.

Hutchins is co-founder of the American Donkey & Mule Society, whose headquarters are in Denton, Texas. And she says that her society's brand of animal is coming up from behind.

"Mules have followed with the recreational growth of the horse," she says. "Our people are using these mules like saddle horses. They've got more character. They've got physical superiority, too -- but I think most of us like them for their insides more than their outsides. Besides, those short ears are so silly-looking."

Whatever the reason, the society, which began in 1967, now has 3,000 members in 20 regional clubs. That first year, Hutchins says, this country had maybe four annual donkey-and-mule shows. Last year, it held around 350.

Which is fitting, she says, because America has by far the most winners. And foremost among those winners, she says, are the mammoth jacks.

"In this century, mammoth jacks are the largest and finest breed of ass in the entire world," she says. "And the best ones of all are in this country. Other countries also have superb horses, but we've got the best jackasses."

And, she adds proudly, we always have.

"George Washington imported the first big jacks that started the mammoth breed. He bred the first high-quality mules in this country. And now interest is growing all the time, and everybody's having a lot of fun with them."

As for the King Don Juan Carlos, Hutchins doesn't know him personally but, going on a description, she confirms he's impressive.

"He's probably the largest one in the New England and upper East area," she says. "Certainly, there are thousands -- but that's a big jack. He certainly may be the largest in New York."

And that's one reason Lloyd Clark has equally large hopes.

Clark is unquestionably devoted to the horse world. Born in Canandaigua and raised in Theresa, Jefferson County, he came to East Bethany about 20 years ago. Soon after, while working as a truck driver, he got horseshoeing lessons from a horse-owning neighbor. In 1968, he started shoeing full time, and he now covers several counties in his blacksmith truck.

He owns 50 acres of land and rents another 50 nearby. On them, he keeps around 20 horses, plus Carlos and two mules. Outside his house, you generally can see a few of those equine residents. And if they're not enough to prove Clark's devotion, just take a look inside his house.

The white farmhouse, which he shares with his wife, Kate, and two of their three sons, is on its way to becoming the Museum of the Horse.

The walls are covered with horse wallpaper, in front of which hang several framed horse prints. The kitchen china cabinet is filled with 100 ceramic and brass miniature horses, donkeys and mules. And near it are boxes with thousands of pictures of real horses, donkeys and mules.

Among the other artifacts are a horse pillow, a donkey clock and copies of "The Quarter Horse Journal," "Horse Bits," "Western Horseman" and "The Brayer: Voice of the Donkey & Mule World." Plus hundreds of ribbons and trophies from horse shows.

And a Hopalong Cassidy watch.

70

The Clarks have been raising quarter horses for more than 20 years; Lloyd breeds them, too, with a horse named Mr. Hill City. Lloyd bought his first mule about 18 years ago, but he first thought of mule breeding around 1980. (Mules, for the record, do come in male and female, but so far all the ones produced have been sterile).

"I read an article in "Western Horseman" telling about how popular mules were, and I read about those mammoth jacks," Clark says. "A lot of times, when you get in on the ground floor, you can make a little money on it. I had the first mammoth jack in the state, and we were the first ones here to produce good-size riding mules. I haven't made a killing on it yet, but it is getting popular."

Clark has had three mammoth jacks, all of which he imported from Kentucky and Tennessee. That first jack, Dodge City, was a little too small and, consequently, so were his mules. The second one, Jesse James, was big enough, but he died of a horse disease. So in 1984, Clark came up with Carlos. He cost $5,000 -- but he's made back more than half.

Clark charges $200 to breed a mare to Carlos and that, he claims is a definite bargain. After all, it costs $400 to breed a mare to his horse stud -- and a big mule can be worth more than a big horse. But not everybody in these parts is sold on mules, so Clark has to do some convincing.

Once he has managed to convince the customers, all he has to do is to convince Carlos.

Apparently, he's not always willing to work.

"You kind of have to talk him into it," Clark says. "He'll come out all excited and then decide he wants to roll on the ground or watch the sparrows flying around the barn. Then finally, for some reason, he'll do his thing."

His thing takes an average of 20 minutes, during which Clark has to hold him by a lead shank. When he's done, he goes back to rolling or watching.

"To him," Clark observes, "it is just a job."

As long as he's willing to do it, however, Clark will continue to rent him out. And if he can't sell customers on mules himself, he evidently can turn to Carlos' progeny.

"We had a horse owner come out in the spring who wanted to breed her Appaloosa mare to the quarter horse," Clark says. "She saw Carlos and said, 'People actually breed to this thing? I wouldn't breed any of my horses to that.'"

Then the woman went out back and saw one of Carlos' little babies.

"The little mule was so friendly," Clark says. "It followed her around -- and she decided she'd breed her mare to the jack."

He remembers that the decision cost him the $200 fee difference.
And he also remembers the horse owner's bemused last question:
"You mean," she said, "you get this kind of baby out of this ugly-looking jack?"

"NEVER TAKE A HINDSHOE FROM A MULE"

This is a parody of a Braham and Harrigan song, from the show *The Mulligan Guard* called, "Never Take the Horseshoe From the Door." The words were collected by Harold Thompson along the Erie Canal and it is also found in the Catskill Mountains of New York State along the Delaware and Hudson Canal.

A story has come down from old Mathusam,
I learned it when I was a boy in school.
You'll make a great mistake and don't forget it.
If you bother round the hind parts of a mule.

Chorus:
So never tickle a mule when he's reposing.
If you disturb his slumbers you're a fool,
If you don't want to visit the undertaker,
Never take a hindshoe from a mule.

The business end of a mule is might ticklish,
Never, never touch him as a rule,
He'll kick you full of holes in seven seconds,
Trust him not, there's mischief in a mule.

(Chorus)

When you see the animal's old and feeble,
Don't you never handle him as a rule.
You'll need a chest-protector on your eyebrow,
They'll lay you on a ton of ice to cool.

(Chorus)

If you touch his caudal appendage, you're a goner,
Asleep or awake you'll find he's not a fool.
Oh, you'll think you were struck by seven kinds of lightning,
If you bother with the hind part of a mule.

A LIFE SAVING CANAL HORSE

According to hoggies, mules had more sense than horses. Yet, on two occasions, Barney Dugan's canal horse, Old Joe, proved a hero.

Annie Ginley was playing on her father's boat at Big Basin on the canal. As Dugan's boat and Old Joe lumbered along, the girl fell into the canal.

Before any other aid could be given to her, Old Joe plunged into the water, seized the girl's dress in his teeth, swam clear across the basin where the bank was low and clambered out with her.

For Old Joe that was enough work for one day. He refused to swim back and had to be taken from the tow line and traveled back a mile to a bridge.

The following day, two hoggies were wrestling on the tow path. One was thrown into the canal. He could not swim; there was no one near him who could. While a boatman looked for a pike pole, Old Joe jumped into the canal and brought the boy safely back to the towpath.

THE RATTLESNAKE HUNTER

All that is necessary to frighten some people is to mention snakes -- and the existence of rattlesnakes scares them cold. That a person would purposely seek out them seems unbelievable, yet here is a tale about just such an individual.

In the early days -- about 175 years ago -- of building the Erie Canal through what is now Lockport, Niagara County, many rattlers were encountered. Where the locks now stand was a portion of a natural glen in the Niagara escarpment. Many rattlesnakes abode on the rocky slopes of this glen. A bit northwest this same creek tumbled through another glen which had even more snakes. The highway down this glen is still known as Rattlesnake Hill. Not far from this was the first sandstone quarry in the area and, because of the prevalence of rattlers, the rock quarried was for some time known as rattlesnake stone.

Our story has to do with an account of a rattlesnake hunter who was a town character in Lockport in 1822. Nearly thirty years later the tale was recounted by one of two young men who had, on a warm and sunny Sunday morning in April, 1822, decided to find a rattlesnake den down the branch of the Eighteen-Mile Creek, "under the gentling influence of such weather and there being no church or other place of worship except that of Friends, and 'it being exceedingly uncertain as to the moving of the spirit.'" (The first religious body in Lockport was the Friends (Quakers) who held silent meetings until someone, prompted by the "moving of the spirit," rose to speak.)

Each of our young men had a good stick and was wearing high boots. Down through the broken ledges into the deep ravine they descended, to a point where they found "tall John of the gaunt hemlock tanned complexion, the rattlesnake hunter who was enemy of the whole reptile race." He was famous in the area as the sole proprietor and vendor of the great remedy known as Rattlesnake Oil. The "Ile" was used as a great rheumatic and gout remedy, which John assured all patrons to be infallible.

John's story was reported in the January 2, 1851, issue of The Niagara Democrat, and was later retold, in the manner given below, in an issue of The Lockport Union-Sun.

John was also notorious for the quantities of scotch snuff which daily was strewed on his waistcoat and besmeared on his face and sandy colored beard as he used it. He carried the snuff in a leather pocket from which he took it by the handful. His long gaunt figure thus covered with yellow scotch rendered him a perfect terror to the whole rattlesnake tribe which was never known to offer any resistance to his attacks because of their antipathy to tobacco.

The first warm spring day he would stealthily approach a den and, having commenced the slaughter, leave only a few to perpetuate the race, thus insuring him a source for his "Ile."

Our young men saw him, armed with a small stick of blue beech and a forked one with which he first secured the snake astride the neck to prevent it from biting itself and thus rendering its oil poisonous. When first observed he was standing motionless, his body half inclined with the wooden fork lifted for a space of two or three minutes. Then there was a thrust of the fork and a blow from the beech, and another writhing victim was tossed on a heap of those already slain.

We had almost gotten to him when he warned us to approach cautiously, and we had crawled almost to him before we saw a snake, although we had the feeling one might be by our heel. He motioned us to stop. Standing still for several minutes, we saw several heads appear. Soon a dozen were within a few feet of us. One large snake a few feet above us made its way down the hill directly for my companion. John stood with uplifted stick until it was almost near, then, losing his courage, he started down the hill, slipping, sliding over the stone, a breakneck pace of "neck or snake" til he brought up on the creek bank.

I remained on a flat stone intending to kill a snake, but as they continued to appear and I counted fifteen hissing heads around my feet, I followed my companion down, bettering his time.

In a short time the snake hunter came down the hill, dragging a string of snakes on a stick as boys string the eels they have caught. "Poor luck this morn," he complained, "but some are pretty fat and larger than the general run." He counted, "Only seventy-one. Poor luck. Less and less every year. By this time another year comes round they'll hardly be worth hunting. The Canawl is going to spile the business, with new settlers, they'll bring hogs and they are wonderful critters for these snakes, sure death on 'em." He took off his hat and wiped the perspiration which was beginning to drop from his face. "They'll be dredful scarce next spring. You see," he continued, in a plaintive voice, "I am a sickly man. Not able to maintain a family on a farm like mine. Ev'ry spring I can get a few dollars to help me get comforts for my family." Tears were visible at the mention of his family. "No use countin' on snakes in the future. Already canawlers thicker'n the trees used to be. I wish I had never heard of a canawl, or that I hadn't settled short of Michigan."

Then, thrusting his left hand in the leather pocket and taking out a quart full of yellow scotch, he besmeared his face with it, not failing to imbibe enough to stimulate his olfactory nerves, and seizing his string of snakes he strode away, dragging them on the ground.

His predictions proved true. In another year his trade in oil was ruined.

Some years later, it was heard that he had moved beyond the great Lake Michigan, where he lived for twenty years. The last tiding of him was that he had moved to the foot of the Rocky Mountains in consequence of a contemplated canal which would run within ninety miles of him.

RATTLESNAKES

Associated with the hardships of early pioneer life are some peculiar recollections. When Rochester was first settled, rattlesnakes were no joke. They were numerous and altogether too socially inclined, not being adverse to seeking shelter and comfort in the houses of our first inhabitants. Either on, or under, the bed seemed to be their favorite cuddling place. Hamlet Scrantom, in a talk before the pioneers' festival, told of his killing a number of rattlesnakes that intruded into his log cabin, built in 1812, on the site of the present Powers Building. Simon Pierson told the same group that, when his wife was lying ill with the ague, the family dog set up a tremendous barking, and, as Pierson told it:

"Behold a famous great rattlesnake was under the bed, which was soon dispatched, but not until he had shown his musical talents. But I did not blame the snake for our floor was made of split logs."

In their <u>Reminiscences</u>, Hosea Rogers said rattlesnakes were common in Carthage and Enos Stone stated that the principal colony of snakes was on the bank of the river below the Lower Falls, at a place called Rattlesnake Point. Their oil was held in great esteem as a cure for stiff joints and the gall for fevers. William Hincher, Jr., said that, alone, he had killed forty rattlesnakes at one time along the banks of the river below the Falls and that on one occasion a group of hunters went up the river in canoes and killed three hundred snakes in one day.

"In the first warm days of spring they would come out, roll and entwine themselves in large coils, with their heads sticking out; so torpid you could kill them easily," he said. This would continue until the weather was settled; then they would go out on their summer rambles, not returning to their dens until cold weather came again."

Edwin Scrantom, in his <u>Old Citizen Letters</u>, had much to say about rattlesnakes. He stated that snakes were plenty all along Buffalo Street, east of Fitzhugh Street to the river, and all the way down the river to the lake, especially among the rocks near the Falls. When Joab Britton was blasting out rocks at Carthage for building the first aqueduct at Rochester, he uncovered a den containing an enormous number of rattlesnakes. Edwin Scrantom also related an amusing story of three Rochester boys who put a pint of rattlesnake oil into a barrel of sperm oil, and succeeded in selling the entire mixture, as rattlesnake's oil, in ounce vials at fifty cents each. The purchasers were all satisfied and wanted more!

ROCHESTER RATTLESNAKES

The old Northampton records show that a bounty of three shillings was voted for every dozen rattlesnakes killed. From 1812 to 1815, while John Mastick was Supervisor of the Town of Greece, the bounty payments were unusually heavy and indicated a fierce warfare upon the reptiles. While, in modern times fraudulent claims are not wholly unheard of, they were hardly to be expected in those primitive days; but human nature seems not to have changed. Professor W.H. McIntosh tells this story:

A man by the name of Shaw, living at Hanford's Landing, one day went to the mouth of the Genesee River, and by raiding a den of rattlesnakes, returned with one hundred and thirty rattles. He took them to Supervisor Mastick, and received the required order for the bounty. After counting the rattles, Mr. Mastick threw them out of the back window into the yard. Jacob Teeples, a local loafer, observed this transaction and at once began to show an unusual activity hunting snakes. Every day he returned with a good string of rattles, upon which the Supervisor gave him his bounty, until he began to be alarmed at the inroads made upon the bounty fund. But one day, thinking he must have a very large pile of rattles below his window he looked out and was astounded to find none. Every one had been taken away, and probably many times, by the enterprising Jacob Teeples!

SNAKES AND IRISH MUD

There was a big passenger business on the Erie Canal when I was a hoggie, but even then the railroads was getting a lot of the travelers away from the packet boats. Back before the war -- the Civil War, I mean -- the westbound boats was loaded with Irish and Germans. There was a packet skipper named Joe who used to get a lot of that business and I've heard that it's on account of him that the snakes left the towpath.

Joe hated snakes. One day his boat was going through a regular school of watersnakes and one of his passengers, an Irish greenhorn, was watching 'em and he fell overboard. The poor devil hadn't a chance to wash since he left Ireland and there was still enough Irish dirt on him so that the water that had touched him was poison to the watersnakes and they curled up and died. That gave Joe an idea. Most of the Irish had a little bowl with them, filled with dirt from their own fields in Ireland, and Joe made every one of them give him a handful of it. He was tired of having his hoggies walk over the rattlesnakes sleeping on the warm towpath and, when he had a bushel or so of the dirt, he scattered it all along the canal bank. They say that from that day to this, snakes keep away from he Canal and I know I never saw one all the time I was canaling.

BIG DROUGHT

Usually the canal feeders supplied enough water to fill the canal prism and float the packets and the freighters. Occasionally, a very dry year caused serious problems. Once it got so bad that the whole of Lake Erie and all the feeders along the Canal couldn't hardly keep it from going dry. They arrested a woman at Palmyra for filling her washtub from the Erie and stranding ten boats. Towpath walkers went along the Canal all summer pulling up weeds and grapevines so their roots couldn't suck water and they carried shotguns to shoot crows and sparrows that tried to take a drink. Down near Utica, farmers got so desperate that they dug up their plants out of their fields and loaded 'em on wheelbarrows and run 'em over to the Canal to dip their roots in water.

There was one fellow who brought over a runty squash vine that he'd kept alive for three weeks by spitting on it now and then and it had two or three nubbin' squash on it. He stuck the roots in the Canal and that vine was so thirsty that it dragged the water out like a big hose and left three miles of bottom bare. The squashes started to swell like rubber balloons and the farmer had to run like the devil for ten minutes to keep from getting smashed. Then a section of the vine went past him, traveling like a racer snake, and he grabbed at it and his hand closed on a flower bud. The bud turned into a flower and then into a squash so fast it blew his hand off like a fistful of gunpowder would. He made a living for years after that peddling sections from the stems of the leaves of that vine. They used to use them for drainage tile.

ENTERTAINMENT AT THE SIDECUT

At the sidecut near Albany there was plenty of entertainment in addition to boxing and brawling. It is said that a certain Davie would allow himself to be knocked downstairs five times in succession with a hammer-blow on the head. I have not learned the reason for his prejudice against a sixth blow.

"Jumpy" Burke's favorite exhibition was to leap clear across a lock with a pair of heavy dumb-bells in his hands. Nelse Carter ambitiously introduced a variety show for his patrons; he is said to have been the first and only one of the old-time hosts to try dancing girls. His patrons preferred a tightrope artist who every night walked from Nelse's place, across the canal and to the top of a tree, pushing a wheelbarrow and at times (by some cantrip which I have not clearly in mind) frying an egg in transit. Jimmy Wood is said to have installed the first telephone in West Troy, as it was called, and insisted upon a large gong in place of the sissy bell usually provided. When someone called him up, the canallers for three blocks would rush up to hear the critter talk.

CANAL STURGEON

The Erie Canal was a grand place for fishing back in the seventies, especially in the Spring when the big pike and sturgeon came in from Lake Erie. Lots of times the captain wouldn't let the boys drop a line in the Canal unless the boat was tied up. I remember once I had a blacksmith make me a hook out of a crowbar, and I put it on a length of old towrope and baited it with a young pig and dropped it in the Canal up near Medina. (We were headed for Rochester with a load of barley.) One of those Lake Erie sturgeon grabbed the hook and hauled us back nearly to Lockport before we could get a rope out and snub it around the 'butment of a bridge. Nearly pulled three mules into the Canal and, for weeks after that, we had to harness those mules with their heads facing the boat, they was so used to going backwards. I'd have had my teeth wrapped around my ears sure if it hadn't been that we sold the sturgeon to a boatman that was headed west. He just put the mules in their stalls and let the sturgeon haul him. The only trouble was that he was just figuring on going to Buffalo, but the sturgeon wouldn't stop there and he ended up in Detroit. He sold the sturgeon for five cents a pound, and got enough to hire a sidewheeler tug to take him back to the Buffalo breakwater. How's that? Well, that's one thing I always forgot to ask him. I never did find out how he got his boat and the sturgeon through the locks at Lockport.

PRIVY

The farmers used to put in claims against the State when a break washed out their crops, and you'd be surprised what good crops there always was in them flooded fields. One of the biggest claims I ever knew of, though, wasn't for crops at all, it was for just an old wooden privy that had maybe ninety cents' worth of hemlock boards in it. But, the man who owned it -- he lived near Bushnell's Basin, north of where the big fill goes over the Irondequoit Valley -- he said it was worth $2,000 to him and he got it, too. He sold farm tools and wagons, and most of his customers didn't pay cash. He told the Court of Claims that he'd take a pencil and write on the inside of the door just who owed him money and how much. It was his bookkeeping system. Then the break came and the water washed his privy down the creek and smashed it into kindling wood, and all his records were gone. He claimed he had at least $2,000 owing him and that he could never collect it now with no scrap of writing to tell him who owed him what.

9 MILLION STONE

In the 1890s and early 1900s, a $9,000,000.00 repair project was started to change the course of the Erie Canal in some places and to deepen it in others. My cousin, Phil, remembers working on this project during college vacations. He tells how stone from his father's farm was brought to reinforce the Canal bed. The stone was weighed at the farm, then loaded onto wagons and drawn to the canal four miles away. The drivers, being in a hurry to make as many trips as possible, did not care how many stones were lost along the way, until the engineers became wise and did not weigh the load until it reached the canal.

THE DAY THE BOTTOM FELL OUT OF THE CANAL

Early in the afternoon of July 30, 1907, I started to cross the bridge over the Erie Canal at Clinton Street in Syracuse. Glancing eastward at what should have been the peaceful waters of the "big ditch," I spied a huge dead cat, yellow in color. It was not unusual to see dead cats floating in the Erie but this one was acting strangely. It was swimming rapidly toward me.

I was fairly certain that my mind was normal, but who of us can be certain? I looked more closely at the strange phenomenon. There was no doubt about it. The animal was deceased and the corpse, evidently long in the water, had undergone considerable deterioration.

Not only was the body approaching the bridge, but the canal which had been content to behave itself ever since it was formally opened by Governor DeWitt Clinton in 1825, was playing unheard of tricks. Suddenly, the usually stagnant water had become a lively stream rushing westward.

It was not long before the late lamented cat had passed out of sight under the bridge where I was standing and I heard a great clatter of fire and police equipment. Looking toward the west, I saw with amazement the cause for all of the excitement. Five canal barges were trying desperately to crowd into an enormous hole. The stern of one of the boats had sunk out of sight and the prow was sticking straight up in the air. In their haste to rush down the opening, the barges had managed to get all tangled up.

Soon the streets were roped off to keep a curious crowd from going down the towpath. Being a newspaper reporter, I was allowed to go close to the scene of the trouble and soon had one of the best stories in my newspaper career. It took considerable questioning to find out what had really happened. The tale needed no embellishment. The facts were fantastic!

Had anyone told me that such a thing was possible, I would have judged him crazy. The bottom of the canal was the earth, just like the bottom of a river. Whoever heard of the bottom of a river falling out? Yet, it had happened. There was a hole in the Erie large enough to accommodate five barges. Moreover, water was rushing from east and west forming a raging whirlpool, then disappearing into the bowels of the earth.

The explanation was simple.

When the canal was built in the early part of the nineteenth century, it was necessary to cross Onondaga Creek, a sizeable stream which in many European countries would rate as a river. To make this crossing, the engineers had to build a culvert over the creek. This had collapsed, letting the water of the canal into the stream.

The five ill-fated barges were tied up within a short distance of each other, loading and unloading merchandise which included coal, lumber and flour. Luckily, most of the people who lived on the boats were taking advantage of the stopover to do some shopping in the city stores. When the canal started to collapse, all the men hot-footed it for safety and no one was injured, save a pair of mules which was drowned.

Not only did the canal cave in but also the rear walls of some of the buildings on the canal banks. Fifty feet of the south wall of Greenway's brewery fell into the maelstrom. Onondaga Creek, suddenly augmented by canal water, looked as it frequently did during Spring freshets. In some places it overflowed its banks.

The break was the topic of conversation for weeks. I overheard a colored man describing the scene to a friend.

"When Ah saw dat big hole filled wid boats, Ah thought dat we had a earthquake. Ah nebber seen a canal dreen down no hole befo'. No Suh!" he said.

It was a difficult task to remove the wreckage from the canal. After everything that could be easily dragged out of the hole was disposed of, the wrecks were soaked with kerosene and burned. For days a huge volume of black smoke and flame drifted upward.

It took several weeks to repair the culvert and to get things moving again. From that time until 1923, when the Erie was abandoned almost exactly 100 years from Governor Clinton's visit, it gave no more difficulty.

However, Syracuse had canal trouble before the 1907 disaster. On April 6, 1901, the Oswego Canal which connected with the Erie, gave the city a thrill when the James Street bridge collapsed under the weight of a trolley car full of passengers. Down went the car to the bottom. Thirty-nine people were bruised, shaken and badly scared but no one was killed. Fortunately, the water had not yet been let into the canal preparatory to the opening of Spring navigation. A man and the horse he was driving also fell into the canal but both escaped death, the man with some bruises and the horse with three broken ribs. In the seat with the driver was his dog, a small animal about one-quarter fox terrier and three-quarters assorted makes. When he felt the wagon sinking and the bridge cracking, he emitted a loud "Yipe!" -- dog language for "I'm gittin' out of here!" He jumped out of the wagon, scrambled back to solid ground and high-tailed it clear to Clinton Square, never stopping until he reached the old Court House.

Hamilton L. Aberdeen, a senior who was taking civil engineering at Syracuse University, stepped on the bridge just as it began to give way. He jumped back and was spared the fate of the trolley car passengers. Aberdeen told newspaper reporters that his experience was worthwhile as he was working on his graduation thesis and had learned something which he could use in it.

"What's the title of your thesis?" asked the reporter.

"A Study of Bridge Construction," was the reply.

I doubt if there was ever a better example of on-the-spot research. His professor marked it "A."

"FINGY" CONNERS AND HIS SCOOPERS

In the last decades of the 19th century, one of the most dramatic and violent chapters in Buffalo-Erie Canal history broke out on the notorious waterfront.

This says a lot because violence had been a common and accepted practice on the Buffalo waterfront for the better (or was it the worst) part of the century.

Reminiscent of a struggle of Greek gods, this was an epic struggle between two Irish titans from Buffalo's Irish First Ward: William J. "Fingy" Conners and Rowland B. Mahany. According to Max McCarthy, a Buffalo writer, they were "two of the most ambitious, determined and intelligent Irish-Americans ever born on the Niagara Frontier." Few who knew them would doubt that. Beyond their Irish heritage, the two men didn't have too much in common but they both had an army of faithful followers and fighters.

To put this Irish "civil war" in perspective, one must understand how the harbor of Buffalo operated during the 19th century. From the opening of the canal in 1825 to about the middle of the 1840's, transfer facilities for people and products at the Port of Buffalo remained in a comparatively rudimentary state.

At the docks, freight was handled manually. Shipments had to be packed in boxes, barrels, bales, baskets and other small containers so they could be carried on the strong backs and in the brawny arms of the Irish stevedores. Even such bulk commodities as grain, in those early days, had to be shipped in bags or similar packaging. If actually carried in bulk in the ship's hold, it had to be shoveled or scooped into barrels or buckets, which were then hoisted by block and tackle or carried on the backs of the "dock walloppers" to canal boats or to the Buffalo flour mills.

In 1839, Chicago forwarders shipped their first wheat cargo to Buffalo. Scoopers shoveled the bulk grain into baskets which they carried on their backs to the docks. It took days to unload this relatively light load. Some forwarders realized that more efficient transfer facilities and methods were needed if Buffalo and the canal could ever be expected to accommodate the flood of grain that would soon be pouring out of the "Bread Basket" of America.

One commission merchant, Joseph Dart, did not believe that Irishmen's backs were the best transfer facilities. He decided to do something about it. What he did in the Buffalo Harbor created a revolution in bulk commodity transfer in ports around the world. He thought that Irishmen's backs were too inefficient to accommodate the anticipated flood of grain from the Midwest and West. He conceived of a huge warehouse with "adjustable" elevators and conveyors to be worked by steam. Dart so arranged his elevator that canal boats could pass under it and be unloaded by elevator. The original elevator had a transfer capacity of 15,000 bushels per day which is insignificant by today's standards, but was revolutionary for its day.

Between 1848 and 1857 the number of elevators increased slowly. The elevator performed three functions: safe, cheap storage; quasi-manufacturing plant for drying, cleaning and mixing grain; and a trans-shipping machine.

Had it not been for Dart's elevators, by the time of the Civil War, Buffalo would have drowned in a sea of grain. Anthony Trollope, an English writer, picturesquely described it:

> An elevator is as ugly a monster as has yet been produced. In uncouthness of form it outdoes those obsolete old brutes who used to roam about the semi-aqueous world, and live a most uncomfortable life with their great hungering stomachs and huge unsatisfied maws. The elevator itself consists of a big moveable trunk, moveable as is that of an elephant, but not pliable, and less graceful even than an elephant. This is attached to a huge granary or barn; but in order to give altitude within the barn for the necessary moving up and down of this trunk, seeing that it cannot be curled gracefully to its purposes as the elephant's is curled, there is an awkward box erected on the roof of the barn, giving some twenty feet of additional height, up into which the elevator can be thrust. It will be understood, then, that this big moveable trunk, the head of which, when it is at rest, is thrust up into the box on the roof, is made to slant down in an oblique direction from the building to the river. For the elevator is an amphibious institution, and flourishes only on the banks of navigable waters. When its head is ensconced within its box, and the beast of prey is thus nearly hidden within the building, the unsuspicious vessel is brought up within reach of the creature's trunk, and down it comes, like a mosquito's proboscis, right through the deck, into the open aperture of the hole, and so into the very vitals and bowels of the ship. When there, it goes to work upon its food and with a greed and an avidity that is disgusting to a beholder of any taste or imagination.

While this invention eliminated the use of Irishmen's backs to transfer the grain, the elevator did need people in the hold of the vessel to scoop the grain into the elevator containers on the endless belt. These Irish scoopers were at the center of this struggle between Mahany and Conners.

The long trunk, or wooden pipe, described by Trollope had two compartments. On one side, loaded troughs ascended on a pliable band while, at the same time, empty compartments descended on the other side. In the hold of the vessel, six laborers shoveled the grain about the base of the trunk so that the empty buckets could scoop it up and carry it to the top of the elevator. It operated very much like an ordinary dredging machine, except that grain, rather than mud, was elevated. At the top of the long trunk the troughs emptied themselves into a chute. At this point, an operator regulated the flow of grain from the chute by a door which was opened and closed by the touch of his finger. Through this doorway the grain ran into a measure and was weighed in units of forty bushels. A recording device at the top of the bin measured out the required units. As the hand of the scale approached close to forty bushels, the door was closed so that only a thin trickle of grain ran through. When the exact measure had been made a teller or tally-man recorded it. The operator then pulled a string releasing the forty bushels through the bottom of the measure and into a chute down which the grain passed to a waiting canal boat at the bottom. The transit of forty bushels from lake vessel to canal boat took one minute and cost one farthing.

In loading a canal boat, the spout from the elevator would run from bow to stern filling it to half level on its return swing to the bow. This prevented the boat from sinking or splitting. Six Irishmen worked in the hold of the ship as scoopers, holding their wooden shovels at an angle so that they could send the grain as it poured in a stream from the chute to any corner of the boat. Boats were often loaded at night by the light of globe lamps. Often they were loaded until after midnight. Few canal boats, however, left after one o'clock in the morning. When two vessels lay side by side at the same wharf, on the same side of the building, and in the same water with the smaller vessel inside the larger one, the grain ran directly from the weighing measure into the chute that communicated with the canal boat. The work of the elevator was not confined, however, to one side of the building. Since there was water on both sides of the elevator, the grain was also elevated from a vessel on one side and reshipped through and across the elevator to a vessel on the other side. It traveled across the breadth of the building through two gutters or channels in which the small troughs, on a pliable band, circulated very quickly. The grain elevated from the lake vessel was poured into these troughs, carried across into the building and emptied into a chute which was connected to the canal boat on the other side. As Anthony Trollope concluded, "The secret of all the motion and arrangement consists of course, in the elevation. The corn is lifted up and when lifted can move itself and arrange itself, and weigh itself, and load itself."

In addition to transfer by land elevators, grain was also moved by floating elevators. This type of elevator, which was actually a boat, would float up next to the lake vessel. The canal boat would lie outside of the elevator. The operators would lower the elevator leg into the vessel and lift the grain out of the hold and into the elevator itself by means of a double bucket on an endless chain, in the same fashion as in a stationary elevator. Within the elevator, the transfer followed the same route as it did in the land elevators. Often, however, grain would not be transferred immediately to a canal boat. In such a case, it would be stored in the elevator to await sale and a transfer to the canal boats.

The canal boats, into which the stored grain was to be loaded, approached Buffalo harbor from the north. At Porter Avenue, about two miles north, the teams drawing the canal boat changed paths. The new path continued as far as Commercial Slip. If the boat had no cargo, it was "pike-poled" down the slip and into the harbor. The pike pole used on the canal for maneuvering the craft in the slips and harbors consisted of a pole 14 to 16 feet long, smoothed down so that it could be handled easily, and into one end of which a pike, or iron rod, was securely fastened by means of a pin through a hole in the pike and in the wood. This pike protruded for about four inches from the end of the pole. The counterpart of this pole on lake vessels, was called a "boat hook." Instead of being inserted into the pole, the rod was fastened in a socket and fashioned at the end into a hook.

The canal boats usually docked in the Erie Canal near Commercial or Prime Slips and upon their arrival the captain of the vessel would report immediately to a forwarder or scalper whose office was located on the Central Wharf and who acted as middleman between the commission merchant and the captain of the canal boat. If a cargo of wheat had been purchased by New York, the commission merchant ordered it shipped from the elevator to that destination. The commission merchant would give a copy of the order to a scalper who, in turn, would give a copy of the order to the tug boat captain. This order, which both the captain of the tug boat and the scalper held in their possession, would indicate the elevator at which the canal boat was to pick up the grain. With these directions in hand, the canal boat would be towed by tugboat to the elevator. During the decade of the 1880's, three small tugs, NEWSBOY, PLAYBOY and SAILORBOY carried on this business exclusively.

Upon arrival at the elevator, the canal boat captain would send an alert member of this crew into the elevator to tally the load. By the 1880's many improvements had been added to the elevator which Anthony Trollope had seen during the Civil War. There were now two loading bins in the elevator, one above the other. The one at floor level had a capacity of 200 bushels; the one above it had a capacity of 2,000 to 3,000 bushels. By standing in front of the lower bin with his foot on an iron balancer, the weighmaster could regulate the flow. From the bottom of the upper bin, above his head, extended a square-shaped funnel through which the grain poured from the upper to the lower bin and which was equipped with an iron cut-off attachment by which the flow of grain could be regulated or stopped. By standing with his foot on the iron balancer and with his hand on the cut-off iron of the funnel, the operator could cut down the flow of grain and finally stop it entirely at that precise moment when the weight of his foot on the iron balancer would cause the scale beam of the bin to balance. By lifting his foot, he could catch the weight to the exact ounce.

A trap door at the bottom of the lower weight bin led to a chute which carried the grain to the hold of the canal boat. This bin had a valve arrangement similar to the bin overhead. This was controlled by a catch over the balance iron near the operator's foot. By kicking the bar, the trap door could be made to fall out, thus sending the grain down the chute to the boat. The weighmaster would call out "tally" for each 200 bushels. For each group of five, he would say "tally five." After having made four parallel marks, for each of four tallies, he would cut the fifth diagonally across the four, thus enclosing the group as a unit of five hashmarks representing a thousand bushels. The tallyman had to be very careful that the amount signed for was the amount in the boat, for the carrier had the responsibility of making up all shortages. One elevator, equipped with a hidden hole at the bottom of the bin so that part of the grain that should have gone down the chute into the canal boat was diverted into another compartment, made it possible for the owner to cheat the carriers for a time.

After the boat was filled, the captain would sign an elevator receipt for the grain. Once again the canal boat would be towed across the harbor up Commercial Slip to the Erie Canal. When the tugboat reached the point where the slip entered the canal, it would give the boat a "kick," causing it to coast slowly down the canal toward Erie Street where the canal-horse barns were located.

By the end of the Civil War, Buffalo Harbor had a total of thirtyone elevators, including two floating elevators. The construction of these elevators fell into two periods: the later 1840's and the war period. Although few elevators were constructed immediately after Dart's successful invention, the tremendous increase in wheat receipts in the late forties led to the construction of eight elevators. Among these were several that were rebuilt after fires and some that were enlarged. From 1861 to 1865, nineteen elevators were built or reconstructed. Almost all of the wooden elevators constructed at Buffalo burned completely or partially at one time or another. Grain is not only highly flammable, but it is subject to spontaneous combustion. In 1865, the elevators at Buffalo, including the two floating elevators, had a total capacity of 6,000,000 bushels.

The elevator represented the mechanical part of the grain transfer business in Buffalo Harbor. The scoopers and dockhands represented the human side. By the end of the 19th Century, the struggle between Mahany and Conners was over the control of the men -- the human side.

Who were these two men locked in combat? William Conners, whose roots dug deeply into the "auld-sod," spent his boyhood in the First Ward with Irish canawlers and their sons. These Irish had dug the canal west to Buffalo. Here, at the end or beginning of the canal, they made their homes.

Born in 1857, Conners had little formal education. At an early age, he was left on his own. He took to the inland seas as a cabin boy on one of the Great Lakes passenger vessels. Early on he lost a thumb and acquired the nickname of "Fingy."

Back on shore, he worked as a dock laborer and stevedore. In later years when his power, position and wealth helped him acquire the title and office of Commodore of the Buffalo Yacht Club, he bragged with Irish good humor that "he was the only man who went from stevedore to commodore in one jump," according to waterfront folklore.

With the death of his parents, Fingy inherited the family's saloon on the Ohio Basin. An additional inheritance made it possible for him to set up a second saloon in the same neighborhood.

He next tried politics in 1882, running for alderman on the Republican ticket in a heavily Democratic ward. He lost. This setback brought him face-to-face with what he knew best: the Lakes and the Buffalo waterfront. What Dart had done for the mechanical aspect of grain transfer, Conners now did for the human component of the business.

He developed a new system of freight handling by middlemen. According to former Western New York Congressman and writer Max McCarthy, he offered to unload freight for companies at a fixed rate. They would no longer have to hire their own crews to do this heavy work. The idea caught on and spread around the Lakes.

At the height of Fingy's operation, he employed 6,000 dockmen. In the 1890's, he expanded into the grain business incorporating the scoopers into his army of workers. He paid them meager wages of which a part was in beer chits redeemable only at his saloons. By controlling waterfront labor, Conners became the most powerful man on the waterfront. His dock roughnecks kept independent unions out of the waterfront. Power brought wealth. He bought two newspapers and merged them into the Buffalo Courier-Express. He moved from the First Ward to Buffalo's "wealthy" street, Delaware Avenue.

His rival, Rowland B. Mahany, was everything "Fingy" wasn't. Graduating in 1881 from Old Central High School, he taught Latin and Greek before matriculating at Hobart College on Seneca Lake in Geneva. In an almost unheard of move for a local youth of Irish immigrant stock, he transferred to Harvard University in Cambridge, Massachusetts. A brilliant student, he was named to

Phi Beta Kappa, the scholarship honor society. Mahany was graduated from Harvard in 1888.

After his return to Buffalo, he served as associate editor of The Buffalo Express and taught history and literature at Central High School. And, if that wasn't enough, he started studying for the Bar. A distinguished appointment by President Benjamin Harrison in 1892 made him envoy to Ecuador where he helped conclude the Santos Convention negotiations that had remained snarled for 20 years.

After an unsuccessful bid for Congress while serving in South America, he returned and won a seat in Congress in 1894 and again in 1896. He served on the Immigration Committee. Mahany lost his bid for a third term when his candidacy was vigorously opposed by Fingy Conners. Continuing his study of law, he was admitted to the Bar in 1899.

In that very year the long-smoldering unrest of the scoopers against Conners' system of labor control caused them to form their own union and to call a strike. A waterfront war broke out, the like of which had never been seen in Buffalo. It attracted national attention and one of the leading mass-circulation magazines, "Collier's," picked up the story.

Here is that story as Max McCarthy and "Collier's" related it:

"Mahany took hold of the rebellion on the docks, crystallized it into a violent revolution against Conners and interested the public outside of the (First) Ward."

"Collier's" recalled that "Mahany interested all the clergymen of Buffalo and especially the Catholics. It was a Catholic matter after all since most of the scoopers were Irishmen -- rough and violent, but faithful sons of their church."

Among the most influential church leaders recruited by the former congressman was the Rev. Patrick Cronin, the scholarly editor of the old Catholic Union and Times. Father Cronin saw the strike as "a fight for Irish homes."

"Collier's" claimed that as the war on the Buffalo waterfront escalated, Conners brought in "bruisers and toughs" from around the Great Lakes to try and break the strike. "Both sides did violence. . . ," the magazine reported. "Three times the Conners heelers cleaned out and demolished saloons in which the union men gathered; every night some striker or other was beaten up or thrown into the canal. . . . The union men fought back. They killed a nephew of James Kennedy, the ally of Conners in his dock work."

The union leaders called a mass meeting at the parish hall of St. Bridget's Church on Louisiana Street. Father Cronin stood up to address the packed hall. He lamented the effects on families of the hard-working, heavy-drinking lives of the scoopers. He alleged that Conners had, in effect, grown rich on such misery. The editor charged that "the diamonds he wears are the crystallized tears of your women."

Then came the most dramatic moment of all, "Collier's" recounted in an article in July 1907: "When he (Father Cronin) finished, a commotion of cheering started at the back of the hall and another man in clericals pushed his way to the platform."

"The strikers rose in a body when they saw who it was -- Bishop (James E.) Quigley, then head of the diocese, now archbishop of Chicago. The men remained standing as he faced them and, in a clear, dispassionate address, set the situation before them. He finished by advising them -- and such advice from him was equivalent to a demand -- never to work for Conners again until he had utterly given over the grain business."

The nationally circulated magazine said that "a committee of citizens, headed by the bishop, met with the carrying companies and arranged a new system." To oversee reform, Rowland Mahany was named harbor commissioner and served in that post until 1906.

Both William J. Conners and Rowland B. Mahany went on to achieve added national prominence. Like Mahany, Conners switched from the GOP to the Democratic Party. Conners captured control of the Democratic Party in Erie County and forged an upstate-downstate alliance with Charles F. Murphy, the famed boss of Tammany Hall. The two saw to it that Conners was elected New York State Democratic chairman.

Conners was a major figure at the Democratic National Convention in Denver that nominated William Jennings Bryan for President. In his third bid for the presidency, Bryan lost to William Howard Taft in the election of 1908.

In 1914 President Woodrow Wilson appointed Mahany as a senior attorney in the Department of Labor. He later named the former congressman as the U. S. representative to the International Commission of Immigration and Emigration, which met in 1920 at Geneva, Switzerland, under the auspices of the old League of Nations.

His experience in 1899 helped to propel Rowland Mahany into the position as the highest labor official in the United States. He ended his government career at the Cabinet table of President Warren G. Harding, where, in 1921, he served as acting Secretary of Labor.

Both Mahany and Conners had long and colorful careers, but nothing either man ever did quite equalled the drama and excitement of the epic strike of 1899 on the Buffalo waterfront.

THE ARCOLE FOUNDRY AND THE COTTON FACTORY

These two establishments, situated on the canal toward Black Rock, are curse to the whole of that neighborhood and to the city at large. The inmates of both, overseers, operatives, apprentices and all concerned, even to the stockholders, conduct themselves more like inhabitants of the Points than like decent people as they ought to do. The two establishments being near to each other and the inmates of different sexes, the consequence is that the intercourse between them is more familiar than the law allows, or virtue will admit of. It cannot be expected, however, that young ladies can long remain in such a place, exposed to so many temptations, without committing some faux pas, that they will regret to the end of their lives, especially when such a man as old as K--ls has the superintendence of their moral education. This lecherous old villain is known to have half a dozen mistresses, and how many more we are unable to say, although we should not wonder if the catalogue included in one-half of those under his charge. He is a mighty sly old fellow, we know, but we are after him and shall be down upon him too "like a thousand tons of brick" if he is not still more so.

Besides these and a hundred other temptations to which operatives in the Cotton Factory are exposed and which one would think enough in all conscience, old Wogan has established a place where semi-weekly shin-digs are half after the Rock Street fashion and into which many of the girls are enticed and there brought into contact with libertines of the most reckless description, who think no more of ruining the reputation of an innocent young girl than they do of drinking a glass of good brandy; indeed, it is fun for them and they boast of it and attend such places for that sole purpose.

"BLACK ROCK PORK"

Black Rock, New York was a small canal town right outside of Buffalo. It was noted for a cured meat product nicknamed "Black Rock Pork." It was a staple of the canaller's diet. Like so many other aspects of canal life, it too had it's own song:

> I shipped aboard a lumber-boat,
> Her name was *Charles O'Rourke*.
> The very first thing they rolled aboard
> Was a barrel of Black Rock pork.
>
> They fried a chunk for breakfast
> And a chunk for luncheon too.
> It didn't taste so goody-good,
> And it was hard to chew.
>
> From Buffalo to old New York
> They fed it to dear-old-me;
> They boiled the barrel and the rest of the pork,
> And we had it all for tea.
>
> About three days out, we struck a rock
> of Lackawanna coal.
> It gave the boat quite a shock,
> And stove in quite a hole.
>
> So I hollered at the driver
> Who was off a-treadin' dirt;
> He jumped aboard and stopped the leak
> With his crumby undershirt.
>
> Now the cook upon this canal boat
> Stood six feet in her socks;
> She had a bosom like a box-car,
> And her breath would open the locks.
>
> Now the cook is in the poor-house,
> And the crew is all in jail,
> And I'm the only canaller
> That is left to tell the tale.

BLACK ROCK TURKEY

One of the characters in Arch Merril's book, <u>Towpath</u>, recalled the generally "good grub on the boats although the crews sometimes tired of too much 'Black Rock Turkey,' which was canalese for salt pork, streak o' lean and streak o' fat."

The following is a letter to Tekla and Newk Steuart from Emma Newcomb Steuart, Newk's grandmother, who lived in Clearwater, Florida, as a reply to a request for information she could remember about the Canal Store, which her father operated in Buffalo from about 1840 on. His name was Harvey Newcomb and is remembered by a few oldtimers of the Erie Canal era.

December 11, 1962

Dear Tek and Newk,

It is more than 120 years since father had his store on the Canal at the foot of Amherst Street and Niagara Street, then called Black Rock. At that time he had 12 clerks working for him, 6 through the day and 6 at night -- store never closed.

He sold hay and oats for the mules; ropes and iron wheels for the ropes (sic); any harness that was needed for the mules while pulling boat. Father also sold dishes, pans, kettles, any need for cooking (while at Black Rock) also wash tubs and wooded board. The boatmen and family had to depend on Father for his wants.

Father <u>always</u> had an open barrel of pickles and crackers, and a cheese, the size of an auto tire (almost) with the largest knife I ever saw, for anyone who came into the store to help himself. Pepper and other spices were sold by pound or ounce; tea $.19/lb., coffee $.15/lb., sugar by lb. or barrel -- more barrels were sold. I think Father was one of the first to introduce Gold Medal Flour. When an agent came to get an order from him, Father had sent a sample home to try a loaf of bread. It came out delicious, so Father from then on was for Gold Medal, which, I think, sold for $1.50 sack of 50 lbs. and $8.00 barrel at that time.

Father owned some boats -- should you care to know, there were boats called HARVE NEWCOM, HARVEY NEWCOMB and W. H. NEWCOMB.

This may be of interest -- for some reason Father would lend to boatmen $500.00 to pay for expenses while in Buffalo, like tugs for unloading. I know I am in trouble trying to explain this; perhaps it included groceries for (the) round trip to New York and return. I only remember there was the lending and when I asked Father why, I do not remember his explanation to me. At that time, I happened to be at store wanting some spending money, age around 12 to 15 years.

When between 7 and 9 years old, I took this trip to New York with Mr. and Mrs. Agan, a girl 16 and Jimmie about 20. When down the Canal a few miles an awning and hammock were put up over the living part of boat. The night Jimmie was steering, he would have me in hammock and sing -- I always remember -- "My Bonnie Lies Over the Ocean." At midnight someone else would do the steering and Jimmie would carry me asleep down to bed. We slept divided by curtains as I remember. I also would ride on the mules when I became tired walking with Jimmie while pulling the boat -- I think I should say driving the mules who pulled the boat. When at Albany, well I was asleep at the time, but when in the morning I awakened to find our boat, along with many others (say 40 to 200) all together being towed by tugs from Albany to New York.

When we got to New York, the whole family of us went to a show at the Bowery. As I recall, there was this big place filled with people at tables and a stage -- drinks were sold too -- those days it was very popular. I am quite sure we all returned to the boat, our home, sober.

When I started this letter to you days and days ago, I would include some of the things Father did to help others. Some of the men driving mules down the Canal came from good families, but drink got them. Do you remember John Wasner? He took the store when we lost Pa. He was one Pa saved and if not too well liked by his brothers, because he was faring too well. He was good to my father and looked after him and the business.

Some more I recall about the food they sold. Coffee was ground to order as many had their own grinders. Candy on sticks only 2 for $.01; potatoes $.10 a peck; 3 heads of lettuce $.05; tomatoes $.50 a half bushel; bread $.05 a loaf; butter $.25; salt pork and mackerel by small keg; bacon by slab and whole hams -- I have no idea of price -- I will say they were cheap and cured better in those days. Much used canned milk was 3 cans for $.25.

After being in Black Rock for more than 20 or 30 years, Father moved the store to the foot of Erie Street. He no longer sold dishes, tins, etc., but cheese, knife, pickles and crackers were still available as usual. It just came to me that we pay $.49 for a box of crackers and $.59 for a half pound of the same kind of cheese now, in silver wrapping and called Cracker Barrel Cheese.

"HASH IS FRIED"

Hash is fried,
hash is tried,
hash is come in with the tide.
(Good for) drunks,
cut in chunks, made of hinges of old trunks.

IV

WHORES, WASTRELS AND WATERFRONT GUERRILLAS!

Republic Steam Presses, Buffalo.

THE BARBARY COAST OF THE EAST

Both Buffalo and Watervliet, near Albany, which were termini of the Erie Canal, claimed to be the "Barbary Coast of the East." Each deserved the title and bragged of Barbary Coast taverns with such colorful names as The Tub of Blood, The Black Rag, The Pigs Ear, Peg Leg House, The Right Bower of Oswego, Free and Easy, Limpy Georges', The Game Cock House, The Newark Goose and some 50 other places of "liquid refreshment and sanguinary encounter."

Not to be outdone, Buffalo had its own dens of iniquity and streets of sin. Read on.

THE OLD CORPORAL

The regular newspapers began to find it increasingly more difficult to tell the full story of Buffalo's seedy Canal Street. Consequently, a newspaper, published clandestinely, made its appearance on the Buffalo streets October 29, 1849. The editors decided it was safer to hide behind nom-de-plumes and so they were listed as J.G. Quick and H.G. Lucky. The paper was called The Old Corporal with a caption slogan "Come and Take Me." In it's first issue it explained its policy as follows:

"The Old Corporal has received his promotion and he now comes to you after having made himself notorious in the service of his country as a soldier, designed to afford you instruction and amusement during the long winter evenings that are approaching and as a fit remedy (to be taken internally) to restore proper exuberance of spirits now, and as a preventative of cholera hereafter. It is our intention to make it emphatically a family paper and in doing so we indulge the hope that we shall be pardoned for saying that we intend to deal principally with family concerns. We shall put forth the best of our humble efforts to make The Old Corporal always a welcome and acceptable visitor among those with whom we are willing to associate and we shall be as choice in our matter as we are in our company. We shall endeavor to furnish those who enjoy a hearty laugh, real genuine pointed wit (no matter if sometimes at their own expense,) with abundant occasion to exercise their risible muscles, in suitable dishes served up to order and at fair prices. But, the principal object which we have on view, is to wage war upon all adulterers, whoremongers, seducers, libertines, fops, candies dead heads, etc. . . etc. . . , and such like, in all, too numerous to mention. Persons moving in respectable circles and practicing their shameful operations without fear of detection or punishment -- a disgrace to society and to themselves -- a reproach upon humanity and a foul blot upon the face of existence. It is well-known that under the fostering hand of the let-alone policy which has prevailed here for several years, these individuals have increased to such an extent that the society of our fair city has become rank with corruption. We speak now of the better classes, if there is any difference, and its moral atmosphere so polluted that the virtuous cannot inhale it without danger to their reputation. Our homes and firesides are polluted with the presence of beings whose only end and aim is to gratify their hellish passions. Daily the seducer practices his subtle arts in the midst of us and the adulterer, emboldened by security from exposure, openly prosecutes his nefarious schemes. Virtuous females are continually exposed to the contaminations of lust and young men are lured away by the more experienced workers of inequity and plunged into the whirlpool of debauchery, whose rapid current soon sweeps them beyond the reach of help. We can point to hundreds, married and unmarried, who make it their regular business to promenade the streets evenings in search of "game" and who do not scruple in the first instance to insult every female who they come in contact with, if an opportunity offers, sometimes by openly addressing them and making their business known -- sometimes by following them to their homes and in various ways giving them to understand that they are of the "bloods." It has become absolutely dangerous for a woman to venture forth after dark without a male protector and, in that case, at every corner of the street they are stared at and their ears are assailed with course jests and obscene observations upon their personal appearance, uttered by well-dressed young men who congregate nightly in front of saloons and fill up the sidewalk for this very purpose. What a disgusting picture of society! What an outline merely of human wickedness is this, but bad as it is, not an item but what is true to the letter. Indeed, it cannot be half-told, for it is not half-known. The details of this picture are so dark that language is inadequate to convey proper understanding of them to the reader. Yet, we promise to corroborate every particle of this general statement by individual instance nor can neither be denied nor gain said and those too from among that class who look down from the dizzy heights of fashion and would faint at a comparison instituted between them and those poor unfortunates whom the cold charity of the world has driven to sell their virtue for their daily bread. For the purpose of checking this monstrous evil and preventing its increase by exposing those engaged in it, we have dared to overstep the limits prescribed by human law and to issue this paper and 'live or die, sink or swim, survive or perish' ship-wrecked , mobbed, mal-treated or shot at, we are bound to go ahead so long as we can keep our heads above water and give all those who do not mend their ways, not only particular fits, but particular jessy, and on this they can most assuredly depend.

" It is our intention, however, to give all who we detect in the path of transgression, an opportunity of retracing their steps and woe unto those who, after our warning comes, neglect to profit by it. We shall drag them forth from their hiding places and hold them up for public condemnation and subject them to the scrutinizing glance of an indignant world. We shall be no respecter of persons. We shall expose with a fearless hand, the libertine, the seducer and the adulterer. We shall hold up to ridicule those men 'whom tailors make' and we shall unmask hypocrasy and strip the cloak from those who 'put borders around the bottom of their garments, that they may be seen of men.' It will go hard with those who 'kick against the pricks,' as we are determined that our beautiful city shall no longer be called 'the Gehenna.' "

TAVERNS AND TRAP DOORS

Love and liquor often meant white legs, and black legs too. Captain Cole found out. . . .

Captain Ben Cole yelled from the bridge to hold fast. The vessel nestled up slowly to the central wharf. Out flew the hawsers. Quickly the hands snubbed them to the dock iron. As the steam was cut, the vessel stopped shuddering and rode softly with the gentle roll of the inner harbor water. Safely docked, Cole went back into the pilot house, took out the roster to see who had ship watch the first night ashore. It was young Mike. The youngest hand always had first watch and this was the first time Mike had shipped out.

With roster in hand, the Captain started down to the crew quarters, called Mike over and reminded him that he was to stay aboard the first night. Mike, of course, had been expecting this duty. Still, it was difficult for him to conceal his disappointment in not being able to go ashore with the rest of the crew. All during the trip the older hands had been telling him over and over the story of the infamous Buffalo waterfront.

Captain Ben read the disappointment on Mike's face.

"I'm staying aboard, son," said Captain Cole. "I'll sit it out with you. Mebee I'll even entertain you with some of my biggest lies." Then turning to the rest of the crew who were making ready to hit the gangplank, Cole shouted, "Now mind the rest of you fresh water salts, stay clear of those 'blackleg' gamblers. They'll skin you for every cent I've paid you. This cesspool has the crookedest crooks on the lake. Worst 'blacklegs' in any port."

With this, the whole crew snorted with laughter but there was none who doubted what he said.

"Hey, Captain!" shouted one of the hands, "you told us to stand clear of the 'blacklegs.' Don't want us to stand clear of the shapely white legs too, do you?"

"Mark me, mateys," Cole said, shaking his finger in warning, "stay clear of the white legs in this port too. They're wors'n the blacklegs."

"Captain, now you know that ain't fair," put in the mate. "The female white legs ain't near as bad as the ornery male 'blacklegs.' Lookee here, the 'blacklegs' take all your money but they don't give ya a damn thing in return. Now the gals take your money, but just think what they give in return."

The crew folded in laughter. When the Captain had quieted his belly laugh to a gentle chuckle, he pointed his pipe at the young sailor and said, "Laddie, you're right. They sure do give you sumpin' in return. Sumpin' you'll try the rest of your life to get rid of. Better stay clear of them white legs too."

"Now, Captain," said the mate, "you yourself told us that Buffalo is a 'lay-over' port. Well, that's just what we we're fixing to do plenty of."

Still laughing, the men scrambled up the ladder to the deck, across the gangplank, and onto the wharf. Captain Cole and Mike stood on the bridge watching them as they darted in, out and around the baggage piled high on the wharf. Soon they lost them in the milling mob of canawlers, lakers and immigrants who clustered on the waterfront streets and wharves.

Cole continued to watch and chuckled a little to himself. Mike, who had been a little bewildered by the banter in the crew's quarters, drew his chair up close to the Captain and said, "Captain, is Canal Street as bad as you and the men make it out to be?"

"Son," replied Cole, "it's worse'n. Here, let me fill my pipe and I'll tell you all about it. But believe me, laddie, this is not one of my yarns. Fetch me that lantern over there so's I can get a light."

Soon the Captain was puffing away contentedly. He knew the waterfront and he loved to talk about it.

"Mike," the Captain said, "let me tell you about the waterfront I knew as a lad your age. When I first came to these docks, everything was in the hands of the canawlers and a sailor cut no figure a'tall. As the sailors grew stronger, there were more and more fights for supremacy. Believe me, Mike, these were real fights -- Spanish knives, stones and fists. Buffalo was a hard place in the early '50s. In fact, a life didn't count for very much on the Buffalo waterfront. There were worse joints around Canal Street than you would believe."

Mike stopped him for a moment and said, "IIow about the police, Captain Cole?"

"T'warn't any police in those days," Cole added. "Only a few watchmen. Often as not they were worse'n the murderers and thieves. Most of them kept their noses out of the waterfront and vice held sway unchecked. Fights and cutting frays were nightly occurrences, and the denizens were as evil a lot of crooks as have ever been collected in one place. Mike, the mining towns in our days are no worse than this waterfront. Gangs of sailors hung on every corner spoiling for a fight. Those were the days when ole Mother Carey's dance hall was famed throughout the land and was the scene of many a fight. In the dark alleys and slips, murders occurred for which no record can be found in the criminal annals of the city. The 'Points' were let alone by the authorities and thievery, licentiousness and vice more than flourished in that awful hotbed.

"Never forget one experience I had, laddie. I was no older than you and for awhile, I thought that was as old as I was ever goin' to be. Shortly after I'd been given my own ship, I went ashore one day with my first mate. I had a roll of money with me but never gave it a thought. The mate proposed to get a drink in the place next to ole Mother Carey's. I agreed and we went in. I was young then and did not know the town very well. After we had the drink, he said 'Come here, Cap'n.' I followed his beckoning finger. He opened a trapdoor in the back of the saloon. I thought I might as well see what was there. We went down and got into a passageway that led about fifty feet. Then we came to a heavy oak door about four inches thick. The mate rapped a peculiar knock on the door and it opened. Inside was a room about twelve feet square. In one end was a bar with five or six black bottles stuck up on it, and at the other end was a table where three men sat playing cards.

"The door closed behind and I knew I was trapped. I had heard of the place. It was one where they fed drugged drinks to the suckers that got in there, rolled them and then poked them out through the slide with a stone around their necks. When they were found, it seemed as though they had committed suicide by jumping into the Canal. I knew where I was and I thought I was a goner. The door was bolted on the other side and I heard it slip into the catch.

"Well, sir, I began to buy them drinks. I made out that I was an awful drinker and said that I could drink the whole lot of them drunk. I poured out big tumblers of the stuff, and poured them down my neck on the outside, instead of the inside. I was fairly ringing with cheap whiskey. They drank the stuff and got paralyzed. I pretended to be boiling drunk and pretty soon everyone except the bartender was stiff. I made him take drinks with me till he got pretty well under. Did you ever see one of those Spanish knives? We all used to have them in those days. Stuck up your sleeves, you know, and bound round your wrist with a thong. I took this out and grabbed the bartender -- I was a husky lad in those days -- I told him I would cut his throat if he didn't open that door. He finally gave the signal and I got out of the place soaked with whiskey. Spent seven dollars for those drinks I bought those cusses, but I was mighty glad to get out of there. You see, the mate knew I had money and he got me in there."

Mike, who was hanging on every word, asked "Whatever became of the first mate, Captain Cole?"

"Well, sir, I saw him a few years ago in Chicago. After I fired him, I don't think any respectable Captain ever hired him again. When I saw him, he was beggin' -- a regular 'wag,' Mike, as I told the men, there ain't no 'blacklegs' anywhere like those on this waterfront."

"But, Captain," Mike put in, "what about the gals -- the white legs the boys were talking about? Ever had any experience with them?"

The Captain sucked in slowly and deeply on his pipe. His eyes looked out over the Canal Street district and he said thoughtfully, as he patted Mike on the knee, "Plenty, laddie, plenty -- but they're all trade secrets."

"HOLE IN THE WALL"
(A Parody)

Improbable lines to the fair damsel who was seen in a saloon called the "Hole in the Wall":

Every day behind the bar
In the "hole that's in the wall"
Is a female standing "thar"
Selling beer in glasses small.

I don't know this dam-sel's name,
But she's brazen-faced and bold.
Still I think she's not to blame,
'Twas her "broughten-up" I'm told.

Maiden, I will sing a song,
If you'll trust a nip or two.
Say, would I be doing wrong
Should I credit ask of you?

When you hear my doleful strain
Pearly tears may dim your eye
Should I strive your love to gain
"Boon" so pleasing, not deny.

She, though human looks divine,
Sandy hair, and ruby nose,
Eyes like lightening bugs do shine,
Cheeks are painted like the rose.

Head gone off upon a "tower"
Left her shoulders clear behind;
Neck the hue of Graham flower,
Hands as rough as baked pork rind.

Such a beauteous lump of grease
Selling beer to all who'll buy,
Love must be on the decrease
If she don't attract each eye.

Oft I'll gaze upon that form
Smiling I behold that smile,
And my heart keeps growing warm
'Till a "brick gets in my tile."

Ask me not, bar maid fair
Why so oft I come to "smile,"
Love and liquor good are there,
Lager tempts me all the while.

THE DRUNKARD MAN

A drunken fellow stumbled into the canal at Rome. After considerable effort failed to "rake" the body up, someone suggested "trolling" for it with a bottle of whiskey for bait. In a short time the drowned man was drawn up clasping the bottle tightly in his lips. He was "cared for" and will recover although he had been underwater over thirty hours.

OLD BEALES AND COFFEE BEANS

If there was any way to make hay while the sun was shining, old Beales the scrounger knew the tricks Fred Emmons had yet to learn. Beales was one of the first salvage men on the western end of the canal and he was truly a fabulous waterfront character. The following story occurred in Buffalo during October, 1844:

Old Beales relaxed contentedly on a hogshead barrel which was nudged snugly against a wood fence. He was wittlin' away. As his eyes took in the little waterfront development in front of him, a smile creased his face. "I ain't giv'n to many," Beales mumbled to himself, "to found a settlement. But this'n's mine and I christened it with my name. Got it right on the sternboard. Bealesville's sure's better'n Sandy Town for a name. Sumpin' a man kin be proud of. Diff'runt from a year ago when I first stranded on these shores. 'Twarn't worth a second look-see. Now take a readin'. Not bad a'tall for an old water-rat the like of me. Not bad a'tall.

"If that ole patched-up canawler of mine hadn't busted the rotten seams that night, I might still of been poundin' the towpath from Ithacy to Buffalo. Come to think of it, it's downright funny. The Ole Erie ditch took one beat-up barge 'way from me, and Lake Erie washed up a dozen to take its place. That's a pretty good deal even for an 'Ole watchstuffer like me. Lucky I sold my cargo the night before. That sure helped launch my land-sailing venture here."   ~

As Beales savored this thought for all the goodness in it, a voice broke his pleasant reverie.

"What ya dreamin' up Beales? Another 'black-leg' deal?"

"Oh, it's you Jake," said Beales as he turned around. "What's eatin' your rotten insides?"

"Nothin'. Loadin's slow on the dock this mornin', so I thought I come over and see who you was fixin' to skin today."

"You, of course, you leather-hided son-of-a-mule," Beales yelled and laughed at the same time.

"My hide wouldn't be worth much," Jake countered. "It's pretty well worn." As he said this, Jake held up his hands. They were the hands of a real water-rat. The mark of the rope could be plainly seen across the palm. Jake belonged. He was part water, part sand, part wind; he was all canawler.

"Jake, I was just 'memberin' a year ago."

"'Twas just about a year ago your ole canal tub went awash at the Rock, if I 'member rightly," Jake said. "You know, Beales, it always seemed a queer bit funny to me that you got rid of your load 'fore she went down. Seems I recall you had the bottom insured but not the cargo."

"Seems I' member sumphin' like that." Beales said knowingly. "But Jake, 'taint always healthy to have too good a memory here on the Buffalo waterfront. But that makes no never mind Jake. You have to give that these were might poor washings before I got here."

"Got to say aye aye to that, Beales. This sandy stretch fore and aft 'twarn't nothin' but a barge graveyard 'fore you took hold."

Beales was thinking. More to himself than to Jake he mumbled, "Yeah, sure was diff'runt a year ago."

Jake and Beales were right. Things had certainly changed in Sandy Town since Beales took over. That morning about a year ago when his boat went down at Black Rock a few miles to the north on the Niagara River, Beales' stock went up. It seemed as if that morning were only yesterday. By the time he reached the Rock his feet were sore. He had spelled off the skinners on the towpath all the way from Ithaca. As Captain of his barge, he was unused to walking the mules because most of his sailing days had been spent at the tiller. That's where he was when the water started gushing in the hold that morning. At sight of the water, he jumped ashore and watched the barge settle to the bottom. As he stared at the barge sitting dumb-like on the bottom of the canal, he decided that he had all he wanted of the life.

While he dangled his tired feet in the cool water, he watched and thought and planned. Although it was early in the morning, the bargers had already begun to move toward Commercial Slip several miles south of Black Rock in the Buffalo Harbor.

What a sight this canal procession made as the barge mules, straining against their sweat-soaked leather traces, dragged their westbound cargo along the last stretch of canal. The mules kicked up puffs of brownish dust as their hoofs bit into the towpath and the skinners fore and aft caught up the slow loping rhythm of the mules in a song of the canal. Alongside the towpath, on the right, the Niagara River plunged swiftly toward the Falls some twenty miles to the north. The French had called these rapids, opposite what one day would be Buffalo, "La Petite Rapids" (the Little Rapids.) On the left side of the towpath, the canal, soft and still by contrast, came to life as the broad blunt bows of the barges rolled up continuous waves which slapped noisily against the towpath. From the other side of the canal, almost in simple counterpoint, came the quiet sound of the same waves as they dwindled into ripples and broke like muffled echoes against the towpath.

When the river water had drawn some of the fire out of his feet, Beales slipped on his faded socks, covered them with what were once shoes, and scrambled up the bank. At the top, he sucked in some fresh Niagara air, braced his shoulders, faced southward and headed down the path toward Buffalo. As he walked, he wondered where the thousands of immigrants had come from and where they were going. It seemed to him that most of Europe, and all of the East Coast, were walking or riding westward on and along the Erie Canal. He wondered how long the immigrants entering

Buffalo that morning would have to wait before they could book passage to the West. He knew that crowded conditions aboard the immigrant vessels sometimes made it necessary for families to wait weeks before they were able to embark. In fact, he had seen many families, unable to book passage or find lodging for the night, sleeping atop their baggage along the wharves. Those with some money took rooms in the cheap hotels which dotted the waterfront and, more often than not, they lost all of their money and were fortunate to get away with their lives.

By the time Beales had reached the outskirts of Buffalo, the morning was well advanced. Some distance from Commercial Slip, the space between the canal and the lake widened. Old Beales noticed that this section of land had changed to a sandy loam. As he scanned the area, an object over to his right caught his eye. It was along the water's edge of the lake. He had heard this region called Sandy Town but he had never examined it closely. He decided now was the time.

As he approached the lake, he was soon able to identify the objects that dotted the shore. Decaying barges and small lake vessels abandoned by their masters had been driven deeply into the soft sand by the pounding lake waves. Their ribs, bleached white by the sun and sand, lay exposed like the skeletons of some prehistoric beast. Traces of once gaudy paint now streaked, blistered and peeled, made hollow mockery of their former fame and fortune. Even now, the faded name printed impressively on the tail board seemed more like a grave marker.

Beales surveyed the barges with the practiced eye of a canawler. Some were old friends. Many brought back to his mind wonderful tales of the raging canal. Perhaps his BETSY would soon join this graveyard of forgotten canawlers. Spotting one barge less old than the others which had just recently been condemned to dry land sailing, Beales decided to explore. He shinnied up the side. On deck, he almost instinctively headed for the Captain's quarters. No more than a gentle push forced the rusted lock catch. Beales found himself inside. As soon as he closed the door, the dust began to settle back to its accustomed spots about the room and the cobwebs relaxed. A water-rat, of the four-legged variety, disturbed in its meal of fresh fish, disappeared quickly into its hold. "That's one rat," said Beales aloud to himself, "who didn't desert the sinking ship." Along the portside of the room, Beales spotted a couch which the rats had used as a source of straw for their nest building. While dampness and age had dulled the luster of its appointments and rotted its paneling, the quarters gave evidence of having been ship-shape the day the barge was abandoned. Beales wondered who the Captain had been. Why had she been abandoned? As these thoughts crossed his mind, he sat down in what had been the Captain's leather chair. He felt at home. As his eye appraised the room, he knew she had been a better tub than

BETSY.

He looked aft through the tiny window toward the Grand Canal. An endless parade of canal boats stretched from the Rock to Buffalo. Atop the barges were men and women of all types; some richly, some poorly, dressed. Some with the costumes of Switzerland and Germany; others with those of the Scandinavian countries. Europe was on the march. Once again as Beales mused, he wondered where they were all going; what part of the West they would make their home in. Perhaps it would be Illinois, Ohio, Michigan or the wild land beyond. He wondered, too, where they would stay that night in Buffalo. Probably the rich could get accommodations at the Mansion House. The poor, but not destitute class, might find cover in some of the waterfront dives. The completely unblessed, however, would undoubtedly sleep atop the cargo tarpaulins on the wharves. Then a thought struck Beales. Like all good ideas, it came swift and sure. "A little fixin' might turn some of these barges into liveable houses. After all, a canal barge was a sort of floating house anyhow. Conversion would be easy." For a quiet while, Beales thought hard on this idea. Then he stood up and opened the door. The lake breeze flurried the room a bit as he stepped out of the cabin. He closed the door, shinnied down the side of the barge and walked between the barges scattered hither and yon along the beach. When he reached the shore he stood a moment watching the rhythmic swells of the lake break into gentle rolls and disappear into the high sands as they reached themselves thin. Still lost in thought, he leaned over, cupped his hand, and drank the cool lake water. It tasted good and felt good as he threw some of it in his face.

As he stood up, still shaking his face, he noticed someone sitting on the shore bank whittling. Beales walked toward the figure slowly. When he was within voice distance, he called out, "Top o' mornin' to ya."

The man raised his head, looked toward the voice, studied the approaching figure for a moment, and said noncommittally, "Mornin'."

"You from here-abouts?" Beales asked.

"Yeah you could say that," the whittler answered.

"Live here?" Beales said.

"Sorta, " came the answer.

"What do ya mean 'sorta'?"

"Well, " said the whittler, "I live a little here and a little there." Then after a very significant pause, he looked straight into Beales' eyes and said, "You're mighty nosey, stranger. What's really eatin' away at you?"

Beales had to smile at the whittler's mind-reading. "I'm a canawler. Name's Beales. Who are you?"

"T'aint none of your damn business, but the name's Jake and I am and have been a canawler, scooper, carter -- hell! I'm a water-rat. Been one since I was knee-high to a whiffle tree."

Beales chuckled at this. It took no mind reading to know Jake spoke the truth. He looked the part. "Who owns this land?" inquired Beales.

"Guess I do," came the unexpected answer.

"You do?" exclaimed Beales.

"Yeah, I guess I do, and if you are a Yorker, it be part your'n too. This is squatter land -- the York State Milestrip. And them's abandoned barges over there belongin' to no one."

The thought Beales had been mulling over in his mind ever since leaving the barge awakened once more and began to take shape. With pioneers moving westward by the thousand, here was an excellent place less than a quarter of a mile from Commercial Slip for the poor and almost destitute pioneers to lay over while awaiting passage to the West on the crowded lake steamers. Beales looked squarely at Jake and said, "Ever handle a hammer?"

"Damn you stranger," said Jake. "Ain't never seen or heard of a canawler who couldn't handle a hammer better'n some who call themselves carpenters."

Beales knew this to be true, but it was just a way of opening the conversation on the point he wished to discuss. "How'd you like to work for me?" Beales offered.

"Look here stranger," said Jake, "I don't know you beyond you sayin' your name's Beales. But 'bout far as I'm concerned you're nothin' but a canawl rat and that is just a mite bit lower than a water-rat. It's probably been so long since you had your paws on the Spanish two-bit piece you wouldn't know what they are. So let's stow the gab."

Beales reached into his pocket and pulled out a bag containing the hard money he had received for the sale of his cargo. He opened the bag and Jake peeked in. Jake gave a low hissing sound that would have been a whistle if he had had teeth instead of their rotting stumps. "Stranger, you've got yourself a man. Let's get at it."

That had been the start of Bealesville. Jake had been in at the birth pains. Taking the best barges first, Jake and Old Beales repaired them very quickly. From the beginning, the venture had been a success. No sooner had the first been completed, than it was rented immediately by a family heading west. The renter, however, secured employment in one of the commission houses the very day he arrived and so never moved on. Beales had himself a permanent tenant.

One by one the barges were completed. None was ever vacant a day. When the barges on shore had been converted, Beales went out and salvaged others and dragged them up onto his sandy land. The little squatter colony grew rapidly. In a very short time, people began to refer to it as Bealesville. This was a significant tribute to Old Beales who by now had become the power behind squatter sovereignty in Buffalo.

Beales began to smile as these thoughts crossed his mind. He had been so lost in recalling the past year, that he had forgotten that Jake was standing next to him. He did not realize how long he had been silent until he looked down at the pile of shavings at his feet, then he knew that it must have been some time. Looking over at Jake, who by now was also whittling, Beales said apologetically, "Sorry Jake, I was just a-thinkin'."

"Bout what?" said Jake.

"Bout the difference."

"So was I," said Jake. "Say, 'member that old stew bum what tried to beat you out of a week's rent? I think if I hadn't come in at the right moment, you'd a 'beat his brains out with that water-logged club you had."

"Think I would have," said Beales. "That dirty piece of seaweed was three parts blackstrap and one part human. All he ever did was suck it up and spew it out. Only man I knew with a continuous two-way gut. I sure thought he had put the bite on me that time."

"What gets me, Beales," said Jake, "is how you ever came to believe in him. All's I was interested in was keeping you from bashing his head in. I didn't believe him when he said he know's how to bring back the face on a smooth Spanish two-bitter."

"Jake, I reckon I dunno why I let him go in return for that witch's brew he scribbled out for me. But I guess it's 'cause I had beat him so close to the edge of his life that I didn't think he had any more lie in him."

"Member the night we mixed that God-awful stuff, Beales? Sure stunk up the barge. Then we took the quarters, dipped them in the brew for a few minutes and pulled 'em out. Beales, you know that drunk must have been somebody once 'cause his brew sure worked. I'll never forget your puss when you saw the image come back on that smooth two-bitter. I think you bought every worn Spanish piece on the waterfront that next week for fifteen cents each. And then dipped 'em and peddled 'em for their face value at twenty-five cents. You ole skinflint, when you gonna tell me how you do it?"

"Jake, you nor anybody else is ever gonna get that brew formula outta me. So far as I know, that stew-bum and I are the only ones who know and I don't guess he'll ever stick his bow in here again."

"Do you still have the water-rats bringing in smooth pieces, Beales?"

"I sure do, Jake, and believe me, business has been mightly good these last six months. You know my Spanish exchange and my rents sure helped to launch my cargo scroungin'. Ya know Jake, I've had plenty of good luck with scroungin'. 'Member the time the propeller PRINCETON got itself stormbound off Fairport?

116

It was hot and muggy and she had a load of 250 dressed hogs. What a load that was. What was it that eastern dandy said, when the Princeton pulled into Buffalo Creek? 'Captain, your meat has acquired a greenish hue and oriental fragrance.' Don't know what he meant by all those big words Jake, but he was sure half right. The hogs was sure green, Jake, do ya ever expect to smell anything that stunk like those hogs? It was worse that the stew's brew."

"Stinkers is right," said Jake. "But as I recall, they brought you a hundred dollars profit at the local lard oil refiners. Not bad dealing for a half hour of dickerin'."

Jake and Beales looked at each other and burst out in belly guffaws that almost rocked them off their barrels.

"But the best damn load I ever scrounged, Jake, was them coffee beans. Do ya 'member? The boat went down over yonder just off the light."

"Yeah", said Jake. "And if I remember my log rightly, you was over there 'fore her belly hit the bottom. And by the time she was scrapin' the bottom, you had yourself a deal. Never did know how you scooped them up, but I sure can remember you spreadin' 'em out right over there on the sand."

"Jake, I dried 'em, roasted 'em, and ground 'em. 'Member the white packages we put them in? I can still see the pretty letterin': Buffalo Pure Ground Coffee. Jake, did you know I made the best haul of my life with those coffee beans in Cleveland? Sold the whole car for 100% profit. A real blackleg haul. From then on, the canawlers tagged me 'Old Beales and Coffee Beans.' You know Jake, those dirty sons of whiffle trees still yell that at me as they float past.

"But here's my pride, Jake," Beales said, as he patted the fence against which he was leaning. This high board fence enclosed an area just off Washington Street near the Canal. Within the enclosure, Beales stored old doors, sash, blinds, mantles, ship chandlery and figurines. In fact, the interior of the warehouse within the fenced area looked very much like a museum of waterfront abracadabra. Here he had gathered, dried and sold the flotsam and jetsam of Lake Erie and the Erie Canal. He furnished his house boats and converted barges with this second-hand furniture.

While Beales patted the fence affectionately, another thought entered his mind. It was a black thought and he always tried to push it aside. But it always kept coming back. With a serious, almost frightened expression on his face, Beales turned slowly to Jake and said, "Jake, ya know, when I see those black devil clouds gatherin' out there over the lake at sundown as they are right now, I get sceered of them waters."

"Why Beales, you ole son of a shady bargain. I never heard tell of you being sceered of anything or anybody."

"You're right Jake. As far as ornery humans is concerned, I

117

always figured I could hold my own against canawler or sailor, fresh or salt. Never feared squatters, floaters, watch stuffers, black legs, migrants, not by a dum sight. Fact is, never feared anything that talked. I understand talk. It's the dumb things I'm scared of. Take that lake yonder. I'm scared to death of Erie when she scowls nasty like she's doin' now."

"Beales, I always thought if any son of a whiffle tree or mast knowed these waters, it was you. Why the canawlers and fresh water boys think you can talk with the waters. Some say they see you."

"Well if they see me on the shore talking, it was to myself, 'cause those dumb waters ain't talked to me or anybody else."

"Beales, I dunno what you're babblin' about. You know damn well Erie's given you all you got. Fetched it up and dumped it in your front yard."

"You're right, Jake," Beales agreed. "These waters have been mighty sweet to my taste. Jake, did you know that the red devils used to call Erie 'The Sweet Waters?' Yeah, I supposed you can say the water's been good to me. But Jake, you know things that talk, give, but by gad they 'spect to get in return. I understand that. But these waters don't talk, Jake. If they give, when are they gonna come to get? Jake, some day they're gonna come and get me and all I got. They plumb scare me. They're dumb things, Jake. I don't know them."

BEALSVILLE POSTSCRIPT

The following was reported in the <u>The Buffalo Commercial Advertiser</u>, October 18, 1844:

"The hurricane storm that swept tidal waves all the way up to Seneca Street, causing great property damage, completely wiped out Bealesville."

For ole Beales, the sweet water had left a bitter taste.

"TALL TALE TELLER"

I landed in Buffalo about twelve o'clock,
The first place I went to was down to the dock,
I wanted to go up the lake, but it looked rather squally,
When along came Fred Emmons and his friend Billy Bally.

Said Fred, "How do you do, and where have you been so long?"
Said I, "For all the past fortnight I've been on the canal,
For it stormed all the time, and thar was the devil to pay,
When we got to Tonawandy Creek, we thar was cast away."

"Now," says Fred, "let me tell you how to manage wind and
weather.
In a storm hug the towpath, and then lay feather to feather;
And when the weather is bad, and the wind it blows a gale,
Just jump ashore, knock down a horse -- that's taking in the sail.

"And if you wish to see both sides of the canal
To steer your course to Buffalo, and that right true and well,
And if it be so foggy that you cannot see the track,
Just call the driver aboard and hitch a lantern in his back."

HAY ON THE SUN

In the slanting beams that silvered the dust in the air, the sun
filtered through the thin morning haze which had settled lazily on the
quiet waterfront. Under the dockboards, the harbor water made
suckling noises. Atop the wharf, with a snub post for a pillow and
a hat on his face, Fred Emmons soaked up the sun and snored out
his contentment. Most of the snores were full-throated and nose-
muted, but intermittently what started out as a well-rounded snore
would get snarled up in his throat pipes and die in a characterless
gurgle. This abortive snore usually set up a mild convulsive
shaking which traveled quickly through his body and ended up in a
wheezing cough which almost, but not quite, succeeded in arousing
Fred Emmons from his sleep.

Fred Emmons obviously took his Sundays seriously. For
this, he made no apologies. The "Good Book" said it was a day of
rest. Fred meant to rest. He felt he deserved one in seven. During
the other six days he practiced hard a profession peculiar to a port
like Buffalo. Some from Delaware Avenue might smile at his work
being dignified by the word profession, but Fred thought it was just
that. Officially (if the city directory could be considered official),
Emmons was listed as a steamboat and hotel agent. He preferred to
call himself a "General Solicitor." Among the soap-lack fraternity of
the waterfront, however, he and his cronies were popularly known

as runners. And well might they be called that because that is exactly what they did. As one waterfront wag put it, the runners put the hustle in the harbor bustle.

Originally, in stagecoach days, these runners brought passenger and freight business to the line of their hire. With the construction of the canal and the creation of steamboat lines, the stages began to die and these agents transferred their allegiance to the place where the money was. Noisy and loud as the waterfront was, high above the usual noises could be heard the voices of the runners singing the praises of this hotel or that steamboat. Living by their wits, competition made them sharp tongued, sharp-eyed, and fleet afoot. In their own way, they were artists. Today, they would be dignified with the title "advertising executives" and would be in demand for newspaper, radio and television work. The stories about these runners were legion. They themselves were legends.

The runner "extraordinary" of Canal Street was Fred Emmons. No one ever admitted outdoing or outwitting Emmons -- at least to his face. His boundless energy was equaled only by his imagination. For example, in the early 1830's, the steamboat PEACOCK burst its boiler a few miles from Buffalo. Many were drowned and many more scalded. Thousands who heard or read about the story hesitated about traveling on steamboats. Not long after the horrible accident, Emmons, plying his trade, approached a group of emigrants and urged them to book passage aboard his nice new steamboat which was about to embark for Detroit and intermediate points. After Emmons had made his pitch, an elderly lady in high dudgeon spoke up, "I don't like steamboats; you bust your bilers and scald folks." "Oh!" countered Fred, "my dear madam, ours is a new steamboat, constructed on a new principle, not one of those high pressure boats like the PEACOCK but a low pressure engine." Then looking her straight in the eye and measuring each word, Fred said, "We use nothing but cold water. In fact, we never let it come to a boil." Emmons as usual got the business.

But not all the stories about Emmons concerned deals on the dock. One night after work, as he made his way home through the dark streets that served the harbor, a robber stepped from between two buildings and leveled a fist at Emmons but missed. Fred quickly turned around and said, "What do you want?" The would-be assailant, slightly abashed, said, "Your money or your life." To this Emmons replied, "See here, stranger, I haven't any money, but if you will step around with me into Perry's Coffee Shop, I will give you my note for ninety days." Apparently the robber had a sense of humor for no harm came to Fred.

Emmons' light touch even affected Samuel Wilkeson, builder of the harbor. He is supposed to have borne the brunt of one of Emmons' quips. It seemed that a new steamer had been built in the Buffalo Harbor. It was magnificent to behold. Apparently

perfect in all parts, it floated gracefully as a swan. Its speed was
unmatched. There was only one thing wrong with the ship: the
engineers couldn't make it back up. The problem was finally placed
in the mayor's office. Emmons was summoned as he was then
acting police chief. After the mayor had stated the problem, Emmons
said quickly, "Well, your Honor, I think that if you just make a
mustard plaster out of some of Felix White's salve and put it on her
stern, that will draw her backwards as lively as anything I know
of." The mayor reportedly never asked Fred Emmons' advice
again.

Perhaps as Emmons snoozed and snored on the dock that
Sunday morning he dreamt of some of his many experiences. At
any rate, when he awoke, he stretched out his arms, emitted a loud
yawn, rubbed his eyes, pinched the back of his neck and slowly
surveyed the waterfront. What to do? Fred missed the crowds, the
noise and the general weekday hubbub. He liked Sundays but he
missed the people. Perhaps, he thought, something was going on
uptown. The thought interested him enough to get him up to his feet
and start him walking toward the Terrace.

The canal boat families were sunning themselves on top of
the barges. Some were doing a little fishing. All seemed to be
relaxing. Not much fun here, thought Fred. So he crossed the
bridge over the canal and made his way up Main Street toward
church. In front of the Episcopal Church was a huge sundial. The
dial had a special appeal for Fred. Shortly after it had been
constructed, Fred applied for the position of Keeper of the Sundial.
In support of his application he submitted to the Board of Aldermen
a universal petition filled on both sides with names that Emmons had
clipped out of the pages of the directory and pasted lengthwise on
the petition. In his petition he promised the people that if he were
appointed he would construct a shed over the dial in order to protect
it from the sun.

Fred parked himself next to the dial. Since most of Buffalo
passed that way on Sunday, Emmons thought it would be the most
likely place for him to receive a dinner offer. There were few people
on the street. Church was not out yet, so Fred bided his time. As
he slouched against the dial with hands in pocket, he noticed a
farmer with a load of hay making his way down Main Street. To
Emmons' experienced eye, the farmer looked like a "green one."
As he drew within hailing distance, Fred yelled, "Hello, there.
What you got aboard?" The farmer reined in a bit, looked at Fred
for a moment and said, "Hay." "Hay?" Fred said in mock surprise.
"Don't you know you have laid yourself liable for arrest?"

The farmer's face blanched in shock and disbelief, but he
finally managed to ask how that could be.

"Well," said Fred, "when you enter the city, you are
supposed to have your hay weighed. But if you will wait for just a
minute, I will fix everything for you. If you will bring your wagon

over here in front of the weigher, I'll check it for you."

Fred motioned the farmer to come over in front of the sundial. When the wagon was centered in front of the dial, Emmons took out a piece of paper and a pencil and started jotting down a few figures. Every so often he looked up at the dial and then wrote some more figures on his paper. Finally he looked up at the "green one," handed him the paper and said, "There, I guess that will do. Here is your certificate and that will cost you 25 cents." The farmer reached quickly into his pocket, fished out a quarter and handed it over to Fred. "Thank you." said Fred, "That will do nicely. Thank you and good day." The farmer give a giddap and the wagon rolled on down Main Street. Well, thought Fred as he flipped the coin in his hand and watched the wagon disappear over the Terrace, there's more than one way to make hay while the sun shines on Sunday.

"THE CHOLERA COMETH"

The Cholera cometh; take care! -- take care!
Look week to thy dwelling; beware -- beware!
He breatheth corruption and loveth the spot
Where offal is suffered to lie and to rot.
Then look to thy cellar, thy closet and yard.
For all kinds of filth he hath special regard.

"IF MR. A"

If Mr. A. or B. get sick,
Send for the doctor, go be quick.
The doctor comes with a free good will
And gives him a dose of calomel. . . .

The patient now grows worse indeed.
Send for the doctor, go with speed.
The doctor comes with a free good will
And DOUBLES the dose of calomel.

The man in death begins to groan,
The fatal job for him is done.
His soul is wing'd for heaven or hell,
A sacrifice to calomel.

O, when I must resign my breath,
Pray let me die a natural death,
And bid you all a long farewell
Without one dose of calomel.

There was another jingle, seldom sung, though it was repeated often enough during the dark days of the Great Plague. It was said to be one of Johnny Appleseed's favorites:

"From the time that you're born till you ride in a hearse,
There's nothing that happens that couldn't be worse."

124

WATERFRONT PIRATES:
DUBLIN, MUGGER, AND THE COTTON HOOK MAN

During the upheaval of the Civil War period, a ruthless clique of Buffalo desperadoes organized themselves into a gang of beach guerrillas. Led by four unholy watermen named "Dublin," Jimmy the "Cotton-Hook Man," Leary Reedy and "Billy the Mugger," they terrorized the Buffalo waterfront. Their lair was Michigan Island in the middle of the inner harbor.

Like Sandy Town, another rivermouth area, the spot was protected by a kind of water ditch and, like Sandy Town, this became a squatter haven. The water moat surrounding the area gave medieval protection so dearly loved by the disreputable waterfront characters whose lawless activities found little appreciation among the police watch or the "Respectability of Buffalo."

Buffalo's original harbor had consisted of a creek that snaked its way into Lake Erie from the rolling hills to the southeast. Western bulk and eastern package freight, together with the greatest mass movement of people the world had ever seen, flooded into Buffalo with such tidal proportions after the opening of the Erie Canal that agitation started at the end of the first decade to increase the inner-creek harbor area.

After much pressure and time, work began on what soon became known as the City Ship, or Blackwell, Canal. This artificial waterway ran almost parallel to the creek, thereby doubling the space of the inner harbor. The cutting of this canal created an artificial peninsula that local habitues of the waterfront dubbed "The Island" because, for most people, the only access to the spit of land in question was by bridge or rowboat. This became the guerrillas' hideout.

At first the guerrillas operated on a small scale, boarding vessels at night and taking only plunder that they could carry in their arms. With success, they grew bolder, until finally they attacked vessels in force, driving off the crew and systematically carrying off the cargo. They had no trouble peddling their loot along Canal Street. In those days, the police force, or "watch" as it was called, was so small that it could not match the strength of the pirates. By simply blowing a whistle, Dublin, or any of the other leaders, could quickly gather a force of one hundred men, armed and capable of resisting any police attempts to capture them. For years, after each raid, the gangsters would retire to their island lair and there, fortified by the natural protection of their position and whiskey, they defied the police to attack them.

On several occasions, the police, despite all the precautions taken by the land pirates, did manage to capture some of the leaders. Even Dublin served time in the Buffalo jail. It happened this way: One night he was leading his guerrillas aboard a schooner loaded with staves. While supervising the operation of heaving the staves overboard onto a tug, which the gang had captured earlier, Charles and Dan Darcy, police officers, crept quietly aboard the vessel. Cotton Hook and Mugger were both aboard the vessel topside helping Dublin transfer the cargo. So quickly and silently did the Darcys steal up on the gangsters that they were taken by surprise. Dublin showed no fight. The others, too, seemed paralyzed.

As soon as Dublin recovered his senses, however, he broke for the railing and dove over it into Buffalo Creek. Since the Darcys were more interested in the capture of Dublin than the others, they jumped over the railing and dropped like a couple of lead plummets on Dublin, who was thrashing in the water. Dublin gave a good account of himself until a water uppercut took the fight out of him. The Darcy boys dragged his almost lifeless body back to shore. Meantime, of course, the rest of the boys escaped. Dublin was committed to jail for a year and, on his release, returned to his old lair on the island.

The year brought many changes. Many of the younger and more respectable men on the island signed up with the Irish regiment formed in Buffalo. The Beach Guerrillas, however, would join up, collect the fifty-dollar bounty, and then jump their enlistment. When Dublin returned, therefore, he found his comrades, Cotton Hook, Leary Reedy and Mugger still operating. One sunny day not long after his release, Dublin sat on the shore bank of the island watching the schooners and other vessels come and go. He mentally noted the size, cargo layout and position of the various boats that pulled in and docked. Suddenly he spotted a trim schooner that caused him to stand up to get a better look. She was loaded to the gunwales with a mixed cargo. Her deck furniture, done in natural dark wood, with the oblong cabin, indicated rich interior comfort. With two hundred and fifty feet overall and a white hull with a gold bead around it , Dublin thought her the trimmest craft e'er to moor along the Island pier. Never had Dublin's eyes seen such graceful lines on a sailing craft. And his eyes had seen almost every vessel then sailing the Lakes. On her stern panel, in proud lettering, was the name, MERCEDES OF SAGINAW. Dublin watched her captain pull her into her proper slip. Then he dashed off to find the Hook, Mugger and Leary.

By the time Dublin reached the shack, he was out of breath. "Hey, Mugger" he called out as he reached the shack, "are the others inside?"

"Sure now and Dublin, you wouldn't be a-runnin' unless the Watch were after the likes of us."

"Wrong, ye Killarney fool," Dublin called out. "But come in. 'Tis a beauty I've spotted." Mugger followed Dublin inside where Cotton and Leary were sorting the loot gotten the night before.

"Listen, ye good-for-nothin' Shanty Irish," Dublin started out good naturedly.

"Shanty, maybe, but jailbird like you be no," Cotton Hook greeted him. And with that, they all roared. Cotton Hook brought his arm down so hard on the table that Leary had to help him pull the hook out.

"Boys," Dublin said, still bubbling over with enthusiasm, "the Saints be praised, our ship has come in."

"T'ain't the first ship that come in that we haven't made like our own." said Leary.

"This be different, lads, she's a beauty. Name's MERCEDES," Dublin explained.

"And so we'll be boardin' her tonight and takin' off her cargo and 'twill be so dark she will look like all the other vessels in the harbor," said Cotton Hook.

"Yeah." offered Leary. "Vessels at night be like women at night -- they all look alike."

Dublin was not to be swerved from his original idea and so he continued trying to outline the plan. "Lads, we board her tonight but we ain't takin' no cargo."

"See here, Dublin, have you seen the Leprechauns, and gone clean daft? What do you mean, take no cargo? How's the likes of us to live?" shouted the Hook.

"Here now," Dublin said in a confidential tone. They all leaned their heads closely toward Dublin and listened while he laid the plan for their new adventure.

127

That night, the guerrillas boarded the vessel, plucked off the crew, hog-tied them and dumped them on the wharf. Once in control of the ship, Dublin signaled to the tug operated by his henchmen. A line was thrown out and the tug pulled them out of the Buffalo Channel and a mile up the Lake. Here they cast off the line to the tug and the men on the tug made their way back to the schooner in a rowboat.

Meanwhile, the guerrilla crew aboard the schooner set to work repainting the MERCEDES in open water. Since the morning sunlight was warm and bright, the paint dried quickly. They painted out the old name, MERCEDES, and replaced it with the name ANNIE, a young love of Dublin's. With painting done, the crew took advantage of a stiff breeze that bulged out the sails and carried the ANNIE to a safe bay on the Canadian shore before midnight the following night. The ANNIE had sailed into the night and into history.

Many an old captain told of seeing the ANNIE. Many described, in glowing terms, her pirate adventures on the Great Lakes. How she could steal into lonely ports, especially along the Canadian shores, raid vessels docked there, and be away before sunrise. Many Lakemen believe that the ANNIE had a part in the attempted capture of the vessel MICHIGAN in 1864. Still other sailors liked to tell of the important part that the ANNIE played in the Johnson Island plot to rescue two thousand Confederate prisoners on that Island in Sandusky Bay. But all this is in the realm of legend and fantasy because no one really knows.

What bold adventures befell Dublin, the Hook, Mugger and Leary may never be known. Should ever the log of this vessel be found there would be a story equal to any pirate story of the high seas: the story of the ANNIE and her crew of Buffalo pirates.

BURNT BREAD AND BROOM HANDLES

Belching smoke, cinders, and fire, the westbound freight slowed as it approached the outer railroad yards of Buffalo. In a few minutes, the lumbering train would grind to a stop with much hissing, clanging and screeching. The stopping of a train always reminded Joe of the last convulsive gasp of some huge thing dying. For Joe, this would be the last time he would have to listen to the cacophony of a freight train for awhile.

Joe had been riding the rails from New York City, spending the last stretch of the journey from Batavia to Buffalo atop a boxcar, the better to see the country near the lake. As the train pulled into the yard near the soot-covered red brick passenger station on Exchange Street, he lowered himself down the steel ladder on the north side of the car. Facing west with a firm left hand on the grabstep and his left foot on the steel step just above the ground, he swung back and using his right hand as a sort of balance, stepped from the train. Looking about quickly to see if there were any rail police around, he dashed across the railyard and out onto Exchange Street.

As he walked west on Exchange Street, he looked over at the train. It seemed to have relaxed from its stopping spasm and only the steady throbbing of the locomotive could be heard. In the early morning, Exchange Steet was quiet. It seemed to be sleeping off its last night's drunk. The sound of the engine idling on the rail siding added the illusion of heavy breathing. An early morning haze seemed to accentuate the stillness of inactivity. Not a soul was stirring. The lonely click of Joe's heels on the cobblestone echoed against the walls of the buildings which line Exchange Street opposite the yard.

If his canawler friend at Coenties Slip in New York had informed him correctly, he would soon be crossing Main Street opposite which he would spot the twin pumps. Beyond this would be the bridge over the Erie Canal which would take him into the Buffalo waterfront district. As he crossed the bridge, he thought of the thousands who had walked down Commercial and Canal Streets on their way to the Old Northwest.

While still a busy and important place, the waterfront's future was in its past. Progress had passed it by. Having crossed the bridge over the canal, Joe turned right off Commercial and Canal Street, once named Cross and later to be named Dante Place. It was like a still picture, nothing moved. In almost all of the alleys, Joe could see drunks sleeping off their whiskey stupor, hair disheveled, clothes dirty and their bodies reeking with the sour smell of cheap liquor. A few buildings away from Commercial Street, Joe turned left down Maiden Lane toward the harbor. Perhaps, he thought idly, I might get a job as a scooper.

The closer Joe walked toward the harbor, the thicker the haze became. The sun, having only started its climb, had not succeeded in dispelling it yet. He sat down on what looked to be some comfortably padded freight and promptly fell fast asleep. A moment later, or so it seemed, Joe was awakened by a voice saying, "Come on buddy, move it."

"O.K.," said Joe, "I'm going." He looked at the fellow for a second and then added, "Don't need an extra hand, do you?" "Nope," said the hustler. "Got too many as 'tis."

With that Joe started back toward the Canal. This time he walked along Commercial Street which edged on the Commercial Slip. In what to him seemed like only a few minutes, the area had been completely transformed. Where there had been only quiet before, there was now the hustle and bustle of noisy confusion. It seemed to Joe almost as if the sailors, canawlers, dock-hands, deck-hands, scoopers, clerks, commission merchants, immigrants and waterfront rats in general had formed out of nothingness. The saloons had already opened their doors in order to catch the early morning trade. There were always those who needed a "starter" and those who had to put out the roaring fires which they had kindled the night before. As Joe pushed through the swinging doors of a saloon, at the corner of Commercial and Canal Streets, such a character had just downed a shot in one sweeping gesture and with perfect synchronization followed it with a water chaser. He grimaced like one in great pain and said, "God, that's good. I always say ya have to fight fire with fire."

Joe stepped up to the bar. "A shot please."

As the barkeeper turned to get it, Joe looked about the room. Over in the corner where just a sprig of light played on a table, someone sat writing. Joe studied his face. He had a feeling he had seen it somewhere before. He looked hard. Then the thought came to him. No, it couldn't be, Jack had left for the coast over a month ago.

Joe turned his attention back to his drink, smelled it for a moment, and then flipped it up to his mouth. As he set the glass down with one hand, he took a swig of water with the other. Turning to the bartender, he asked him who the lone customer was over at the table in the corner.

"Dunno where he came from," said the barkeep, "but he asked me when the next westbound freight was leaving and I told him that one had arrived from the East early this morning and would be pulling out in about an hour. I reckon he's fixin' to skip along."

While the bartender talked, Joe continued to study the man's face closely. It couldn't be, he thought to himself, but by God, it was. It was his old pal Jack. Joe quickly walked over to the table.

"Why, you silver-plated bum," Joe yelled. "What in the hell are you doing in Buffalo? I thought by now you'd be in Frisco."

The person at the table dropped his pencil, looked up at Joe and a broad, warm smile broke across his face.

"Joe, you rod-riding son-of-a-rail. It's good to see you. Watcha doing here?" said Jack as he stood up from the table and grabbed Joe's hand.

"Not fair, Jack. I asked you first. Let's have it. What happened? You didn't get a job and go respectable on me, did you?"

"Yes and no, Joe."

"You mean you did get a job? Who'd ever hire the likes of you?"

"Now look here Joe, I'm not so bad when you get to know me. I can think of a number of people who might hire me. As a matter of fact, a number of people did hire me."

Joe looked steadily at his friend for a moment and in mock disbelief said, "Who?"

"Erie County," replied Jack with a straight face.

"Erie County?" said Joe, no longer faking his disbelief. "What do ya mean, Erie County?"

"I mean," Jack insisted, "Erie County hired me."

"Now wait a minute, Jack, what in hell have you got that Erie County could possibly want?"

"Me, I guess," Jack said, trying to keep a straight face.

"All right, all right, Jack. I'll admit I was never quite as sharp as you and now you got me tied for sure. Come clean. What really happened?"

"Well, I'll tell you, Joe, I have just spent thirty days as the guest of the Erie County jail."

"No," said Joe. "You can't really mean that. I know you're capable of a great many things. I never thought you would stoop to stealing. Not one who can talk people out of money the way you can."

"Truth is, Joe, just the opposite happened. I was picked up at the Falls on a vagrancy charge and tossed into the Erie County jail with all the trash and garbage of the Buffalo waterfront."

"Well I certainly am surprised," Joe said, "I always thought you'd make your own way. Never thought you would stoop to having the Government take care of you. How does it feel to have had a well-fed and slept vacation?"

Whatever humor had been in Jack's face now melted away and in its place an expression of deep revulsion appeared.

"Joe, believe me, there has been no humor in my experience of the last month. This so-called jail where they housed me for thirty days is located on the canal. The prisoners are made to carry huge stay-bolts, railroad ties, stone and other heavy freight boated in on the canal. They kept us at it for eighteen hours a day. The work was hard, too hard considering the prison diet. Bread and water, that was all that was given us. Once a week we were supposed to get meat, but this meat did not always get around, and since all the nutriment had been boiled out of it in the making of soup, it didn't matter whether we got a taste of it once a week or not.

"Furthermore, there was one vital defect in the bread and water diet. While we got plenty of water, we did not get enough bread. A ration of bread was about the size of one's fist and three rations a day were given to each prisoner. There was one thing I must say, about the water -- it was hot. In the morning it was coffee, at noon it was dignified as soup, and at night it masqueraded as tea. But it was the same old water all the time. The prisoners called it water bewitched. In the morning it was black water, the color being due to boiling it with burnt bread crust. At noon it was served minus the color, with salt and a drop of grease added. At night it was served with a purplish-auburn hue that defied all speculation; it was darn poor tea but it was dandy hot water."

Joe laughed and said, "What are you complaining about? Look what it's done for your waistline."

"Joe, perhaps I can make light of the food situation, but believe me, there is nothing, absolutely nothing, to mitigate the utter brutality prisoners are forced to endure in the Erie County penitentiary. Joe, if I had not seen it with my own eyes, I would never have believed that such conditions existed in America in this year of civilization, 1890. That prison was a living hell. The treatment of prisoners was not only unprintable, it was unthinkable. Because of insufficient personnel, certain inmates are made to trustees. They are called hall-men. I suppose considering the nature of the

132

waterfront brutes they picked up, it was impossible to rule by kindness. Yet some humanity could have been employed. Their rule was to hit a man as soon as he opened his mouth -- hit him hard; hit him with anything. A broom handle, end on in the face, had a very sobering effect. I remember a young mulatto about twenty who got the insane idea into his head that he should stand for his rights. Eight hall-men took the conceit out of him in just about a minute and a half -- for that was the length of time required to travel along his gallery to the end and down five flights of steel stairs. He traveled the whole distance on every portion of his anatomy except his feet, and the eight hall-men were not idle. The mulatto struck the pavement where I was standing watching it all. He regained his feet and stood upright for a moment. In that moment he threw his arms wide apart and emitted an awful scream of terror and pain and heartbreak. At the same instant, as in a transformation scene, the shreds of his stout prison clothes fell from him, leaving him wholly naked and streaming blood from every portion of the surface of his body. Then he collapsed in a heap, unconscious. He had learned his lesson, and every convict within those walls who heard him scream had learned a lesson. So had I learned mine. It is not a nice thing to see a man's heart broken in a minute and a half."

Jack looked over at Joe for a fleeting second. Joe had been hanging on his every word. There was a look of horror on his face.

Then slowly Joe said, "Jack, there are no brute animals as inhuman as human beings. I have never had such a deep feeling of revulsion as I had when you told that story. But I could not help also thinking that you have a great gift for story-telling. You seem to be able to make the things which you see and experience live again for others through your words."

"Joe, I always felt that I had some ability along that line. That's why I was writing when you interrupted me a few minutes ago. I did not want to lose the story I just told you and you know, Joe, I would like nothing better than to see a printed title on a book one day with the name Jack - Jack London - after it."

"Well, Joe, my train leaves in a few minutes. After what I've just told you, you don't want to stay around this town, do you?"

Joe took a letter out of his pocket, looked at it for a moment and then tore it up. "You're right, Jack, let's hit the road."

Jack turned with this to Joe and after a few seconds said, "You know, Joe, maybe that's what I'll call this book, The Road, by Jack London."

V

CANAL
ENTERTAINMENT

Republic Steam Presses, Buffulo.

CANAL STREET ENTERTAINMENT

Each canal port from Buffalo to Albany had a canal street by name or reputation. These were wild and weird, some more than others. They were all fascinatingly sinful, but none more so than in Buffalo and the Albany area.

"BUFFALO GALS"

As I was lumb'ring down de street,
Down de street,
Down de street,
A handsome gal I chanc'd to meet;
Oh! she was fair to view.
Buffalo gals, can't you come out to-night?
Can't you come out to-night?
Can't you come out to-night?
Buffalo gals, can't you come out to-night?
And dance by de light ob de moon?

I ax'd her would she hab some talk,
Hab some talk?
Hab some talk?
Her feet covered up de whole sidewalk
As she stood close to me.
Buffalo gals, can't you come out to-night?
Can't you come out to-night?
Can't you come out to-night?
Buffalo gals, can't you come out to-night?
And dance by de light ob de moon?

I ax'd her would she hab a dance,
Hab a dance,
Hab a dance,
I taught dat I might get a chance
To shake a foot wid her.
Buffalo gals can't you come out to-night?
Can't you come out to-night?
Can't you come out to-night?
Buffalo gals can't you come out to-night?
And dance by de light ob de moon?

I'd like to make that gal my wife,
Gal my wife,
Gal my wife,
I'd be happy all my life,
If I had her by me.
Buffalo gals, can't you come out to-night?
Can't you come out to-night?
Can't you come out to-night?
Buffalo gals can't you come out to-night?
And dance by de light ob de moon?

PEG-LEG HARRISON

How he lost his leg no one knew, but it gave him his nickname "Peg-Leg" to go along with his formal name of James Harrison. Peg-Leg was a black man, a man of towering height, prodigious strength and amazing musical talents. His feats became legendary on the Buffalo waterfront in the 1830's and 1840's and in those days the whole world seemed to be pouring through the narrow funnel of the Canal district.

The waterfront was awash with a babel of tongues. The variety of dress that once was brightly colored was a confusion of cultures and customs of people adrift, cut off forever from home and things familiar. They faced a future unknown and frightening. Nothing was normal; nothing ordinary. Yet, in this teeming life, Peg-Leg Harrison stood out bigger than life itself, a more than ordinary man.

Often he would stride into one of the many taverns and announce in a voice that quieted the crowd that he could twirl his body one foot above the tallest man with the tallest stovepipe hat in the tavern. Bets were quickly made. The crowd settled down making a circle about the tallest man and Peg-Leg. Peg-Leg, with a flourish of his crutch, would plant it in the barroom floor. Grasping tightly the top with his powerful arms and giving a tremendous kick, he would twirl his body a foot above the stove-pipe hat and come down, standing right side up.

Nor did Harrison's one leg hinder him from developing into a remarkable swimmer of Olympian class. Daybreak often found him swimming in the lake, just off the harbor. Many unfortunates, unable to swim, who fell in owed their lives to him.

One day he had a spat with his wife. In cuffing her about the ears, she backed away and tumbled into the lake. Peg-Leg jumped in immediately, treading water with his one leg and holding her head above the water until help came.

He met his wife in the old Vine Street Black Methodist Church where he was the conductor and soloist of the church choir.

138

Peg-Leg did not confine his musical talents to church. In the 1840's, he became acquainted with E. P. Christy and his son, George, singers and musicians who owned a tavern-theater on the waterfront. How their idea of a musical mode started, no one knows for sure, but soon the Christys were meeting regularly in Peg-Leg's home for music "sessions."

Probably it came from Peg-Leg who recalled his plantation days. Certainly, he had shared his stories and songs of the Deep South with the Christys. Undoubtedly, none of them realized that the shows they were creating in that Canal Street tavern would revolutionize musical entertainment not just on the waterfront, but around the world.

Harrison taught the Christys "down-South" talk and plantation dances. From the canawlers and sailors, they learned the songs of the lakes and canal. Finally ready, they opened to standing room only with their toe-tapping theme song, "Buffalo Gals, Won't You Come Out Tonight." Thus was born Christy's Minstrels, claimed by their proud Buffalonians, Lakers and Canawlers of the waterfront, as the pioneer minstrel company in America.

After entertaining local crowds, they soon traveled to New York via the canal, where the Christys' musical format enjoyed even greater success. Before long they were performing before the crowned heads of Europe. The minstrel show deeply influenced the Broadway musical theater.

Peg-Leg was not only agile on his one leg, but equally well-balanced in the saddle. One day in May, a few gentlemen relaxed in big arm chairs in the shade of trees in front of Stevenson Brothers' big yellow wooden livery stable on Pearl Street at the rear of the old American Hotel overlooking the Terrace.

Their reverie was broken when Lt. Hamilton, of the Regulars (stationed at Poinsett Barracks on Delaware Avenue), ordered Jimmy, who was in charge of the livery, to saddle and bring out the new horse. Hamilton wanted to ride out to Black Rock along the beach road between the Lake and the Canal to see if the animal would pass inspection.

He mounted the horse with the disparaging remark that the horse had eaten too many oats. The instant Hamilton's bottom touched the saddle, the horse reared up in a war dance "with a sawing on the bit, a bracing in the stirrups, a flying of heels and dirt in the air." The officer's limbs seemed to be flying in all directions with little attachment to his body.

Fearing disaster, John, one of the hotel proprietors, rushed up, seized the bridle and loudly suggested that Lt. Hamilton come down and that they try another horse. He then added, "we will turn this horse over to Peg-Leg Harrison," who happened to be watching from across the street with growing amusement, the whole ungainly exhibition.

Hamilton obeyed the order, but his Southern blood was fired-up and in his best dueling voice demanded to know what John meant by his insinuation SAH!

John should have remembered that it was part of a West Pointer's education to stay in the saddle of all bucking broncos, under all conditions. It was the code of the Corps.

Before the incident developed into a matter of honor to be dealt with dueling pistols, cooler heads suggested to the officer that they refer the matter to landlord Hodges of the American Hotel.

Everyone walked through the backway to the American Hotel and there "the affair was settled according to the old Kentucky code: 'bourbon and branch water,' with a bit of lemon peel to ward off scurvy."

Meanwhile, Peg-Leg, using his crutch as a pole, vaulted into the saddle and taught the bucking colt who was master.

Riding a horse had become second nature to Harrison. While the waterfront saw one side of him, uptown people saw another side. Mounted on his horse with the reins in one hand and an old tavern hand-bell in the other, he moved from street corner to street corner, crooning a plantation melody and ringing his bell to the rhythm of the horse's hooves. On hearing his voice, window sashes would fly up and his stentorian voice would break the stillness and blackness of the night.

"Oh, yes! Oh, yes!! I have lost a little girl, three years old, with a yaller calicer dress, blue check apron, pink sun bonnet, red stockings and blue morocco shoes. Whoever will deliver her to me shall be well rewarded." Then he would proceed to the next corner until the child was found.

One day, Major Berry, the old tax collector, saw Peg-Leg coming down the street all cluttered up atop his horse. He stopped at Hargreave Lee's old store opposite the Kremlin Block and there delivered, to an almost distracted family, one little boy and one little drum which, along with his crutch, bell and reins, he had managed to balance gracefully on his one-stirrup saddle.

For a man of such talents who seemed to want only good for his fellow man, it is unpleasant to add a sad postscript. In later years, Harrison became depressed. For an intelligent, creative black man in those years, society offered little recognition, reward or understanding. He undoubtedly became completely frustrated. One day he lost control of his temper according to accounts of the period. History does not record what he did, but he ended his life in the Auburn (New York) State Penitentiary.

A century or so later, another man of comparable physical, mental and musical gifts, Paul Robeson, found America had little changed.

MILLSTONE MINUET

Once upon a time, a Buffalo dance-house flourished on the Lower Terrace, facing the canal. The upper story of the structure was even with the ground at its rear, where there was a lone window. Capt. Frank Wheeler, with companions, were passing by one evening, when they observed through the rear window a party of dancers skipping the light fantastic in high glee. On the ground nearby lay an unmounted grindstone, some four feet in diameter. The grindstone was raised and taken to the bank in the rear of the dance-house, to which the downgrade was about forty degrees. When the stone was started it rolled accurately, passing through the window and speeding on through the maze of dancers and through the front of the building into the canal, where, perhaps, it remains imbedded in the mud bottom. The consternation of the dancers at the sudden invasion of the grindstone may be imagined.

"TOWPATH CIRCUS"

Canalers on the Ohio-Erie Canal often referred to the Nye family boats as the "towpath circus:"

One day on the towpath I was scared for
a billy goat aimed right at my rear,
but I jumped quick upon a mule,
He looked at me just like a fool,
But soon he followed me with his bleat,
I knew enough to keep my seat,
So quiet, yes, just like a bird,
'Twas better seen but not heard.

What fun that old canal,
'Twas something new each mile.
my parents oft would laugh,
when I met a frisky calf.

Sometimes we'd meet a sow and pigs,
If she showed fight we used our legs,
And on the mule you bet we'd climb,
So often 'twas just in time.
The old gander with his hearty brood,
We're a bunch, we youngsters though so good,
Sometimes he'd get our seat of pants,
And would he make us yell and dance.

When Buzzard's Island we would pass,
Whate'er hour, 'twas none too fast,
The sky was filled with these old birds,
Their young quite often would be heard,
Sometimes they would get us awful mad,
They'd try and give us what they had,
But Oh, that carion rotten stuff,
They'd cough it up, that was enough.

Such times and fun I can't forget,
Whate'er my lot, they linger yet,
There everybody was so gay,
'Twas sure a picnic everyday.
But I can not bring back the past,
Tho' it was great while it did last,
I know such thoughts are often vain,
But I love to live o'er again.

PIGS AND PLAYERS

Mr. Connolly of Hornell, who is head of the Community Theater, tells this one:

A troupe of actors was stranded in a small town along the Erie. Not having much money, they couldn't afford to pay regular rates. Finally they booked passage on a boat carrying hogs. While the boat was going along the Erie, the captain was hailed by the captain of another boat who asked what cargo he was carrying. His reply was, "Hogs and actors." At this, one of the actors who was on deck said, "Well, he might at least have give us top billing."

COCKFIGHTING

Cockfights were popular with canal men. One chief gathering place seems to have been Leonard's saloon on the "Dyke," or lower Cohoes, where canallers frequently paid off their debts in fuel, thus keeping the enterprising saloonkeeper in winter supply. The sport of cockfighting finally became illegal in New York State, and by 1880 newspapers carried accounts of raids on the cockfight "arenas." Bulldog fighting used to be another sport which an SPCA would not have tolerated. The haunches of the dogs were sandpapered until they were raw in order to get the dogs fighting mad and cause them to tear into each other.

KOONIN'

The following is taken from the <u>Buffalo Express,</u> August 3, 1870. It is a sketch of the "Popular Country Juvenile Sport" and was written by a boy correspondent, Happy Holler.

Probably, Mr. Editor, you don't know where Happy Holler is, or you don't know who I am. Wull, I'm a member of the Happy Holler Club and the Happy Holler Club is a 'sociation for mutual enjoyment of its members. We don't limit our doins' to poker and sich, but we sometimes goes koonin', or go off to another town and have a good time. We went koonin' a week ago tonight; thar was about ten of us; we took a couple of boats and floated down the river to old farmer Hardy's grove about a mile and a half from town, whair we made a fire and sent Sammy Green and Jimmy and Tommy Jones after the koons. I suppose you know that koons ain't koons at all, but green corn or anythin' you can lay yer hands on that's good to eat. Wull, in about fifteen minutes they come back with their arms full of corn and the nicest lot of melons I ever got my eyes on. We all took the corn and commenced. We was on the second ear when we heard a "bow-wow-wow" of Hardy's dog about a half a mile off. Sich a scatterin' you never saw. I ran for the boats, but the rest must suddenly hev taken leave of their senses, for they ran in all directions. I pushed off the boat but didn't hear the dog any more so I come back and the fellers was jist comin' to. Sam Green was up in a tree and in gittin' up had torn his pants off. I come dern near a hollerin' right out but thoughts of the dog suddenly sobered me, and lookin' around I saw Zeke Smith comin' out of a old holler log that had been burnt out in the middle and he was black as coal; he had caught the corner of his coat pocket in the log goin' in and had torn it almost off; jist Al Tousing came out of a lot of berry bushes (where he had throwed himself) with his hands and face all scratched so that he looked as if he had the small pox. The rest come from behind trees and we concluded to vamoose that place but took the melons along to eat on the way. Next nite we was all on hand but Al Tousing had stayed at "Sam's" (that's our rendavoo) for we had had enuf of koonin' to last us most a week. We don't always have such bad luck. We manage to enjoy ourselves in spite of an occasional dog or sich.

KITTY ON A PEDESTAL

Canal Street, in particular, and the Buffalo waterfront, in general, always wore the carnival air of a holiday. On holidays, therefore, the festive spirit knew no bounds. Of all the celebrations, none received the attention and treatment reserved for Independence Day. This holiday traditionally began on the second and lasted through the fifth. The days were filled with activity around the clock the celebrants were filled with blackstrap and rot gut.

To mark the day as something special, tavern keepers brought in thousands of maple trees and stuck them in the ground. As if by magic, it touched the area with a bit of nature, which was normally lacking. Viewed from the Upper Terrace, the waterfront took on the appearance of maple forest. The extremes in decorations during this period were matched only by the decor of the participants. The canawlers and sailors, who lived a lusty, brawling life demanded entertainment to match.

As the Fourth approached, captains aboard lake vessels and canal boats bent their efforts to reach the waterfront in time for the fun and festivity. Drinking bouts, among other forms of indoor sports, were the order of the day. Rival crews tried to out-drink each other. The best bouts, however, were those between canawler and laker. For no respect or love was lost between these groups.

As soon as the crew had their ship fast at dock, off they went to their favorite haunt, which would be one of the many concert halls which flourished on the waterfront during the '70's and '80's. Many found the Only Theatre at the corner of Canal and Commercial Streets, to their liking; the Olympic Theatre at 157 Canal St., appealed to others. There were enough on Canal Street to appeal to the most discriminating taste of the watermen. Upon entering these concert halls through swinging doors, customers would find a bar which extended the length of the hall. At the far end, away from the door, was a small stage lighted with kerosene lamps. Along the side of the tavern or hall, opposite the bar, were booths where girls entertained the men who could pay the price. About fifty tables on the open floor provided places for those who could not afford the luxury of a booth. In some of the concert halls, customers sat on long benches on the back of which were small ledges. Waiters selling drinks and cigars would slide them along this ledge to the purchasers. So adept did these saloon salesmen become that they could stop a drink in front of the prospective buyer.

Owners during the holidays usually tried to out-do themselves with entertainment. Unless the entertainment was out of the ordinary, however, the sailors were content with black strap and women. In the drinking bouts, one table of sailors might challenge a table of canawlers in the same tavern. Under the watchful eye of

several impartial observers the drinking would begin. Careful count was kept of each shot drunk by the participant. If one member of the team could no longer sit up at the table, his teammates would place him gently on the floor next to the table. According to the rules, he could still participate so long as he could open his mouth and swallow. His friends, therefore, would continue to pour the liquor into his mouth. When both eyes and mouth finally closed and the participant was completely paralyzed, the tavern bouncer would drag the drunk off the floor into a special room where the "stiffs" were dumped like ten pins after a strike. The game proceeded until only one man remained. That team was then declared the victor. The tavern, as a reward for such outstanding performance, would buy the victor a drink.

On occasion, the professional entertainers managed to steal the attention of the crowd away from these drinking bouts. On the Fourth of July (circa 1881), word spread quickly through the infected region that Kitty O'Neil would do her famous dance that night. As the hour approached, waterfront characters pushed their way into the tavern where she was scheduled to dance. By the time Kitty began her dance, the spectators had packed themselves in so tightly that, as the drunks passed out from the influence of heat, liquor and lack of oxygen, they remained in a standing position propped up by the tightly packed mass of humanity about them. There in the center of the theater, atop a white Grecian pedestal, stood a beautiful young woman whose lithe body would carry her to the top of the entertainment world. When no other person could be packed in, the dance began.

The dance was most difficult , and was made more so by its being performed atop a pedestal which measured only twelve inches in diameter. For one hour and twenty minutes, Kitty danced. She danced in the nude. No one moved. No one could move. When the dance was completed, and Kitty had made her bows, the doors of the theater-tavern burst open. The compressed mass of humanity exploded into Canal Street. The applause and roars of the audience were punctuated by the thud of the dead drunk bodies as they hit the floor after their human props had been removed. It was some time before the tavern could sweep the human debris into the sobering room to make way for the paying customers.

Yes, the Buffalo waterfront took its Fourth of July seriously. Poet Thomas Love Peacock summed it up well:

> He is not drunk, who from the floor,
> Can rise again and drink some more.
> But he is drunk who prostrate lies,
> And cannot drink or cannot rise.

SAM, SAM, THE JUMPIN' MAN

It all began in 1826 at the other end of the state in New York City. Sam started jumping from the mastheads of ships anchored in the North River. His passion for notoriety encouraged him to risk his life in even greater jumps. As his reputation spread and the crowds grew larger, Sam tried higher masts. The day came when there were no higher masts in the North River. So he began to look around for new heights to conquer.

At the western end of the state, especially at Niagara Falls, hotels and shopkeepers needed publicity. Now that the Erie Canal made transportation across the state comparatively easy, they wanted to lure people to the Falls. These entrepreneurs had read, with the interest borne of money, the newspaper stories of Sam's jumpin' feats. Soon arrangements were made between them for Sam to jump the Falls.

In September, 1829, widespread coverage was given to the announcement. It became the chief topic of crackerbarrel conversation whenever people gathered at the general store. Many allowed that it just couldn't be done. Arguments grew heated. Betting was heavy. While it had to be admitted that he had successfully jumped a number of times from great heights into the North River, his detractors quickly pointed out the difference between the calm waters of that river and the turbulent waters of the Niagara River at the foot of the Falls. Through all the loud debate, Sam remained confidently calm and cool. To those who pointed to their head in a knowing gesture, Sam replied in priceless prose, "Some things can be done as well as others."

At Niagara, preparation went forward. A large platform projecting out from the Biddle staircase was constructed 125 feet above the water. Interest mounted. People from all over made arrangements to be on hand to watch "Crazy Patch" jump. Finally, on October 6, 1829, the day had arrived. When all was ready, Patch climbed the ladder to the platform. All eyes were on the tiny figure atop the aerial stage. Many wondered if some things really could be done as well as others. There was no doubt in Sam's mind. To show his utter contempt for the danger, he danced a jig and sang a song:

> I wish I were in Buffalo,
> Good friends along with me
> I'd call for liquors plenty
> Have Rowling bowls on every side;
> Hard fortune never grieved me --
> I am young and the world is wide.

Then Sam took another swig from his flask of rum and concluded, " Good liquor in a poor man's house, is a pleasing thing to view."

As he finished his song, he stepped to the edge of the platform and, without hesitation, jumped. His body shot through the air toward the water 125 feet below. All the way down he managed an erect position. He cut the water feet first and disappeared below the surface. As if they were under the water themselves, everyone seemed to be holding his breath. When his head bobbed to the surface all seemed to exhale a sign of relief. Sam had conquered the Falls. He was a hero. When the man in the rowboat picked him up and asked him how he was, he said, "It's like I told you, some things can be done as well as others. Now give me a swig of whiskey to take the chill out of my bones."

According to the story, Patch remained in the Falls for a few days and made a second successful leap, just to show the doubters that the first was not an accident. Offers now poured in to Sam asking him to appear here and to jump there. He soon announced that he would jump the Falls at Rochester. The scene was much the same as it had been at Niagara. Only this day, as he stood atop the platform overlooking Genesee Falls, he sampled the flask too heavily and too often. He was very drunk. If anything, he showed more bravado than at Niagara. After he had finished all his preliminaries and the flask, he stepped to the edge, spread his arms, and jumped off. As he fell through the air, he waved his arms wildly. Partway down, he lost his balance. His body flopped crazily in the air. When he struck the water, it tore his arms out of their sockets and broke his body like a toothpick. People looked on in frozen terror. It was Sam's last jump. Sam had learned that some things can be done, but not always as well as others.

(Another version of this story appears in the chapter notes of this book.)

VI

WATER, WINE AND WHISKEY

Republic Steam Presses, Buffalo.

WATER, WATER EVERYWHERE

When England was outfitting her Lake Erie fleet, which eventually met defeat at the hands of Perry in the Battle of Lake Erie in 1813, the Admiralty sent over to all the lake ships water casks for carrying fresh water. So strong was the tradition of salt water sailing, that the Admiralty did not realize that a bucket over the side of the boat would have tapped an almost inexhaustible supply of fresh drinking water.

On one occasion a crew of old salts returned to their ship after a long pull in a rowboat under the burning sun almost perished from thirst. They had never thought of tasting the cool spring water which their oars were every moment splashing and flashing in the sunshine.

FRESH WATER AND FREE WINE

In the early forties of the last century, shipping on the Great Lakes out of Buffalo was riding a crest of unprecedented business. Shipping companies should have been making money but they were not. A price war was on. Competing lines ran steamers alongside the rival vessels, slashing prices at every port in a wild endeavor to secure the business offered. Travelers took advantage of the rate warfare.

Each steamship line had its own set of runners who worked the docks attempting to secure trade for the lines they represented. As the battle for business grew in intensity, it challenged the ingenuity of the most imaginative "runners" and captains. Armed with advertisements and spieling out unfounded claims, "runners" would attempt to persuade the travelers, first verbally, and then physically, to take passage on the vessel which they represented. Frequently, several "runners" would pounce upon some hapless prospective traveler and succeed in tearing off most of his clothes. For years the city attempted to abate this nuisance but was unsuccessful.

Immigrants, ignorant of English and baffled by the customs and manners of this rough inland port, became easy prey for the slick wharf salesman most of the time. The price war, however, had now given the traveler a temporary advantage. By September of 1842, prices had fallen so that it was possible to book passage from Liverpool to Detroit for seven dollars. The Journal of Commerce quoted a price of four to five dollars for emigrant passage from Liverpool to New York in the finest ships afloat. From New York to Buffalo that year, travelers could purchase transportation for one dollar and fifty cents. It had even dropped as low as one dollar and twenty-five cents. A dollar more would take the westbound emigrant from Buffalo to Detroit. Added all up, it meant the Europeans could pass from their shores far into the interior of America for seven dollars.

Buffalo's Commercial Advertiser in 1842 estimated that provision for the ocean, canal, and lake trip would cost about seven dollars. By adding a dollar more for emergency, the entire cost including food, transportation and incidentals would amount to about fifteen dollars. "There is no use calling," said the editor of the paper, "upon past ages to come and see what is doing now. They would not believe it if they saw it."

Low as the prices had dropped, however, the bottom had not yet been reached. One day a man asked David Wilkinson, Captain of the steamer COMMODORE PERRY, the price of cabin passage to Detroit. Wilkinson quoted him an amount which was considerably less than one-half the price of the regular rate. Anxious to please the prospective passenger, he invited him aboard

154

for a drink at the ship's bar. Despite the pleasantries of Wilkinson's hospitality the traveler could not be induced to book passage.

A little later, while the Captain was walking along the wharf near his vessel, he again met the stranger who informed him that a rival steamer had offered to carry him to his destination for nothing.

Not wishing to be outdone by the rival line, Wilkinson turned to him and with a gesture of great magnanimity said, "Oh well, if that's the case, I'll carry you for nothing and board you. You will go with me, won't you?"

"Well, I don't know," came the unexpected answer. "I think his wine is preferable to yours."

DRINKING WATER

For drinking, of course, there was always water. But sometimes they didn't want to take a chance on it. . . .

I'D RATHER DRINK BUTTERMILK

Now, I ax you, fellers, who's the best citizen? Him who supports Government or him as doesn't? Why, him as does, of course. We support Government; everyone as drinks supports Government -- that is, if he swollers thay is taxed to pay the salary of them'ar grate officers, such as mayours and corporationers, his constables, presidents and custom-house gentlemen. S'pose we was to quit drinkin? Why Government must fail; it couldn't help it no how. That's very resun I drinks. I don't like grog -- I mortality hate it. If I follower my own inclination, I'd rather drink buttermilk or ginger pop, or Dearborn's sody water. But I likkers for the good of my country to set an example of patriotism and virchuous self-denial to the rizun generation.

MIXING AN ERIE CANAL COCKTAIL

You will see at Brighton Village Cemetery the tomb of William C. Bloss, who in early days ran the three-story red brick tavern that stood beside the canal until the subway came. It was known as Miller's and then as Sheehan's. Bloss sickened of the business and, as is recorded on the stone, dumped all the liquor from his tavern into the canal. He became a foremost temperance advocate as well as a champion of the anti-slavery and woman suffrage causes. He died in 1863.

RECIPE FOR WHISKEY

You take one barrel of Erie Canal water, and two gallons of alcohol. Then you add two ounces of strychnine --because strychnine is the greatest stimulant in the world -- and three plugs of tobacco to make them sick -- any Canawler wouldn't figure it was whiskey unless it made him sick -- and five bars of soap to give it a head, and half a pound of red pepper, and then you put in some sagebrush and boil it until it's brown. Strain into a barrel, and you've got your Canal Whiskey.

DRINK

But how they could drink and dance, and drink and dance, and drink, and drink, and drink, and...

Drink is in itself a good creature of God,
and to be received with thankfulness
but the abuse of drink is from Satan,
the wine is from God, but the Drunkard
is from the Devil.

THE AMERICAN TOAST

The Frenchman likes his native wine;
The German likes his beer;
The Englishman likes his 'alf and 'alf
Because it brings him cheer.
The Irishman drinks his whiskey straight
Because it brings him dizziness,
The American has no chance at all,
He drinks the whole damn business.

FIVE REASONS FOR DRINKING

In the early days, many a canawler needed no excuse for a drink. Beers' Calendar published the year the Canal opened offered them five reasons for drinking.

(It must be remembered that about the time the Canal was completed, the Temperance Movement swept across New York State along the Canal. . . .)

> Good wine -- a friend -- or being dry --
> Or lest we should be by and by --
> Or -- any other reason why.

From the 1825 edition came the following:

"The Drunkard's Character" -- A drunkard is the annoyance of modesty; the trouble of civility; the spoil of wealth; the distraction of reason; he is only the brewer's agent; the tavern and ale-house benefactor; the beggar's companion; the constable's trouble; he is the wife's woe; his children's sorrow; his neighbour's scoff; his own shame; in summer, he is the tub of swill; a spirit of sleep; a picture of a beast, and a monster of a man.

The newspapers continued the theme over the years.

TEMPERANCE -- INTEMPERANCE

A MORAL AND PHYSICAL THERMOMETER.

A scale of the progress of Temperance and Intemperance.—Liquors with effects in their usual order.

TEMPERANCE.

70 — Water,	Health and Wealth.
60 — Milk and Water,	
50 — Small Beer,	} Serenity of Mind, Reputation, Long Life, & Happiness.
40 — Cider and Perry,	
30 — Wine,	
20 — Porter,	} Cheerfulness, Strength, and Nourishment, when taken only in small quantities, and at meals.
10 — Strong Beer,	
0 —	

INTEMPERANCE.

	VICES.	DISEASES.	PUNISH-MENTS.
0			
10 — Punch,	Idleness, Gaming,	Sickness,	Debt.
20 — Toddy and Egg Rum,	peevishness,	Tremors of the hands in the morning, puking,	Jail.
30 — Grog—Brandy and Water,	quarrelling Fighting,	bloatedness, Inflamed eyes, red nose	Black eyes, and Rags,
40 — Flip and Shrub,	Horse-Racing,	and face, Sore and swelled legs,	Hospital or Poor house.
50 — Bitters infused in Spirits and Cordials.	Lying and Swearing,	jaundice, Pains in the hands, burn-	Bridewell.
60 — Drams of Gin, Brandy, and Rum, in the morning,	Stealing & Swindling,	ing in the hands, and feet Dropsy, Epilepsy,	State prison
70 — The same morning and during day & night,	Perjury, Burglary, Murder,	Melancholy, palsy, appe- plexy, Madness, Despair,	do. for Life. Gallows.

The "Moral and Physical Thermometer" of temperance and intemperance. Rush did not insist that particular levels of drinking corresponded precisely to the matching vices and medical and legal complications. Nevertheless, he did try to convey, in a way that a popular readership could understand, the progressive nature of alcohol addiction and its personal and social implications. In this regard, Rush's views come strikingly close to modern conceptions of alcoholism.

SKELETON IN THE CLOSET:
LEGRAND MARVIN

Anyone named LeGrand might be expected to be an unusual person. LeGrand Marvin was such a person. He lived his name to the fullest. When his parents named him, they must have been conceitfully aware of his potential, or they named him as an act of wishful thinking. Perhaps they liked the sound of the name. Whatever the reason, LeGrand Marvin certainly turned out to be different. Buffalonians of his day claimed that he held "the distinction of being the queerest character who ever lived in Buffalo." Since this city, with its floating population, had its fair share of such people, this was no small tribute.

He was born November 9, 1807, in Clinton Valley, New York. After graduation from Hamilton College, he taught school in Maryland for a few years and then came west to Buffalo where he studied law under Philander Bennett. He successfully invested his law earnings in Buffalo real estate. In 1838, after financing his brother George's college and professional education, he opened a partnership with him which lasted from 1838 to 1864. This venture brought them both wealth and reputation. In 1864, however, the brothers had a serious disagreement over the disposition of property originally belonging to their mother. The property was in the waterfront district and, therefore, was among the most valuable property in Buffalo. The litigation which resulted dragged through the courts for 25 years, ending only in the death of LeGrand. Little satisfaction seems to have been gained from the dispute. Law fees drained away most of LeGrand's fortune. In his later years, he almost became a public charge. Like his law firm, his marriage also dissolved. He had married Julia Reynolds, of Syracuse, in 1854 and they separated seven years later.

The mere recital of these facts in no way reveals the interesting and eccentric personality of LeGrand Marvin. In stature, he was tall and angular and moved with a slow but determined gait. His dress caused people to stop and gape whenever he walked down the street. During the winter, he wore an old fashioned cap with dangling flaps which covered his brown wig. He adorned his face with spectacles customarily worn on his forehead while out walking. Circular whiskers covered his chin and cheeks. In summer, he wore a brown-glazed Panama hat attached to his alpaca coat by a string. His trousers were linen and he always carried a palm leaf fan in his hand.

It took him a long time each year after the coming of summer before he made the change-over from winter to summer apparel. In fact, it was always well into summer before he abandoned his winter cap and artics. Law students watched for this change as a harbinger of warm weather. The usual saying after LeGrand had finally made the change was "Now we can count on warmer weather." No one who ever saw LeGrand Marvin ever forgot him. No one ever knew him to tell a joke or crack a smile. He seemed to have little wit and less humor. A drooping eyelid caused by an attack of apoplexy gave his face a forbidding look.

LeGrand Marvin distrusted all forms of organization. He condemned all churches, political parties and professions. Women he found "full of guile." Men "were wicked conspirators against his property and peace of mind." Being an independent thinker himself, he held that "every person should investigate for himself to learn the truth." In religion, he was a deist; in politics, a Republican, although he deviated to vote for his fellow townsman, Grover Cleveland.

In philosophy, he seems to have been a pragmatist. His belief in utilitarian principle during his life helped him to cheat the grave on his death -- at least for a little while. He willed his body to the Buffalo Medical College, stipulating that his skeleton be handsomely mounted for use by the medical students. The skeleton saw many years of use until it was finally relegated to a closet. There were probably some in Buffalo who believed that Marvin gave his skeleton to the college specifically to haunt his enemies, of which he had many.

In writing, he developed a style that almost defied reading or understanding. In his younger days, however, he wrote with clarity. His feeling against drinking which caused him to write "Benefits of Rum" apparently was aroused when he learned, shortly after coming to Buffalo, that the local habitues purchased annually from retail stores 6,000 gallons. This figure, of course, did not include the thousands of gallons of liquor purchased from wagons which peddled whiskey and rum on the streets.

If he left his skeleton behind to haunt his enemies, as some seem to think, perhaps he left behind this paper on the "Benefits of Rum" to haunt the drinkers of Buffalo. Whatever his purpose, his paper is amusing to us because his satire is so heavy and extreme that it lends itself easily to burlesque.

BENEFITS OF RUM
by LeGrand Marvin

We are free. It is our boast that ours is a land of freedom.
We sit and sleep under our own roofs and apple trees, without fear
of molestation. We can eat when we are not hungry; drink when we
are not thirsty. If we have wit and good philanthropy mixed well in
our souls, we can break and wear other people's clothes, ride in our
creditors' carriages, and live upon another man's money. We have
the superlative right of raising a president from an honest man to
newspaper garbage; we can better his messages by throwing away
his sense; can suspect his honesty and begrudge him his pence; we
can slander his wife, mistrust his mates, keep away his foes and
drive away his friends. We can revile congressmen, run down
senators --despise assemblymen -- speak lightly of squires --
criticize priests -- and make all men waddle like geese. However a
man may be -- we have the liberty of saying of his character "Well, I
don't know."

It is not our intention to illustrate, at the present time, the
importance of each one of the inestimable rights; which, by the bye,
our much honoured red forefathers, unaccountably neglected to
incorporate into our ever memorable "Bill of Rights." We shall
attempt only to show a few and the shortness of our time forbids our
showing but a very few of the drinking benefits when we are not
dry or, as it is vulgarly called, the Benefits of Rum.

Perhaps the speaker may incur the displeasure of some of the
honorable friends of temperance, who are raising such a hue and cry
throughout the land. And for what? Why, forsooth lest some of
their own party should desert them and go over to the opposite side.
It always appeared to me that the party attacked should give the
alarm; -- but here the boards are turned and they are going about --
just like the silversmiths of Ephesus went about, stirring up the
people and shouting, "Great is Diana of the Ephesians. Great is
Diana of the Ephesians."

Now, in the first place, we ought to determine whether we
have a right to Rum; -- lest we fall out, by the way, -- and preclude
the possibility of a good understanding thereafter. In addition to the
certainly very strong evidence of right already mentioned on the
score of freedom; -- Hume says that "Custom is the constitution,"
and therefore it's "law" and that "custom confers a right." For
instance, in some of the East India islands, there is a custom of
sending people, when they become a little too old to perform their
task -- upon a tree. The children and relations then gather under the
tree and begin the song of:

The seed did sprout
The tree did grow
The fruit did ripen
and down it fell.

Then the old victim is tumbled down and devoured by his own devout kinsmen; therefore this custom, according to Hume, confers a right to eat one's parents. Again, among the Aborigines of this country, it was customary to roast and eat their enemies, when taken. Hence upon the same principle -- to roast and eat human beings is right. Now, since it appears, according to Hume, that custom is law and confers a right; we shall only refer you to your everyday observation and experience for the criterion of the right to drink Rum.

Wherefore, since the most skeptical need not doubt respecting the right to drink, let us consider for a moment, what we pay for it, and be, thereby, quickened to greater diligence to improve that right. The quantity of distilled liquors consumed in our towns (is) from 4 to 10 thousand gallons, annually. In this village, however, according to the estimate of gentlemen, as well able to judge as any other, who, without knowing to what purpose it was going to be applied, there are retailed 6,600 gallons every year. We must recollect that this 6,600 gallons is the retailed quantity and does not include the liquor purchased from wagons by consumers which is perhaps much more. However we will put down but 6,600 gallons at the low price of half a dollar a gallon (look at the dram and retail prices at the taverns and stores) amount to $3,000; a sum not only greater than all of the taxes of the village -- but also more than three times greater than the taxes even of the district; a sum greater than you pay for all of privileges; civil, religious, and literary; for your state, your priests and your schools. In less than 100 years you would drink up your town; and should you get trusted for fifty years and allow simple interest upon the debt, the sale of the whole town at the end of that term, could not pay your Rum bills; you would drink the value of all the landed and personal property, which has been acquired by wearing out your own body as well as those of your family. And what a sublime thought it must be to drink down, not only hod farms and swallow houses; but to gullup down one's arms and body, in comparison with which Jonah's whale is but a small fish.

Besides, in the United States there are computed to be not less than 60 mils. gallons of distilled spirits drunk annually. The 60 mils. gallons --at $ 1/2 a gallon, amounts to $30,000,000.

But you will please to recollect we have taken but the price of the bare liquor. "The cost of the liquor is but a small part of the cost of intemperance." "Time," says Dr. Franklin "is money," and who can doubt that the time spent by the intemperate over their cups, and in recovering from the "glory" of intoxication, is worth many

162

times more than the petty trifle they pay for the dram. When it is remembered that whiskey enough to prostrate an ordinary drunkard for six hours can be purchased for six cents, will it be thought extravagant, if we estimate the time killed by the 60,000,000 gallons of spirits consumed in the U.S. at as many millions of dollars? But we will suppose but the one half of this to be consumed by drunkards, and that one pint of spirit destroys only six hours of the drunkard's time; the value of time destroyed, reckoning it at only four cents an hour, would be $57,600,000. This added to the $30,000,000, the cost of liquor permits us to charge Master Rum for cash and time $87,600,000.

But this is not all. In the U.S. the estimated number of paupers is 2,000,000; their cost to the public $10,000,000 every year. Now from official document of the number and expenses of the paupers in the cities of Baltimore and Philadelphia and in the states of New York and Massachusetts, we learn that a full three-fourths were made paupers by ardent spirits. According to this, we may put down 3/4 of the $10,000,000 -- the cost of the paupers in the U.S. -- which $7,500,000 to the aforementioned cost of the liquor and value of the time described; and we have the pretty little sum about 4 times the whole expenses of the general government; more than three times the receipts of the U.S.; more than sufficient to excavate annually, one dozen canals as long as the great Erie Canal through the capital state of New York; enough to make railroads from Baltimore to the Ohio, every year; and would supply every family on the earth for eighteen months; and would make a silver wire to reach around the earth.

Come lovers of good cheer, rally around the "jolly club," spend not your pence in trifling; assemble round some table; sit it out; and turn to your course; and face the frowning world. Oh, you have friends a plenty yet; you will never want for Good Cheer: Look yonder, see that merchant, 'Ah,' He sighs, 'what a lamentable thing this drunkenness!' Friend of the Jolly Club, never mind what he says; you will just recollect, it is one thing to preach, and another to practice; as long as you have money enough, you will get enough to drink even were it arsenic water.

So down the seller will pour it;
Though it grieve him sore
For, loss of pence full well he knows,
will grieve him much more.

Do you see that squire there, with a Sheriff and a constable at his elbow? Don't be frightened; for the clerk of the New York City court says that three-fourths of all the cases brought before this court originated in drunken sprees, or were caused by a man's being a drunkard; don't mind if Squire does frown, now and then; You don't suppose he would chuck his bread out of his hungry jaws?

163

No, nor will he chuck the good cheer out of your mouth. What, they wish you to quit sipping? No such thing; but the contrary: let us reason upon it: In the first place, squire and sheriffs and constables; yes, and lawyers and judges, jailors, prison keepers and prison builders should destroy drunkenness, three-fourths of their own profession would be turned out, with their families, upon the world.

Mad-house physicians, too, and mad-house keepers and mad-house builders want business. Well from those confined in the insane hospitals in the cities of New York and Philadelphia, it is ascertained that one-third were rendered insane by the use of ardent spirits. Hence should drunkenness be stopped; one-third of all the mad-house visitants and mad- house physicians and servants, and builders of mad-houses, with their families, would be forced out into the griping world. Furthermore, from what we have said before, we learn that should the Rum be stopped, three-fourths of all of the overseers of the poor, and poor-house physicians, and builders and servants and keepers of poor-houses with their families would be thrown out upon the merciless world. And then see the coopers, employed in making barrels to keep the good liquor in; thousands of them would be thrown out of employment, and their poor families. Then the thousands of grog-shop owners and grog-shop tenders and barkeepers and distillers and waggoners and pump makers and a world more would be thrown out of business and their families after them, and they would all be forced to become honest farmers, or to engage in some other injurious occupations, such as pedagogues, and preceptors or industrious mechanics. Why, what misery there would be in the world? And then, if the drinking should suddenly be stopped, what would become of the immense capital in our distilleries and stores and villages and cities and counties and states invested in distilled liquors? Why, the man would be found weeping for his money, and behold it was -- Rum. Oh, it must be poured down the throat of men to save it; just as after dinner, the frugal mother would stuff the full fed boy with the fragments, lest the swine should hurt by having too much. And, 'sure, there can be no harm in all this, says one "for if the jolly fellow does not buy of me, he will buy of some other one." So, if you think a neighbor is going to kill a certain man soon, do you lay to and kill him first? For sure, at farthest, someone will kill him and a few moments just before death you know is of no consequence.

Then what a host of dinner speeches would be lost, and newspaper devourers would be greatly puzzled to find what to do with their time. We all know what a fine thing a little good cheer is to enliven dull minds and fill empty heads at social tables and public dinners and to spin, as it were by magic a half dozen column speech and thus how it clears up the misty ideas in the peericraniums of the candidates and members of our legislatures and of our congressmen, not forgetting traveling secretaries and other cabinet officers.

Well, lovers of good cheer, I hope you are convinced of the right to drink; of the importance of being duly active to get the worth of your money and time; and of the vast misery that would be produced by forcing people to honest businesses. Now, let us mark the comfort of drinking, when one is not dry. How complaisant, a lover of good cheer is, when he is just so far that he cannot tell whether the moon has three or five "horns." He is then just capable of being initiated into the jolly club, ready for a song, or a jest, or a repartee; a pattern for delicate and particular taste, or bachelor whims, a table, or a bench or a floor, answers for a bed, or some kindly corner of a serpent fence offers a fine place to turn in his weary bones for the night. Unlike the raised couch, he can roll and tumble without breaking his bones, by too sudden an embrace with the floor. He is not forced to breathe the confined air of a narrow chamber, but he can shove upon the fresh pure dew of the night, with the wide earth for his bed, and the starless heavens for his bed curtains. What a splendid place to contemplate the slowly turning lights of the sky; the polar star, the sailors' guide, just about to be hid by a beautiful black cloud, Anon, the candles of heaven being put out; the darkness invites to repose. Now the water pours into the thirsty mouth, and all of this, without the least trouble or interruption, except mayhaps a gentle jog from the hoof of some neighborly cow or the hooting of some snorting brother. And, then, the next morning, how free and nimble he is? Why he feels like dancing a reel with a lively barn-door post for a partner. Just now, watch him, entering his own house; how prettily, his loving wife comes forward to salute him; presents her cheek or tongue or club but we can go no further toward the affectionate scene. Then, his children, how familiar they are; how prettily they hang around his knee; and his fences, cattle can but just get over them, and his crops, his swine have saved him the trouble of gathering.

Lover of good cheer, I have come to thee. Stand forward. Let us draw thy picture: a pale visage, thou oughtst to plaster a little French rouge (red paint) upon thy cheeks; thy eyes, how white; thy step how firm; thy tread how majestic. Perhaps the ladies, ever benevolently disposed, would lend a little assistance to our Jolly Club. It gives such a modest blushing look: cheeks, dyed with a mixture of the lily and the rose; clear, soft, loving eyes; a breath like the gales of Persia wafted over the spicy garden of Arabia.

Besides there are other blessings to be derived from Rum, some of which the celebrated Dr. Rush left us; such as loss of appetite and sickness at the stomach and obstructions of the liver and jaundice, and red irruptions upon the face and other parts of the body and fetig, and rhumatism, and chills and agues, and palsy and apoplexy and paralitic affections and many other pretty things, too numerous to mention. Furthermore, they have left us many signs of lovers of good cheer, who, from their badges, may be at once known as a member of the Jolly Club. For instance, tattered clothes and ragged garments hanging upon the body, paper lights, and broken windows in a house, and sashes stuffed with rags are as plain badges of membership as the American flag upon the mast is evidence of a vessel's being American. And, then, how mercifully blessed is the man who drinks a little, in never being obliged to lug about with him any money, that root of all evil, and do you see a man always complaining of hard times and never ready to pay his bills. You need not ask whether that man sips, for he has told you one of the watch words of our Jolly Club and has saved you the trouble of inquiries. Now, how happy a man, half sea's o'er is; how happy, no jargons, no contention, no broils, no uninterrupted scene of jocularity, every soul thinks he is far on the way to heaven, just entering the gates of happiness. Friend, did you ever visit the election polls or the race ground; what lovers of good cheer and harmony and affectionate embraces are there. 'Tis true, there are sometimes some knocks, followed by red rivers; but those are nothing but the taps of love and streams of affection.

> Come, come away, ho,
> To the bar-room go,
> Play a little at high-lo
> Take a drink at every throw
> For sure to heaven you will go.
> Come ho, Jolly foe.
> Why delay you to go?

But stop, friend, a moment, you will recollect before you get in, that some particular propensities are requisite, before a person can be constituted a member of the Jolly Club, for instance, never to refuse the passing bowl, and at the meeting, to take the Ace of Spades, if he can.

Now, some may have some qualms of conscience respecting entering upon such proceedings at once, and would, perhaps, like a little advice on the subject before they should be initiated.

Have you ever tasted of the inspiring liquor? Do you say no? Well, then you sometimes visit? When you enter a neighbor's house, be careful not to neglect out of compliment to your host; to carry the glass to your mouth and wet your lips and tongue. Do you meet an old acquaintance? Don't forget to take him to a bar and cement the friendship with a couple of toddies; bind it as strong as liquor is and make it as lasting as the fumes of whiskey are. When you go to a tavern to have a horse fed, recollect to call for a glass to please the landlord. When you travel, get but two meals in the day and drink the value of the third to please the hosts; be careful not to feed your horse with too many oats, but take yourself, their value, in the milk of rye.

But have you ever taken a sip? Frequent public meetings and attending barroom assemblies; cock your hat upon your head, prime your whistle, with a segar; 'Sir, a bottle of your best? Turn around to your Jolly companions and vow I can stand so much, a little more pour in, that's just the gage' -- then down it goes. Follow these prescriptions for a short time and my word for it, you will soon be capable of becoming an efficient member of the Jolly Club.

Many persons are very much afraid that they will be buried alive. Do you fear such a thing? Take some grog and you will have a sure remedy. Attend a moment, I will tell you a story that will allay your fears, if you have any, upon this head. "It is the case" of a woman, eighty years of age, exceedingly meager, who had drunk nothing but ardent spirits for several years. She was sitting in her elbow-chair, while her waiting-maid went out of the room for a few moments. On her return, seeing her mistress on fire, she immediately gave an alarm and some people coming to her assistance, one of them endeavored to extinguish the flames with his hand, but the flames adhered to his hands as if they had been dipped in brandy and oil on fire. Water was brought and thrown on the body in abundance, yet the fire appeared the more violent and was not extinguished until the body was consumed. The lady was in the same place she was accustomed to sit every day, there was no extraordinary fire, nor had she fallen from her chair. "This with nine other cases related and proved by Trotter, was a consumption of the body produced by the use of ardent spirits." Besides these I could mention scores of instances where, not only drunkards, but even moderate drinkers breath has caught fire from coming in contact with a candle. One, in particular, the body burst and not a piece an inch square could be found. But enough has been said to convince the most timorous that he need not be buried alive, if he only proceeds systematically, or if he will but just follow his natural inclination after having been initiated into the Jolly Club.

If your conscience condemns you for taking a sip, here is a palliative: as soon as you begin to hesitate, look about you; you will find plenty of professors of religion who take hearty sips. Mayhaps, too, you may find some priests that do the same and are not ashamed of it either and these are good men, you know. For nowadays there are no wolves in sheep's clothing as there were in Christ's time. If, however, your conscience is not quite quieted, search out a certain doctor, or doctors, should your conscience require more than one. Recollect beforehand and be wary to get the right one! Let him feel of your pulse. He understands your system and a hundred to one, if he does not humour your constitution so that your qualms of conscience shall be entirely drowned. He will confute to your great edification that notion of the great Dr. Rush's, that ardent spirits can be administered without injury in but two cases. And those two, cases of persons likely to perish and yet their substitutes may be applied with equal effect. We will prove it to be nothing but a whim, a fantasy of the old Doctors and would verily

167

make you believe you have the honor of addressing a greater than a Rush or a Zimmerman or a Polycarp or a Galen or a Herbus or an Aesculapius and that Hippocrates was a school boy to himself. He will flatly deny the assertion of Dr. Bell of the hot West Indies who declares that Rum, whether used habitually or moderately, increases, instead of lessens, the effects of heat upon the body and renders it more susceptible to disease. Your doctor would spit in the face of the Captain of the vessel wrecked on an intensely cold night a few years since off the port of Newbury Port in Massachusetts, who affirms that he entreated his crew not to taste of ardent spirits. Many of them nevertheless did. The result was that, of those who used the spirits, some lost their heads, some their feet and some perished, while the rest survived unhurt. Now, your doctor will convince you, at least, attempt to do so, which, you know, will be the same -- that liquor has rare qualities. For example, in winter it will make your body warm; in the summer, make you cook; and in the temperate weather, it will make you better.

Now, lover of good cheer for I suspect thou art here, if your rumifications have not been spoken, I pray you next time to send them in your letter and they will not be unreasonably neglected by a friend to all good undertaking.

DRINKING AND THINKING

If a man would be dry, let him drink, drink, drink. . . . My hearers -- to keep constantly dry, always wear an oilcloth dress, carry a good umbrella and practice rum drinking. The first two articles are only essential in protecting rum drinking. The first two articles are only essential in protecting the outside from super abundant moisture, but the latter keeps the inside as dry as a stove pipe. I never saw a drinker but was eternally dry -- dry in all kinds of weather. He goes to bed dry, gets up dry, and keeps himself dry through the day. It's not to be wondered at; for how can he be otherwise than dry, when he keeps the blue blazes of hell constantly burning in his bosom, by pouring double distilled damnation down his throat. In fact, my friends, the drunkard is forever dry. The more he drinks, the dryer he grows; on his deathbed he cries for "one more drink for the last" and then goes out of the world as thirsty as tho' he lived on codfish all the days of his life. I should not wonder much if he called for a cocktail at the bar of judgment; and there is no doubt but what he would prefer going to Tophet to abiding in Heaven, -- if they only sold liquor there. . . .

"CONVENTION OF DRUNKARDS"

Yes, go I will to find a home,
Where drunkards, live, and swim in rum.

My brother sot, who planned the race,
Said, Western New York is the place.
O, happy people, happy land!
They keep a world of stuff on hand!
Poor drunkards have some freedom there;
Can sprawl in mud, and howl in air!
What I here state I do not know,
But my dear friends informed me so.

Yes, Uncle Sam, Aunt Peg and Sal,
Took passage on the great canal
To go out west; they fixed a plan
To see the glorious Michigan.
So on they went, they seemed to know,
As far as wondrous Buffalo.
Thence they returned through day and night,
And had a fest of sweet delight.
With many smiles they told around
What pleasures in the west abound.

169

Said, Western New York crowns the nation,
It is sublime; a grand location
For sots, and jilts, and men of leisure;
There all can have their fill of pleasure.
Things so handy, and so nice,
It seemed to them a paradise;
No trouble found in all the way
With any thing like sabbath day;
All days were filled with toil and care --
Sal guessed they had no sabbath there!
The boats were passing every hour,
Pressed down with whiskey, rum or flour,
By horses drawn that could not tell
Which way fools went to go to hell.

Throughout the state it seemed a fair;
All life, all spirit everywhere.
Enchanting scenes, hoped to bewitch,
Adorned the banks of the great ditch.
There splendid stores, and public halls,
And public cells, and public stalls,
Stood open to their ratputred view,
By night and day -- and Sundays too!
Yes, boys they saw learning to swear,
And drunkards drinking freely there.
Proud liberty controlled the day,
Without a bar to obstruct its sway.

Lo, there they saw the drunkards' cause
Sustained and sanctioned by the laws.
What! temperance men -- they heard of some,
But guessed that they had gone from home!
Or lost their skill to speak and think,
By using too much tasteless drink.
Sam thought they went on reason's plan,
And let alone the rights of man.
They all seemed free -- as free as air
To gamble, fight, and drink, and swear;
And showed their reason, skill and might,
In a tremendous point of light.

170

So, Uncle Sam came home, you see,
Quite charmed with western liberty.
His face was red, his nerves were strung,
And freely went his licensed tongue.
The whiskey stalls inflamed his eyes,
And made delightful visions rise;
His stomach felt the happy steam --
And that, in fact, was all his theme.

Now, wretched sots, let us prepare
To leave our homes, and settle there;
Friends we shall find, and freedom too,
And as we please, so we can do.
If I don't err in what I say,
The motion is, to run away --
If we strive on we shall all fail,
And take our lodgings in some jail;
Or be compelled to curse our cause,
And argue for the temperance laws.
To shun the evils, great and small,
Is to depart and leave them all.
Then temperance men will feel their sin,
And know what useful men we've been.

PENN YAN

In 1822, a Penn Yan jury decided that a man was not a
"habitual drunkard" unless he was drunk more than half the time.

171

SMELLING OF THE BAR RAG

Instead of saying a man is a habitual drinker, you say that he has "fourteen drops every fifteen minutes." If his conduct is indecorous, you observe that he has been "smelling of the bar-cloth," though this phrase is sometimes used by practiced drinkers in scorn for the inexperienced.

"TEMPERANCE RHYME"

Mental suasion for the man who thinks,
Moral suasion for the man who drinks,
Legal suasion for the drunkard-maker,
Prison suasion for the statute-breaker.

HOW THE TEETOTALERS GOT THEIR NAME

During the second quarter of the 19th century, a variety of religious and social reforms swept Upstate New York creating what history has called the "Burnt over Region." The people were consumed by emotional fire, not unlike the burning of the growing fields after harvest to refertilize the land.

Hector, a village on the Southeast shore of Seneca Lake which is a part of the Erie Canal system, became caught up in the anti-alcohol movement sweeping the area. A temperance society was formed there in 1818. The founders aimed at total abstinence as the cure for the evils of drink; but, they omitted wine and beer from the pledge lest they defeat their purpose.

In the 1820's other New York State societies incorporated the ideal of total abstinence in their constitutions. In 1826 the Hector society voted to offer its members the choice of two pledges, one for abstinence from distilled spirits and the other for total abstinence. In recording the choices, the secretary placed a "T" before the names of those who had signed the total pledge and they were called "T-Totalers" Teetotalism spelled the temporary decline of the local temperance organizations; many which would have subscribed to abstinence from hard liquor but would not relinquish a glass of wine or a scuttle of suds. But Hector remained a desert for many years.

TEETOTALERS' OATH
(The Massachusetts Ministers' Oath)

"Recognizing the evils of drunkenness and resolved to check its alarming increase, we do solemnly pledge ourselves not to get drunk except on Christmas, at Sheepshearing, Independence Day and Muster Day."

"Nobody could get from waterfront to the Capitol without a score of accosts from these well-meaning zealots," Grandfather told us.

A stock argument for sobriety was that only two out of the total four thousand temperance members had died of the cholera.

"Probably a lie," said Grandfather who, though an ardent abstentionist himself, was a stickler for facts.

Gradually the comforting faith that the respectable elements of society were immune -- the credo so industriously promulgated by the authorities -- weakened. Early in August that influential national periodical, The Niles Weekly Register, a powerful prop of the thesis, acknowledged with obvious dismay, " several worthy and prudent persons have lately died at Albany of the Cholera."

In the minds of the best medical authorities, the plague had clearly surmounted the barriers of class and character and was striking right and left. Three emergency pest-houses, hastily put into commission, filled and overflowed. People fell, writhing, on the streets. Houses were found with forgotten dead in them. Coaches arrived empty and departed full. Theaters and museums closed. Stores boarded their windows. Food became scarce; potatoes went to a dollar a bushel. Camphor, which was highly regarded though a wholly inert medicament, rose from thirty cents to five dollars a pound, with calomel and brandy following suit. Physicians, who were normally satisfied to get four shillings for a night call or a dollar for reducing a fracture, demanded and received six dollars a day for serving the city. Burials rose from fifty cents to two dollars per cadaver. Half the homes in town were in mourning.

Though disturbed by the news from their capital, the York Staters were too sturdy a breed to be stampeded into panic. But they did take a more serious view of the threat than at first. Pious folk attributed the visitation to the vengeance of Heaven upon the sins of the people. The remnant of the old Federalist aristocracy ascribed it to President Andy Jackson and his "blasphemous Democracy." The Sober Societies blamed it upon the national habit of tippling. "Flagitious youth," said the purist. "Freemasonry," cried the militant anti-Masons. Some cleric with a knack of the dramatic catchword preached a sermon on "The Monster of Epidemy," and the phrase was taken over as a text in a score of pulpits. These "cholera sermons" were complained of by Rochester's Liberal Advocate as being a potent auxiliary of the disease. Because of

173

them "consternation seized the inhabitants and thousands fled,"
recorded the editor under his nom-de-plume of Obadiah Dogbery.

TEMPERANCE TO DRY

On the basis of the preceeding story, teetotalers carried their
point. At a subsequent national temperance convention in Saratoga,
New York in 1836, the delegates formally endorsed total abstinence
as the movement's interpretation of temperance. There was still
some resistance among the rank and file, but by the end of the
decade the issue was virtually closed. Temperance reform had, for
the first time, gone fully "dry."

"TO A POOR OLD BUM"

I'm going, I'm going, for I know my time has come!
And to the workhouse I must go, a poor old bum.
As a free-lunch destroyer, I'm the terror of the route
I can wrastle with the sausage or a plate of sauerkraut.
And when I get a plate of beans, oh, don't I make them
hum!
They're such a solid comfort to a poor old bum.

LOAFER JIM

The worthy mentioned above has, for time immemorial,
been a drinking philosopher. Dynasties have changed, new
constitutions have been adopted, magistrates have risen to eminence
and passed away, the ordinances have been revised -- but here is
Jim unchanged, uncontaminated by the march of improvement -- a
living landmark of the loaferism of the seventeenth century. What
some sensitive minds of this degenerate age would shrink from, Jim
glories in. Men now pride themselves in keeping sober; Jim is the
very opposite in his lofty aspiration -- he delights in getting drunk.
Temperance societies he considers a modern innovation of most
pernicious tendency, because they bring things down to a sober
reality, destroy the delight of imagination and loaferism, and have a
tendency, to make man a working animal. "Man was made to
drink," reasons Jim. "He is one of the fluid imbibing species, and
commencing with baby's milk, he gradually rises to the elevation of
corn juice -- as his powers increase his desire for steam, and then

174

the holy danger to be apprehended is that he should get too great a hand on."

"Why don't you quit drinking, Jim?" inquired a member of the moral reform society, who was lecturing him the other morning through the bars of the calaboose. Why don't you quit and become a useful member of society?"

"Cause it's agin' natur'" answers Jim. "Natur' created me a ornamental animal, a philosopher of fluidity, a teacher in her hydraulic high school, and I'm in the top class, up head; all the other fellars have gone down tail because they didn't know how to drink. They wasn't philosophers, old fellar -- they drinked their liquor all in a heap, and got through quick; now I take mine moderate, and when it's strong and hard to carry, I doesn't like the green ones, struggle along and wear my precious self out, but I lays down along side of it and waits till it gets easier. That's the way to last. Liquor, in the particular view, is a preservative. 'Cause why? Don't they put peaches in liquor when they want to keep 'em? Don't they preserve every juicy vegetable with liquor, and ain't I a juicy vegetable of the male sex? In course I am, and Liquor's good for me. Now these fellers that mixes up their liquor ain't educated. I never mix -- I begin corn and I sticks to corn; there's a beautiful consistency about havin' a drink and stick to it; it betrays the difference between your philosopher of age and experience and your feller what don't know a treat when he get it for nothing."

"But you get locked up here for indulging and such philosophy," remarked his adviser.

"That ain't nuthin'," says Jim. "I'm used to it -- it's a part of my teachin'. A fellar as doesn't know how to loaf, meanly hides hisself in some place so the official fellars can't git him. I doesn't do so. I scorns to be so mean, 'cause it's cheatin' a fellar what watches at night out of his livin', and that isn't a becomin' act for a white man to do. I lays down on pavement and has myself took up reg'lar and respectable -- they then fines me accordin' to law, and of course I doesn't pay it. I carries my system out to the work house, and wins my way back again to liberty be breakin' rock. That's the way I do it, old sobers! Let every fellar foller his own business, loafin' is mine, and I likes it."

Thus, reasoned Jim with the reformer, and when his name was called he acknowledged the "corn," and went out a reg'lar.

DEACON WORMWOOD AND THE DRUNK

Among the retired lake captains who resided in Buffalo some few may recall Wormwood, commonly known as Deacon Wormwood, who became a pillar of the Methodist Church on Niagara Street, where the Masonic Temple now stands. The Deacon was a Christian of the stern unbending type and in his store, near the wharf, where he sold sailors' outfits, he often had occasion to vindicate his religious principles. His customers, when sober, respected his scruples, but one day a drunken fellow became abusive and blasphemed horribly. Deacon Wormwood, marching up to the offender with fire in his eye, cried, "Drop that, you rascal; another word and I'll backslide for five minutes and give you the damndest hiding you ever had in your life."

DESCRIPTION OF WHISKEY

A Congressman was once asked by a constituent to explain his attitude toward whiskey:

"If you mean the demon drink that poisons the mind, pollutes the body, desecrates family life and inflames sinners, then I'm against it," the Congressman said. "But if you mean the elixir of Christmas cheer, the shield against winter chill, the taxable potion that puts needed funds into public coffers to comfort little crippled children, then I'm for it. This is my position, and I will not compromise."

"THE ER-I-E"

This is one of the few canal songs that is presently well known. Its popularity is probably due to its simplicity.

We were forty-nine miles from Albany
Forget it I never shall.
What a terrible storm we had that night
On the Erie Canal.

Oh! the Erie was a rising,
And the gin was a getting low.
And I scarcely think we'll get a drink
'til we get to Buffalo-o-o,
'til we get to Buffalo.

We were loaded down with barley,
We were chocked up full of rye,
And the Captain he looked down at me,
With his Gol-durned wicked eye.

Our cook she was a grand ol' gal,
She wore a ragged dress,
We hoisted her upon the mast,
As a signal of distress.

Lay me on the horse-bridge,
With my feet up toward the bow,
And let it be a Lockport Laker,
Or a Tonawanda scow.

Our Nell has got the blind staggers,
And Maude has got the heaves,
Black Tom has thrown his off-shoe,
And our driver's got the weaves.

Two days out from Syracuse,
The vessel struck a shoal,
And we like to all been foundered,
On a chunk of Lackawanna coal.

I hollered to the driver,
On the towpath treadin' dirt,
He jumped aboard and stopped the leak,
With his old red flannel shirt.

As we got into Buffalo,
It was but four o'clock,
The very first man we chanced to meet,
Was Gilson on the dock.

Well, our Captain he got married,
And our cook, she went to jail,
Now I'm the only son-of-a-sea-cook,
That's left to tell the tale.

TAVERN TIPPLING

A canaller who stopped by the McClare Hotel in Rexford bet the barkeeper a dollar he could down a gallon of hard cider without taking more than three breaths. When the barkeeper took him up on it, the canaller excused himself for several minutes, then returned, gave the jug a full tilt and emptied the contents. The bug-eyed bartender handed over a dollar, shaking his head that he had not thought it could be done. "T' tell the truth, neither did I," said the Erie canaller, wiping his sleeve across his mouth, "'til I ran down to the neighbor tavern to find out!"

TAVERN IN A TREE TRUNK

Travel across York State after the American Revolution was by foot, horseback, wagon or stage coach. Taverns along the tiring way provided lodging, food and drink (especially drink) about every ten miles or so. Such accommodations were often not much more than enlarged family homes and were operated by mom and pop.

When the canal opened, traffic moved north from the Western Turnpike, now Routes 5 and 20, and a new string of taverns stretched along Clinton's Ditch at locks, aqueducts, villages or whatever caused traffic to pause or stop for a spell. Actually, the hoggies who drove the mules didn't even have to stop if they were thirsty, and they were always thirsty, from towpath dust or habit. These mule skinners would drop the lines, dash into a towpath tavern, down a shot of liquor, pay up, then run out and pick up the lines while the mules continued to walk without benefit of the hoggies. Most taverns were of the ordinary canal variety, principally a room, a bar and tables.

The most curious tavern connected with the Erie Canal was the famous Tavern in a Tree Trunk. As the canal was dug west from Rome in 1817, there stretched out through western New York a wilderness of giant trees. These ancient trees, estimated by some to be 500 years old, had been revered by the native Americans.

Hezekia Niles, editor and publisher of the <u>Niles Register</u>, told of "a walnut tree in the wilderness of New York that had fallen to the ground during a storm...." This forest giant had stood 80 feet tall. Its lower branches were as large as mature trees, some three or four feet in diameter at the trunk. At its base, the tree was 12 feet in diameter, 36 feet in circumference. If chopped into firewood, there would have been 37 full cords; 50,000 board feet. Its bark covering measured 12 inches thick.

In 1822, a Lake Erie gale blew off the top of the tree about 12 feet above its trunk. Its owner cut off the top about 10 feet from the ground then excavated, with axes and chisels, the sound heartwood down to the ground level. A portion of the wall was cut out as a door. A window was cut out and a lead casement placed in the opening. The tree trunk was hollowed out and transformed by its owner into a barroom capable of serving up to 31 persons at a time.

After being furnished with a Brussels Medallion Carpet, portraits of Washington and Lafayette, splendid mirrors and suitable furniture, the owner announced his unusual "tavern in a trunk" to the world.

When business slacked off there, the tree tavern was hauled by ox team to Buffalo, serving for a time as a grocery store. When business slacked off there, it was shipped off to Rochester where it became a barroom again. It was then moved to New York City via the Erie Canal causing wonder and amazement to those who saw it. In 1827, it attracted 30,000 paying customers.

No one knows what finally happened to the Tavern in a Tree Trunk.

"LIQUOR AND LONGEVITY"

The horse and mule live 30 years
And nothing know of wines and beers.
The goat and sheep at 20 die
And never taste of Scotch or Rye.
The cow drinks water by the ton
And at 18 is mostly done.
The dog at 15 cashes in
Without the aid of rum and gin.
The cat in milk and water soaks
And then in 12 short years it croaks.
The modest, sober, bone-dry hen
Lays eggs for nogs, then dies at ten.
All animals are strictly dry:
They sinless lie and swiftly die;
But sinful, ginful rum-soaked men
Survive for three score years and ten.
And some of them, a very few,
Stay pickled till they're 92.

                                    Unknown

TALE OF THE PICKLED PORKERS

South of Lake Ontario, in the northwestern section of York State, the ghostly shoreline of a prehistoric lake forms a ridge on which red men, and later white, have worn paths and built roads. Quite naturally, it is called "The Ridge." When the waters receded from this old beach, they left behind fertile fields, rutted with a few creeks and blotched with some swamps. Across these fields, the water had spread its rich silt along with a mixture of small stones and rocks, some rough and sharp, others water-washed smooth and round. These latter became the building stones for the sturdy and decorative walls of central York State's famous "Cobblestone" houses which give so much character to the Ontario country.

The real life of this country, however, seems to have moved along The Ridge. In proper sequence, it has felt the soft step of the Iroquois, the beat of horses' hooves, the roll of stage and wagon wheels and now the speed of the motor car. Today, as the cool breeze from the present lake sweeps over the plain and across The Ridge, only in the inner ear of imagination, keen and finely attuned, can the ancient waves of the lost lake be felt and heard. To learn of man-made times, however, there is needed only an attentive eye and appreciative ear. Old-timers with good memories and better imaginations can still recall, for those who will listen, stories of The Ridge when the wagon wheels rolled over the road to the Niagara River.

Located as it is, midway between the Niagara escarpment on the south and Lake Ontario on the north, The Ridge became a land route to the West for the pioneers before the Erie Canal provided a waterway westward. For those along the highway, who from their windows have watched history go by their doors, The Ridge is also a road back to the past; its taverns the stopping-off places to tell its tales.

The pioneers built these tavern-inns at convenient stage-coach distances, most frequently at crossroad corners, west to the Niagara River. Some of these still stand. In fact, some are still lived in. One such is located at Warren's Corners; that is, the map calls it Warren's Corners and for good reason. Despite this almost official recognition, however, (and I suppose it is duly and officially registered and recorded elsewhere) some natives there-abouts think it ought to be called Forsyth Corners for what they consider even better reasons. But that is all part of the story.

At the back of this tavern the ground falls away sharply. In wet seasons the low land is swampy. About the center of the backyard area a huge four-trunked willow tree spreads its cover over much of the yard.

One afternoon I stood there drinking in the charm of the surroundings (that's about the only kind of drinking that tavern had seen since 1825, if the stories I had been hearing were true).

183

"Quite a tree, isn't it?" said a voice which startled me. I answered, "Yes," almost automatically as I turned my head quickly toward the direction of the voice.

"This your farm?" I asked the approaching figure. "You bet it is. My land on both sides of The Ridge."

"Well, it certainly looks like rich land to me, although I am really no expert in such matters," I said.

"It is rich," he readily agreed. "Rich for crops." Then, with a smile which crept slowly up his cheeks, he added, "rich for stories, too. I guess since I own the land, I rightfully own the stories, too. What do you think? At least, I ought to have the right to tell them. The fact is, stories are really no good unless you share them with someone else."

"I certainly agree with you on that," I said.

"Take that tree over there, the one you were looking at. Must be over 100 years old. Notice its four trunks. It's no ordinary tree," he insisted.

"No it certainly isn't. It's a real beauty, and huge too, " I said.

"I don't mean that exactly," he spoke seeming to feign impatience. "I mean it just ain't an ordinary tree."

"Well," I said, somewhat amused, "what is it if it isn't a rather good ordinary tree?"

"It is a buggy whip," he shot back at me. "At least, it was a buggy whip."

"A buggy whip?" I repeated in amazement.

"Yes," he explained, "an honest-to-goodness, overgrown buggy whip, come to life. As I get it from those who have passed on, this was one of the important stagecoach taverns in the old days. Often the drivers would come out in the back here to stretch their legs before they went into the tavern to bend their elbows. One driver apparently stuck his whip in the muddy ground and went in to have just one for the road. Apparently, he had more than one (road-dust being what it is) and when he left he forgot his whip. No one thought any more about it until a month or so later. Then one night, as the tavern owner threw out some food scraps and slop (as he was accustomed to do each night) he noticed it sticking in the ground. Something drew him over to the whip. As he approached he could hardly believe his eyes. The whip had apparently taken root. It was actually greening and growing. And that's how a buggy whip grew up to be that four-trunked willow over there.

"At least," said my friend with a chuckle, "that's the story they tell hereabouts."

"Quite a story for a tree," I said. "Certainly shows the fertility of the soil along The Ridge." I was about to add "and the fertility of imagination" when he interrupted my thought .

"Well, yes, in a way it does, but that's only part of the story. You see, it has never been clear to me from the story whether the buggy whip grew before or after God visited the tavern.

This stopped me cold for a moment and I must have stood there with my mouth slightly ajar.

"What do you mean," I stuttered, "before or after God visited the tavern?"

"Well, maybe," the farmer said, "I had better tell you the whole story from beginning to end. And I guess I ought to start at the beginning. 'In the beginning' say, that does fit in rather well when you are talking about a visit from the Lord, doesn't it? In the beginning," he started and then interrupted himself by saying, "well, if we are to begin that way, we ought to go around to the front of the house and really start from the beginning."

From the front the house still retains some of the general appearances it had as a tavern. Modifications have taken place on the inside but very few on the outside. The house, or tavern as it used to be, is now located on the southwest corner of the junction of Stone Road, Ridge Road, and the Lockport-Cambria town line. It all began when John Forsyth, his wife and two children left Batavia in 1805 with an ox-sled, loaded with household goods and food, at the head of a procession of pigs, sheep and a cow. Mrs. Forsyth and the two children rode the horse while Forsyth himself followed on foot at the rear of the wagon train to prevent any straggling animals from getting lost. It must have been a lonely trip, for they saw only three or four families along the way. When he came upon this very spot he knew it was the place for him. Like other pioneers, before or after, he followed the pattern of claiming the land. He drove a stake into the ground. This was now his land, his home and his future. But it was still a real wilderness. He set to work to clear the land. He built a log cabin for his family and himself and a log shelter for the animals to protect them from the wolves which infested the region. Nevertheless the wolves killed all the sheep the first year.

Snakes caused trouble too. To the north and east of the Forsyth cabin, beaver dams plugged many of the creeks that flowed to the lake, thereby swamping much of the land. So thick were the rattlesnakes, that Forsyth, whenever he cut swamp grass for his livestock, wore leather boots to protect himself on the outside from snake bite and took several stiff shots of whiskey to protect himself on the inside. The snakes even crawled into the house. On her return to the cabin one day, Mrs. Forsyth found a rattler curled up beside her child, who was asleep on the floor. Quickly, quietly, she picked up the axe standing near the door, moved toward the snake, raised her arm and brought down the axe right behind the head of the snake and a fraction of an inch away from the child. Then she sat down to catch her breath. The child slept on.

The Forsyths met their daily problems well. Slowly pioneers settled the country. In 1808 a surveyor laid out Ridge Road. With the possibilities of a road junction in the offing at this point, John Forsyth built the frame tavern through whose door we were about to pass.

"That stone," said the farmer turning partly around as he crossed the porch, "is the same one that DeWitt Clinton stepped on when he stopped at the tavern on his trip to the West in 1810. You recall he was trying to get the lay of the land for his famous ditch."

To an old "canawler" like me, it seemed almost sacrilegious to step where the "patron saint" of the Erie Canal had stepped almost 150 years ago. I did it, but with reverence.

"And here," said my friend, pointing to a slit in the right side of the porch, "is where the stagecoach mail was pushed through."

We entered. Once inside and seated comfortably, he told the stories of the tavern as generations had told them before.

Beginning in 1816 the stagecoach made regular stops at the "Corners" with mail and passengers. Forsyth himself, however, never lived to see this. In fact, he died June 2, 1812, just before the War of 1812 began. The war brought that tavern a thriving business, and only one slight interruption in its service. This occurred on December 19, 1813 when the British raids across the Niagara River drove practically all of the settlers out of the western half of the county. The widow Forsyth sent her children east of Batavia, to her brother's, while she remained at the Corners.

The Ridge became a road of safety for the fleeing people. Unfortunately, it also served as an avenue of desertion for some regular army and some militia men. As a result, an Ezra Warren, sergeant in the regular army, along with two other soldiers, was stationed at the tavern in order to watch for stragglers and deserters. In a short time Warren fell in love with the widow Forsyth. Following his discharge from the Army, even before the end of the war, Warren returned and they were married. After that, the place became known as Warren's Corners although there are still those who insist it should be called Forsyth Corners.

The war's end saw growing numbers of pioneers on the move westward through York State. Conestoga wagons lumbered over the Genesee and Ridge Roads carrying an old world westward to the new -- to the lake country and beyond. Politicians renewed agitation for a canal; legislation followed. Several surveys were taken, and finally the digging of the canal itself was begun. Meanwhile, Ezra Warren did well at his tavern on The Ridge.

Along with the completion of the canal and the great thrust of people westward, a strange phenomenon occurred. An outburst of highly charged religious emotions engulfed central and western parts of the State. Millerism, Mormonism, Spiritualism, Utopianism and Anti-alcoholism swept over the land like wildfire. In time, the reform movement left behind "a burnt over region" of spent

]emotions. But while feelings burned brightly, many people were fired with the passion of zealots. The "fire" reached Warren's Corners one night in 1825.

That night Mrs. Warren persuaded a reluctant Ezra to go with her to a service at the Methodist Church at the "Corners" to hear a hell-fire and brimstone, total-damnation preacher curse the sinful evils of liquor drinking. It was said he held the power to open the heavens and loose the wrath of God with his fervent voice. Understandably Ezra was none too eager to attend the service. After all, he liked his whiskey and made a good living selling it to others of like mind. But in the end, he went anyway.

When he walked out of the church that night, he was not the same man who had entered earlier. He was deeply troubled. His soul seemed to be wrestling with the habits and desires of a lifetime. Man does not change easily the old patterns of living. For hours, disturbing thoughts kept him from sleeping. Finally he fell asleep. This was even more frightening. Suddenly he sat up bolt-like (or was he dreaming?). A shaft of light flooded the room blinding Ezra for a few moments. Out of the light came a deep and commanding voice. A body-outline took shape. By now Warren had fallen to his knees prayerfully. He stiffened in terror. He was struck dumb. The Voice told him to go forth throughout the land, to preach the Gospel and the evils of liquor to whomsoever. Then the figure placed his hand on Ezra's head in a gesture of blessing and baptized him. Ezra in his own mind had been reborn. He took the name "Father Warren." From then until the day he died at age 90, he refused ordinary baptism, claiming the "Lord had baptized" him.

The next morning like a man possessed, Ezra went down to his liquor cellar below his bar. One by one he rolled his liquor barrels over the stone floor toward the rear. He pulled the latch string on the door, opened it and pushed them out to the top of the gully. Then with his axe he smashed in the barrel heads. Out spilled whiskey, brandy and brandied cherries. Ezra stood, axe in hand, and watched the barrels empty themselves of their evil contents. At the end (like the barrels) he felt purged and clean. Then he went inside and closed his bar forever.

Now in those days of unfenced farms, farmers let livestock wander about the fields, roads, village streets and yards. The law required only that they be registered with the town clerk. This particular morning, as usual, the pigs from the adjoining farms made their way over to Warren's swampy gully for their daily meal of tavern garbage and slop. With all the greed of pigs, they swilled the liquor and lapped up the brandied cherries. Their normal appetites must have been even sharper than usual that morning. Soon the spirits took effect. The pigs started to wobble but they kept on drinking. Finally one by one they fell over in a drunken stupor and lay contentedly in the swampy ooze. When Warren came out later, he found the pigs lying in the gully, not dead, as he first thought,

187

but dead drunk. He set out immediately to tell his neighbors to come, bring their "mud-boats" and get their drunken pigs out of his yard.

"Well, that's it," said my story teller. "That's the Tale of the Pickled Porkers."

Then after a moment, he turned and said, "Now you can see my confusion. If the liquor spilling happened just before the willow whip incident, it probably wasn't just the fertile ground that caused the buggy whip to take root and grow but the special irrigation Ezra gave it that morning after the 'Lord's visit.' For the fun of it I like to think that it happened that way. One way or the other that whiskey-brandy-swamp water drink must have been about the most powerful shot in York State."

"Well," I agreed partially. "It sure must have been powerful stuff. But don't be too sure about your comparison. I've heard that Erie 'Canawlers' used to claim "Canawl" water and whiskey (Erie brand, of course) the breath of it would open all the locks at Lockport. But fair minded as they were, I'm sure they would agree with you that, if your swamp water and whiskey from The Ridge were strong enough to make the blood run hot in hogs and the sap run high in a dead dry buggy whip, it would have been a fit companion for their 'Canawl' water and whiskey -- but only as a chaser."

"ODE TO A DRUNKARD"

How well do I remember, 'twas in the late November,
I was walking down the street quite full of pride.
My heart was all a-flutter as I slipped down in the gutter,
And a pig came there and laid down by my side;
and as I lay there in the gutter, all too soused to even mutter,
A lady passing by was heard to say:
"One may tell a brute that boozes by the company he chooses."
Hearing this the pig got up and walked away.

-- Unknown

189

"COME, COME AWAY, HO"

Come, come away, ho,
To the barroom go,
Play a little high-lo
Take a drink at every throw
For sure to Heaven you will go.
Come, ho, jolly foe.
Why delay you to go.

So down the seller will pour it;
Though it grieve him sore
For, loss of pence full well he knows,
Will grieve him much more.

THE CASE OF THE STIFF CANAWLER
Originally published in 1956

Of all the tales that came out of the western end of the canal, this is perhaps the strangest. It happened at the turn of the century. I first heard it from an eighty-year-old Niagara river man who had the look of the river on his face, a spark in his eyes and a tongue for telling tales. Henry told this story as he relaxed in what must certainly be the last rendezvous of the towpathers on the Niagara Frontier: Mutz's Old Saloon on what used to be the old canal towpath.

Tug tows and power barges had long since pushed the hustling hoggies, with their mules and horses, off the canal towpath and all. The canal itself at Riverside years ago, took to the Niagara River. At Frank Mutz's Saloon, man has filled the canal bed. Years have erased its markings and the State has taken away its liquor license.

Still the towpath tavern stands, mothering a line of tumbled down fishing shacks, gaily named sporting clubs and just plain cottages on both sides of the saloon along the river bank. The name "towpath" sticks. A fierce pride of oneness with the water marks this colony as a community apart with its own elected mayor. But the towpath is doomed. In another year Thruway bulldozers, making way for the new days, will bury it all in its past.

For now, however, the tavern still stands. Topside it's rainsoaked and sun-baked; below, water-logged and ice-scarred; overall it has weather-stained gray, matching the foggy overcast that often rides in on the river and seeps into the wood as it does into your bones.

The two-story building leans crazily in all directions, as if it were too tired to hold itself up; as if it were in a state of momentary hesitation before falling into the river. Attached to the side, a bowling alley, already completely collapsed, seems to be tugging at the rest of the building to join it. In the far corner of what still remains of the alley is a chalk inscription: "Cap Summers rolled three hundred July, 1895."

In its young days (1892 and immediately thereafter) when the saloon stood erect and fronted proudly on the towpath just a few feet from the canal, many a thirsty driver, as he neared the swinging doors, dropped the reins of his mule team, ran into the tavern, grabbed his schooper of beer, gulped it down, slapped his money on the bar, dashed out and caught up with his well-trained mules as they continued to walk driverless toward Canal Street and the Buffalo Harbor.

When the towpath died with the birth of the Barge Canal, life naturally turned to the river. The backs of the saloon and the canal cottages became more important than the front. Seen from the

191

waterside it looked as if the river itself had drawn out the backs of the shacks like an accordion and then spread them over the spindles and spiles which stick out of the river.

As I sat listening to my friend, in the back room of the saloon, I could see the river through the cracks and holes in the floor. Stringy green seaweed clung about the spiles, climbing up and down with the gentle swell of the water. But the river-man was telling his story and my mind went back with him to the old canal days.

When dropping temperatures gradually froze the commercial life of the canal, the canawlers gave up and their kids and other kids took over. With enough water left in the bottom for ice cover, children and adults alike had a ready-made ice rink, 70 feet wide and 365 miles long. Often, the boys who lived near the towpath region at Riverside would skate from the old Black Rock Lock past Mutz's Saloon and onto the double flight at Lockport, miles to the north. On the way back, if the wind was right, they nailed two sticks together like a cross, spread a sheet over them, fastened it tightly, and sailed home on the wind and ice.

South of Mutz's Saloon, where Conjockety's Creek (Scajaquada Creek today) emptied into the canal behind Squaw Island, was a slack water pool that made a fine ice pond. Now, a ship canal lock operated by the Army Engineers lowers northbound canal and lake boats into the river or lifts southbound vessels up to lake level, on their way to the Buffalo Harbor and Lake Erie. In 1899, the lock at this point compensated for the same level but the canal stayed inland all the way along the Niagara River. The pond at this point was well protected from the wind so that the ice was unusually smooth for skating.

The winter of 1899 came suddenly with a week of turbulent weather; a severe drop in temperature, a violent sleetstorm, snow, thaw, rain, and again freezing temperatures and snow. Then it cleared and stayed cold. In a few days the boys were skating on the pond. From time beyond their remembering they always sat on one certain spot on the side to put on and take off their skates. This year, to their delight, they discovered near the pond edge an ice hummock, shaped like a chair and just right for changing skates.

Young and old alike enjoyed a great season of skating. The ice chair became the gathering point for the gang and the prize to be won in contests. The winner could sit first on the chair to take off his skates.

For them, the days lengthened too soon. The sun climbed higher. The canawlers and watermen grew impatient to hit the path. The boys knew their skating days were ending.

Still the ice stayed firm enough on the pond. They kept skating, fearing each day would be the last. Their ice hump melted some and, although still more than man-size, it kept getting smaller. The strange feeling Henry had when he first sat on the ice hump to

change his skates seemed to grow stronger. One day, the last it seemed for the year, Henry again sat down on the ice chair. As he finished clamping on his first skate, the strange fear gripped him again, so strongly now that he was not able to put on his other skate. He had a strange feeling, like the feeling one gets on a warm summer evening when a cold blast of air strikes suddenly and dies quickly, or the feeling that sometimes drains the strength from legs for no apparent reason. Uncontrollably, Henry turned his head to the back of the ice seat. Terror loosened his face and glazed his eyes. Looking at him out of the ice cake was the face of a man frozen stiff. The chair-like form of the ice hump had followed the sitting contour. Here the canawler had sat down, tired, sick or drunk. Here he had died. The rain and snow had enveloped him for the whole winter.

As Henry finished his story, he took a long, satisfied draw on his pipe, looked at me for the effect of his story and then added, "Seen many a stiff canawler in my day, but never saw any except old 'ice hump' who didn't ask for another shot to take the cold damp out of his bones. That really would have been 'whiskey on the rocks!

VII

LIFE ON THE RAGING CANAL

Republic Steam Presses, Buffalo.

COMMENDING MY SOUL TO GOD

New Englanders first came to New York State on foot through the wilds, sleeping nights upon the ground. Many went back and forth on foot; some with ox-teams and covered wagons. Is it any wonder that we feel deeply thankful to the men who dug the "Big Ditch," thereby giving them ease in transport? Many pioneers became firm friends during the journey, changing their proposed locations so they might become near neighbors. The journal of an old pioneer contains the following item, written as he was about to take his first journey by the Erie Canal: "Commending my soul to God and asking His defense from danger, I stepped on board, and was soon flying toward Utica."

LEAVES WIFE IN SYRACUSE

Since the Old Erie's ports furnished the most abundant sources for answers to questions, scarcely did a packet ever pull out without leaving behind a passenger or two, lost in conversation. Even the canallers themselves were guilty of this. News item: "Mrs. Captain Hawkins was so deep in conference with Mrs. Captain Jones while their husbands' boats lay in fleet at Syracuse, the Jones' towrope was picked up and headed west without either woman noticing, causing the disgruntled Captain J. to proceed west a full month, wifeless."

"PASSING THE LOCK"

The activity of the canal itself broke the tedium of traveling. "Everything on the Canal is life and motion," wrote a Bostonian as he rode west on the Clinton Line in 1846. "Every moment the boats pass loaded with western produse (sic). A packet has just passed filled with passengers and a man playing the violin and Gentlemen and Ladies dancing on Deck."

Though there might not always be dancing on the deck, some of the packets carried bands for the entertainment of the passengers. And the following poem entitled "Passing the Lock" suggests that some New Yorkers found traveling on their Grand Canal very exciting indeed:

> The Grand Canal! how proudly o'er
> Its glorious tide we're riding now!
> The bright waves dance along the shore,
> Or gaily kiss our fairy prow --

The Trumpet's warning notes ring out
With high-tones flourish loud and brave;
And then comes back the "tender's" shout,
"All ready!" up the glancing wave.
Now bear thee bold, and bear thee well,
Thou pilot at the building helm!
If fail thy hand, O! who can tell
What dangers dire our bark may whelm?
"Hold up" -- the slackened traces drop,
And down the narrowing way we run;
Till curbed and checked, at last we stop --
Hurrah! hurrah! right bravely done!

We're in the lock! We're in the lock!
With many a restless thump and bang!
With gurgling splash, and watery shock
The gates are closed, and down we sink
Into the twilight depth below,
Where gushing streams from every chink,
Like rich and sparkling fountains flow!
A moment now of dim repose,
A moment's space of calm we win --
Then wide the sweeping door unclose,
And let the welcome daylight in.
The "bowsman" stands upon the deck
In his high place of power and pride,
His tin-horn dangling on his neck --
And shouts "go on!" and forth we glide.
Then lightly o'er the waters far,
We take our glad and devious way --
For freight we've codfish, salt and tar,
And paving stones and potter's clay.

What soul so full as needs be told
That to high themes my harp is strung,
Which ne'er inspired the bards of old,
When Dante and when Milton sung.
Old Homer made what we may call,
In liberal phrase, quite decent rhymes;
But ah! there was no grand canawl
To wake the muse in those dark times.

When the passing of a lock became more an interruption than
an adventure, many passengers welcomed a lock-side walk while
the boat passed through.

"LOW BRIDGE, EVERYBODY DOWN"

This song has found its way into folk tradition, although it is really a Tin-pan Alley tune written in 1905 by Thomas S. Allen.

I've got a mule, and her name is Sal,
Fifteen miles on the Erie Canal,
She's a good ol' worker and a good ol' pal,
Fifteen miles on the Erie Canal.
We've hauled some barges in our day.
Filled with lumber, coal and hay,
And we know ev'ry inch of the way
From Albany to Buffalo.

Chorus:
Low Bridge ev'rybody down.
Low Bridge for we're comin' to a town.
And you always know your neighbor,
You always know your pal,
If you ever navigated on the Erie Canal.

We'd better look around for a job old gal,
Fifteen miles on the Erie Canal,
You bet your life I wouldn't part with Sal,
Fifteen miles on the Erie Canal.
Giddap there gal we've passed that lock,
We'll make Rome 'fore six o'clock,
So one more trip and then we'll go,
Right back home to Buffalo.

Chorus:
Low Bridge, ev'rybody down,
Low Bridge, I've the finest mule in town.
Once a man name Mike McGinty,
Tried to put it over Sal,
Now he's way down at the bottom of the Erie Canal.

Oh, where would I be if I lost my pal?
Fifteen miles on the Erie Canal,
Oh, I'd like to see a mule as good as Sal,
Fifteen miles on the Erie Canal.
A friend of mine once got her sore,
Now, he's got a broken jaw.
'Cause she let him fly with her iron toe
And kicked him into Buffalo.

Chorus:
Low Bridge, ev'rybody down,
Low Bridge, I've the finest mule in town.
If you're looking for trouble,
Better stay away from Sal,
She's the only fightin' donkey on the Erie Canal.

I don't have to call when I want my Sal,
Fifteen miles on the Erie Canal,
She trots from her stall like a good old gal,
Fifteen miles on the Erie Canal.
I eat my meals with Sal each day,
I eat beef and she eats hay,
She ain't so slow if you want to know,
She put the "Buff" in Buffalo.

Chorus:
Low Bridge, ev'ry body down,
Low Bridge, I've the finest mule in town.
Eats a bale of hay for dinner,
And on top of that, my Sal,
Tries to drink up all the water in the Erie Canal.

BRIDGES LOW

The bridges on the Canal are very low, particularly the old ones. Indeed they are so low they scarcely allow the baggage to clear and, in some cases, actually rub against it. Every bridge makes us bend double if seated on anything, and in many cases you have to lie on your back. The man at the helm gives the word to the passengers: "Bridge, *very* low bridge. The lowest in the Canal," as the case may be. Some serious accidents have happened for want of caution. A young English woman met with her death a short time since she, having fallen asleep with her head upon a box, had her head crushed to pieces. Such things however do not often occur and in general it affords amusement to the passengers who soon imitate the cry and vary it with a command, such as "all Jackson men bow down." After such commands we find few aristocrats.

"OH! DAT LOW BRIDGE"

Most of these canal songs were not sung by canal boatman, but by entertainers along the canal. This song was written for an 1880's vaudeville show called, "The Grip." Music is by Dave Brigham and lyrics by Edward Harrigan.

It's many miles to Buffalo, Oh, dat low bridge.
Balky mule he travel slow. Oh, dat low bridge.
Dars gravel on de tow-path, Dars hornets in de sand.
Oh, pity poor canallers, dats far away from land.

Den look out, dat low bridge, (Look out, dat low bridge.)
Look out, dat low bridge, (Look out, dat low bridge.)
The captain, cook, and all de crew, Oh duck your head
way down.
The fastest boat in all de fleet, two sisters come to town.

Dars many locks to shut you in. Oh, dat low bridge.
Ev'ry worm must learn to swim. Oh, dat low bridge.
We're loaded down with barley, and lumber from de West.
Oh, ev'ry poor canaller, Now do your level best.

We're froze up in the winter time. Oh, dat low bridge.
Summer how de sun do shine. Oh, dat low bridge.
In rain or stormy weather, De captain's on de poop.
All huddle up together, like chickens in de coop.

Dars' groceries in de cabin dar. Oh, dat low bridge.
Never leaks, she's full of tar. Oh, dat low bridge.
Dar's freckles on de children, Dars' glanders on de mules.
Mosquitoes by de million, Who keep de golden rule.

CORNS CURED

After dinner, a brisk young man entered the boat and in a loud voice asked if any lady or gentleman wanted to have "corns cured." He was asked his terms, and said they were half a dollar for one corn and less for each additional. He offered to remove the corn by the root instantly, without pain, and engaged that it should never grow again. After a great deal of bargaining and bad wit, one passenger made an agreement with him to have one corn extirpated, for which he was to pay 25 cents (1s. sterling). The operator, who was dubbed by the passengers, "the Doctor," pulled out a bottle, borrowed a pen-knife, applied some sulphuric acid to the corn, received his 25 cents, paid 18 cents for his fare, and left the boat. The lent knife was destroyed by the acid, but "the Doctor" was fairly beyond reach before its owner made this discovery. The best piece of wit elicited on the occasion was a remark that this was in every sense "a toeboat." The master of the boat told me that "the Doctor" had done a small business today, but that yesterday he cleared $9.00 in the boat going east. . . .

TO BED ABOARD A CANAL BOAT

There remains still another condition which arose during the process of going to bed on a crowded canal boat. When the floor and tables were all occupied, as well as the shelves, it became necessary to erect a zigzag series of clotheslines back and forth across the cabin, on which the discarded garments of the passengers might be hung. The scenic effect produced in the sleeping room when this process had been completed somewhat resembled that displayed by the back yard of a modern tenement house on wash day. Finally, after all the travellers were spread out upon their berths and on the tables and floor and the light had been put out, the unhappy assemblage subsided into a restless but unseen throng in which the stillness was only broken by faint moanings, the creaking of the boat and an occasional stentorian snore.

After suffering for several hours amid the conditions here outlined, it was a common occurrence that some passenger abandoned his endeavor to obtain rest in an upper berth and decided to quit it for the better air and greater comfort to be found on the roof. He, therefore, cautiously lowered his feet in the direction of some table whose position as it stood when he went to bed was remembered by him. He would try to perform this operation of getting a foothold with utmost quietude in order that he might not disturb his fellow travellers. Hanging from his shelf by his elbows and feeling in the darkness with his foot for the table he was seeking, he might at last find it, only to step on the prostrate form of some belated passenger to whom it had been allotted. Then the mischance occurred -- and being anxious to comply with the sudden protest which it evoked -- he would hastily try to shift the position of his feet, only to discover that he was astraddle of one of the clotheslines. He then abandoned further hope of a peaceful solution of his difficulties and let go, without caring where he alighted, or how.

FAT MAN IN A BERTH

I awoke in the night with a dreadful feeling of suffocation. Cold perspiration stood on my forehead, and I could hardly draw my breath; there was a weight-like lead on my stomach and chest. I attempted to cry out -- in vain. I lay almost without consciousness. At last I became quite awake, and remembered where I was, and in what circumstances I was placed. The weight remained immovable. Above me was a noise like distant thunder; it was my companion of the upper story, who lay snoring over my head and that the weight which pressed on my chest was caused by his body no longer remained a doubtful point. I endeavored to move the Colossus -- impossible. I tried to push, to cry out -- in vain. He lay like a rock on my chest, and seemed to have no more feeling. As all my attempts to awaken him were ineffectual, I bethought me of my breastpin, which luckily I had not taken out of my cravat the night before. With great difficulty I succeeded in moving my arm and reaching the pin, which I pressed with a firm hand into the mass above me.

There was a sudden movement, which procured me momentary relief; but the movement soon subsided. The weight was growing heavier and more insupportable, and to prevent being utterly crushed, I was obliged to reapply the pin. "What's that?" "Murder!" "Help!" cried a deep bass voice above me. Feeling myself free, I slipped like an eel from under the weight, and saw, by the dim light reflected from a lamp hanging under the deck, a sight of no common occurrence. A stout heavy man, who slept in the upper frame without a mattress, was too much for the canvas which spanned the frame and it had given way under the weightiest part of his form, which descended til it found support on my chest. The thrust of my breastpin had caused him to make an effort to move, which gave me that opportunity of making my escape I so gladly seized. As he returned to his former position with greater force and weight, from the exertions he had made, the support being gone, the canvas split still wider and, more than half asleep, he was sitting on my bed, while his head and feet remained in his own. He soon began to call out, "Help!" "Murder!" Everybody started up to see what was the matter, and to laugh heartily at the extraordinary attitude of this stout gentleman.

LIKE A "WORKING" BARREL OF BEER

There is no philosophy in snoring -- none that we can see -- and yet you must make the music go all night. Can't help it? Would stop if you could? We don't believe a word of it. How do you help it in the daytime? We verily believe nature intended you for a hog, and made a mistake. For the life of us, we can't tell whether or not there is a grunter in our room when we awake -- only the hog is more musical -- that's the difference. But a hog does all his grunting in the daytime and when he is awake; but most of yours comes at night when a poor fellow is tired, and such sounds grate upon his ear. If you were not so snappish and growlish in the daytime, we should have more charity for you at night. We never knew a person of a good heart and kind disposition, to snore and keep another awake. The good angels that attend and watch the bed of such would be frightened at the noise you make, and never come near the bed again. You will never cease to disturb your bedfellows, while you are so morose and crabbled in the daytime. The malignant feelings you cannot grunt out when you are awake, belch forth in torrents while you are asleep. Like a working barrel of beer, your body can't contain your bad feelings, and so at night where they find a hole in your head, they squirt out to the provoking of all who sleep in the house. There's no one who would consent to become your wife?

AGRICULTURE

The Canal cut through farms and gave the passengers a look at barnyard life. Unlike ocean sailors, canawlers learned about agriculture. There were, now and then, amusing incidents that occurred along the line of the old waterway. One time when Mark Hollister was canal collector at Rome, a boatman came in the office and requested Hollister to write a letter for him to his wife. This was often done by boatmen, for some of them were deficient in education. The collector commenced as in the usual way, but soon stopped and asked the boatman if he had any endearments to send his wife.

"Oh yes, I have. Just write as you would to your own wife and put in some big words. Now there is AGRICULTURE. That is a big word, and put it in often. That will please her."

GAME TO THE LAST

Two years ago last "pulling fodder time" (when farmers pulled corn stubble out of the fields for fodder) Uncle Josh B. had a bucking goat that he brought up in the lot next to the house. The boys had, by fooling with him, taught him to 'butt' as hard as a mule's kick, and 'butt' he would at everything that came his way until it seemed he would 'butt' everything off the lot.

So, Uncle Josh concluded to see if he couldn't give him his fill of butting. Out he goes and takes a big hickory maul and hangs it pretty well up in an oak tree, letting it hang just low enough for the goat, Mr. Bucking, to take a fair crack at it. He knew that he would take a buck at anything pushed toward him -- taking such move always as banter. Uncle Josh waited patiently until the buck goat came around, when he gave the signal and here he came with such a force that it would have knocked down a bull! Away flew the maul, and back bounded the buck. "Go at it, my good fellow," sings out Uncle Josh. "If you can whip that maul, your head's a hard'un."

Seeing the motion of the maul as it commenced its returning swing, he met it again at about the same meeting place, driving the maul about twenty feet in the air and bouncing from it himself like a cricket ball! "Hurrah, my little wolly!" said Uncle Josh, who began to get interested in what he considered an equal fight. "There's very little goat in your head if you stand another lick, certain."

207

But here comes goat and maul again, with nearly the same result as before, except the blow did not seem quite so heavy on the part of the buck. "At him again, my hard head," sang out Uncle Josh. "Take your fill in butting." And at him again the little fellow went and kept repeating until Uncle Josh thought the very devil was in the head of the goat, sure enough. But back went the maul and goat went back and, to the astonishment of Uncle Josh, the buck still showed no signs of quitting. "Well," says he, "if you choose to butt your brains out, go ahead." Whack-whack, went head and maul. By this time, it was near night and no sign of quitting. Uncle Josh left. Next morning, he got up early and saw the maul swinging back and forth and the 'buck goat's' tail hopping at it being all that was left of the butting bucking goat.

FROG IN STONE

He told of the live frog the stone cutters found when they split a great slab years ago:

"Some people thought the frog had been there thousands of years. Others said it never happened; that he made it up. But I saw it with my own eyes. I think it is easily explained. There was a crevice in the stone and water coursed through it. The frog might have passed into the fissure when tiny. He may have lived there only a matter of months or a few years. But he was there all right and it caused a lot of talk in the quarries at the time."

THE EMPEYVILLE FROG

Red McCarthy found Joshua in the Erie Canal along South James Street while he was still a polywog. As soon as Joshua lost his tail, as polywogs do, and after developing legs, he hopped away.

For a while no one knew where he was, but several years later he turned up again at his old pond at Empeyville off the canal. For 100 years Joshua continued to grow. When he reached his full height, his hind legs were six feet long and his front legs three feet long. Each time he jumped in his Empeyville Pond, he splashed water thirty feet into the air and the pond became six feet wider. Joshua's food consisted of chipmunks, squirrels and sometimes rabbits. He ate whatever overgrown insects he could capture.

Old Joshua was constantly in demand. For a time, he was employed as assistant sawman at Empeyville. He hauled logs and pulled things too heavy for a horse to draw. Probably most importantly, he straightened out roads. It was a simple matter. A chain was hooked to the road and fastened around Joshua's middle. Joshua would huff and puff and then make one mighty leap. The road was stretched and straightened. They say he moved the town barn about 33 1/2 feet without straining a muscle.

The last time that Joshua is known to have been seen was in the summer of 1934. Floyd Esch's account of the event is reprinted from a clipping from The Rome (NY) Sentinel:

"I had been north of Empeyville building a picnic table for a Roman business man at his camp and this Roman will vouch for the following event. As we were returning home late one evening and arrived at the Busy Corner in Empeyville, old Joshua sat under a tree catching for his supper some of the monstrous insects that inhabit the region. We waited nearly half an hour for him to get his fill. While we were waiting, the pond filled with water. As Joshua turned and entered the pond, the pond overflowed and washed the road out so that we had to rebuild it before we could proceed home."

Joshua has not been seen since that night, but he may still be alive. At least no death notice has been seen in the local papers. Four of old Joshua's grandsons are known to be owned by a man in Rome. Charles Beacraft says that they are busy, having been employed by the city to pull stumps. Not many people see the frogs, for they are allergic to strangers. Many of Joshua's descendents, however, are still living in the Empeyville pond, but none has reached the size and fame of old Joshua.

MARK TWAIN IN BUFFALO

Buffalo likes to claim Mark Twain, but Mark never liked to claim Buffalo. During his short stay in Buffalo, he seemed to experience little but unhappiness. The unpleasant memories of Buffalo eventually forced him to leave the city. Originally, he had come to Buffalo in August 1869, one month after the publication of his successful book, <u>Innocents Abroad</u>. He had purchased a part ownership in the <u>Buffalo Express</u>.

On February 2, 1870, he married Olivia Langdon of Elmira. His father-in-law gave them a beautiful house on Delaware Avenue, then the most expensive street in Buffalo. It did not, however, prove to be a happy home. During the summer of 1870, Olivia's father took ill and on August 6, 1870, died. This cast the Clemens' household in deep grief. Shortly thereafter, a school friend of Mrs. Clemens visited them, contracted typhoid fever and died in their Buffalo home on September 29, 1870. Two months later, their first child was born prematurely. This left Mrs. Clemens in a very weakened condition. In April 1871, Clemens had all he wanted of Buffalo. He sold out his interest in the <u>Express</u> at a loss and moved to Elmira. Mrs. Clemens was so sick she had to be carried from the house on a mattress.

Mark's opinion of Buffalo was as frank as it was uncomplimentary. From Elmira on September 15, 1871, he wrote to his lecture agent:

Dear Redpath -- I wish you would get me released from the lecture at Buffalo. I morally hate that society there, and I don't doubt they hired me. I once gave them a packed house free of charge and they never even had the common politeness to thank me. They left me to shift for myself, too, a la Bret Harte at Harvard. Get me rid of Buffalo! Otherwise I'll have no recourse left but to get sick the day I lecture there. I can get sick easy enough, by the simple process of saying the word -- well, never mind what word -- I am not going to lecture there.

Yours,
Mark

211

"LET THE STORM COME DOWN"

The sun is no longer in view,
The clouds have begun to frown,
But with a bumper or two,
We'll say, let the storm come down.
And the song we'll sing, one and all,
While the storm around us pelts,
A life on the muddy canawl,
Oh, we don't want nothin' else.

A STORM ON THE CANAL

It has been the fortune of many to travel on the canal, when its calm waters slept in undisturbed tranquility and the soft breath of the summer air scarcely excited a ripple upon its peaceful bosom. But when old Boreas has awakened from his slumbers and is stalking furiously over its dangerous depth, lashing its waters to madness, throwing up huge billows high upon its banks and engulfing everything in its boiling whirlpools, with threatening water-spouts and roaring tornadoes -- at such a time, we question whether many have dared the dangers and perils of the "Raging Canal."

It was a calm night in June, when it was my fortune to be traveling with a goodly number of passengers upon that staunch and thorough sea-boat, the *Dolly Maria*. Nought was heard to break the silence, save the sleeping passengers in the cabin, who seemed combined to "roll the deep eternal bass of Nature's Anthem," in one general snore which shook the boat from stem to stern and reverberated along the wooded banks like muttering thunder.

The grim sons of Neptune who navigated the boat were dispersed about the deck in various attitudes and the skipper was pacing by the weather gangway, quietly smoking his cigar. Suddenly, he stopped short in his walk and his eye rested upon a small black cloud which had appeared in the western horizon and was growing larger and blacker every moment. He gazed but a moment and, then, his voice rung with clear and startling tones. "Every man to his post!" "Aye, aye," growled the old waterdogs, who were soon ready for the approaching storm.

Shortly it burst upon us in all its violence -- "Hard up your helm," shouted the captain. "Aye, aye," growled the old Muskrat in the stern, and for a few moments she rode the gale nobly; but, suddenly a heavy sea gave her a "side winder," carrying away the wash-dish and ducking the cook and the gallant craft began to settle to leeward.

"Haul taut the towline. Box-haul the main setting pole and square away the woodbox!" thundered the captain, whose spirit seemed to rise superior to the emergency.

The storm was now terrific, the waves running mountain-high, often rising to the very summit of the towpath and it was soon seen that the *Dolly Maria* was no match for such a tempest and was gradually drifting before the wind.

"Breakers ahead!" shouted the bootblack.

"Where away?"

"Over the off row-lock!" was answered.

The decisive moment had now come and the captain saw that desperate measures alone would avail and through the canal horn shouted, "Steerman, take another tack in your unmentionables. Cook, double reef the stove pipe and get up more steam on the tea kettle. Cut away the gangway. Furl the jib-boom. Unship the taffrail and let go the boat-hook!" But the anchor still dragged. The danger was every moment becoming more imminent; the roar of breakers was distinctly heard and orders were given to lighten the ship.

"Discharge overboard your tobacco quids, every man of you. Steward, throw overboard the boot-jack and the coffee pot," upon which she was very perceptibly lightened, the anchor caught, and a faint gleam of hope broke upon our dispairing souls.

But soon came the appalling cry, "the best bower has parted and we are adrift!" Then all hope was gone and a wild shriek rose high above the ragin' storm; but anon was heard the calm voice of the captain exhorting us to be quiet for we might yet be saved. The towline had been secured to a stout post-and-rail fence on shore, a running bow-line was got upon the cutwater, a double turn was taken upon the caboose, the helm jammed hard apart, and the *Dolly Maria* once more brought up in the wind and rode out the gale in safety.

THE RAGING CANAL

From 1825 through the Civil War era, immigrants by the thousands crossed the stormy Atlantic to America. The voyage was often filled with discomfort and very real dangers.

Upon landing in Boston or New York, these new Americans looked forward to their smooth trip westward on the relatively danger-free Erie Canal. After all, the Canal from Albany to Buffalo was only four feet deep. To a waterway wag, the Canal seemed not much more than a damp cloth stretched across the State. That's a good picture and an acceptable folklore exaggeration. While records show a number of accidental drownings over the years, it would take the most determined effort of a suicidal person to drown. It was almost as hard to drown in the Erie Canal as it was to drown on dry land.

The narrow width of the Canal, forty feet, meant that the steersman hugged close enough to the towpath to permit passengers top side to pick leaves from the low-lying branches that overhung the Canal. Perversely, these relatively safe conditions tickled the funny bone of Canawlers and minstrels who wrote imaginatively and satirically of fighting their way to port on a stormy night on the "raging canal." Farmers, plowing near the towpath, were more than amused by these Canal sailors singing of the dangers they faced.

By 1844, in one form or another, this song-poem was a part of the Erie Canal folklore. According to William Hullfish, it became "the most famous and popular Canal song of the Nineteenth Century."

In 1884, "This ludicrous satire about storm-swept crafts," was published by C. G. Christman and billed as "written and sung by the most celebrated comic singer, P. Morris:"

"THE RAGING CANAWL"

Come listen to my story ye lands-man one and all,
I'll sing to you the dangers of that raging canal.
For I am one of many who expects a watery grave,
For I've been at the mercy of the wind and of the wave.

I left Albany harbor about the break of day,
And if I rightly remember 'twas the second day of May;
We trusted to our driver, altho' he was but small,
For he knew all the windings of that raging canal.

It seemed as if the Devil had his work in hand that night,
For all our oil was gone, and our lamps they gave no light,
The clouds began to gather and the rain began to fall,
And I wished myself off of that raging canal.

The Captain told the driver to hurry with all speed,
And his orders were obeyed, for he soon cracked up his lead;
With the fastest kind of driving, we allowed by twelve o'clock,
We'd be in old Schenectady right bang against the dock.

215

But sad was the fate of our poor devoted bark,
For the rain kept on pouring, and the night it grew dark;
The horses gave a stumble, and the driver gave a squall.
And they tumbled head over heels into the raging canal.

The Captain came on deck, with a voice so clear and sound,
Saying, "Cut the horses loose, my boys, or else we'll all be
drowned,"
The driver swam to shore, altho' he was but small,
While the horse sank to rise no more in the raging canal.

The cook she wrung her hands, and she came upon the deck,
Saying, "Alas, what will become of us, our boat it is a wreck?"
The steersman knocked her over, for he was a man of sense,
And the bowsman jumped ashore and he lashed her to a fence.

The Captain came on deck with a spy glass in his hand,
But the night it was so dark he could not discover land;
He said to us with a faltering voice, while tears began to fall,
Prepare to meet your death this night on the raging canal.

The sky was rent asunder, the lightening it did flash,
The thunder rattled up above, just like eternal smash;
The clouds were all upset, and the rigging it did fall,
And we scudded under bare poles on that raging canal.

We took the old cook's pettycoat, for want of better dress,
And rigged it out upon the pole as a signal of distress;
We pledged ourselves hand to hand aboard the boat to bide,
And not to quit the deck while a plank hung to her side.

At last that horrid night cut dirt from the sky,
The storm it did abate, and a boat came passing by;
It soon espied our signal as each on his knees did fall,
Thankful we escaped a grave on the raging canal.

We each of us took a nip and signed the pledge anew,
And wonderful as danger ceased, how up our courage grew;
The craft in sight bore down on us and quickly was 'long side,
And we all jumped aboard, and for Buffalo we did ride.

Now, if I live a thousand years, the horrors of that night,
Will ever in my memory be, a spot most burning bright;
For nothing in this whole wide world will ever raise my gall,
Except the thought of my voyage on the raging canal.

"THE AGED PILOT MAN"

Amused by the ironic humor of this song-poem, Mark Twain, who lived in Buffalo for a brief period, wrote a companion piece entitled "The Aged Pilot Man." Of his poem, Twain said, "The idea (not the chief idea, but the vehicle that bears it) was probably suggested by the old song called the 'Raging Canal' but I cannot remember now. I do remember, though, that at this time I thought my doggeral was one of the ablest poems of the age." It follows here:

On the Erie Canal, it was, all on a summer's day,
I sailed forth with my parents, far away to Albany.
From out the clouds at noon that day, there came a dreadful storm,
That piled the billows high about, and filled us with alarm.

A man came rushing from a house, saying, "Snub up your boat, I
pray,
Snub up your boat, snub up, alas, Snub up while yet you may."
Our captain cast one glance astern, then forward glanced he,
And said, "My wife and little ones, I never more shall see."

Said Dollinger the pilot man, in noble words, but few --
"Fear not, but lean on Dollinger, and he will fetch you through."
The boat drove on, the frightened mules, tore through the rain and
wind,
And bravely still, in danger's post, the whip-boy strode behind.

"Come 'board, come 'board," the captain cried, "Nor tempt so wild
a storm."
But still the raging mules advanced, and still the boy strode on.
Then said the captain to us all, "Alas, 'tis plain to me,
The greater danger is not there, But here upon the sea."

"So let us strive, while life remains, to save all souls on board,
And then if die at last we must, Let . . . I cannot speak the word."
Said Dollinger the pilot man, tow'ring above the crew,
"Fear not, but trust in Dollinger, and he will fetch you through."

"Low bridge! low bridge!" all heads went down, the laboring bark
sped on,
A mill we passed, we passed a church, hamlets, and fields of corn;
And all the world came out to see, and chased along the shore,
Crying, "Alas the gallant ship and crew, can nothing help them
more?"

217

"Ho! lighten ship! ho! man the pump! Ho, hostler, heave the lead!
And count ye all, both great and small, as numbered with dead!
For mariner for forty year, on Erie, boy and man,
I never yet saw such a storm, or one 't with it began!"

So overboard a keg of nails, and anvils three we threw,
Likewise four bales of gunny-sacks, two hundred pounds of glue,
Two sacks of corn, four ditto wheat, a box of books, a cow,
A violin, Lord Byron's works, a rip-saw and a sow.

A quarter-three, tis shoaling fast, three feet large, three feet,
Three feet scant, I cried in fright, Oh is there no retreat?
Said Dollinger the pilot man, As on the vessel flew,
"Fear not, but trust in Dollinger, and he will fetch you through."

A panic struck the bravest hearts, the boldest cheek turned pale,
For plain to all, this shoaling said, A leak had burst the ditch's bed,
"Sever the tow-line. Cripple the mules. Too late, there comes a
shock,
Another length, and the fated craft would have swum to the saving
lock.

Then gathered together the shipwrecked crew and took one last
embrace,
While sorrowful tears from despairing eyes ran down each hopeless
face,
But of all the children of misery there on that poor sinking frame,
But one spake words of hope and faith, and I worshipped as they
came,

Said Dollinger the pilot man, O brave heart, strong and true,
"Fear not, but trust in Dollinger, for he will fetch you through."
Lo! scarce the words have passed his lips, the dauntless prophet
say'th,
When every soul about him seeth a wonder crown his faith.

For straight a farmer brought a plank, mysteriously inspired,
And laying to unto the ship, in silent awe retired.
Then every sufferer stood amazed, that pilot man before,
A moment stood. Then wondering turned and speechless walked
ashore.

VIII

HERE, THERE & EVERYWHERE

Republic Steam Presses, Buffalo.

THE IRISHMAN AND THE FALLS

As the Irishman looked at the falls, he turned slowly to his companion and in a level voice thick with brogue said, "Faith and what's unusual about this. Indaid, Ireland too has water that runs downhill. Now if you can show me some water that runs uphill...."

GOD MADE NIAGARA FALLS

God made Niagara Falls. The Erie Canal made it a tourist attraction.
Mark Twain made it the Garden of Eden.

It is thought Mark Twain worked on "Adam's Diary" in Buffalo during 1870 for an unfinished book entitled Noah's Ark Book. It was finally printed in 1893 as part of the Niagara Book. Eventually, it was copywrited by Harper Brothers and issued by them in 1904.

Mark Twain's own opinion of this story is interesting. He revealed his thoughts on it in a letter to Frederick Duneka, general manager of Harper Brothers:

I wrote Eve's Diary, she using Adam's Diary as her (unwitting and unconscious text, of course), since to use any other text would have been an imbecility -- then I took Adam's Diary and read it. It turned my stomach. It was not literature; yet it had been literature once -- before I sold it to be degraded to an advertisement of the Buffalo Fair. I was going to write you to ask you to melt the plates and put it out of print.

But, this morning, I examined it without temper, and saw that if I abolished the advertisement it would be literature again.

So I have done it. I have struck out 700 words and inserted five pages of new matter (650 words), and now Adam's Diary is dam (sic) good -- sixty times as good as it ever was before.

I believe it is as good as Eve's Diary now -- no, not quite that good, I guess, but it is good enough to go in the same cover with Eve's. I'm sure of that . . . .

Yrs ever,
Mark

GARDEN OF EDEN

MONDAY -- This new creature with the long hair is a good deal in the way. It is always hanging around and following me about. I don't like this; I am not used to company. I wish it would stay with the other
animals . . . . Cloudy to-day, wind in the east; think we shall have rain . . . We. Where did I get that word? . . . I remember now -- the new creature uses it.

TUESDAY -- Been examining the great waterfall. It is the finest thing on the estate, I think. The new creature calls it Niagara Falls -- why, I am sure I do not know. Says it <u>looks</u> like Niagara Falls. That is not a reason, it is mere waywardness and imbecility. I get no chance to name anything myself. The new creature names everything that comes along, before I can get in a protest. And always that same pretext is offered -- it <u>looks</u> like the thing. There is the dodo, for instance. Says the moment one looks at it one sees at a glance that it "looks like a dodo." It will have to keep that name, no doubt. It wearies me to fret about it, but it does no good anyway. Dodo! It looks no more like a dodo than I do.

WEDNESDAY -- Built me a shelter against the rain, but could not have it to myself in peace. The new creature intruded. When I tried to put it out it shed water out of the holes it looks with, and wiped it away with the back of its paws, and made a noise such as some of the other animals make when they are in distress. I wish it would not talk; it is always talking. That sounds like a cheap fling at the poor creature, a slur; but I do not mean it so. I have never heard the human voice before, and any new and strange sound intruding itself here upon the solemn hush of these dreaming solitudes offends my ear and seems a false note. And this new sound is so close to me; it is right at my shoulder, right at my ear, first on one side and then on the other, and I am used only to sounds that are more or less distant from me.

FRIDAY -- The naming goes recklessly on, in spite of anything I can do. I had a very good name for the estate, and it was musical and pretty -- GARDEN-OF-EDEN. Privately, I continue to call it that, but not any longer publicly. The new creature says it is all woods and rocks and scenery, and therefore has no resemblance to a garden. Says it <u>looks</u> like a park, and does not look like anything <u>but</u> a park. Consequently, without consulting me it has been new named -- NIAGARA FALLS PARK. This is sufficiently high-handed, it seems to me. And already there is a sign up: "KEEP OFF THE GRASS." My life is not as happy as it was.

SATURDAY -- The new creature eats too much fruit. We are going to run short, most likely. "We" again -- this is <u>its</u> word; mine, too, now, from hearing it so much. Good deal of fog this morning. I do not go out in the fog, myself. The new creature does. It goes out in all weathers, and stumps right in with its muddy feet. And talks. It used to be so pleasant and quiet here.

SUNDAY -- Pulled through. This day is getting to be more and more trying. It was selected and set apart last November as a day of rest. I already had six of them per week before. This is another of those unaccountable things. There seems to be too much legislation, too much fussing, and fixing, and tidying-up, and not enough of the better-let-well-enough-alone policy. (Mem.--Must keep that sort of opinions to myself.) This morning found the new creature trying to clod apples out of that forbidden tree.

MONDAY -- The new creature says its name is Eve. That is all right, I have no objection. Says it is to call it by when I want it to come. I said it was superfluous, then. The word evidently raised me in its respect; and indeed it is a large, good word and will bear repetition. It says it is not an It, it is a She. This is probably doubtful; yet it is all one to me; what she is were nothing to me if she would but go by herself and not talk.

TUESDAY -- She has littered the whole estate with execrable names and offensive signs: "THIS WAY TO THE WHIRLPOOL." "THIS WAY TO GOAT ISLAND." "CAVE OF THE WINDS THIS WAY."

She says this park would make a tidy summer resort, if there were any custom for it. Summer resort -- another invention of hers -- just words, without any meaning. What is a summer resort? But it is best not to ask her, she has such a rage for explaining.

FRIDAY -- She has taken to begging and imploring me to stop going over the Falls. What harm does it do? Says it makes her shudder. I wonder why; I have always done it -- always liked the plunge, and the excitement and the coolness. I supposed it was what the Falls were for. They have no other use that I can see, and they must have been made for something. She says they were only made for scenery -- like the rhinoceros and the mastodon.

I went over the Falls in a barrel -- not satisfactory to her. Went over in a tub -- still not satisfactory. Swam the Whirlpool and the Rapids in a fig-leaf suit. It got much damaged. Hence, tedious complaints about my extravagance. I am too much hampered here. What I need is change of scene.

SATURDAY -- I escaped last Tuesday night, and traveled two days, and built me another shelter, in a secluded place, and obliterated my tracks as well as I could, but she hunted me out by means of a beast which she has tamed and calls a wolf, and came making that pitiful noise again, and shedding that water out of the places she looks with. I was obliged to return with her, but will presently emigrate again, when occasion offers. She engages herself in many foolish things: among others, trying to study out why the animals called lions and tigers live on grass and flowers, when, as she says, the sort of teeth they wear would indicate that they were intended to eat each other. This is foolish, because to do that would be to kill each other, and that would introduce what, as I understand it, is called "death"; and death, as I have been told, has not yet entered the Park. Which is a pity, on some accounts.

SUNDAY -- Pulled through.

MONDAY -- I believe I see what the week is for: it is to give time to rest up from the weariness of Sunday. It seems a good idea, in a region where good ideas are rather conspicuously scarce. (Mem. -- Must keep this sort of remarks private. . . .) She has been climbing that tree again. Clodded her out of it. She said nobody was looking. Seems to consider that a sufficient justification for chancing any dangerous thing. Told her that. The word justification moved her admiration -- and envy, too, I thought. It is a good word.

THURSDAY -- She told me she was made out of a rib taken from my body. This is at least doubtful, if not more than that. I have not missed any rib . . . . She is in much trouble about the buzzard; says grass does not agree with it; is afraid she can't raise it; thinks it was intended to live on decayed flesh. The buzzard must get along the best it can with what is provided. We cannot overturn the whole scheme to accommodate the buzzard.

SATURDAY -- She fell in the pond yesterday, when she was looking at herself in it, which she is always doing. She nearly strangled, and said it was most uncomfortable. This made her sorry for the creatures which live in there, which she calls fish, for she continues to fasten names on to things that don't need them and don't come when they are called by them, which is a matter of no consequence to her, she is such a fool anyway; so she got a lot of them out and brought them in and put them in my bed to keep warm, but I have noticed them now and then all day and I don't see that they are any happier there than they were before. When night comes I shall throw them outdoors. I will not sleep with them, for I find them clammy and unpleasant to lie among when a person hasn't anything on.

SUNDAY -- Pulled through.

TUESDAY -- She has taken up with a snake now. The other animals are glad, for she was always experimenting with them and bothering them; and I am glad, because the snake talks, and this enables me to get a rest.

FRIDAY -- She says the snake advises her to try the fruit of that tree, and says the result will be a great and fine and noble education. I told her there would be another result, too -- it would introduce death into the world. That was a mistake -- it had been better to keep the remark to myself; it only gave her an idea -- she could save the sick buzzard, and furnish fresh meat to the despondent lions and tigers. I advised her to keep away from the tree. She said she wouldn't. I foresee trouble. Will emigrate.

WEDNESDAY -- I have had a variegated time. I escaped that night, and rode a horse all night as fast as he could go, hoping

224

to get clear out of the Garden and hide in some other country before the trouble should begin; but it was not to be. About an hour after sun-up, as I was riding through a flowery plain where thousands of animals were grazing, slumbering, or playing with each other, according to their common wont, all of a sudden they broke into a tempest of frightful noises, and in one moment the plain was a frantic commotion and every beast was destroying its neighbor. I knew what it meant -- Eve had eaten that fruit, and death was come into the world. . . . The tigers ate my horse, paying no attention when I ordered them to desist, and they would even have eaten me if I had stayed -- which I didn't, but went away in much haste . . . . I found this place, outside the Garden, and was fairly comfortable for a few days, but she has found me out. Found me out, and has named the place Tonawanda -- says it <u>looks</u> like that. In fact I was not sorry she came, for there are but meagre pickings here, and she brought some of those apples. I was obliged to eat them, I was so hungry. It was against my principles, but I find that principles have no real force except when one is well fed. . . .She came curtained in boughs and bunches of leaves, and when I asked her what she meant by such nonsense, and snatched them away and threw them down, she tittered and blushed. I had never seen a person titter and blush before, and to me it seemed unbecoming and idiotic. She said I would soon know how it was myself. This was correct. Hungry as I was, I laid down the apple half eaten -- certainly the best one I ever saw, considering the lateness of the season -- and arrayed myself in the discarded boughs and branches, and then spoke to her with some severity and ordered her to go and get some more and not make such a spectacle of herself. She did it, and after this we crept down to where the wild-beast battle had been, and collected some skins, and I made her patch together a couple of suits proper for public occasions. They are uncomfortable, it is true, but stylish, and that is the main point about clothes. . . . I find she is a good deal of a companion. I see I should be lonesome and depressed without her, now that I have lost my property. Another thing, she says it is ordered that we work for our living hereafter. She will be useful. I will superintend.

TEN DAYS LATER -- She accuses <u>me</u> of being the cause of our disaster! She says, with apparent sincerity and truth, that the Serpent assured her that the forbidden fruit was not apples, it was chestnuts. I said I was innocent, then, for I had not eaten any chestnuts. She said the Serpent informed her that "chestnut" was a figurative term meaning an aged and mouldy joke. I turned pale at that, for I have many jokes to pass the weary time, and some of them could have been of that sort, though I had honestly supposed they were new when I made them. She asked me if I had made one just at the time of the catastrophe. I was obliged to admit that I had made one to myself, though not aloud. It was this. I was thinking about the Falls, and I said to myself, "How wonderful it is to see that vast body of water tumble down there!" Then in an instant a bright thought flashed into my head, and I let it fly, saying, "It would be a deal more wonderful to see it tumble up there!" -- and I was just about to kill myself with laughing at it when all nature broke loose in war and death and I had to flee for my life. "There," she said, with triumph, "that is just it; the Serpent mentioned that very jest, and called it the First Chestnut, and said it was coeval with the creation." Alas, I am indeed to blame. Would that I were not witty; oh, would that I had never had that radiant thought!

NEXT YEAR -- We have named it Cain. She caught it while I was up country trapping on the North Shore of the Erie; caught it in the timber a couple of miles from our dug-out -- or it might have been four, she isn't certain which. It resembles us in some ways, and may be a relation. That is what she thinks, but this is an error, in my judgment. The difference in size warrants the conclusion that it is a different and new kind of animal -- a fish, perhaps, though when I put it in the water to see, it sank, and she plunged in and snatched it out before there was opportunity for the experiment to determine the matter. I still think it is a fish, but she is indifferent about what it is, and will not let me have it to try. I do not understand this. The coming of the creature seems to have changed her whole nature and made her unreasonable about experiments. She thinks more of it than she does of any of the other animals, but is not able to explain why. Her mind is disordered -- everything shows it. Sometimes she carries the fish in her arms half the night when it complains and wants to get to the water. At such times the water comes out of the places in her face that she looks out of, and she pats the fish on the back and makes soft sounds with her mouth to soothe it, and betrays sorrow and solicitude in a hundred ways. I have never seen her do like this with any other fish, and it troubles me greatly. She used to carry the young tigers around so, and play with them, before we lost our property, but it was only play; she never took on about them like this when their dinner disagreed with them.

SUNDAY -- She doesn't work, Sundays, but lies around all tired out, and likes to have the fish wallow over her; and she makes fool noises to amuse it, and pretends to chew its paws, and that makes it laugh. I have not seen a fish before that could laugh. This makes me doubt. ... I have come to like Sunday myself. Superintending all the week tires a body so. There ought to be more Sundays. In the old days they were tough, but now they come in handy.

WEDNESDAY -- It isn't a fish. I cannot quite make out what it is. It makes curious devilish noises when not satisfied, and says "goo-goo" when it is. It is not one of us, for it doesn't walk; it is not a bird, for it doesn't fly; it is not a frog, for it doesn't hop; it is not a snake, for it doesn't crawl; I feel sure it is not a fish, though I cannot get a chance to find out whether it can swim or not. It merely lies around, and mostly on its back, with its feet up. I have not seen any other animal do that before. I said I believed it was an enigma; but she only admired the word without understanding it. In my judgment it is either an enigma or some kind of a bug. If it dies, I will take it apart and see what its arrangements are. I never had a thing perplex me so.

THREE MONTHS LATER -- The perplexity merely augments instead of diminishing. I sleep but little. It has ceased from lying around, and goes about on its four legs, now. Yet it differs from the other four-legged animals, in that its front legs are unusually short, consequently this causes the main part of its person to stick up uncomfortably high in the air, and this is not attractive. It is built much as we are, but its method of traveling shows that it is not of our breed. The short front legs and long hind ones indicate that it is of the kangaroo family, but it is a marked variation of the species, since the true kangaroo hops, whereas this one never does. Still it is a curious and interesting variety, and has not been catalogued before. As I discovered it, I have felt justified in securing credit of the discovery by attaching my name to it, and hence have called it <u>Kangaroorum Adamiensis</u>. . . . It must have been a young one when it came, for it has grown exceedingly since. It must be five times as big, now, as it was then, and when discontented is able to make from twenty-two to thirty-eight times the noise it made at first. Coercion does not modify this, but has the contrary effect. For this reason I discontinued the system. She reconciled it by persuasion, and by giving it things which she had told it she wouldn't give it before. As observed previously, I was not at home when it first came, and she told me she found it in the woods. It seems odd that it should be the only one, yet it must be so, for I have worn myself out these many weeks trying to find another one to add to my collection, and for this one to play with; for surely then it would be quieter and we could tame it more easily. But I find none, nor any vestige of any; and strangest of all, no tracks. It has to live on the ground, it cannot help itself; therefore, how does it get about without leaving a track? I have set a dozen traps, but they do no good. I catch all small animals except that one; animals that merely go into the trap out of curiosity, I think, to see what the milk is there for. They never drink it.

THREE MONTHS LATER -- The Kangaroo still continues to grow, which is very strange and perplexing. I never knew one to be so long getting its growth. It has fur on its head now; not like kangaroo fur, but exactly like our hair except that it is much finer and softer, and instead of being black is red. I am like to lose my mind over the capricious and harassing developments of this unclassifiable zoological freak. If I could catch another one -- but that is hopeless; it is a new variety, and the only sample; this is plain. But I caught a true kangaroo and brought it in, thinking that this one, being lonesome, would rather have that for company than have no kin at all, or any animal it could feel a nearness to or get sympathy from in its forlorn condition here among strangers who do not know its ways or habits, or what to do to make it feel that it is among friends; but it was a mistake -- it went into such fits at the sight of the kangaroo that I was convinced it had never seen one before. I pity the poor noisy little animal, but there is nothing I can do to make it happy. If I could tame it -- but that is out of the question; the more I try the worse I seem to make it. It grieves me to the heart to see it in its little storms of sorrow and passion. I wanted to let it go, but she wouldn't hear of it. That seemed cruel and not like her; and yet she may be right. It might be lonelier than ever; for since I cannot find another one, how could it?

FIVE MONTHS LATER -- It is not a kangaroo. No, for it supports itself by holding to her finger, and thus goes a few steps on its hind legs, and then falls down. It is probably some kind of a bear; and yet it has no tail -- as yet -- and no fur, except on its head. It still keeps on growing -- that is a curious circumstance, for bears get their growth earlier than this. Bears are dangerous -- since our catastrophe -- and I shall not be satisfied to have this one prowling about the place much longer without a muzzle on. I have offered to get her a kangaroo if she would let this one go, but it did no good -- she is determined to run us into all sorts of foolish risks, I think. She was not like this before she lost her mind.

A FORTNIGHT LATER -- I examined its mouth. There is no danger yet; it has only one tooth. It has no tail yet. It makes more noise now than it ever did before -- and mainly at night. I have moved out. But I shall go over, mornings, to breakfast, and to see if it has more teeth. If it gets a mouthful of teeth it will be time for it to go, tail or no tail, for a bear does not need a tail in order to be dangerous.

FOUR MONTHS LATER -- I have been off hunting and fishing a month, up in the region that she calls Buffalo; I don't know why, unless it is because there are not any buffalos there. Meantime the bear has learned to paddle around all by itself on its hind legs, and says "poppa" and "momma." It is certainly a new species. This resemblance to words may be purely accidental, of course, and may have no purpose of meaning; but even in that case it is still extraordinary, and is a thing which no other bear can do. This imitation of speech, taken together with general absence of fur and entire absence of tail, sufficiently indicates that this is a new kind of bear. The further study of it will be exceedingly interesting. Meantime I will go off on a far expedition among the forests of the north and make an exhaustive search. There must certainly be another one somewhere, and this one will be less dangerous when it has company of its own species. I will go straightway; but I will muzzle this one first.

THREE MONTHS LATER -- It has been a weary, weary hunt, yet I have had no success. In the meantime, without stirring from the home-estate, she has caught another one! I never saw such luck. I might have hunted these woods a hundred years, I never would have run across that thing.

NEXT DAY -- I have been comparing the new one with the old one, and it is perfectly plain that they are the same breed. I was going to stuff one of them for my collection, but she is prejudiced against it for some reason or other; so I have relinquished the idea, though I think it is a mistake. It would be an irreparable loss to science if they should get away. The old one is tamer than it was, and can laugh and talk like the parrot, having learned this, no doubt, from being with the parrot so much, and having the imitative faculty in a highly developed degree. I shall be astonished if it turns out to be a new kind of parrot; and yet I ought not to be astonished, for it has already been everything else it could think of, since those first days when it was fish. The new one is as ugly now as the old one was at first; has the same sulphur-and-raw-meat complexion and the same singular head without any fur on it. She calls it Abel.

TEN YEARS LATER -- They are boys; we found it out long ago. It was their coming in that small, immature shape that fooled us; we were not used to it. There are some girls now. Abel is a good boy, but if Cain had stayed a bear it would have improved him. After all these years, I see that I was mistaken about Eve in the beginning; it is better to live outside the Garden with her than inside it without her. At first I thought she talked too much; but now I should be sorry to have that voice fall silent and pass out of my life. Blessed be the chestnut that brought us near together and taught me to know the goodness of her heart and the sweetness of her spirit!

THE TAILOR AND THE FALLS

Probably more words have been written about Niagara Falls by more people than any other single spot in the United States. Some of it is truly inspired; most of it is mediocre. Of the thousands of words written and spoken nothing is perhaps more apt than the immortal words of an unknown tailor who said as he looked at the falling waters, "Gods! What a place to sponge a coat!"

CAVE OF THE WINDS AND A BREATH OF WHISKEY
Tyrone Power, "Impressions of America"

"Och, blur an' 'oon! Mr. Power, sure it's not yer honour that's come all this way from home!"

An explanation took place; when I found that our guide, whom I had seen some two years before as a helper in the stable of my hospitable friend, Smith Barry, at Foaty, was this summer promoted to the office of "Conductor," as he styled himself, under the waterfall.

And a most whimsical "conductor" he proved. His cautions and "divil a fears!" and "not a hap'orth of danger!" must have been mighty assuring to the timid or nervous, if any such ever make this experiment, which, although perfectly safe, is not a little startling.

His directions -- when we arrived at the point where the mist, pent in beneath the overhanging rock, makes it impossible to distinguish anything, and where the rush of air is so violent as to render respiration for a few seconds almost impracticable -- were inimitable.

"Now, yer honour!' he shouted in my ear -- for we moved to the Indian file -- "whisper the next gintlemen to follow you smart; and, for the love o' God! shoulder the rock close, stoop yer heads, and shut fast yer eyes, or you won't be able to see an inch!"

I repeated my orders verbatim, though the cutting wind made it difficult to open one's mouth.

"Now thin, yer honour," he cried, cowering down as he spoke. "Do as ye see me do; hold yer breath, and scurry after like divils!"

With the last word away he bolted, and was lost to view in an instant. I repeated his instructions however to the next file, and, as directed, scurried after.

This rather difficult point passed, I came upon my countryman waiting for us within the edge of the curve described by this falling ocean; he grasped my wrist firmly as I emerged from the dense drift, and shouted in my ear.

"Luk up, sir, at the green sea that's rowlin' over uz! Murder! bud iv it only was to take shlope in on uz!"

Here we could see and breathe with perfect ease; and even the ludicrous gestures and odd remarks of my poetical countryman could not wholly rob the scene of its striking grandeur.

I next passed beyond my guide as he stood on tiptoe against the rock upon a ledge of which we trod, and under his direction attained that limit beyond which the foot of man never pressed. I sat for one moment on the Termination Rock, and then followed my guide back to my companions, when together we once more "scurried" into day.

"Isn't it illegant, sir?" began the "Conductor" as soon as we were well clear of the mist.

"Isn't it a noble sight intirely? Caps the world for grandness any way that's sartain!"

I need hardly say that in this opinion we all joined loudly. But Mr. Conductor was not yet done with us -- he had now to give us a taste of his "larnin."

"I wish ye'd take notice, sir," said he, pointing across the river with an air of authority and a look of infinite wisdom. "Only take a luk at the falls, an' you'll see that Shakespeare is out altogether about the discription."

"How's that, Pat?" inquired I, although not a little taken aback by the authority so gravely quoted by my critical friend. "Why, sir, Shakespeare first of all says that there's two falls; now, ye may see wid yer own eyes that it's one river sure, and one fall, only for the shtrip o' rock that make two of id."

This I admitted was evident; whilst Pat gravely went on:

"Thin agin, only luk here, sir; Shakespeare says, 'The cloud-cap tower' why, if he'd ever taken the trouble to luk at it, he'd seen better than that; an' if he wasn't a fool, -- which I'm sure he wasn't, being a grad poet, -- he'd know that the clouds never can rise to cap the tower, by reason that it stands up above the fall, and that the current forever sets down."

Again I agreed with him, excusing Shakespeare's discrepancies on the score of his never having had a proper guide to explain these matters.

"I don't know who at all showed him the place," gravely responded Pat. "But it's my belief he never was in id at all at all, though the gintleman that told me a heap more about it swears for sartin that he was."

This last remark, and the important air with which the doubt was conveyed, proved too much for my reasonable faculties, already suffering some constraint, and I fairly roared out in concert with my companion, who had been for some time convulsed with laughter.

Whoever first instructed the "Conductor" on this point of critical history deserves well of the visitors so long as the present subject remains here to communicate the knowledge. Indeed, I trust, before he is drowned in the Niagara, or burnt up with the whisky required, as he says, "to keep the cold out of the shtomach," the present possessor of this curiosity in literature will bequeath it to his successor, so that it may be handed down in its integrity to all future visitors.

AT NIAGARA FALLS

At Niagara Falls some just crossed the bridge back and forth. All they really wanted was to get to the other side. . . . with a bit of the "creature" (whiskey) snuggled in their clothes. Or was it smuggled in their clothes?

HOLY WATER AND WHISKEY

Another Irish woman crossed the Niagara Gorge border with a bottle of whiskey hid in her valise. When she reached the customs inspector he asked what was in the bottle. She replied "Holy Water." "Be good enough to open it up," said he. She unscrewed the cap and he touched a drop of it to his tongue. "That's whiskey," he exclaimed in amazement. "Glory be to God," said the Connemara woman, " A miracle already."

A WHISKEY SMUGGLER

I once tried to talk temperance to a washer-woman whom I detected smuggling whiskey in flat bottles, and who was "half seas over," but she insisted that when she had to work so hard a quart of whiskey made her stronger!

"Stronger!" said I, "I should think not, you can hardly walk straight now! It makes you weaker!"

"An' faith, now! Is it ye's sayin'? An' doesn't it make my breath stronger? An' mus'n't ye brathe strong if ye's workin' at all, at all?"

"But it will kill you to drink so much whiskey," I replied.

"An' if it does, then I shan't have to kill meself a workin' to get me livin'! Ye see I ain't much valye meself, anyway."

"But, madam, it is against the law for anyone to bring whiskey from Canada in this way, as I've told you before this!"

"An' sure it's not that, now, you'll make me be after belavin'! Fur hasn't meself the right to bring me own clothing, and whatever is in me own pocket, for me own use, without bein' stopped by a dacent man like yourself, now!"

"Well, madam, I have taken you to the lady examiner and found you smuggling bottles of whiskey too many times to overlook it much longer."

"Indade it's your own fault that you have found it! An' it's no country at all, at all, if we haven't the liberty of our own pockets!"

THE GHOST OF LOCK HERKIMER

Wherever the Irish have made their home, loveable little leprechauns and garrulous gangling ghosts have joined them. When the Irish moved from the Isle, they brought Irish spirits (ethereal as well as liquid) with them. Disbelievers over the years have, of course, come to doubt the strange and wonderful Irish world of crying banshees and wispy ectoplasm, but never, God bless them, have the Irish been disbelievers. It's all very simple. They believe because they've seen. And they've seen because they have the "power." Anyone ought to be able to understand that without too much trouble.

When the Irish came to the new world to help dig the Erie Canal, they naturally brought the light-footed inhabitants of the nether region with them because they knew the little men would come anyway. As they dug the Canal, as they piled stone upon stone for the lock walls and scooped out mud from the ditch for berm bank and towpath, they built and buried their pixies into the Canal with loving care. Along with the Irish imagination, York State soil proved rich for such a planting. The ghosts of Erin Isle had found a snug home on the Erie Canal. "Bogs is bogs," they used to say to those who could understand ghost language.

Only the Irish diggers knew exactly where their invisible friends were buried. And only Paddys knew how to get them out

234

and at what hours they would come out without asking for help. Under certain auguries (and especially for non-believers) the Irish talked rather freely about their non-terrestrial friends. Much of the Erie Canal folklore therefore has grown up around the Irish.

Unfortunately, your Irish friends today will probably not be much help in introducing you to too many (if any) of these Canal ghosts. Most of the modern Irish seem to have lost the "gift." Distance in miles and years in time from the "auld sod" have decreased the power of the "power." Some have, alas, listened too long to the disbelievers of the new world. Those who still know of such things claim that the Canal ghosts are getting restless. Sealed tomblike for long years in stone and dirt with no exercise has not, to say the least, kept them in the best of spirits.

The present anemic ghost "power" would have been a disgrace in the old days. In the Grand Years of the Grand Canal -- (the "Old Ditch" as well as the improved) -- the "Grand" Irish had the power in full amperage. There were giants in those days, to coin a phrase. Among them was a driver boy. Nothing then, and it must be admitted today, is more Irish than an O'Brien, unless, of course, it is an Erie Canal Irishman named O'Brien. John O'Brien was such a man: he had the power. He knew all about ghosts -- canal and general variety as well. He had a first name talking acquaintance with most of the Canal ghosts; leastwise, the most interesting.

When there were no genuine ghosts around, that is, when they were busy haunting (they referred to it as "visiting other places") John O'Brien and the other drivers "jured" some up. New boys on the path got the full treatment. A favorite haunt for such activities was the swamp near Rome. Whenever they tied up there for the night, the old hands made for the marsh and the new boy or boys tagged along.

They gathered swamp wood, piled it, set it afire, sat circled about it and started telling ghost stories. The long orange fingers of the fire painted strange figures, gave form and substance to dancing shadows and touched gnarled trees with life and movement (to be sure, of a ghost-like quality). As the fire grew tired, content just to glow, the shadows began to hide behind the trees, to soften and melt back into the bushes, the trees, and the cat-o'-ninetails. Meantime, the Irish driver boys talked of their easy acquaintance with Canal ghosts -- the good ghosts, of course, hinting there were bad ghosts, also, too frightening to talk about.

At the proper moment, however, John O'Brien would start ever so slowly to tell the weird and horrible story of the swamp ghost. So terrible was this creature from the bogs, John emphasized, that the sight of him would turn every hair on the head of the beholder snow white, and the scream that tore itself deep from the throat of the victim on the sight of the ghost would be the last human sound he would ever make. As the new driver boy sat stiff and white with fear, the older boys would slip away one by one. As

John told the story, eerie sounds and weird movements came at precisely the right time from the dark edge of the firelight. The climax of the story would be accompanied by a moan which issued forth from the woods. With that, a white shape would float up from the swamp in full sight of the scared driver. With a Yess!!! the driver boy would run for the boat, head down, eyes shut, mouth open.

But the ghost story John O'Brien and his wife Alice liked best to tell their niece in later years was the tale of the Herkimer locktender and his wife. There was nothing lighthearted about this canal story. It seems that a locktender near Herkimer loved his wife very deeply. And well he might have, for a prettier lass would have been hard to find anyplace along the Canal from Waterford to Buffalo. As the tender "tended" business, his beautiful wife would pass the time of day in woman's talk with Canal cooks and wives. Every boat that passed through carried news along with its regular paying cargo, for in these years the Erie was the busiest trade route in America. Through it passed the wealth and resources of America -- the world's young giant. On its waters, through its valleys, the old world moved into the new to build a modern nation in a wilderness. Locktenders needed no special qualifications beyond a strong back and the ability to guess right on Election Day. If they guessed wrong, they were out of a job. If they were right, they were sure of a job for about seven months or as long as their politics were in good order. Their job was fairly simple. When they saw a boat coming, they leaned their back against the gate and shoved. The tenders stayed in a shanty 10' x 10'. The state provided lodging for the locktender and his family in a lock house generally in full view of the incoming boats.

The locktender's wife found fun in talking to the captains, especially the young ones. They generally looked her way when they could safely steal a glance. As the days passed, the locktender husband, sharply jealous to begin with, could no longer stand to see his wife looking at other men, let alone talking to them. Unable to bear it longer, he finally made his wife a prisoner in their own house.

One night when he went to her room he found her packing her clothes. Convinced that she was running away with the young captain whose boat was tied up just below the lock, rage filled his mind and blinded his reasoning. His body seemed almost possessed. Madness streamed from his eyes. He picked up the iron poker from the floor and brought it down on her head, blow after blow. Caught in the grip of compulsion and terror, he dragged the smashed body of his wife to the lock wall, attached some stones and dumped her into the lock. Slowly the madness left him. He felt drained. He watched the body sink below the surface. A semblance of reason returned. For a moment he thought he saw the body move by itself toward the edge of the wall under the water. But no, the light was fading and his mind was playing tricks on him. In panic, he stumbled back from the lock and ran for the door of his house. Quickly, awkwardly, he tried to sop up the pool of blood, but it had already stained deep into the soft wood. Blood had splattered about the room and on his clothes. Finger lines of blood were streaked down his front where his wife, in desperation, had grabbed at him to ward off the blows. He looked about crazily, then dashed for the door. He ran right into the arms of several men who had heard the screams of the murdered woman. The sight of the blood, the wrecked room, his disheveled appearance, and the telltale poker with a blood-matted clot of hair stuck to the end told a very convincing story. A bloody trail led to the edge of the lock.

"Go get the constable," said one of the men. "We'll start walking him down toward the village."

"Wait 'til morning, we'll drag for the body when it's light."

They marched the locktender off to jail, and in due time justice had its way. But, strangely, the body was never found.

The day following the murder, a new man took over the lock duties. All day long he listened to stories about the murder. That night he felt considerably uneasy about going to bed in a murder room still smelling of fresh blood. Nevertheless, he slept soundly. The next night, knowing they had not found the body, he found himself more upset. That night his sleep was not undisturbed. He dreamt that the murdered woman had come for dry clothes and had laid down in the bed to rest. He awoke in a cold sweat.

He sat up bolt straight. When he knew it was only a dream, he sank back into the bed, weak but relaxed. Then by habit, he stretched out his arms and yawned. At the same time, his arm fell naturally over onto the pillow next to him. It felt wet. He stiffened. He turned quickly. It was wet. And there was the shape of a head on the pillow.

Panic seized him. Then slowly, his reason began to take over again. Perhaps, he thought, he had rolled over on the pillow during the night. Feeling better, he swung his feet out over the edge of the bed and again, by habit, scratched himself and rubbed his face. His face felt funny. He looked at his hands as he took them down from his face. Long strands of wet hair hung from his fingers. With a yell, he ran from the house. When he had gushed out his story, the men around the Canal only laughed at him. Most canawlers felt locktenders were a bit tetched anyway. Perhaps it all had been his imagination. With their laughs ringing in his ears, he went back to his work. That night, he placed a wood brace across the door, made sure the windows were secure, took several shots of whiskey, went to bed and eventually, to sleep. Again, he had the same terrifying dream. It woke him. He was almost too afraid to feel the pillow beside him or to touch his face. Slowly, paralyzed with panic, he inched his hand over to the pillow. It was wet. He scraped at his face, long hairs clung to his cheek. The last the boatmen saw of the locktender he was running west along the Canal.

In a few days a new man took over the job. He, too, knew the story of the murder and the ghost. His mind preyed on the story. The next morning he came screaming out of the house saying he had seen the ghost of the lock. A captain grabbed him, shook the fear out of him and sat him down. But all he would do was blubber out the same story, the dream, the wet spot on the pillow and the long hairs on his face. If they wanted him to stay on the job they would have to build him a new house. Finally, to humor him and to avoid the difficulty of getting a replacement, they built a new locktender house. Never again did the ghost visit the house.

"How can people believe in ghosts, Uncle John?" little Shirley would ask at the end of the story.

"Well, child," John O'Brien would say to her, "perhaps you can't, but when a body spends a lifetime on or near the water, in the wheel house, standing on the bow, on the towpath or on a lock wall, listening to the rhythm of the water, peering into the dark, seeing pin points of light streaking out of the black marking channels and boats that can't be seen, feeling loneliness sink deep into his bones, then it's not hard to believe in other things you can't see. Especially," he would add with an Irish grin, "if you have the power."

WHISKEY AND THE GHOST

In the early days of settlement, when transportation costs were high, grain was too bulky to be shipped to market and was therefore turned into whiskey, much of which was consumed on the spot. There is a local story about a farmer's wife who tried to cure her husband of excessive drinking by accosting him one night wrapped in a sheet. But he met the situation with a drunken calm, addressing the ghost thus: "If you 're a good spirit, you'll do me no harm; if you're the devil, as I suspect, I've married into your family, and as you're much too much of a gentleman to injure a relative, I fear no danger from the quarter; so I pass."

SWAMP WATER AND GALLINIPPERS

This night I found it impossible to look in upon the cabin. I therefore made a request to the captain that I might be permitted to have a mattress on deck; but this, he told me, could not be. There was an existing regulation which positively forbade sleeping upon the deck of a canal packet. Indeed, he assured me that this could only be done at the peril of life, with the certainty of catching fever and ague. I appeared to submit to his well-meant arguments but inwardly resolved, coute-qui-coute, not to sleep within the den below, which exhibited a scene of suffocation and its consequences that defies description.

I got my cloak up, filled my hat with cigars, and planting myself about the center of the deck, here resolved, malgre dews and mosquitoes, to weather it through the night.

"What is the name of this country we are now passing?" I inquired of one of the boatmen who joined me about the first hour of the morning.

"Why, sir, this is called the Cedar Swamp," answered the man, to whom I handed a cigar in order to retain his society and create more smoke, weak as was the defense against the hungry swarms surrounding us on all sides.

"We have not much more of this Cedar Swamp to get through, I hope?" inquired I, seeking for some consolatory information.

"About fifty miles more, I guess," was the reply of my companion, accompanying each word with a sharp slap on the back of his head, or on his cheek or forehead.

"Thank Heaven!" I involuntarily exclaimed, drawing my cloak closer about me, although the heat was killing. "We shall after that escape in some sort, I hope, from these legions of mosquitoes?"

"I guess not quite," replied the man. "They are as thick, if not thicker, in the Long Swamp."

"The Long Swamp!" I repeated. "What a horrible name for a country! Does the canal run far through it?"

"No, not so very far, only about eighty miles."

"We're then done with swamps, I hope, my friends?" I inquired, as he kept puffing and slapping with unwearied constancy.

"Why, yes, there's not a heap more swamp, that is to say, not close to the line, till we come to within forty miles of Utica."

"And is that one as much infested with these infernal insects as are the Cedar and Long Swamps?"

"I guess that is the place above all for mosquitoes," replied the man grinning. "Them's the real gallinippers, emigrating north for the summer all the way from the Balize and Red River. Let a man go to sleep with his head in a cast-iron kettle among them chaps, and if their bills don't make a watering pot of it before

239

morning, I'm d----d. They're strong enough to lift the boat out of the canal, if they could only get underneath her."

I found these swamps endless as Banquo's line "would they had been shadows only, but alas! they were yet to be encountered, horrible realities not to be evaded." I closed my eyes in absolute fear, and forbore further inquiry.

Here I remained throughout the whole night, dozing a little between whiles, but never forgoing my cigar for a minute. Toward daylight the dew descended like rain, but brought with it no coolness to earth or man. It felt exactly as though it had been boiled the day before, and had not been left long enough to get cool.

During this day many of our men frequently threw themselves overboard, clothes and all on; that is, in shirt and trousers, these being all of habiliment that could be worn. I really feared that some of them who had been a little too free in their cold applications, that is, of iced water and brandy, would have gone mad.

This blessing of ice we were seldom many hours without, the poorest hovel on the canal being commonly provided with it in sufficient abundance to give us a supply. The inhabitants, I found, were suffering from the unusual continuance of heat as much as strangers. At night they built huge fires of pine before their doors so that the thick smoke might penetrate the dwelling and scour the infernal mosquitoes out of it. At these fires we would find the poor women sitting in the smoke at the risk of suffocation: pale, haggard, with their hair neglected and dishevelled, looking like worn-out ghosts rather than living beings. The oldest inhabitants on the line of the canal assured us they never remembered any heat of three days' continuance which could compare to this; and I believe them, since no man could long endure such a visitation.

This evening our condition was in no way improved, except that we heard the sound and felt the presence of a strong current of northerly wind. But it blew as though issuing from a furnace, and afforded no present relief. The sky continued to show "fiery off," and the mosquitoes of that ilk did credit to the genealogy my informant ascribed to them. But there is a period beyond which even suffering ceases. This happy insensibility I had attained and when after midnight we were landed at Utica, I felt as though I could have slept soundly and well even beneath the heated deck of our canal packet.

BUNIONS, BLISTERS AND BOOTLIKKER

Many of the settlers in the Ontario Country of Canada came originally from Pennsylvania. Like their New York counterparts, they were Pennsylvania Germans or Pennsylvania Dutch. On occasion they would make their way back home for a visit across the Niagara River. After boating across the river, they would travel the rest of the way on foot.

A Dutchman from Canada was on his way back to Pennsylvania for one of his visits when he fell in with a group of Irish canal diggers who were walking from the Erie to the Union Canal. At one tavern, the landlord gave each guest, as he departed, a half-pint of whiskey. The Irishmen drank theirs, but the Dutchman poured the contents of the bottle into his boots. All the Irish became footsore, but the Dutchman walked merrily along, for he was untroubled by bunions, corns, blisters or any of the ills that beset the feet. If living today, I suppose the Dutchman would be Minister of External Affairs for Canada and the Irishmen would be in charge of the Department of Internal Revenue in the United States.

THE DEVIL WORE A CANE AND CRUTCH

How endless the waiting seemed; even when death waited too. Grim-faced men, the youthful and the old peered across the dark water seeing nothing but blackness -- that and moving shadows cast by their uneasy minds. They waited. They were the invaders. What a frightening and formidable name for peaceful farm boys from the north country of York State, from the Mohawk Valley, from villages and towns upstate and downstate and from neighboring states. Many of them had wanted no part of this Niagara invasion. Most of all, they had wanted to get home to their farms and families.

But for them this year there would be no farming. It was October 13, 1812, the beginning of the war that would forever bear that year's name. Although history had not yet decided to call it the War of 1812, American patriots referred to it as the "Second War of Independence." Some politicians bitterly denounced it as "Mr. Madison's War." Canadians fighting for their land and feeling the first glow of nationalism described it as a "War of Survival." To the militia men, however, it didn't matter much what anyone called it. It was still war. That they knew, and they now stood on the American shore waiting for the signal to enter the small boats hidden beneath the thick brambly underbrush that edged the Niagara River. They were ready to move; some even eager. Since they were here to fight, they were all for getting the fight started and over with. They, like the armies of all ages, feared the waiting more than the fighting.

Across the river lay Canada -- now enemy country. Beneath the sharp Niagara escarpment lay the Queen's Town, shortened in usage to Queenston. Above it were the Heights where the dramatic battle would take place. At Lewiston opposite, on the United States side, the army of invasion stood poised at the bottom of the escarpment. Between the two settlements the Niagara River flowed and eddied, dark and deep toward Lake Ontario. Here, where the River splits the mountain, the waters of Niagara find peace after their turbulent struggle to fight their way through seven miles of narrow rock gorge. Smoothly, the water glides into the open lands, leaving behind the roaring sounds of the lower rapids bouncing against the steep stone cliffs. In fifty thousand years, according to some geologists, Niagara Falls has cut this canyon 275 feet deep at this point and at lesser heights back to the present site of the Falls. Atop this escarpment, high above the heads of the men, Niagara Falls had been born. From here, it had eaten its way back through the hard Lockport dolomite and Medina red sandstone.

At the moment, however, there was no place in their thinking or feeling for contemplating the Falls and gorge of Niagara. The men were filled only with the gnawing emptiness of fear. They scuffed their feet against the loose stones. In front of them the invasion boats tugged nervously at their lines as if they, too, were tired of waiting.

One man alone could end the waiting. His name was General Stephen Van Rensselaer, scion of the Hudson Valley patroons. On him rested the awful decision of invasion. The demoralizing delay had been caused not by his indecision, but by the infamous treachery of a river pilot. Earlier it had been discovered that the pilot in charge of the crossing had apparently turned traitor, cut the invasion boats loose and presumably escaped to Canada. Questions of doubt, that had not entered Van Rensselaer's mind originally, now shook his confidence: How much did the Canadians know now about his plans? Only with surprise could the Americans hope for a gambler's chance of success. Otherwise, the operation, conceived in complete violation of almost all accepted military principles, could prove tragically disastrous. Eventually, however, Van Rensselaer, in his own conscience, resolved his fears and decided to go ahead according to plan. Fortunately, the General had in the meantime bolstered his confidence by securing the valuable services of the loyal Cooke brothers, Lemuel and Lothrop, of Lewiston.

A long decade before, these two pioneers had built the first log cabin in Lewiston not far from the present invasion encampment. Later, while his brother Lemuel bought land east of the village of Lewiston, Lothrop, hearing of cheaper land across the river, bought a section of it in Canada. The war found him in enemy territory. Refusing to swear allegiance to the English King, Lothrop and his family escaped forty miles across the Lake and up the river to Lewiston. Not many people knew the river and the land that held it better than the Cookes. Few, if any, loved it more. The General knew he could depend on the Cooke brothers.

With the boats ready, the men anxious, and the pilots on hand, the General gave the signal. In the darkness, the men quietly entered the boats. The first into the river carried the Cookes and Colonel Solomon Van Rensselaer, kin of the General, and in charge of the beachhead operation.

To assault and dislodge a determined enemy securely entrenched atop a 275-foot cliff required courage and agility. Rather than risk a deadly frontal attack, Van Rensselaer planned a flanking movement that followed the fisherman's path to Queenston Heights. Slowly, the pilots picked their way by sound and feel across the river. They took fifteen minutes before they touched land. At the very instant Colonel Van Rensselaer stepped ashore a volley of shots cut him down. He was struck four times. Lothrop tried to grab him and get him into the boat. As he did so, his foot slipped on a stone and he fell against a jagged rock which tore a deep wound in the fleshy part of his leg. Still he managed to pull the colonel into the boat. Soon he had the colonel safely back on the American side.

244

Giving no thought to his own wound, Cooke continued ferrying men across the river as fast as he could make the round trip. Despite the heavy Canadian fire, the Americans succeeded in establishing a beachhead. They fought their way up the path to the Canadian entrenchment on the heights.

With the heights secured, the General called for reinforcements to meet the anticipated counter-attack. On his next trip back, Lothrop carried the order to an American major in charge of the second wave. Incredibly, at the moment of apparent victory, the major refused to order his men across. Abandoned on top of the escarpment, the American men, faced with armies under Brock, McDonnell and Sheaffe, surrendered. Half a thousand Americans were taken. The Battle of Queenston Heights was over. Born ignominiously in treachery, it ended in treachery. America's first invasion attempt had failed.

Many battles later, the war ended. For most, memories of the river crossing dimmed. Lothrop had cause not to forget the tragic morning of battle. Intent on his ferrying work that morning, Lothrop Cooke had neglected to have his wound treated. Finally in exhaustion he turned for medical attention. It was too late. Infection had set in deeply. Only amputation could save his life. With several stiff swigs of whiskey to ease the pain, and a lead ball between his teeth to bite on, he watched the medics saw off his leg. Lothrop lived through the ordeal, but it was months before the shock and weakness left him.

Over the years following the war, his tall, powerful, six-foot figure became familiar and respected on the Niagara Frontier as he moved about on a leg, a cane and a crutch. When the state separated the counties of Erie and Niagara in 1821, Governor DeWitt Clinton appointed Lothrop Cooke Sheriff of Niagara County. He served in that official capacity and, later, as Deputy Sheriff. Peaceful citizens loved, and lawbreakers feared, "Ole Cane and Crutch." He soon came to personify law and order. Day by day Cooke performed the duties of his office.

One of those days he experienced a delicious and ironic twist of history that happens only infrequently in a man's lifetime. For some time, a despicable character had been abusing his neighbors by poisoning their horses and oxen.

With a warrant in hand, Lothrop set out to bring him in. He found his man hoeing in his field close to the fence where the road ran. Riding up close to him, Cooke engaged him in idle but disarming conversation. He knew this man always carried a pistol and never hesitated to use it.

After some minutes of small talk, Cooke, in a voice of surprise and a gesture of direction, exclaimed, "What is that vessel doing so near shore? She will go aground." The farmer looked up quickly. As he did, Cooke leaped from his horse, pushed the man to the ground, drew his pistol and handcuffed him.

As they rode back, Lothrop looked at his prisoner and smiled. He had reason to be pleased. Of all the men he had ever arrested, this man deserved most to be brought to justice. He glanced down at the stump of his leg, he thought of that battle night many years ago, of the dying and the dead. Memory sent a sharp pain through what remained of his leg; disdain dropped from the corners of his lips and hardened his face. He felt slightly nauseous as he looked again at his man. This was the man, the Major of the Militia, who, on that October 13, 1812, had refused to cross the river to reinforce the Americans on the heights. His cowardice in large part had cost America the battle. Cooke, indeed, had reason to be more pleased with that day's work than any other. No days were unexciting for Lothrop Cooke. It was just that some days were more exciting than others.

In the 1820's the tempo of that excitement increased noticeably. Those years saw the coming of the Erie Canal. During the digging, an estimated two thousand laborers, mostly emigrants from Ireland, worked in and around Lockport. Being from the north and south of Ireland, their politics and religion differed. Stimulated by cheap whiskey drunk almost as freely as water (and far safer than some water), the workers, who labored hard twelve hours each day, frequently found themselves in fights in or near the shanties built along the canal bank west of the village. The natives lived in constant fear that the brawling would sometimes spill over into the village.

One day, it did. A full-scale riot broke loose. Several hundred canal workers, fortified on the inside with whiskey and on the outside with sticks and stones and picks and shovels, threatened the villagers. Cooke was called in immediately. "How many men do you need?"

"None whatever," came the quick answer. "You have not enough citizens to make the arrests if they resist, but they will not look on a single one-legged man as a defiance."

Before the staff recovered, Cooke started out the door and on toward the edge of the village where the diggings were located. In slow rhythm, Lothrop swung his huge frame forward on his cane and crutch. Towering like a tall tree with half a trunk, his massive form swayed and moved magically and most untree-like. At a distance, as the rioters came out of the lock basin, the lone figure lumbering across the field toward them seemed grotesque and ridiculous: a "cripple" sent to stop them. They shouted taunts and they belly-laughed as they charged across the field, yelling like banshees and brandishing their picks and shovels. Cooke's tall powerful figure and long limbs grew taller, longer and stronger as the distance closed. The mob began to slow its pace as it looked and wondered. To the superstitious Irish, the dishevelled hair, determined chin, set lips and blazing eyes made the figure less a man and more a demon.

Cooke clutched the warrant in his fist. He worked his cane and crutch like instruments bent on destruction. The leader hesitated. The gang stopped. For a moment, Cooke stood thirty feet away, glaring at his adversary. At that instant he dropped his cane and crutch, swung his arms over his head in an arc and lunged forward. With three prodigious leaps on his one powerful leg, Cooke, all six-foot-five of him, landed on top of the bug-eyed leader. In terror, he had stumbled and fallen as he started to run. Cooke pinned him to the ground with his stump. Screaming for mercy, the gang leader called out to his men, "Run, run, the devil with one leg is after me."

Turning to the huge form over him, he cried, "I surrender, I surrender." Cooke's face softened and he said, "Send the rioters back to work and I'll tear up the warrant."

The man looked up and said "Sheriff, you are a brave and kind man. I will do it."

The villagers always remembered that day. Lothrop Cooke became a legend among them. And the Irish story tellers, too, with their fine sense of delightful exaggeration never forgot the day the devil came on a cane and a crutch and just one leg to chase the canal diggers back to their diggings.

ADIRONDACK STORIES

What did the big canawlers tell the little canawlers at night? Well, they told them stories of the Canal, of course. But sometimes, as they drifted along beside the Mohawk through the forest lands and watched on a clear night the Adirondacks climb northward to the St. Lawrence, they told stories about hunters. One hunter in particular. Maybe James Fenimore Cooper heard these tales, too . . . .

Over the years, the Adirondack Region of New York State has claimed to be the coveted habitat to some of the greatest hunters east of the Mississippi River. Of all white men, Nat Foster was probably the greatest hunter of all. Many claim, with good evidence, that Nat Foster was the Natty Bumpo of James Fenimore Cooper's Leatherstocking Tales.

According to Harold Thompson, New York State's greatest folklorist, Nat Foster appeared in 1787 at St. Johnsville on the Mohawk "to celebrate Independence Day, clad in buckskin . . . claiming he had come a long distance and that his name was Leatherstocking." (This was 26 years before the first of Cooper's Leatherstocking Tales appeared). Rev. A. L. Byron Curtiss who wrote an enchanting biography called Life and Adventures of Nat Foster, Trapper and Hunter of the Adirondacks in 1897 feels that Cooper knew Nat Foster. Certainly, some of Foster's exploits appear in Cooper's works, thinly disguised.

For 30 years, Nat lived on a 150-acre farm at Salisbury, Herkimer County, on the edge of the Adirondack Forest a few miles northeast of Little Falls, a village on the Mohawk River-Erie Canal waterway. Here in spring and summer, he farmed. Come autumn and winter, he hunted and trapped north through the Adirondacks to the St. Lawrence River. According to Jeptha R. Simms, author of Trappers of New York (1850) and the aforementioned Byron Curtiss, Foster killed more deer, bear, wolves and panthers than any other white man in the history of York State.

From such exploits is folklore born. It is said and written that Nat Foster in one season killed twenty-five wolves, seventy-five or seventy-six deer and, with the aid of several assistants, set 300 to 400 muskrat traps. In three seasons, he killed ninety-six bear and a number of panthers. Nat Foster firmly believed these "varmits" had to be killed to make the frontier safe. He also collected a handsome bounty for some identifying part of the dead critter.

It would not have been so bad if Foster had limited his hunting to animals, but he didn't. For good reasons, he hated the Indians and for equally good reasons, they hated him.

Foster vowed bloody vengeance against all Native Americans. In turn, they tried to kill him.

They did not succeed. Foster died of natural causes on March 16, 1840, at Ava, New York, not far from where the Mohawk rises. He has been enshrined as a York State folklore character.

Charles Atwell, a son of the Adirondacks who lived near Foster's home, collaborated with me in writing these two stories.

Apart from the Canal, the Adirondacks region has a folklore of its own. So, even as the Canal was making its own folklore, it was traveling through country rich in folklore.

Here are two stories, among many, of Nat Foster, the hunter-extraordinaire.

THE BUCKSKIN RIFLEMAN

The peaceful countryside near the little York State town of Mannheim was the scene of noisy activity. For nearly two months now the talk of war with Britain had been as common a topic as the weather and the approaching harvest; and today, soldiers had come swinging up the old turnpike -- soldiers from the Carolinas, on their way to Canada.

Captain Benjamin Forsyth, commanding, had spotted a wide clearing along the bank of West Canada Creek and with a wave of his hand had turned his men off the turnpike. It was an ideal place, and a night's camp here would give the men a much needed rest and an opportunity to bathe in the creek and to wash their clothes in the sparkling water.

Although dust-stained and weary, the military bearing of these troops was imposing. They went about the routine business of making camp with a smartness and precision that spoke well of their training. Sharp commands mingled with the metallic clatter of equipment. A scattering crowd of curious townsmen gathered to watch.

One, bolder than the rest, approached a stand of stacked rifles and examined them with interest. Shorter than the average hunter's flintlock, these guns were a product of the Harper's Ferry Arsenal. All rifled and with a heavy barrel they were, in the hands of a marksman, even deadlier a weapon than the far-famed Ferguson rifles once used by the British. Seeing soldiers equipped with such rifles amazed the York State man and, though taciturn by habit, he could not resist a question.

"Is the gov'mint," he asked, "givin' these guns to ever' man that jines up?"

A soldier driving tent pegs nearby stopped and looked at him. The answer came in a slow drawl, rich with the twang of the southern mountains. "Not by a dum sight, it ain't! We-uns gets 'em. But we-uns ain't jest ordinary sojers. We-all is riflemen."

"Huh!" The Yorker's grunt was highly skeptical. "Riflemen, eh? I ain't never seen a soldier yet that a good hunter couldn't outshoot!"

A soft voice spoke from just behind the skeptic and the soldier stiffened to attention. "What makes you think we're not hunters?"

It was Captain Forsyth speaking. He motioned the soldier at ease with a nod and, without waiting for an answer to his question continued, "Almost every man here has hunted the Car'lina hills since he was old enough to carry a rifle! We're not soldiers by profession. We're only soldiers from necessity."

The tanned face of the York Stater still wore its skeptical frown. "Well," he said, "I remember t'other war. Soldiers that come through here then was 'bout as handy with a musket as a cow would be -- and slow to boot."

"That was some thirty years ago," Forsyth said. "Times have changed!" He reached for one of the rifles and handed it to the townsman. "This doesn't look much like the muskets they used in '76 now, does it?"

The townsman examined the rifle closely. When his curiosity had been satisfied, he looked up. He said admiringly, "That's a right smart rifle but it need a right smart man behind it to make 'er talk the way she could talk." He grinned. "I ain't seen nobody here that looks like he could do it! All them fancy uniforms and sech -- they're purty but they don't make a man a shot!"

Forsyth frowned slightly. "Our riflemen are the pick of the Car'linas, suh," he said flatly. He pointed to a soldier nearby, a man seated on a log, cleaning his rifle. "See that man there? His name is Robinson. Some claim he's the best rifle shot in the world. Whether or not that is strictly true, we have no way of knowing, but it is true that so far no man has been able to disprove it!"

The Yankee looked hard at the soldier, then turned back to the Captain. "Best in the world takes in a heap of territory, Cap'n. It includes York State. We got a hunter over Salisbury way, name o' Nat Foster. Nat's done a heap o' huntin' 'round these parts. Trapped and shot all the way from the St. Lawrence to the Mohawk. I reckon there ain't many critters ever got away from him neither.

251

Leastwise, he's got a mess o' skins in his shed right now that ain't there by accident!"

"Have you ever seen him shoot?" the Captain asked.

"Some," the townsman admitted, "Just t'other day I seen him win a nice shiny powder horn off'n a stranger, bettin' he could fire his old flintlock six times in a minute, startin' with the gun unloaded. He done 'em too. Fastest shootin' I ever did see."

Forsyth looked thoughtfully at the Yankee. "Do you suppose Foster would agree to a match with Robinson?"

"Reckon so," the Yankee said. "Never know'd Nat to turn down a sportin' offer."

"Excellent!" said the Captain. "Ask Foster to be here tomorrow and we'll settle the argument."

The York State man's furrowed face softened slightly and a glint danced in his eye as he realized that he had succeeded in his purpose. He had goaded the Captain into accepting a Yankee bargain! With a quick handshake to seal it, he turned and in the deepening twilight started through the camp on his way to Salisbury and to Nat Foster.

Even before taps news of the contest had spread through the camp and the countryside and by reveille it was evident that more than Robinson's reputation would be at stake on the morrow. Pride of the regiment and staunch belief in Robinson's ability on the one side was matched on the other by the shrewd faith of the York State men in Nat Foster. The bets mounted.

The next day's sun had just begun its westward slant when Foster presented himself at the Captain's tent. The field had been paced off and the bark targets set up one hundred and sixty feet distant. There were scant formalities; a brief introduction, a quick handshake, and then Foster and Robinson walked to the firing line.

As the contestants took their places, Forsyth outlined the rules of the contest. "The man who first hits the target six times will be the winner." He held up a pistol he had brought from the tent. "When I fire, you will begin loading. Is that clear?" The men nodded and Forsyth stepped back.

Standing side by side, the soldier and the hunter presented a striking study in contrasts. Robinson, who took his stance opposite the left target and nearest the line of "spit and polish" soldiers, was nattily attired in a well-fitting cutaway coat of bluish-gray faced with buff lining and lapels blending neatly with tight breeches of light blue. Two broad white bands were drawn tightly across the chest and over the shoulders. Topping this bright regalia was the gaily decorated cylindrical hat, replete with visor and pompon. From shiny gaiters to the well-brushed hat, Robinson looked sufficiently starched to lead a dress parade at West Point.

Nat Foster must have felt a bit conspicuous among the brightly colored uniforms of those Carolina riflemen. His dusty buckskin edged with fringe fell loosely about his tall form, and

252

beaded moccasins and coonskin cap completed his utilitarian uniform.

Forsyth raised his pistol. A hush fell over the regiment and over the townsmen, each group fixing its gaze upon its champion. It was the same tense silence that had so often been Foster's companion in the hills and woods.

As the pistol shot rang out, both men's arms moved with almost the same motion and two powder-horns flashed upward. Robinson released his horn first and reached for his bullet pouch. Unhurried, Foster charged his rifle with powder. By the time the hunter's powder-horn had fallen back to his side, the soldier was already seating his bullet. Then, mysteriously, Foster cupped the muzzle of his rifle with his left hand, tapped the butt sharply against the palm of this right hand and brought the gun to his shoulder.

The two shots rang out simultaneously. A hole appeared in each target dead center. One question was in the mind and on the lips of every soldier. Where did Foster get his bullet?

None had seen the hunter reach into pouch or pocket. Had his hand moved faster than their eyes could see?

One soldier, more observant than the others, said dazedly, "Why, hell! That Foster rascal don't even have a bullet-pouch!"

Even as he spoke, the woodman's rifle came to this shoulder for its second shot. The high-pitched crack of the long-barrelled flintlock preceded the loud crash of the soldier's rifle by a split second. An awed silence gripped the onlookers as they strained their eyes to solve the mystery of Foster's loading. Again the Yorker's rifle dropped to his side. It received its third charge and this time the spacing between his shot and that of the soldier was more appreciable. Foster was gaining!

Watching closely the rhythmic action of Foster's arm, the soldiers caught a variation in his loading technique now. After charging his gun for the fourth shot, he placed his right hand, instead of his left, over the muzzle of the gun, tapped the stock, and brought the gun to his shoulder.

As the seconds sped by, Robinson's plight became more evident. The smoothness of his loading was gone now. He was amazed and hurrying. In contrast, Foster's tempo quickened. While the Carolinian reloaded for his fifth shot, Foster's flintlock bored its fifth hole in the target. Reloading this time with even greater speed, Foster swung his gun to his shoulder just as Robinson did likewise. Foster's sixth shot matched Robinson's fifth!

With the smoke still curling from the muzzle of his rifle, the soldier stared at the targets. With a half smile that conquered the bitterness of defeat, he turned and grasped Foster's hand.

As if at a prearranged signal, wave upon wave of frenzied cheering burst from the close drawn ranks of soldiers. They were good sportsmen, these Southerners, but more than that each man was a rifleman -- burning with curiosity. How did this woodsman load?

They lifted Foster to their shoulders, then to a plank hastily laid across two water kegs, and clamored for an explanation. The hunter thrust his hand into his jacket. The men fell silent. From his pocket, Foster drew six well-aged rifle balls, shiny as agates. He held his hand high for all to see, and slid the bullets one by one into the sockets between his bony fingers.

"Thar's how she's done, boys. 'Course it takes time t' grow sockets to hold 'em, but thar's times when it's worth the trouble."

Practiced since boyhood, this method of carrying rifle balls had so warped Foster's hands that virtual pockets concealed the balls, held them without effort, and gave him free use of both hands.

"You boys know, bein' hunters -- some critters won't wait if ye're slow in reloadin'. This way, jest tap your hand on the muzzle and the ball rolls into it!"

Suddenly embarrassed by so much talk, Foster leaped down from his pulpit. He was grinning shyly as Captain Forsyth met him. Forsyth's hand gripped Foster's paw.

"Join the company, Foster, and I'll pay you thirty dollars a month." It was a handsome offer, but Forsyth's next words topped it. "What's more, by the eternal, you'll eat at my table. Is it a bargain?"

Foster's gaze rested for a moment on the rifles stacked before him. But there was the scent of an early Adirondack autumn in the air and the hunter's eye drifted off to the blue haze of the mountains. He shook his head.

Benjamin Forsyth followed the receding figure with his eyes. He said softly, "Give me a regiment of riflemen like that -- one regiment -- and in close action I could decide the fate of a battle!"

THE DEER OF PANTHER LAKE

By the time Nat Foster reached Panther Lake, the sun had already begun to stretch dark shadows across the well-worn path which generations of bucks and does had pushed to the lake. As he quietly made his way through the thick woods whose fall leaves had splashed so indiscriminately with gay, bright colors and then down along the narrow shore strip, he paused for a moment to watch the soft lake waters gently rearranging the shiny pebbles on the beach. A breeze ruffled the surface of the lake and sent a shower of colored foliage cascading from the tops of the trees that closely ringed its shores. Off to the northeast the country rolled in long sweeps of hardwood ridges and spruce filled valleys toward the mounting heights of the Adirondacks.

Anyone less a part of the forest would have felt a sense of guilt by this untimely intrusion into one of nature's quiet sanctuaries. But not Foster, for the woods were his home and his place of occupation. He belonged there. He loved the forest and perhaps that is why he knew it so well. Nature, with all her clever tricks of camouflage, hid little from his keen eye, his sharp ear or his reliable gun. From the Fulton Chain to the Finger Lakes and from the land of the Hurons to the land of the Andastes, the fabulous reputation of this Adirondack hunter had already begun to take on the aura of romantic legend even as he made his trip to Panther Lake in the early 1820's. His admirers -- and they were legion, as well as his enemies and they were mostly Indians -- would probably have told that he was the best hunter by far in York State and that was no accident that his name contained the same letters as the word "forest."

Dressed for the long trek he had already made, Foster was comfortably clad in a loose fitting buckskin jerkin with pants to match, ideal for warmth, wear and quick shooting; a coonskin cap whose tail dangled noiselessly down the back of his neck and soft skin moccasins which carefully cushioned his step in silence. About his waist a belt held a sharp knife and a hatchet, while from a rawhide shoulder strap hung a large powder horn and bullet pouch with sufficient ammunition for his hunting expedition. His pack contained a few essentials for comfort and sustenance: a blanket, a frying pan, a little salt and some Indian meal.

His rifle was a never ending source of envy wherever hunters gathered and its bark had silenced the howl of many an Adirondack wolf. Designed and made expressly for Foster, it was a sample of the fine craftsmanship of Willis Avery, a gunsmith of more than local reputation. When Avery moved into the small frontier town of Salisbury, New York, Foster's fame as a rifleman had already become common tavern-talk along the Mohawk Frontier. Living in the same community, it was only natural that these two men, one a master in the fine art of rifle shooting, the other equally at home in his chosen craft, should become close friends.

Not content with the everyday type of flintlock, Foster commissioned his friend to make a hunting rifle whose accuracy and ease of handling would match the skill of its owner. Intended for hunting and not target shooting, it was light at the muzzle and heavy in the stick. To decrease the danger of damp priming when death could so often result from a misfire, Foster had asked that it be equipped with the new lock for percussion pills. The uniqueness of its design, however, lay in the fact that it had not one, but two locks. The upper one was placed far enough above the lower so that the barrel would contain two balls with the upper charge resting on the lower bullet. The locks were so arranged that when the upper charge had been fired, there was no danger of firing the lower one until the pick had been cocked again.

It was this "double shotter" which rested easily in the crook of Foster's left elbow as he stood on the shore of Panther Lake. A sudden crackling of dry leaves and the rhythmic thud of flying feet turned Foster half around with his rifle poised mid-way to his shoulder. Through the slender hardwood saplings, he caught sight of a streak of brown and a flash of white. Not twenty yards away, a large buck bounded through the air in a long arcing leap that carried it again beyond the range of his vision. Had Foster chosen to squeeze the trigger, the deer would have crashed to its death at the end of the very leap that carried it out of sight. But in that fleeting instant, Foster was aware that something was wrong. He had not been moving when the deer startled him, nor had the wind been at his back, so he could not possibly have frightened it. But something or someone had frightened it and Nat Foster's practiced eye had caught the unnatural force behind that terrified leap. With his rifle still in mid-air, he stood motionless, intent on detecting the approach of whatever animal or human had started the deer on its headlong flight. Moments later it came. Two wolves, mouths flecked with foam, sped into the clearing and halted abruptly at sight of Foster, their flanks heaving with exertion. A sheet of flame leapt from the muzzle of the "double shotter." The foremost wolf clawed the air with his forelegs, twisted half around and sank to the ground, his head twitching in a pool of blood. The other had turned and was just disappearing when Foster's swift and deadly fire overtook it. The hollow 'thuk' of lead against flesh told the fate of the second wolf.

Before he moved, Foster poured a charge of powder into his rifle. Holding his left hand over the muzzle, he gave the stick a light tap against the ground. Leaning his rifle against a tree within easy reach, for long experience had taught him that the smell of blood might well attract other game, he took out his knife and began skinning the animals. He chuckled with satisfaction at the thought

256

that these two would bring him sixty dollars in bounty alone. He had only partially finished his work when down the deer path some eighty feet away, a she-panther of medium size broke through the thick underbrush and, with an easy lope, trotted through toward the fresh wolf meat which hung half skinned from a branch. Slinking along behind the female were two mangy looking cubs. Foster quickly seized his rifle and drew sight on the female's head. The gun cracked sharply and the first panther slumped to the ground. So swiftly did Nat recharge his gun that the two small panthers had no more than turned to run when his rifle stopped them quite dead in their tracks.

While smoke still curled out of the muzzle, Foster dropped in another double charge for he anticipated other visitors. Versed in the ways of the woods, he knew that the she-panther's mate would soon hit the trail in search of her. Hardly had he dragged the three carcasses back to his makeshift camp than a crunching noise just off the path told him that his expected guest was already on the way. He lifted his gun to ready position. Louder and closer came the sound. Suddenly not one, but two panthers, pushed through the berry bushes onto the path. The first, Foster later contended, was the largest cat he had ever seen, and he had seen many. The other, tagging along behind, was a small one. As they trotted briskly down the path, both presented equally good shots, but by chance the cub crossed his intended line of fire first. A single charge brought it down. Instantly the other screamed wildly as it leaped over the path and up the trunk of a dead tree which had lodged at an angle against another. Silhouetted against the darkening sky, the huge panther made an almost amateur shot. Confidently, Foster fired then relaxed to watch the animal fall. To his bitter amazement, it continued its mad scramble up the tree and cut over a low hanging branch. As Foster recovered from the shock, he began to feel not a little ashamed. In all his shooting, this was the first time his rifle had failed to score a hit. Just as he prepared to fire again, however, the animal reached the end of the branch and plunged to the ground in a dead heap. Foster walked cautiously over to the prostrate form and discovered that he had actually shot the animal right through the head, exactly where he had intended to hit him. Apparently, the brain set and the muscular reflex had carried the panther up the tree and out on the limb before its mortal wound finally stopped it. Foster's record was still intact. Seven shots had brought him seven animals within less than an hour. This was shooting worthy of Foster's reputation.

Having filled his pack with skins which would bring him a tidy sum on his return to Salisbury, Nat turned his attention to securing food. He left the scene of his recent killings and moved slowly along the deer path which hugged the shore. As he had expected, the deer which had been the source of his good fortune was resting in an Alder thicket just off the trail. At his approach, it

257

sprang to its feet but before it could move twenty paces, the unerring fire of Foster's rifle stopped it with a bullet just below its ear. It was but a few moments work to dress it out and secure the meat he needed. With the two quarters tied together with a rawhide thong and slung over his shoulder, he started back to his camp. The twilight of early evening had spread its mantle over the forest and for a few hours the woods would be free from the staccato bark of his rifle. The heavy pack under which he labored along the trail was filled, not only with the skins of five panthers, two wolves and a deer, but with the facts of another hunting experience which soon would become a picturesque part of the kit and kaboodle of northern York State hunter legend.

THE WATERWAYS OF NEW YORK

A young artist and a young writer booked passage on a canal boat bound for Buffalo in June 1873. Each was at the start of a career which would bring him international fame. Edwin A. Abbey, then twenty-one, had been an illustrator on the staff of "Harper's New Monthly Magazine" for the past two years. His companion, William H. Rideing, was twenty. Rideing's first article for "Harper's" was in the press as their boat headed westward. It dealt with sailors' life on shore in the port of New York. While collecting material for this story, Rideing had come across the "city" of canal boats wintering in Brooklyn's Atlantic basin and learned something of the inland boatmen's world. Now with Abbey he would explore the canal and report to "Harper's" readers. Here is his account, omitting descriptions of scenery, dialogue humor and much of the gracious literary phrasing of the period:

The boat was lying in the Atlantic basin and would be brought over to the New York side and attached to one of the evening tows to Albany. We had scrambled over several other boats and were on the broad deck of our own. The captain led the way to the cabin. It measured about six feet by ten but was exquisitely neat and cozy. An oilcloth was spread over the floor and several engravings hung upon the walls. Apart from the larger room was a galley and two sleeping berths, one of which was assigned.

There were two men and a boy in the crew. The captain was a farmer as well as a boatman and worked his forty acres "up to Oneider" with profit. The purest democracy exists among boatmen; obedience is necessarily exacted, but otherwise the employees have little reverence in the treatment of their superiors. They eat at the same table and are waited on by the captain's wife. While the captain was dozing on deck, one of his men would coolly take his pipe out of his mouth and use it himself.

Our boat was towed to the New York side and attached to the rear of a tow led by the steamer NIAGARA as it was intended that we should drop off at Newburgh and there load with coal. Passing up the North River at two miles an hour proved to be not at all wearisome. After sundown, lights gleamed out from the long train of white boats, the green and red steering lamps of the steamer diffusing their colors over all. From the windows of some cabins floods of hospitable light poured, revealing domestic groups at supper, reading and sewing. With the voices of men and women, mingled the soft, swelling tones of a parlor organ and the less musical clicking of several sewing machines. Contentment and tranquility rested upon these water-homes, a gentle spirit pervaded them, and though they were ever-moving, the bonds within seemed permanent and strong. There was no riotous conduct, little loud talking, scarcely anything stirring but the water rippling about the stern. Mothers were hushing their children to sleep on some decks and a young boatman was bending over the side of his own craft to clasp the hand of his sweetheart on another.

We visited the men's quarters next to the stable in the forward part of the boat. They were the smallest sleeping compartments in which men were ever herded. From an aperture in the deck about three feet square, we lowered ourselves and found a space not more than large enough to accommodate both our bodies when upright.

At Newburgh, as soon as the boat had been hauled beneath the high trestle-work railway to coal, we disappeared for a ramble about the town. When we returned, the decks had been scoured to their ordinary whiteness and the hatches battened over the cargo. Next morning when the tows came in sight, we were prepared to continue our journey.

On the Hudson, the boatman's duties are light and the men sing, dance, and otherwise make merry but the women are busy. Early in the morning, in a uniform dress of brown calico and a red sunbonnet which hides their features, they wash clothes and hang them out to dry. Later, chubby children are brought on deck and scrubbed. Toward noon they are peeling potatoes or dressing the meat for dinner. In the cool of the evening, when the crew have been served with supper, they are to be seen in spruce attire alternating sewing with conversation or reading. Social gatherings sometimes take place in the tows and Mrs. Captain Frank Reese sends her compliments to Mrs. Captain Jake Boardman and begs the pleasure of her company to tea at 7 p.m.

The only lonely people in the tow were the men on scows who form a distant class. The scow has neither shape nor color nor comfort and is sworn at every time she is passed on the canal. If a boatman would wound a rival, he calls his boat a scow. Sometimes they steal up the canal with loads of coal, stone or lime; but they are mostly used for lightering. They are usually manned by a desolate old man and a very profane boy who live in dark quarters somewhere in the hold and cook their own scant provisions.

The inevitable peddler is not missing from the tows. In the neighborhood of Rondout a punt starts from the eastern shore, pulled by a hearty old man. As she nears the foremost boat in the line, he sounds a dinner-horn. A rope is thrown out and the marketman hauled in. He has strawberries, potatoes, lettuce, radishes, ice, milk, peanuts and figs. Loud petitions are made to him for an honest five cents' worth of ice, two cents' worth of peanuts, a quart of milk with no water in it and a basket of berries with no false bottom. In half an hour he has passed down the length of the tow, his stock is depleted and he drops astern.

The boats are detached from the line at Albany, near the great basin. The disbanding of the tow is done clumsily and a terrible clamor is raised. In the end, the boats are escorted by a steamer, one by one, to the locks at Troy or to the branch entrance of the canal at the great basin in Albany. Here they receive the third man of the crew who has been attending to a pair of horses while the boat has been down the river. The routine of canal life then begins. The crew is divided into two watches, each of which, with a pair of horses or mules, is on duty six hours. Most of the boats travel night and day, making about forty miles in twenty-four hours.

Six hours are occupied in the first three miles of the canal at Troy in passing through sixteen locks, only a few hundred feet apart. Both banks are lined with miserable wooden buildings used for trade with boatmen. Most of them, beneath the sign indicating their business, have the additional announcement, "Highest price paid for old rope and iron." In one, the business of a restaurant was successfully combined with that of the junk dealer. In another, veterinary, dental and photographic services were modestly offered by one man on one shingle. The most unsightly of these unsightly structures are the "day-boat barns," which bear misspelled legends in straggling characters. "HORSE KEP WHILE BOT TO YORK" appears on one; upon another, "HO BOATMAN HORSES PROMPTLY SHOT!"

Congregated in this neighborhood is the rough material of canal life, the tramps and unemployed hands. "Crew all full, cap'n?" a hiccuppy voice inquired, as a beery face thrust through the cabin window while we were at breakfast. "Please God, they aren't as full as you be!" At which evasive retort the disagreeable animal slouched away.

The collector's office, a pretentious building in the Corinthian style, is near the portals of the canal. One-half of it forms an arched passage in which there is a lock. Here the vessels are weighed, the tolls paid, and clearance is given. "Comin' up , they ain't so rough on us as comin' down. First, the State takes a

260

small skelp off of you at Buffalo; and then the reg'lar and professional skelpers helps themselves to a big slice," lamented the captain. "There is miles of middlemen at Buffalo who makes it a business to obtain loads for the boats and charges heavy commissions for it. Sometimes they holds back stuff ontil the boatman is glad enough to make terms with 'em and there's not a load comes to the Atlantic but they gits five per cent."

We crossed the Lower Aqueduct which carries the canal over the Mohawk River and entered a dream land of pastoral beauty. At one store the boat stopped. A bubbling stream rose in front, from which our water-casks were filled. On a small table, beneath the thin spray of a syringe, an assortment of fresh vegetables was arranged.

Further on, we came upon a raft nearly eighty feet long and six feet wide, formed of spruce and pine hewn in the Black River country. The timbers are bound together by ropes and in the center a caboose of thin planking is erected for horses and men. Sometimes two boys navigate a small raft down and spend days and nights without shelter and without food.

Once in a while the passing boat is owned by a neighbor of the captain and, as the two vessels move in opposite directions, a string of questions is asked and answered until the voices can no longer exchange questions of home, wives, children, trade and weather. An unfriendly boat now and then strikes us and dire threats are uttered on both sides but neither crew evince an intention to execute them.

In the night we passed over the Higher Aqueduct and early next morning we are at Schenectady. Thence, the canal follows the track of the Mohawk. The New York Central Railroad keeps company with us on one side and the track of the proposed West Shore line to Chicago is marked out on the other. Remnants of the old canal are scattered here and there along the route-- a moss-covered lock or a patch of towpath nearly obliterated by weeds and grass. It is a luxury to lie on deck and feast on the never failing panorama. A boat comes along with a hard-worked woman seated in a rocking-chair at the stern; a wild lily is drooping in a tumbler of water on a common box which serves as a work-table; and in an enclosure of rope and wood on the cabin roof, a group of plump children of one to five years are playing.

The locks on the canal are drearily alike, not in masonry alone, but also in the structures surrounding. One cannot help wondering why the opportunities for beautifying them are persistently disregarded. Perhaps it is because women do not live near them. The tenders for the most part are uncouth and unintelligent men who hold their positions through political influence and are often unqualified for their duties, to the great inconvenience of the boatmen. An ugly caboose shelters them and in it they add to their incomes by dispensing magic oils, balsams and liniments for man and beast.

A sparse collection of shabby buildings is also near the lock, foremost being the canal grocery, a squat shingled structure with a portico in front. Here a pack of vagabonds and idlers in tilted chairs seem to pass their worthless lives. The interior is gloomy and has a very insalubrious atmosphere; but there is no article in the range of an ordinary boatman's necessities that cannot be obtained. Dry-goods, fresh meat, poultry, groceries, liquors and literature are combined attractions. A sagacious dog is attached to most of these establishments and as each boat arrives, he marches to the galley window and it is impossible to resist his pathetic importunities. A small dry dock and boat yard adjoin the grocery. We see a scow on the stocks but most boats are built at Albany and Rochester and cost from $3,000 to $5,000 each.

At Little Falls, the locks are worked by hydraulic power. At Syracuse, a floodgate that turns over as the boat passes has been substituted for the old gate which swung aside on hinges. As far as Syracuse, the locks are double. Above that point, the commissioners are at present doubling them to meet the demands of traffic. At Lockport, five locks lift our heavy cargo seventy-five feet in a few minutes.

Night on the canal has the enchantment and mystery of night on the ocean. Each boat carries a brilliant lantern in the bow, which disperses a circle of yellow light on the watery track ahead. In advance you hear the steady thud of the horses' hoofs or the low cry of the driver as he urges them forward. At the stern the helmsman is singing in a plaintive measure, until a lock engages him. His voice is then deepened. "Lock be-l-o-o-w!" he calls to his mate; "Ste-a-dy, ste-a-a-dy!" to the driver. There is a momentary clatter of feet upon the deck; we rise smoothly to the new level; the lock lights fade; quiet again, and we are traveling with the softness of a dream toward the amber morning.

At Buffalo our boat rapidly discharges her cargo of coal and we are speeding homeward in the Pacific Express while she is hauled to an elevator and deeply laden with grain.

The boatman calculates to make six round trips in a season, and at the end he retires to his farmhouse, if he has one, and passes the winter in the bosom of his family. A large number of boats are quartered at the Atlantic Basin, throughout the winter, and form in themselves a city with denizens who have social ethics, occupations, and habits. The boats -- over 200 of them, closely nested together -- form a white plain. Children play and loiter, run from boat to boat and leap distances over water with astonishing daring and security; women pass to and fro with market baskets; there is every sign of a thrifty and happy town.

Humorous and kindly, these people are worthy of study and deserving of respect. They are temperate, industrious and energetic.

They are clean and moral. In wandering from hamlet to hamlet and city to city, they have acquired singularly varied knowledge and habits at once creditable to themselves and interesting to the observer. Their lives are simple but picturesque. In the length of our journey we did not once meet with a discourteous word or a rude action.

IX

MAYHEM, MURDER, MYSTERY AND MISCHIEF

Republic Steam Presses, Buffalo.

THE PHILOSOPHY OF CRIME
(c. 1869)

If dishonest men would use half as much effort to make a living by labor as they used to make it without, they would be surprised at their success. Thieves, burglers and highwaymen do not possess more courage than other men; yet they will expose themselves to personal perils for a few dollars that an honest man would not encounter for hundreds or thousands.

The labor of breaking into a store or dwelling is no careless affair. The policeman in the vicinity must be dodged; the door or shutter must be opened without noise; then there is the groping through the dark halls and rooms, with the probability of being fired at with a blunderbuss from the head of the stairs; and there is a labored search for the coveted treasure, through drawers, safes, sideboards, trunks and garments, with the constant necessity of conducting the difficult process without a noise that would alarm the sleepers. Through every step of this perilous work, the burglar takes his life in his hand, and many a one falls a bloody corpse on the window he is escaping from, or hobbles painfully away with a bullet in his body, and a trail of blood in his returning footsteps. Yet, in the face of all these dangers, the burglar plies his trade as faithfully as if he were bound to it by a necessity which he cannot escape.

Horse stealing is one of the most dangerous of crimes in the West, and yet one of the most common. The loss of a good horse is a calamity which farmers will not endure, and the horse thief is their most hated foe. They have no mercy on him, and give him no quarter, and there are few horse thieves who do not sooner or later swing by the neck from a tree -- victims of the rude and terrible vengeance of the husbandman they have despoiled. But for this, horse stealing has always flourished and always will flourish in these regions where it is attended with most danger, and where the penalty is almost certain death.

Robberies of banks, express companies and brokers' offices -- those daring, brilliant feats that startle the community, and excite a feeling of admiration for the genius which planned and the skill and boldness which executed them, are rarely successful in the end. The robbers carry off their prize, leaving apparently no traces of their flight and, for a time, the transaction is forgotten. But there are detectives who understand the shrewdest thief better than he understands himself. They know his haunts and his habits, and they get to work cooly and deliberately to find him. The heavy reward offered is their incentive, as the stolen treasure is the thief's and though the task may require weeks and months and even years of labor and vigilance, they are pretty sure to find him at last and bring him to justice.

But in spite of all the dangers and anxieties of the criminal's life and the tragedy with which it ends -- in spite of the demonstrated and not denied fact that (the morality of the matter entirely out of the question) the hardships of a vocation of crime and vice are greater than those of a vocation of labor and virtue, crime flourishes and grows without abatement and even furnishes examples of genius, enterprise and skill, which honest business can hardly excel.

Civilization corrects many evils and wrongs by proving that they are hurtful to health, injurious to society, or unprofitable to the person. But crime thrives best right under the shadow of our highest civilization. It is proved to be disgraceful, injurious and unprofitable, but for all that is pursued as a vocation, as indefatigably and resolutely as if it were a legitimate and exemplary industry. No amount of "progress" or "advancement" no increase of that "human development" that promises to work such wonders for us can banish it from society, or even tame it into decency.

Perhaps when that model and unexceptional animal, the "coming man" shall have arrived, and the world shall have reached that beautific condition which some philosophers promise, this mystery will be explained. At present, human philosophers and human laws throw no light upon it.

There are theories which impute to insurrections of crime the property of perdicity, and made them dependent on electrical conditions of the air and earth -- which, in short, assume that there are fixed and irrevocable laws governing crime, just as there are laws governing the movement of the planets and the operations of trade. Perhaps, when the world shall have been fully "developed," and these occult laws prescribed and defined, we may be able to harness crime into such tractable and manageable conditions that the front doorstep will be a safe depository for money and jewels.

We may -- perhaps -- for the delightful goal seems to recede farther from us with the very agencies that were to bring it near. The contest between the right and wrong, virtue and vice, in all the hearts and lives of men appears to be as fresh and as far from its end as it was thousands of years ago. The enemy exhibits a tenacity and vitality of so innate attribute, and he struggles for possession of the human heart with the imperial perseverence of one who claimed the domain as his own by right or possession. No dogmas of human perfection have yet beguiled him into yielding his claim and withdrawing from the contest, and, very probably, they never will.

IRISH SENSE OF HUMOR

The Erie Canal was constructed mainly by Irish immigrants under local superintendents -- often of English stock. One day, as Mr. Colt, superintendent of one of the links, was passing through a company of these laborers, he gave one of them a smart kick on his rear exposure for some real or supposed offense. The man instantly let go of his barrow, and while with his left hand rubbing the seat of attack, with his right he very respectfully raised his hat, and rolling the quid in his mouth, with a peculiar knowing twinkle of the eye, said in the richest Irish brogue: "Faith and be Jesus, if yer honor kicks so hard while ye're a colt, what'll ye do when ye get to be a horse?"

CHIPPY CONNOLLY

If you ask an old canaller about those fights which Mr. Edmonds has made so vivid, the reply will usually be, "Oh, there wasn't much fightin' in my time," or, "All the fightin' was at Buffalo and West Troy, when the men had nothin' else to do." But once in a while you may meet someone like Mr. George Denniston of Waterloo, who can remember the decade of 1860-70 when, as a lad, he drove for his father, the tall, brown man with a white beard known along the Erie as "Uncle Billy." Here is Mr. Denniston's story:

In my day we had mostly slow, heavy boats, ninety-six feet long, carrying heavy loads of coal, lumber or salt.   Most of the fighting was before that, when the packets were running. They were light passenger boats, built for speed. It used to be that if one canal boat got within two hundred yards of a lock, another boat couldn't pass it. But the packets wouldn't wait for two or maybe three hours -- time was important to them. So all the packets carried fighters. Sometimes they were men who didn't do anything but just sit around 'til they came to a lock, then they'd fight to see who'd go through first.

"Chippy" Connolly was known as Champion of the Erie Canal; he wouldn't hire a man that wasn't a fighter. He challenged any man between Buffalo and Albany, but nobody would fight him if it could be helped. One time I saw his boat near Montezuma. Connolly's driver wouldn't let another boat pass him. The driver of the other boat started calling names, and pretty soon the two of them got to fighting. The other fellow ran away, and Connolly's driver threw stones after him.

The champion before Connolly was John McMan (McMahon?). I saw him once when he was an old man at Troy -- tall and broad shouldered, with a great big head on him. One time

269

his driver got into a fight -- his name was Bill Stewart -- it was up at Centerport, and the other drivers licked him. John said, "Bill, I didn't think you'd let him roll you around in the dust like that." Bill said: "Well, Captain, you know, before breakfast I can't seem to fight right." So John took him over to a canal store and bought him some beer and bread and cheese -- all he wanted. When he'd finished eating, Bill called the other driver off his boat and licked him easy.

Jerry McCarthy was known as the Champion of the Chemung Canal, a branch going down from Seneca Lake to Elmira that is closed now. I seen this Jerry with a black man at Geneva -- a fellow named George Taylor. McCarthy's boat with a load of lumber on it was tied up at the dock. Taylor had his towline out and his team drawing; the towline caught in the lumber and threw some of it into the canal. McCarthy wanted Taylor to get the boards out of the water; he wouldn't do it, McCarthy hit him, and they began punching around. First one would be on top and then the other; neither one could get the best of it. Finally some men standing around watching separated them -- they generally did this after a fight had lasted some time. Taylor said, "If I'd knowed you was a champion, I don't believe I'd have started; but as long as I did, I'd just as soon finish it."

The biggest fight I ever heard of was at Memphis, a little town about thirteen miles from Syracuse. I was two-three miles away, near Peru, when I heard there was a big fight going on. The way it started was, there was this brand-new boat, and this old boat came along side and scratched the paint. This made the captain of the new boat pretty mad, and he said to the captain of the other boat, "Say, I'd like to punch your jaw for that!"

The other captain says: "Why, I got a driver that kin lick you!" This was an insult, because the drivers were generally young boys.

The first captain says: "Where is he? I'd like to see the driver that can lick me."

The driver spoke up from the towpath and says, "Here I am. Come on out, and I'll show you."

The captain jumped off his boat, and they went to fighting on the grass. Then a man jumped off and joined them, then one off the other boat, until both crews were out there, mixing in. There's generally five men on a crew -- the captain, two steersmen and two drivers -- so pretty soon here was the whole ten of them, fightin' to beat the deuce. After they fit for long time, they was all knocked out except one man on one side and two on the other. The two of them couldn't knock this one man down; so after a while one of the two went over to the boat and asked the cook to give him a heavy stick or something. She handed him a heavy iron bar. He went back with it, watched his chance, and gave the fellow a crack on the head along by his jaw, and it killed him. There wasn't any jail in

Memphis; so they locked the men up in a barn till they could take them to Syracuse to be tried. I never heard what happened to that fellow that killed the man.

YOU EAT IT

It is not to be supposed that fighting was confined to ancient times or to the east end of the canal. Mr. Oviatt McConnell of Buffalo likes to tell of the late Captain Ed Scouten, who died in 1922 at the ripe age of ninety-three.

Cap'n Ed was a Civil War veteran who knew the canal intimately for half a century and who lived to command one of the modern "hoodledashers," powered boats which surge along with a barge in front and a couple behind. The Cap'n used to stop fights by stepping in and thrashing the combatants one at a time or, if they preferred, together. When he was about seventy-five, he decided to follow a general custom by hiring a fighter. On the first voyage out, it occurred to him that he hadn't tried his slugger to see whether he was up to canal standards; so he picked a fight and knocked out the professional. It is told of him that in the seventies he was walking through a canal town, his luxuriant whiskers waving. Approaching some loungers, he predicted, "One of these fellows is going to say Baa to me on account of my whiskers, and I am going to pop him." The prediction was immediately fulfilled.

The classic tale at Buffalo is of the big battle between Charley and Jack. Jack bit off a piece of Charley's ear and spat it on the deck whereupon there followed the following curt dialogue:

"There's your ear, Charley."

"You bit it off, you cuss, Now you eat it!"

BUCKO BEN AND SLEEPY FRANK

The National Hotel at Cuylerville, New York, puts out a sheet explaining its history. The following section, reprinted here, deals with canawlers.

The Genesee Valley, Indian paradise, birthplace of Utopian dreams and projects, has no more colorful edifice than the National Hotel, at Cuylerville. This famous inn and tavern has been much else beside: Underground Railway Station, dance hall, town hall, Sunday school, whiskey distillery.

Built in 1837 by Charles Phinney, the hotel was first called The National Exchange. Truesdall Lamson, an abolitionist, took it over in 1843 and, until the enactment of the strictly enforced Fugitive Slave Law of 1850, the hotel was an important station in the Underground Railway between Pennsylvania and Canada. James G. Birney, a converted Alabama slave-holder who ran for President of the United States on the Liberty Party ticket in 1840 and again in 1844, directed the movement of fugitives up the valley from the hotel. In an attic stairwell, there is still an old hiding place for a slave -- usually only one fugitive at a time could be helped to freedom. In 1848, traffic was brisk: twenty-eight fugitives were harbored at the hotel.

W. Scoville took over the management from 1850 to 1871 and called it the Scoville House. With the completion of the twenty-year project of the Genesee Valley Canal from Rochester to Olean in 1856, the hotel reached the zenith of its fame and glory. Here the boat captains and their ruffians (crew members hired for their fistic ability) fought, danced, prayed, bought their supplies, drank whiskey by the tin cup, and slept if off.

The first boat to be pulled down the canal when it was opened September 1, 1840, from Rochester to Mount Morris was piloted by "Bucko Ben" Streeter, known as the Terror of the Valley and the Rochester Bully. He had fought for a straight hour in the old Reynolds Arcade in Rochester with a Negro called Sleepy Frank. On the second boat which pulled into the Cuylerville Basin in front of the hotel was Bucko Ben's old opponent, Sleepy Frank. "Let's get this damn thing over with," yelled Bucko Ben and he stripped to the waist. The only rule was that the loser was to buy five rounds of drinks for the house. The fight started in the Hotel barroom and ended in the horse stables, lasted two hours, and it was Bucko Ben who bought the drinks. He never returned to Rochester, sold his canal boat and became a law abiding citizen of Cuylerville.

272

MURDER A DAY

It is an exaggeration to say that there was a murder a day on the Buffalo waterfront during its hey-day. Probably there was not more than a murder every other day. Some statistics show that seventy to eighty percent of the major crimes in the United States occurred along the Erie Canal, in Buffalo and Rochester, during the years 1830-1836.

MAN ON A MULE

Perhaps the strangest murder on the Erie Canal happened near the Eastern lock at the Little Falls line lock. Up and down the canal, the Little Falls lock had a saloon as unsavory as any of them.

At one time a man disappeared, a not unusual occurrence along the canal. People assumed correctly that the man had been murdered. Careful search for days, however, failed to find the body until one day a mule was found floating in the canal near the saloon. Upon checking the mule, it was found that the mule had not drowned, but had died on shore. Close examination revealed that the mule's belly had been sliced open, disembowled, the body of the man pushed inside and the belly sewn up.

THE MAN WITHOUT A SLEEVE

The immigrants needed protection from more than the Indians. Now take the man who wore one sleeve. . . .

Weather-wise, it had been a rare day. A day with a smile on its face. Everyone and everything seemed to like it. On the towpath even the mules stepped livelier. Their skinners sang much faster but no sweeter. On deck, the captain wore a grin as wide as an open lock. Even the Erie Canal wore its best. The water seemed to blend the deep blue of a spotless sky with the earth-green of growing things. As the barge moved forward, pushing aside the water, silver streams ran off to the side, breaking for a moment the solid water color and then just as quickly melting back into skyblue and earthgreen. It had been a June day and rare was, indeed, the word for it.

William Nowlin drank in the beauty. The breeze gently spanked his cheeks as he stood on the bow of the barge looking southward toward Buffalo less than a mile away. He felt that this was really it. This was the great moment he had hoped for, planned for, and worked for. The Nowlins were headed west. Here was the great adventure. Looking out on the horizon south and west, a feeling of destiny gripped him. It was more than a personal feeling. It was something outside of him and his family. He felt a part of something great. He knew now that it had been in the air like a contagion since they had first boarded the barge at Albany. No one tried to talk about it. Probably no one could. It was just there. You knew it.

Nowlin's eyes studied the men standing on the topside of the barge. His mind took in the wives and children in the cabins below. They and the Nowlins were a part of a great mass movement westward. They came from the hinterlands of Europe and from the tidelands of America; from old England and New England. They were new America on the march. They and, more especially, their children, were the bright, brave New World. They were the pioneers.

These thoughts crowded his mind as he looked westward across the Niagara River and watched the setting sun paint the sky a beautiful afterglow. For some minutes, Nowlin's eyes remained fastened to the western sky, hypnotized by the changing colors. It was fascinating to watch the dark blue of the night sky press down on the orange-red of the fading day sky. Suddenly, his reverie was broken by the all too familiar yell of his little girl. "Daddy, Daddy." Nowlin turned around just in time to catch her under the arms as she jumped at him. Playfully he swung her out in wide circles so that her legs flew out over the water. Her little nose wrinkled as she giggled in the delight of danger. She staggered a bit as Nowlin set her down on her feet. Pointing a warning finger at her, which he waggled good naturedly under her nose, he said, "Now see here, young lady, you'd better rein in a little when you come running toward the edge of something. You might trip and fall some day."

"But, Daddy," she protested, "I knew you would catch me."

"Oh, you did, did you? Well sometime I might fool you and then what'll you do?"

"Get wet," she laughed. Her laughter tinkled like gay little bells.

"That's exactly right," Nowlin said. "Now tell me, if you have any breath left, what's all the excitement about?"

For a moment the girl had forgotten what she was excited about. Then suddenly it came to her like the rush of water when a dam bursts. The words tumbled out of her mouth so fast it sounded to Bill Nowlin like some kind of gibberish.

"If you really want me to know what you want me to know, you had better check rein your tongue a bit."

The little girl laughed at her father's words and then with a little less excitement, but still with a high pitch of expectancy in her voice said, "Well, where are they?"

"Where's what?" her father questioned.

"Where are the Buffaloes?"

"What Buffaloes? What are you talking about?" Nowlin asked.

"Why, I heard the big people down below talking and they said we would see the Buffaloes in just a few minutes."

Nowlin chuckled, "so that's it." Crouching down beside her and slipping his arm around her tiny waist, "I'm afraid, my dear, they didn't say 'Buffaloes,' they said 'Buffalo.'"

"Oh, all right, where's the Buffalo then?"

Nowlin smiled again. "Baby, I'm afraid you're in for a disappointment. Those people down below were talking about Buffalo, the city, not the animal. So far as I know, there are no Buffaloes in Buffalo."

The little girl tried to push back the cloud of disappointment that darkened her face but it wouldn't budge. "I don't think it's very nice to call this place Buffalo when there aren't any Buffaloes here."

Nowlin smiled at his little girl's protest and said, "Well, dear, it hasn't always been called that. Matter of fact, the captain told me just a few minutes ago that the original settlers called it New Amsterdam, since the area was originally owned by a Dutch Company. Would you like New Amsterdam better?"

"Well, I think it's a much better name than Buffalo, especially since there are no Buffaloes here. I can't see why they changed the name."

"Well the good Yankees hereabouts probably thought that the name 'Buffalo' was more American than the name 'Amsterdam.' And, since the creek which now forms its harbor was so important in the development of the city, they probably decided to name it Buffalo after Buffalo Creek."

"Well, but Daddy, how did . . . ."

Nowlin did not let her finish the question. "I know. You want to know how the creek got its name. The captain told me he didn't rightly know. Some people claimed that there were really Buffaloes here at one time. Others say that the stream was named after an Indian. Still others contend that Buffalo was the sound the Indians made when they tried to pronounce the French name for the creek."

Nowlin looked at his little girl. He could see that he hadn't lifted her expression of disappointment. Picking her up so she could see better, he pointed to his left and said, "Over there is the creek -- Buffalo Creek. You can see the masts of the various vessels. Some place yonder in that tangled mess of masts is the MICHIGAN and we'll be aboard her tomorrow headed west."

These words sent a new thought racing across her mind. As if by magic it erased her downcast look and once again her eyes danced.

"Oh, Daddy," she said, squeezing him tightly and nuzzling her face against his neck. "Could we sleep on the boat tonight?"

"Would you like to?"

"Very much."

"Well, I don't know, my dear," he said, letting her slide down gently. "We'll have to ask your mother and see what she says." Then pointing to the stairs he said, "Why don't you go below and get her? We'll be docking in a few minutes."

The little girl was off like the wind, her blonde curls flopping against the back of her neck. In a few minutes she was back hand in hand with her mother.

"Well, my dear," said Nowlin as he took his wife's hand and slipped his other arm around her, "the first leg of our trip is just about over. They'll be 'pike-poling' the canal boat around the corner into Commercial Slip in just a moment. Is everything shipshape below deck?"

"Yes, Bill, everything is ready to be taken off."

"The willow basket -- where is it?"

"It's safe. Timothy is watching it."

"We have to be very careful with that basket. We can't afford to lose it."

"I know, but Timothy's a dependable boy. Nothing will happen to the willow basket with him watching it."

"Look quickly over there, dear," Bill Nowlin shouted and pointed at the same time. "You can see the harbor and, oh! -- look! -- doesn't that say 'Michigan' on that ship straight ahead?"

Mrs. Nowlin squinted her eyes a bit, "Why it does say 'Michigan'!"

"Well, that's it! That's the boat we'll be on tomorrow. Isn't she a beauty?"

"Well, I wouldn't know about that, Bill, but it does look strong enough to stay afloat and that's what I'm interested in, staying dry inside and out."

"What do you say, Mother, shall we sleep aboard her tonight? I know the kids would enjoy it."

"Well, I suppose it would be fun," said Mrs. Nowlin as she tried to think the problem through. "But don't you think we had better save our money and take a cheaper place? We're going to need every penny to keep going our first year. 'Member how the Smiths had to give up and come back after their first year. I don't think I could face the folks back home."

Nowlin tightened his arm around her just a bit and with the other arm patted her gently on the forearm. "Well, my dear, maybe you're right. We probably will get a better night's sleep in a public house here on the waterfront." Bill went over to the railing, eyeing carefully the establishments along Commercial Street.

"Well, from the noise and confusion 'round abouts I don't think we'll get very much sleep in a boarding house or aboard the Michigan. Have you ever seen anything like it?" Mrs. Nowlin asked.

"What did you say?" Bill asked as he turned and cupped his ear.

"I said, "Have you ever seen anything like it?" Mrs. Nowlin shouted.

No, Bill Nowlin had never seen anything like it. It seemed as if the roads of the nation crossed here where the Erie Canal joined the Commercial Slip and the Buffalo Harbor. On both sides of the canal, two and three deep, were canal barges. Commercial Slip was completely clogged. One could walk dryshod from one side of Commercial Slip to the other. All along the line big, burly Irishmen with burnt brown skin carried bags, barrels, packages and household goods out of the holds of the barges and piled them high on the wharf. In some places along Commercial Slip, whose one side acted as the wharf, freight was piled above the second story of the buildings which lined the side opposite the canal. As the stevedores struggled up the narrow, ribbed gangplank with their loads, you could hear a thick Irish brogue demanding a clear road. Along the street people pushed and pulled and tried to keep from being swept along in the opposite direction. Serious-minded clerks gave the impression of importance and wore serious expressions on their faces as they clutched business papers in their hands. They ran swiftly in and out of the various business houses and commission rookeries where the commercial business of the port was transacted.

Nowlin had never seen anything like it. The other ports along the canal had had an exciting hustle and bustle about them, but here on the Buffalo waterfront it seemed that all the noise of the whole canal had been brought together in one continuous wild sound that seemed to pulsate against your ears. There seemed to be no order in the seething mass of humanity which filled Canal and Commercial Streets.

To Nowlin it seemed as if every language and every accent could be heard in the swirling, Babel-like confusion. Reaching out high above the crowd noises, he noted, were the voices of the "runners" or "solicitors" (as they were professionally called) trying to get various passengers to stay at this hotel or to take that boat. In the melee, coats and dresses were torn, sometimes the baggage of immigrants ended up in one place and they in another. The runners were indeed, a breed apart.

Nowlin noticed another waterfront breed. These characters, members of the "soap-lack" fraternity, leaned up against the taverns and saloons that lined the street. They were the drunks, the beggars, the thieves, the blacklegs and prostitutes, looking over the new arrivals to pick out the most likely-looking suckers. Nowlin made a mental note to be thankful to the Almighty if they got out of the Buffalo waterfront with their lives and their money.

Nowlin broke himself away from these thoughts for a moment and said, "Well, Mother, I guess I'll go down and get Timothy and the baggage."

Minutes later the four Nowlins found themselves standing on the wharf listening to the runners singing out the praises of their respective hotels and boats. Then they made their way along Commercial Street, down Canal Street to Maiden Lane. There,

Nowlin saw a house which offered rooms at what he thought was a reasonable rate.

"Mother, how does this look to you?" Nowlin asked.

"Well, I don't know, my dear, it doesn't look too clean but it is cheap."

"Well, I guess we can stand it for one night. I'm so tired I could sleep any place. Let's go in."

In the dingy entrance just off to the left was a little table that had once been an elegant piece of furniture but, like the fat woman who sat behind it, the table had fallen on evil days. Her blotched face had been made uglier by liberal doses of paint in the wrong place. As Nowlin looked closer at her pimpled face, however, he realized that there could be no right places on her face. Nowlin asked her if his family could rest in that room for a few minutes while he went down to the MICHIGAN to make sure of his arrangements.

Soon after Nowlin left, the woman came over toward Mrs. Nowlin, reached down to the willow basket as if to move it a little, then lifted it and said knowingly, "You must have plenty of money, your basket is very heavy."

Mother Nowlin stood dumblike. She just looked at the woman who now quickly turned on her heel and walked out of the room with the air of someone who suddenly remembered that she had something that needed to be done quickly. Mrs. Nowlin was frightened. She felt surrounded by evil. But she kept her fear away from the children. She thought her husband would never return. When he finally did enter the door, her fear melted away but the concern was still there. She told him immediately about the woman and the willow basket.

"William, I'm scared," she said. "I don't like the idea of staying here, especially with that five hundred dollars in silver in the willow basket."

"Well, my dear, I think we're stuck. I've checked at the other places on my way down to the steamer. They're all filled. I even asked the captain of the Michigan if we could stay aboard that boat tonight, but he told me that was out of the question. They were making some minor repairs and no one would be allowed aboard until morning. So I guess we'll just have to worry it out here."

Nowlin no more than finished that sentence, when the fat woman returned. Bill asked if they might have a sleeping room with three beds. "Well, mister," said the woman as she tried to fit her backside into the chair behind the desk, "we're pretty well crowded, but I do have a small room on the third floor with three beds and you can have it if you want it."

"Well, I guess we haven't much choice. We'll take it."

With that Nowlin turned, walked back to his family, picked up the baggage and led the way upstairs. It was three flights up through a narrow, rickety staircase. On the third floor they found the door to their room. It opened into a dark, dismal, windowless room. The door through which they entered was their only entrance and exit. Bill Nowlin did not like the looks of things, but he also kept his fears to himself.

"Well, kids, we'll all have a big day tomorrow, so we'll all pile in and get some sleep." Mrs. Nowlin helped the children with their clothes, tucked them into bed, and put the willow basket with the silver in between them -- she thought that would be the safest place.

After looking over the situation downstairs, to see if everything seemed safe, the older Nowlins went back up to their room and prepared for bed. Though they were gone only a few minutes, the children were sound asleep by the time they came back.

Bill and his wife had not been long in bed when he thought he heard footsteps outside the door. Before he could get up, the door opened a crack and the light cut the darkness of the room like a knife. A man with a candle tiptoed into the room. Nowlin started to get out of bed, but Mrs. Nowlin put a restraining hand on his arm as if to say, "Quiet, don't jump him yet." The man with the candle went to each bed to see who was in it. Bill Nowlin's bed was last. As the intruder went around his bed, Nowlin sat up bolt straight and asked the man what he was doing in the room and what he wanted.

"I'm looking for an umbrella," said the man with the candle.

"Here, I'll give you an umbrella," said Nowlin and with that jumped from the bed, grabbed at the man and caught hold of his sleeve. The man tried to jerk away but Nowlin had a firm grip on his sleeve. As he lunged forward, the sleeve ripped at the shoulder, but the man kept running out of the door and down the stairs as fast as he could go. Nowlin sat on the edge of the bed with the sleeve in his hand.

Nowlin and his wife knew that there would be no sleep for them the rest of the night.

Turning to his wife, Bill said, "I'm going to put my knife above the door just in case our friend returns."

Everything remained quiet for about three hours. Then once again the Nowlins heard something.

"Do you hear what I hear?" said Bill Nowlin.

"Yes, it sounds like footsteps doesn't it, but without shoes."

"How many do you think there are?"

"Sounds to me like two or maybe three."

As they got to the top stair, Nowlin picked up a chair, held it above his head and stood at the side of the door. As soon as Mrs. Nowlin heard the latch turn, she yelled so that they could hear her, "John, have the pistols ready. The moment they open the door, shoot them." Mrs. Nowlin's stratagem worked. The door closed and the footsteps descended the stairs quietly and quickly.

Bill Nowlin put down the chair, threw his arms around his wife and planted a big kiss on her mouth. "Aren't you the cool one, my dear? What would I ever do without you?"

"Well, I did it, my dear, so that I wouldn't have to do without you. I figured that with that chair and your knife, you probably would have killed one of those men and the other two would have killed you."

"Well, maybe, my dear, they won't come back anymore."

"Don't be too sure of that. I think we'll have to stand guard all night."

"Yes, I know we will," said William Nowlin.

They both settled back to wait. In just about three hours they heard footsteps again. As the door opened, Mrs. Nowlin said, "All right, my dear, be ready now and mow them down the moment they burst open the door."

Again they went away only to return just before dawn. If possible, this time they were even quieter than they had been before. Again Nowlin took his place beside the door with the chair in hand. Just before they started in, they were greeted again by Mrs. Nowlin's voice. "All right, John, shoot the first one that enters. We'll blow them to kingdom come."

For the fourth time the scheme worked; the thieves left. Mrs. Nowlin breathed a sign of relief, her husband put the chair down and sheathed his knife, the only weapon they possessed. That was the last visit of the night. Soon Bill could hear noises out on the street. Since there were no windows in the room, it was the only way they could tell it was time to get up. They quickly got the children out of bed. After dressing and getting the children dressed, they collected their baggage and started down the long flight of stairs to the rooms on the street level. Nowlin walked over to the woman behind the desk and complained about the man who had entered the room. He held up the broadcloth coatsleeve as evidence. The woman said that it must have been the old man who usually slept in that room.

"Well, from now on, you'd better be careful to inform him when the room is occupied. And I'm telling you, if I find a man around here with one sleeve I'm going to give him the beating of his life."

Nowlin never found his man and he never forgot the story of his one-night layover in Buffalo. Often in later years, when he entertained his friends in his Michigan home, he told all who would listen (and even some who wouldn't) the story of their escape from the man with one sleeve.

EPITAPH

Dr. Robert M. Palmer, Fulton County historian, copied the following inscription in the Prospect Hill Cemetery, Gloversville:

In memory of
Mr. Philo Mills

In the mysterious providence
of God: he was suddenly removed
from life while on his way
to Schenectady on the night
of Dec. 30, 1835 in the 45 year
of his age. He was driving on
the bank of the canal where he
is sleight upset & he was thrown
upon the ice, caught under a
part of his load & there found
the next morning alone,
helpless, dead.
It shocked the soul when first we heard
The dreadful new P. Mills is dead.
Be still and know that I am God.

Ps. 46-10

"This epitaph," Dr. Palmer says, "has long been considered a curiosity by the people here. I have copied it just as it appears on the gravestone."

OF SAND AND TIME

A bright moonlight streaked the lake water. It shimmered gently as the soft wind tried to spread its sparkling sheen over the sandy beach. Along the canal and river, dozens of grain elevators reached skyward, like the towers and parapets of medieval castles. In the water, the barks and schooners with sails furled rolled gently to the soft lullaby of a lake breeze. Here and there steamers with fires banked for the night seemed to be breathing slowly and contentedly in their slumber. On the other side of the river harbor, the oil lamps of the Canal Street groggeries painted grotesque shadows which danced crazily on the walls and the cobblestone streets. The drunken noises tried to reach across the river and canal to the south beach but the clear moonlight, the lake breeze and the slowly moving creek seemed to filter out most of the animal-like noises leaving only the faint suggestion of sound -- a pleasant background to the quiet of the south beach.

Across that beach this night, a lone figure hurried toward a darkened house that fronted on the lake. He pounded loudly on the door. After several minutes a light came to the window on the second floor. The window flew open and an angry voice yelled down, "What in hell do you want man? Don't you know it's two o'clock in the morning?"

"Yeah, I know it is," admitted the voice on the lawn. "But I gotta see Charlie Payment right away."

"Oh, you do, do you? Well the Captain's sleeping and I'm not going to disturb him for the likes of you." With that, the man on the second floor slammed the window shut. As he turned from the window and started back through the hall toward his room, he saw the Captain in his nightshirt coming down the hall with a lighted candle in his hand. "It's all right, Jack. That voice sounded like Captain Hubert's." With that the Captain opened the window and

283

holding the candlestick above his head hollered down. "That you down there, Tom?"

"Yeah, Charlie, I've got to see you right away."

"Sumpin' troublin' you Tom?"

"Yeah, and it's mighty big trouble. Hurry up will ya, I ain't got much time."

"Well what in hell's wrong with you anyhow? The door's open, why don't you walk in?"

"I don't wanta come in, Charlie. I wanta talk to you out here."

"Okay, Tom, I'll be right down." Captain Payment thought Tom's behavior was very strange. He was not ordinarily so excitable or mysterious about his actions. As the Captain started down the stairs, he wondered whether his friend had been hitting the bottle. "No, that couldn't be it," Captain Payment mumbled to himself. Tom never took more than one or two drinks and then only to be sociable with his crew. Matter of fact, that was one of the reasons why Captain Payment hired him as the skipper of his vessel after Tom lost E.S. BEMIS in a wreck the year before. No sir, something must be very wrong with Tom to come calling at two in the morning.

Captain Payment pushed open the door and walked over toward Tom standing in the yard. The full moon highlighted Tom's face; his eyes seemed to have a strange glaze. He looked at Charles as if he weren't really there. Beckoning him over, Tom whispered to him, "Charles, I just killed a man."

Payment stood there, numbed by this blunt confession. "You're joking, Tom. How could you murder anyone?"

"I'm not joking, Charlie. I had a scuffle with some wharf rat in a tavern on lower Main Street; lost my temper; hit him over the head with a bottle."

"Come on, Tom, get hold of yourself. How can you be sure he was dead?" Charlie placed his two hands on Tom's shoulders as if to reassure him and then said, "Here, I'll tell you what I'll do. I'll walk over and see what really happened."

"No need to, Charlie. He's dead; I'm sure of it. Just as dead as the bottle he'd been drinking." Tom paused for a moment and then said, "You know, Charlie, there's a certain dumb look a man gets when he's dead. This guy had it." The tone with which Tom Hubert made this statement convinced Charlie that the man surely must be dead.

There was silence for a moment and then Captain Payment, looking straight at him and in a reassuring tone said, "What do you want me to do, Tom?"

"I want you to get word to my first mate on the COLUMBIAN. I can't go over there because the Watch will be laying for me."

"You want me to go, Tom, is that it?"

284

"You gotta go for me, Charlie. It's my only way out."

"Okay, if that's what you want, I'll go in and dress. Be back in a minute." As Charlie walked back into the house, he was still trying to make himself believe that Tom had killed a man. Tom was his best friend. Only last Saturday, Tom had had dinner with the Payment family in the very room through which Charlie walked on his way to the stairs. As he started up the stairs he remembered pleasantly how often he and his wife had visited Tom Hubert's family in Detroit. And he remembered the many times that he had raced his ship, the H.S. WINSLOW, against Captain Hubert's E.S. BEMIS. After the BEMIS went down, Hubert seemed like a lost soul -- a Captain without a ship. Unless a person had been master of his own vessel he could never know the gnawing feeling a skipper gets when his ship goes down. It's like losing the most precious thing in the world. It's like losing the dearest member in the family. No wonder, he thought, captains go down with their ships. In the long hitch, it's much better that way.

As Charlie started down the hall toward the door, he remembered how Tom looked that summer day in 1870 just after the BEMIS sank. He remembered also seeing him a few days later, sitting on the wharf gazing out over the lake as if he expected the E.S. BEMIS to come sailing in as she had for many a year. As if it were yesterday he could remember the conversation.

"Tom, I'm mighty sorry about the BEMIS."

"Thanks, Charlie," said Tom Hubert, as he looked up from the wharf, "but it won't bring her back."

"I know it won't, Tom." Then Charlie paused for a moment and said, "You know, Tom, The BEMIS had the prettiest lines of any schooner in this harbor, unless of course it was my own WINSLOW."

Tom looked up at Charlie Payment. There was no humor in his face. "Look Charlie, I ain't in the mood for comparisons and I don't want to be reminded of the BEMIS."

"Sorry, Tom, I meant no offense. I liked the BEMIS and thought maybe you liked the WINSLOW too."

"Well I do, but I just don't want to talk ships today," said Tom Hubert.

"Okay, Tom, if that's the way you feel. But I wanted you to know that there's a skipper's job open. If you hear of anyone interested, let me know." Captain Payment turned and started across The Beach.

Tom jumped up from the wharf, started after Payment and said, "Come here, you old carbuncle. You know I'll die of plain dry-rot if I don't get a ship."

"You mean you'll take the job, Tom?"

"As of now, you've got yourself a skipper, Captain Payment." Tom stuck out his hand and Charlie took it.

That was a year ago. Tom stayed with the ship the rest of the season. Then this year he was appointed master of the COLUMBIAN which now lay in port. A better skipper, the WINSLOW and COLUMBIAN had never had.

"How could such a man be a murderer?" thought Charles. Whatever it takes to commit a murder, Captain Payment was sure Tom didn't have it. Maybe it was self-defense -- that's it, self-defense. The drunk swung at Tom and to protect himself he hit him with the bottle.

By now Charles Payment was lacing up his shoes. That done, he put on his light jacket and started down the stairs as quickly as possible so as not to waken Mrs. Payment. As he passed the kids' door at the top of the stairs he stole a quick look and saw that his two boys were sleeping soundly in their snug harbors. Outside, Tom and Charlie started for Hubert's skiff which would carry them over the Blackwell Canal to the spot where the COLUMBIAN was moored.

For almost a minute, as they walked along, neither one said a thing. Then Tom started mumbling, half to himself and half to his friend, "Charlie, why did this thing ever have to happen to me?"

"Take it easy, Tom. I've got it all figured out. He swung at you and in self-defense you hit him with the bottle. It was as simple as that. Self-defense! A man's got a right to defend himself ain't he?"

"Charlie that would be all right, but it wasn't self-defense. He was just sitting there drinking," Tom said. "Some uncontrollable urge seized me. It was as if someone else were making my actions for me. I picked up the bottle and slammed it over his head. Then I plunged the jagged edge of the bottle again and again into his head. He screamed, pitched forward face down on the table and then rolled over on the floor. His eyes were open and sort of bugged out. There was a frozen expression of terror on his face. Then the blood started rushing down over his face."

Charles took a good look at Tom again. He noticed that same dazed look in his eyes -- the same look one gets when he's taken a hard right to the jaw. Then in measured words, almost not believing that he could be asking the question, Charlie said, "You mean to tell me, Tom, you killed a man in cold blood?"

"Well if that's what you mean by a cold sweat, yes I did."

"But Tom, how could you do such a thing?"

"I don't know, Charlie, but it's done and you've got to save me."

The two men had walked across the sandy waste which sloped down from the bank of the Blackwell Canal to the lake. At this point along the canal, the salt dock was located. Large sheds had been built on the dock to protect the salt from bad weather. Beyond these sheds lay the path to the rowboat Tom said would be waiting to take them over to the COLUMBIAN on the opposite bank. As they approached the sheds, Payment was perhaps a step in front of Tom Hubert. He could hear Hubert mumbling to himself how sorry he was for having committed such a horrible deed. Just as they walked into the shadow of the sheds, he heard Tom say, "Stop!" He wheeled about quickly and found himself looking into the barrel of a revolver. Tom Hubert's finger was on the trigger. Before Captain Payment could say a thing, Hubert said in clipped words, "Payment, get down on your knees unless you want your brains blown out right away."

"Tom, what's the matter with you? Have you gone mad? Aren't you in enough trouble as it is, or is this just a bad joke?"

"This is no joke, Payment, and neither is this revolver. Now down on your knees and start praying. And Charlie, pray good, because you only have two minutes to live."

"Now wait a minute, Tom."

"I said I'd wait two minutes, didn't I, Charlie? Say, that's pretty good, isn't it." With that Hubert pushed Captain Payment to the sand. "Now listen here, Payment, I warned you. You've got less than two minutes to live. You'd better make your peace with God, because you're going to meet Him."

Charlie Payment knew Hubert meant business. The cold steel barrel and the look in his eyes convinced him that this was no joke.

"Tom, for God's sake, what is the meaning of this? Are you going to commit two murders in one night? Put that pistol down and let's stop fooling."

"No, Charlie, not two murders, just one -- yours. And you'd better start praying because your time's getting short."

How can this be, thought Payment. It must be a nightmare. Less than an hour ago I was sleeping in my bed. This must all be a bad dream.

"I don't hear you praying, Charlie. If you have any sins to confess, I will be your confessor."

Where the line is between hope and despair is difficult to know, but wherever it is, Charlie knew he had crossed it. He felt absolutely helpless -- weak and drained. Think of it, he was about to die. For the first time in the last agonizing minute he began to think about that. He was going to die and there was nothing he could do about it. Die -- he, Charlie Payment, about to die. What was it they said, "Ashes to ashes and dust to dust?" Just think, he had been born, lived, married, raised a family and now he was going to die. Just like that. Here on this lonely sandy beach without his family about him. He was going to die without his ship under him. He grabbed a fistful of sand and let it trickle out of his hand. Like the sand his time was running out. He was going to die. The more he dwelt on the idea of dying, the more it began to intrigue him. Would the bullet hurt when it pierced his brain? Then a crazy thought. Would he hear the explosion or would he be dead before the sound reached his ears?

He looked up at Tom whose face now wore an almost satanic expression.

"You know I am without arms and within your power, so if you want to murder me I cannot prevent it," Charles said. With that he closed his eyes and waited. It was quiet. It was very quiet. He could feel the blood beating in his temples. His mouth was dry and his throat almost closed. Droplets of sweat appeared on his face. Still nothing happened. It was quiet, so quiet he could hear the water gently lapping against the shore and still he waited and waited. "For God's sake, Hubert, pull the trigger and get it over with."

After an eternity Charles Payment felt Hubert grab him by the arm saying, "Get up and be quick about it. We're going across the flat and over the sea wall to the lake beach. It will be easier to dispose of your body over there." Still holding the pistol at his temple, Hubert then ordered, "Hold your hands above your head. Walk straight. One false move and you're dead."

Payment started to walk forward toward the sea wall. Hubert followed close behind. Beyond the sea wall the two had to walk close to several houses. Payment resolved to make a break away. He knew he could not turn around to see when the best moment might be. It would have to be a leap and a prayer. Then he said to himself, This is it. With all the energy he could muster he sprang forward. He had not taken one full step before Hubert pulled the trigger. Charlie knew, for he heard the sound of the revolver hammer. It took him a split second to realize what had happened. He had heard the sound of the hammer but not the explosion.

Now he was running with all his might. Hubert was close behind. The next shot was not a dud. It creased the air so close to Payment's face that he could feel the wind from it. Stumbling and falling, but always moving forward. Ball after ball whizzed by him, kicking up the sand in front of him. Never had he run so fast. Finally he made the street but he didn't stop running until he was sure there was a safe distance between him and Tom Hubert. Then for the first time in an hour, Payment sat down. His lungs felt as if a hot poker had been thrust into them. His stomach was tied in knots. He was sick; very, very sick. He emptied the contents of his stomach several times over. When he was drained, he lay down in the sandy field close by the road. The cool lake breeze felt good on his face. All he could think of was how good it was to be alive.

Once again he grabbed a fistful of sand and let a thin strand trickle out of his hand. Now there would be more time.

"I DISCOVERED AMERICA"

(Harry J. Siemsen, Sawkill)

The first part of this song was given to me by a man in Fort Ewen who had heard it as a boy. He said the simple little tune was a barroom song from the time of the Delaware and Hudson Canal and that was all there was to it. It was too short for me so I added to it.

I discovered America
You discovered beer,
Long before Columbus
Ever landed over here.

You discovered the Adyrondacks,
And I placed them where they are,
Sold whiskey to the Indians
Behind my little bar.

I took the Catskill mountains
And I rounded all their tops.
Went up into Schoharie
And started raising hops.

Where I drug me home some hoop poles
To build myself some barrels,
That's where the Irish later
Dug the D. and H. Canal

BLACK BECOMES THE BRIDE'S GHOST

Slowly, as if moved by an unseen hand, the huge boulder rolls aside. Up from beneath the rock, the Indian Princess and her warrior Prince, dead these many years, arise. Once again the two ghost lovers walk hand in hand along the bank of their creek. For an hour, they walk the earth again. Then they return to their watery grave under the rock. Again the rock moves back into place and the stream resumes its peaceful flow around it.

What better testament of the immortality of true love! At Claverack, in the Hudson Valley, they call this The Legend of Spook Rock of Claverack Creek. If you're a willing listener, the people thereabouts will tell you this story in a number of variations as well as many another ghost story from the haunted Valley of the Hudson. But before the stories, a word or more about ghosts in general and more particularly the Hudson Valley species.

In that valley of spring and summer green, across from the lore-filled Catskills whose peaks the summer sunsets paint a deep purple, there are those -- the very young, with the inner glow of pink on their cheeks, and those -- the very old, with the sky color of sun and the soil color of earth on their faces -- and all those natives in between, who will tell you that the Headless Horseman still madly rides the hills and hollows along the sunrise shore of the Hudson River. In the land Washington Irving peopled with lovable lazy characters, good and ill-humored ghosts, the hapless Horseman always returns on moonful nights, especially when the frost is on the pumpkin and the wind howls down from the mountains.

To most, the ghostly ride may seem a bit overdone and rather theatrical; just a tale made up to frighten people and sell books. It did well. It did both. So thoroughly were the valley people frightened that many of them, especially the young and the old (and all those in between) became ardent ghost believers. Remember, of all ghost believers, a scared ghost believer is the very worst -- or is it the very best? With such an historic background, the Valley became a favorite haunt for ghosts. At least the believers, particularly the affrighted believers, thought so. After all, ghosts are (or rather were) people. They like to go where they are believed. Belief in ghosts among the young probably comes from an over-active imagination, among the middle-aged from an over-active thyroid and among the old, sometimes from indigestion or intoxication. Being Irish helps, too. And for some who live in the Hudson Valley, too much reading of Irving has had the same effect.

Since most ghosts live on forever, the ghost in our story, vintage 20th century, is relatively modern and young. As ghosts go, this one has not gone very far. Unlike the Legend of Sleepy Hollow, and to keep pace with the modern period, no horses dash through this story unless, of course, one wants to make a very feeble joke about the steam locomotive in the story being an iron horse.

It is also probably true that our young ghost could do with more aging. But, in this day of speed, who can wait, even for a ghost? Still, aging would help as it always does with the better ghosts. Ghosts, unlike people, are like good wine. They seem to do better with age. In the process, they acquire more spirit and less body. This helps them to get around more quickly, more easily and, to more people. With ghosts this is quite desirable, for they like people -- all kinds of people (why else would they return?). Everything ghost writers have dug up recently in their research seems to substantiate this. But enough of this lengthy ghost lore. Let's get on with the stories.

Since our ghost isn't old, it can at least be a woman: beautiful, and a bride. As the story has it, she is all of these. What daring but frightened group of boys first found the haunted honeymoon house, who first told the tale to the townfolk, who learned the secret of the ghost girl and actually unraveled the meaning of the story? All these are now lost, probably forever, in the heavy haze of the Hudson. All the historic details have dissolved in that misty past where ghosts like to gather and where there are no footprints or footnotes. Only the skeleton of the story remains, and it has been rattling around for twenty five years. Here it is, as I remember hearing it then, from one who claims to have been there:

According to him, it all began, as these tall telltales sometimes do, around a Boy Scout campfire in the Mid-Hudson hinterland, east of the river. This particular night was a good one for telling ghost stories. Black clouds blotted out large chunks of sky. A storm was in the making. The boys could see it, smell it, feel it coming. After a session of spinning ghost stories from all over the world, the camp counselors started with the local genre of ghosts: the Hudson Valley variety. They ended with the sad, sad story of Spook Rock of Claverack Creek. It went something like this:

In the time before the coming of the white man, the Konosioni wore deeply the trail through the valley of the Great River that flowed to the Big Water. One day a lone Iroquois warrior happened upon an Indian maiden of a river tribe, resting not far from her bark hut. He first saw her through a break in the brush as she knelt on the bank beside a quiet pool just off the main stream of the creek. She was gently scooping up handfuls of its crystal water. After drinking for a while, she continued to palm the water, letting the coolness trickle through her long, graceful fingers. Sunshine filtering through the trees sprinkled diamonds in her dark hair.

For a moment the warrior watched her face and form in the water. She was indeed a lovely creature -- far the loveliest he had ever seen. As the gently agitated water stilled and smoothed itself to a mirror, her image grew even lovelier. Soundlessly he moved closer, not wishing to disturb anything. The water caught his handsome reflection with hers. At the same instant a leaf dropped into the pool, rippling the waters and blending their faces prophetically. The forest girl was startled at first, but not frightened, by the picture in the water of the man standing behind her. Slowly she turned her head to look up at him. Then with graceful dignity she rose to face him. As the changing light caught her deep dark eyes, they flashed brightly, sparkling like star fires chipped from flint. They looked at each other for a long time. They felt much. They said nothing. Here was understanding without the need for words. From that moment on, they knew they were meant for each other.

For them there were many other days to follow, filled with the happiness of young love. But in the end, their love could never be. She was the daughter of a chieftain, a Princess. He was a Prince. Their nations were enemies to the death. They knew this as surely as they knew their love from that first day. Where love should be life, their love could be only death or even worse, life without love -- a living death. The Iroquois despised the tribes of the Hudson Valley as weaklings, especially the Mohicans. They had subjected them; found them useful only to pay tribute to the warriors of the Long House. Under no circumstances would they sanction such a corruption of the good blood of the Iroquois. They tabooed the marriage.

Still in love, yet still loyal to their people, the young couple knew that only death could give them what life had denied them. For the last time they walked beside their creek, then climbed the pathway that led to a rock ledge high above the stream. On the top of the cliff a huge boulder balanced precariously and delicately. It seemed held by an invisible hand. Finally by climbing carefully they made it to the very top of the huge stone. For a moment they held each other with their eyes and arms. Silently they turned, looked up, and then stepped off into space and eternity. At the same instant the added weight and sudden motion on the rock caused it to teeter and break loose. Small stones and shale stirred up by the moving rock rained after it and a cloud of dust followed it down the side of the mountain. With a crashing, crunching roar, the boulder plunged after the lovers, crushing their bodies beneath it in the creek. In a few minutes the noise quieted, the dirt and dust settled, and the creek took a new course around the rock.

Did the lovers really take their own lives by their own wish and will? Some say not. According to another version of the story, the Indian Princess and her Prince had planned to run away, hoping to find in another land the happiness their fathers denied them. One night, she escaped from the castle when all were asleep and met her lover at an appointed place. As they neared the cliff a storm struck. They sought refuge near the rock. Then with the suddenness of anger, a blinding flash and a thunderous roar broke out of the heavens, shaking the mountain, loosening the rock and hurling the Indian lovers to their death below. The rock tumbled after them. It landed on top of their bodies, crushing them into the bed of the creek and sealing their grave.

All this happened before the white man began recording his history of the valley. Today the creek flows as it did then. The erosion of time has changed it little; man has changed it some. But the huge rock still rests in Claverack Creek, in precisely the same spot. For all who would like to see, they can see it. For almost all, however, that is all they'll see -- the rock and the creek -- nothing more. For them, the deep mystery will always remain.

Only a rare few have found the true secret of Spook Rock of Claverack Creek. This is the story some of them tell:

Each night at the Angelus Hour, or whenever the church bells of Claverack toll for death, a deadly quiet descends on the creek. The rock rolls over. Up from beneath it the Indian lovers arise and move once again along the bank of the creek. When the Angelus Hour has run its time, when the bells have ceased their ringing, they disappear under the rock. Then as slowly as it moved away, the rock slips back in place.

Now lest any of you Boy Scouts think you, too, might see the ghost lovers of Spook Rock, remember this: they are only for the eyes of young lovers still pure in heart, whose love is truly as undying as the love of the Indian girl and her beloved warrior.

This tale ended the storytelling for one night. One of the counselors put a period on the session by blowing his whistle. Slowly the boys arose to make their way to their tents.

As the circle broke up, one of the more adventuresome and experienced of the scouts whispered to a few of his friends that after "lights out" they sneak out of camp on a ghost hunt. But they wanted none of the love stuff of Spook Rock. They wanted ghosts without girls. As it turned out, they were to get only a part of their wish.

With the dying fire still in sight, the ghost stories fresh in mind, and the approaching storm all about them, the boys had the proper mood and atmosphere for their trip. The boy who suggested the expedition had already mentioned that he thought he knew a likely hideout for ghosts, an abandoned house across the lake on the other side of the railroad tracks. Not a boy among them could have known that they were about to uncover one of the most fantastic ghost stories of all time. They made their way across the pond and over the tracks. As if they were actually stalking a ghost, the boys crept up on the house very slowly. Finally they reached the house. In the dark it was hard to make out its shape. There was the musty smell and feel of age -- actually decay -- about the house. Yet it didn't seem to be too old, just very sad.

Since the windows were too high to peer into from the ground, one of the boys shinnied himself up to the sill, brushed aside the dust covered webs and dried bugs, spit on the glass, wiped it clean and peeked in wide-eyed. The flashlight revealed nothing but an empty room. Even the boy's imagination and delicious desire to be scared couldn't conjure up anything resembling a ghost.

Then, just as he started to lower himself to the ground, wondering whether he was relieved or disappointed in not finding a ghost, a hideous shriek shattered the air. Terror drained his strength, loosened his grip. He fell to the ground. Frightened for the moment, the boys huddled together in a pile beneath the window, scarcely daring to breathe. Then the one on top dared to look up. He shined his light at the window. Staring down at him, through the clear spithole in the glass, was a ghost -- a sheeted figure jumping up and down and waving his arms wildly at the boys. That was enough! The boys wasted no time. They untangled and took off. The ghost, his white sheet billowing out behind, flew through the door, down the steps, over the tracks and across the field after them. Almost to the boats, one of the boys took courage to look back. He was just in time to see the ghost stumble and fall, and what was even worse than for the ghost to lose his sheet. He played his flashlight on the crumpled figure, then called to his companions to stop running. The ghost turned out to be one of their companions who had given them the slip in the dark when they first circled the house.

Laughing and joking, the boys returned to their haunted house for a last look for ghosts -- this time for real ghosts. In the distance, they could see and hear the approaching storm getting nearer and nearer. They knew they had very little time. At the house the boys tried the front door, but it had slammed shut when their ghostly friend bounded through in pursuit. The back door had been bolted by him as he changed to a ghost. They were locked out.

So this time they fixed a board across two cut stones several feet above the ground. Now they could all see in the window. Look they did. Again they saw nothing, just an empty room with a stairs flat against the side. The stairs and stair wall were painted white.

Then the storm broke with such violence it seemed the heavens would rip apart. As the hard wind hissed through the branches in sweeping gusts, it sucked the leaves after it. The wind stretched out the branches and the leaves like fingers and arms eager to flay and grab the unwary. It turned over the light colored underside of the leaves. The lightning flashes reflected on the whitish green palms of the leaves and changed the trees to a kind of ghostly ashen.

Sticking close to the house, under the eaves, the boys kept out of some of the rain. The lightning cracked and the thunder rumbled back and forth against the Catskills and the Berkshires as it rolled down the valley. On the roof and the side opposite the boys, the rain beat an ominous staccato. The boys wondered whether to break in where it was dry or to try to make it back to camp. Then a flash of light and a sound like thunder, only closer and steadier, stopped them still. And all at once they saw it in the room. They were stunned and stone silent. This was it! Whatever it was. This was it! There was no laugh in the boys now. This was not one of them playing ghost. This was the real thing! The boys stood stiff with fear. They stared unbelieving in a kind of trauma. The stair end of the room was filled with a flood of light. Then, forming out of nothing at the head of the stairs stood a beautiful girl with a bouquet in her arms, a veil over her face and a flowing dress. It was certainly a bridal gown, but it was black. In one flowing motion, almost as she formed, she floated down the stairs moving, yet not seeming to walk; there in form, yet transparent. Near the bottom of the stairs she dissolved into the nothingness from which she came. The light passed by and faded. The darkness, now deeper, enveloped the room. A bolt of lightning crackled across the sky. It painted grotesque shadows of dancing trees on the walls and stairs. At almost the same time with the sound of thunder that follows a bolt of lightning, a train rushed down the tracks near the house and disappeared in the distance, blending its mournful sound with the wind and the rain.

Not a word was spoken. None had to be spoken. The boys needed all their breath for running. Where there had been no motion, now there was all motion. Run they did, pell mell for the pond. This time no one looked back. They made it back across the water much faster than they had made it over.

At camp, all were asleep. But for these boys there was no sleep that night. They lay tense, tight, excited, silent. How good it felt to be dry and warm and safe under the covers. The bunks never felt better. Next morning, the camp buzzed with the incredible story; more exactly stories, for each telling by each boy brought more embellishments. As much as they didn't want the counselors to know, the story was too good to keep from their friends. By nightfall, everyone knew at least one variation of the "Phantom Bride" story including, unfortunately, the counselors. They, of course, treated the whole episode with amused cynicism except for their discipline of the boys for being A.W.O.L. after "lights out." The ghost hunters were confined to camp. It did not matter much to them, however, because to their bunk buddies they were heroes.

At chow time, the counselors tried to be casual about the ghost story. They covered up their curiosity by making fun of the "kids" story. Finally one dared to say what they were all thinking.

"Well, I don't know about you guys, but I'd like to have a look at that house after we get the kids bedded down."

No vote needed to be taken. This was what they all wanted to say and do. That night, those counselors who could be spared from the night operations at camp, started off for the haunted house. The sky was cloudless, filled with pinholes of light. The full moon had clear shining. They had no trouble finding the house. Even with the moon shadows playing on it, it did not look ghostly.

The doors were still locked. The windows were weather wedged. As their flashlights washed away the darkness, they could see nothing unusual about the empty room. Like the boys the night before, they noted the stairs and stair wall had been painted white; the rest of the walls had been papered.

They waited. Nothing happened. Off in the distance they heard the sound of an approaching train. As it grew closer, the sound grew louder. Then just about the time they would have turned their heads to watch the train go by, one said. "Look!" and pointed inside the room. Light flooded the stair case. Then they saw it. Just as the boys had seen it they were seeing it and not believing it. The figure of a woman formed at the head of the stairs, moved footlessly down the stairs, melting into the darkness as the light moved away, leaving the room and the counselors to the night. At the same time, the train curved by the house and rushed into the night, too.

The ghost had not been imagination. If there be ghosts, this was one of them. No one doubted that. There must be an explanation, but night time was no time for finding out. The counselors had not been so much frightened as mystified. They were happy, however, when one of their number suggested going back to camp. Tomorrow they would return during daytime. There is always more courage in daylight.

Early the next morning they were back. This time they went inside the house. They examined the house upstairs and downstairs. Nothing! Suddenly one shouted, "Look, I think I've found something!" There in the wall was an opening much larger than a peephole, but smaller than a porthole. The glass that covered it looked like a lens. There between the lens-like glass, they found their ghost -- a picture of the bride. As a light played on the glass on the outside, the picture was projected on the stair wall opposite. The light obviously came from the train.

But why all this? Investigation later revealed a strange story. A man had once brought his bride to this house. A few weeks later a tragic thing happened. Crossing the tracks near the house one night, she fell. The train bore down on her, killing her instantly.

In his melancholia, the husband built the lens-like window and put his wife's bridal picture in it. Each night when the head light of the train flashed against the window lens, it played the picture on the opposite wall. As the train followed its curve around the house, the light moved away causing the image to descend the stairs. The train that had taken his loved one away, brought her back each night.

Though centuries and civilizations separated the ghost story of the Indian lovers and tale of the modern lovers, the themes were exactly the same -- the immortality of true love. May it ever be thus!

But why, in the modern theme, you ask, did the bride wear black? Well, picture prints are opaque and negatives are transparent. Since only transparencies project, the negative and not the positive had to be used. In such cases, white is black and black is white. Come to think of it, perhaps this is the way it is in the ghost world, too. Things are not what they seem. Often they are just the opposite.

There may be even more to it than that. If at weddings, for purity and the promise of life, white becomes the bride, then for death, it follows that black becomes the bride's ghost.

So be it for this story. So be it here. So be it.

WHISKEY CARGO AND JOHN WILKES BOOTH

To most any Chicago barkeep at the turn of the century, a call for a shot of "Mary Smith" meant the best whiskey in the house. It marked the buyer a judge of good liquor and the bartender an expert in whiskey folklore -- that is, he knew the whole story behind the name of the whiskey. Few did. Those who did know always told the story. It went with the drink like a chaser. It was quite a tale -- this story of the MARY SMITH and her cargo.

It all began (the man behind the bar would usually say) one stormy night on Lake Erie -- April 17, 1859, to be exact. The schooner MARY SMITH, out of Chicago, ran into bad weather and heavy seas not too far west of its Buffalo destination. With the good and experienced hands she had before the mast and tiller, the schooner should have ridden out the storm. Strangely enough, she didn't. Only the mate and two hands managed to escape in a small boat before the schooner sank a little before daybreak in deep water twenty miles from Buffalo. Save for these three, all hands were lost along with forty-thousand gallons of the choicest spirits from mid-western distilleries. This wet cargo on the bottom of Lake Erie was, of course, the point of the story.

The whiskey remained undisturbed in the hold of the MARY SMITH for 14 years -- at least undisturbed by humans. The deep water discouraged salvage attempts and as the years rolled on, the

299

story of the MARY SMITH grew. As her whiskey cargo aged, the price increased accordingly. What could be better, thought many a tippler as he wetted his lips with a whiskey bearing the name Mary Smith, than a taste of the real "Mary Smith" whiskey aged in oaken barrels for 14 years and cooled all that time by the bottom waters of Lake Erie. It was enough to make some men want to go diving for it. None did, however. They just talked about it. Occasionally they lifted their glasses in a toast to the cargo of the MARY SMITH -- "May her barrel seams stay tight and her whiskey never be watered."

The men, however, who sell whiskey and drink whiskey have long memories for their favorite liquor. Now and again those with the longest memories and keenest taste for both spirits and money would speculate on the constantly increasing value of the whiskey cargo. One such man lived in Chicago in those years. His name was Ralph Bayne. Though he had accomplished little else, he had, at an early age, acquired a goodly inheritance from his family and an exacting taste for fine liquor.

Across famous bars in Chicago, he had heard with many a drink the story of the lost cargo of the schooner MARY SMITH. Being an adventuresome sort of fellow, he inquired about the location of the wreck and the possibility of raising the cargo. He found out exactly where it was and how it could be raised. From a Chicago firm he negotiated a contract that would pay him $20 a gallon for all the MARY SMITH liquor he delivered. With this contract, a good crew and a lively retinue, Bayne sailed out of the Chicago River April 17, 1873, fourteen years to the day that the MARY SMITH met her fate.

Bayne brought with him aboard the sloop a father and son team of divers named Falcon. In those days, Chicago marine interests considered these two the best divers around the city. To take care of his legal and business interests, Bayne engaged a lawyer named Luther Laflin Mills. For just plain fun around the poker table, Bayne invited a whiskey-drinking friend. History and the story leave him nameless.

The trip proved uneventful. They played poker, drank and sang. In idle moments, Bayne multiplied 40,000 gallons by $20 per gallon. The result always came out the same: $800,000. The thought of the money warmed the cockles of his wallet and the thought of the whiskey whetted his taste buds. He found both thoughts pleasant. Finally, on a still, warm day, the sloop dropped anchor at what had become the hallowed spot of some whiskey drinkers: the place where the MARY SMITH sank. The elder Falcon wasted no time in donning his diving suit. His son manned the air line. Being French, the Falcons were understandably demonstrative. The father loved the boy very deeply. Not knowing the water's depth, or the full risk involved, just before he stepped over the side he grabbed his son impulsively, pressed him close against his chest in a warm embrace, then pushed him out at arms length, looked at him tenderly for a moment and then kissed him quickly and softly on both cheeks.

Watching this touching scene from the taffrail, Bayne's poker-playing friend, filled with plenty of whiskey, removed his hat, clutched a rope with his left hand, extended his right hand, palm up, struck a dramatic pose and declaimed,

> Oh! Give him a sepulchre broad as the sweep
> Of the tidal wave's measureless motion;
> Lay our hero to sleep in the arms of the deep
> Since his life was as free as the ocean.

The quiet waters seemed to magnify his voice. It made majestic what he had meant to be mockery.

Falcon was already disappearing below the surface as the words floated over the water. Part way down a kink developed in the air line. Desperately the elder Falcon tried to get it out. On the bottom he signaled for slack in the line hoping this would clear it. It failed. With his air supply cut off, his moments were now numbered. He began to grow faint. Still he struggled to straighten the line, but to no avail. Just before he blacked out he frantically pulled the air line three times, the danger signal. Young Falcon and the crew worked fast. They pulled him up as quickly as possible. When they stripped off his helmet the old man was already unconscious and almost lifeless. They applied artificial respiration immediately and in time the old man came around. Understandably he would have no more diving for that day or that trip. So, reluctantly Bayne weighed anchor and returned to Chicago. Since that unsuccessful attempt, there is no record of anyone trying to reach the cargo of the MARY SMITH. For all anyone knows, she is still there with 40,000 gallons of aged whiskey which may or may not be watered. Old-timers among Buffalo mariners, however, do not recall her name or story. Newspapers of her time carry no reference to her and histories of the Great Lakes list no schooner of that name. Yet the story by a Chicago correspondent of the New York Sun appeared in the Buffalo Enquirer May 24, 1898.

Ordinarily, this would have ended the story if it had not been for something said the day of the unsuccessful dive. Luther Mills, the lawyer on the trip who later attained great stature in that profession in Chicago, had been struck by the beauty of the words spoken by the friend at the taffrail as Falcon disappeared into the water. Anxious to learn the whole poem and the name of the author, Mills, some years later, found Bayne's friend and asked him about the lines quoted on that memorable day. All he knew of the poem was what he quoted and that it had originally been printed in the old Chicago Times and signed "Arrington." He had not committed to memory the entire poem. By his own admission he would not have recalled the lines or spoken them if it had not been for old man Falcon's strong emotions and Bayne's strong whiskey.

Mill's curiosity was piqued at this point. He started a search for the poem and its author. He soon discovered that the Times files had been lost. He had, however, known a brilliant lawyer of uncertain habits who had been dead for three years by the name of Alfred W. Arrington. Perhaps, he thought, this could be the author. Mills, however, could find no one who had heard Arrington read the poem much less claim authorship of it. Finally, in his search he located Arrington's son. Unfortunately, young Arrington had no knowledge of the poem or his father's connection with it, if any. He suggested, however, that a poet-lawyer from Ottawa, Illinois, named Oliver C. Gray might know something about the poem. This proved to be the key to the mystery. From Gray, Mills learned the whole story of the poem and its author. His hunch had been quite right. It was Arrington. But the story behind the poem was as interesting as the story behind the cargo of the MARY SMITH, and not as disappointing:

In the early days of the Civil War, Alfred Arrington had strong loyalties to the South. As the war turned more and more against the Confederates, his deep sense of sympathy for the underdog and his love for a lost cause made him a rabid secessionist. Most people treated him with good-natured tolerance. In 1863, let it be remembered, it took more than a little courage to hold and express such feelings in the North. Arrington lacked nothing of courage. He wore his unpopularity like a badge of honor. Sometimes he wore a black eye to match it. The end of the war brought Lincoln's tragic death. The nation mourned and hunted the assassin. John Wilkes Booth's name became a vile word. People screamed for vengeance. They soon had it. Booth met his death in a burning barn.

The night the news reached Chicago, a man with a pale face, disordered attire and drunk with alcohol and anger, rushed into the editorial rooms of The Chicago Times. Later in the day, Arrington, wanting more liquor, walked into the barroom of the Sherman House at Randolph and Dearborn Streets. Federal troops filled the tables and lined the bar. Many were happy about the capture and killing of Booth. They knew Arrington's strong feelings and excused them. That day, however, they had been drinking -- perhaps too much. Besides, it was a different day. Arrington joined them in drinking several glasses of whiskey and then announced to all that he was going to recite an original poem. He jumped up on a table and started reciting the poem he had written the night before:

302

Oh! Give him a sepulchre broad as the sweep
Of the tidal wave's measureless motion;
Lay our hero to sleep in the arms of the deep
Since his life was as free as the ocean.

It was Liberty slain that maddened his brain,
To avenge the dear idol he cherished;
So it's meet that the main, never curbed by a chain
Should entomb the last freeman, now perished.

He dared break the rod of the blackamoor's God --
All the hosts of the despot defying
May not swell in the sod by a Nation's feet trod
That he shamed with his glory in dying.

Yes, hide him away from the sad eyes of day
In the coral of sea-green abysses.
Where the mermaidens gay as they fly through the spray
Shall purple his pale cheek with kisses!

As the ocean-streams roll from the Gulf to the Pole,
Let them mourn him with musical surges!
Let the tempest-bell toll the repose of his soul
More sublime than the sound of its dirges!

He has written his name in letters of flame
O'er the archway of Liberty's portal
And the serfs that now blame shall crimson with shame
When they learn they have cursed an Immortal!

With each of the words anger mounted in the soldiers at the bar. They sensed the meaning. When at the end he announced that the poem was dedicated to John Wilkes Booth, a roar went up from the soldiers. They dragged him from the table and hurled him to the floor. Arrington would have been trampled to death if it had not been for the quick intervention of the proprietor who grabbed him away from his attackers and shoved him out the back door. Apparently, Arrington never again acknowledged the poem.

But that is not the end of the story. In 1866 he visited Texas. His pro-secessionist sentiments made him a welcome guest among the leading men of Texas. After that sojourn, he returned to Chicago and died; but the story of the poem did not die with him.

In 1888 a Texas paper printed the poem and erroneously credited it to Alexander W. Terrell. Five years later this same Terrell, prominent in public affairs in Texas, was appointed Minister to Turkey. In an attempt to defeat his confirmation in the Senate, his enemies reprinted the poem and attributed the authorship to him. The maneuver, however, failed. Terrell became Minister to Turkey.

Significantly, the poem, which was discovered in an abortive attempt to raise a cargo of whiskey near Buffalo, had in a sense come back almost to the same spot. For the President who appointed Terrell Minister to Turkey was Grover Cleveland, formerly Mayor of Buffalo and Sheriff of Erie County.

And that is the story of how a lost cargo of whiskey helped to find a lost poem dedicated to Lincoln's assassin. There will always be those of certain tastes who will never consider it a fair exchange.

FREEDOM IN THE WOODPILE

In the years before the Civil War, it is said that some four thousand slaves moved out of the northern port of Pultneyville, N.Y. across Lake Ontario to Canada and freedom. Many were the stories behind the escapes -- as many perhaps as the slaves that gained their freedom. Out of their escapes came the story behind the vulgar phrase "Nigger in the Woodpile."

According to some of the people in the village of Pultneyville this is the way it all happened one particular night (leastwise, this is the way they told it to me.)

It was that kind of night when dark clouds scudded across the moon, smudging it with ugly figures which the wind quickly washed clean again. A crowd of people, not distinguishable in the brush and shadows, waited for the cloud-darkened intervals to slip forward to the next cover. As the eye accustomed itself to the dark, one man among the group could be seen leading the way. Minutes before, they had all left the dusty road which had brought them from the southern part of New York State. Now they picked their way along a secret path, holding the branches each for the other to keep them from snapping in the person's face next in line.

Like hunted men, they moved quietly, nervously -- never quite sure. They threw haunted glances over their shoulders whenever an unfamiliar sound broke the night air. The leader, apparently, knew his woods. Without false step or wrong direction, he brought his people to a spot where a large canoe nestled under the bank of a stream he called Salmon Creek. Now, all answering to a silent arm motion, they stepped into the canoe (a large one of the freighter variety,) settled themselves, trimmed their weight for balance and, at the command, pushed off from the bank into midstream. Expertly turning the paddle for more power and less noise, the man in charge cut, rather than broke, the water. The boat slid forward down the middle of the narrow winding creek. The water folded smoothly in behind the canoe.

A soft breeze shook the leaves. Willows and silver poplars caught it with a sharp high pitch, like tingling bells. The other trees harmonized with a deeper more mellow rustling. A flash of light would burst out, as clouds occasionally brushed past the face of the moon. Through the breaks in the trees, it streaked the creek with a shimmering silver and lighted the faces of the men in the boat. The paddler's face seemed to reflect more light than the others. No wonder. Close inspection showed his skin to be white; the others were black. Such momentary glimpses, like flashing pictures, made the darkness that followed deeper than before, and through it all remained the same awful quietness.

The canoe moved on along the narrow pathway of water, and overhanging branches scratched against the men and the boat. Suddenly, a crunching sound broke and startled the silence. Motion froze. Everyone stiffened. No one breathed. Everyone looked, listening intently. The black men turned quickly and instinctively to the paddler. After a moment of tight concentration, his body relaxed, his paddle motion resumed. Thus reassured, the others started breathing again.

"A woodchuck," he whispered in relief.

What a pity, he thought, after all these long miles of hardship and escape, if these poor wretched souls were now to be captured so close to freedom's shore.

The minutes and quarter-hours slipped by under effortless stroking. The creek curved gently northward through the woods to Pultneyville. Soon, at a sharp right-angle turn, the white man reached out, grabbed a branch and pulled the boat over to the shore where he crawled out of the boat and scrambled up the shallow bank. There for a long time he lay, bellydown, awaiting a signal from one of the three houses whose yards backed onto the creek.

Idly -- as they waited out the long minutes in the canoe -- one of the Negroes, ever so softly, stripped off a little piece of bark from a bank tree, handled it fondly in the cup of his hand for several minutes and then, almost in reverence, dropped it into the water.

With a faint smile and almost a murmur, he thought, "Go down to the lake, little boat, go down to freedom." For a few minutes the bark strip floated toward the lake in the general direction the canoe had been traveling. The Negro soon lost it in the darkness.

Minutes later, still gazing hypnotically at the water, he wondered whether his boat, like himself, would ever reach Canada. Huddled in the canoe, he bethought himself as tiny and as helpless as the little piece of tree bark on the water. Still lost in his reverie, he suddenly thought he saw what looked like the same strip floating back. The clean, cream-like inside of the strip had caught the light.

"No, no," he thought almost aloud, catching himself just in time. "It couldn't be the same piece."

Intently, he watched it disappear. Sure enough, a few minutes later, the little bark boat returned once again, moving in its original and, what he thought was, its right direction.

For a long time, with gnawing fright, the Negro watched the ebb and flow of the water and the bark. The more he watched, the more terrified he became.

"A spell, the water's bewitched," he thought. Fear of capture dried his throat. Every small sound was thunderous. Even the moon seemed crazy with mysterious figures dancing on its face. He gripped himself tightly to regain his courage.

Just then, the awaited signal from the house appeared. Cautiously, they all climbed out of the boat and up the bank, following the leader. The man who had been frightened looked back at his piece of bark floating back and forth in the stream. Prayerfully to himself, he said, "No time now, Lord, to be afraid."

They crossed Pig Lane, moving toward the backs of the three houses. One stood in front of them; the other two were off to the left. Farthest to the left was a cobblestone house; next, a large, white dignified New England-type frame house; and finally, the one toward which they made their way, a small, white frame salt-box style house. In later years, a brick addition in the front, topped by a cupola and a widow's walk would cause this house to be known as the "Little Brick" but now it was just a salt-box. All three of these houses backed on Salmon Creek, faced on Washington Avenue and overlooked Lake Ontario. Much of the village activity centered here. These houses occupied the three original lots of the village of Pultneyville, a village which once promised to be a large port east of Rochester and in the years before the Civil War still held its head high with such hopes.

Through its harbor, farmers and commercial merchants shipped produce -- fruit, fresh meat, potash and wood -- carted and floated in from the interior of the state. Steamers made four regularly scheduled calls a week. Schooners arrived frequently and unannounced.

But to many, during the critical pre-war days, Pultneyville was more than an active and promising port; it was an underground railroad station -- the last station on the land route from the South and the jumping-off place for Canada and freedom. This "runaway" route reached northward from Bath on the Cohocton River, along Canandaigua Lake, then crossed the east-west Erie Canal, Seneca Turnpike and rail lines. Finally the underground railroad left the wagon road as it approached Lake Ontario and took to Salmon Creek, which flowed northward to Pultneyville. Other fugitive slave routes, some perhaps more important, carried the slaves northward to Buffalo, Rochester, Oswego and the St. Lawrence River. Freedom was across the rivers and the lakes in Canada. Besides the three houses near Salmon Creek in Pultneyville, the Hallet and Cuyler houses owned by distinguished Pultneyville families were also underground stations -- the end of the slaves' long and arduous journey to freedom.

This night the slaves were to find haven in the salt-box house on lot three. As they approached the back of the house, the door opened. The leader entered and the others followed. They crossed the room to the stairs in the right-hand corner. A few steps took them to a right-angle turn, and then more steps carried them up to the second floor. Another right turn brought them to a bedroom with a ladder leading to a small trap-door in the ceiling approximately 15 inches wide and 27 inches long. Each slave mounted the rungs as he was told. As the last one placed his foot on the rung, he turned to the guide and, no longer able to contain himself said, as he slowly shook his head, "Judge, there's sumpthin' awful wrong about that branch water out there." The Negro went on to excitedly tell the local Justice about the bark strip that seemed to float both ways.

The Justice looked at him for a moment and then said evenly, "Yes, 'tis a strange thing. Seems to be no accounting for it. Salmon Creek sometimes just seems to flow in both directions. Don't ask me why. We're close to where it empties into the lake. Perhaps the lake has something to do with it. I really don't know."

"Judge, don't you see, that means no good to us. That going back and forth means the Sheriff's men will catch us and carry us back in chains. It's a powerful bad omen."

The Justice replied, "Don't you worry yourself. I don't know why the creek flows both ways. But I do know that the courage which has brought you this far, with God's help, will take you to freedom."

The Negro seemed to get more assurance out of the Judge's manner and expression than out of the words he used. For a moment longer, the Negro studied the Judge, tried a smile and then climbed the ladder to the attic. The crawl space under the eaves above the rooms was just that. The slaves had just enough space to slip in and lie down. They stretched their tired bodies across the rafters and fell asleep. The heat of the day was still in the attic, but already the night air coming through the dwarf windows in the front had begun to cool and freshen it. At this underground station when space permitted, they kept the slaves in the attic by night when it tended to be cool there, and in the cellar during the day for the same reason.

Before daybreak that particular morning, a knock on the trap door awakened the men. As the one farthest to the front of the house opened his eyes, he noticed the early morning light filtering in through the tiny windows. From the window lights he saw the lake stretching east, west and north. It disappeared into the distance. Beyond that horizon line lay freedom. Two wharves stretched out into the lake. They bent toward each other like arms, almost enclosing a part of the water to form an artificial harbor. It was as if Pultneyville had embraced the lake. Several white-sailed schooners rolled at anchor. The steamer ONTARIO was tying up at the dock. The western wharf, just east of the mouth of Salmon Creek, had several warehouses. The dock itself was large enough for a yoke of oxen to turn around.

Many a captain and his boat called Pultneyville home port. Perhaps the most famous of all was Captain Horatio Nelson Throop, a descendant of Connecticut Yankees, builder of boats, lake captain extraordinary and it's said, the first person to be born in Pultneyville. His was the substantial cobblestone house on lot one. It was one of the three houses on Washington Avenue that backed onto the creek. A cobblestone house fitted the Captain. The stone had been washed smooth and dredged up out of his beloved Ontario. What better material for building a lake captain's home than the stuff the lake water helped to fashion? His sailing days were mostly over now, but on rare and important occasions, he took command again, along with his faithful friend Jeppa, his beloved Italian greyhound. This day and this night was such a time for Captain Throop. As the slave looked out of the harbor from the attic, lost in the promise of it all, he wondered if that steamer, snug at the wharf, might be his boat to freedom. Already he had mused too long. A tug on his leg and a whispered word started him crawling backwards toward the trap door. One by one, the Negroes retraced their steps of the night before to the first-floor room where they had originally entered. In the corner, diagonally opposite the stair well, a long narrow trap door approximately six feet by four feet was lifted up. One by one, the men dropped through the trap door to the cellar below. The trap shut and normal household duties resumed.

Soon the village was awake and up and doing. Farmers' wagons, having started out the night before, moved out to the dock to unload apples, peaches, grapes, grains -- all of the produce of the rich hinterland farms. In the Sessions House, diagonally across the street from the underground station, official looking men walked through its doors to start their daily work. The local Justice of the Peace entered. Only a few knew that he had already done a worthy night's work. There were also Federal men entering the Sessions

House -- the Customs men charged with the duty to enforce the Federal laws -- including the Fugitive Slave Act, among others.

Also that day, the Pultneyville natives would see a few strangers walking along Washington Avenue. They were the Sheriff's men from the South -- slave owners' agents looking for runaway slaves. These were the men the underground tried to avoid. They were the hunters, the Negroes the hunted; men on both sides from the North and from the South trying to outwit each other. For each the gain was worth the effort.

Inside and outside the salt-box house and the other beautiful homes along Washington Avenue chore work went on as usual. Villagers along the street passed the time of day with farmers. Those who had unloaded had more time to chat. Those just pulling into the wharves had time only for a quick "hello."

In the cellar of the small frame house with only wisps of light coming in, the slaves could hear the chatter of voices on the village streets, the rumble of oxen carts and the many footsteps of household activities on the floor above. Several times during the day, a shaft of light would force them to huddle against the stone wall in front of the cellar. Assured that it was food being brought to them, they would move back toward the trap door to get it. For the villagers, the day passed fast, filled with the hundreds of tasks to keep life going. Outwardly, it was just like any other day. For some, however, huddled in dark places, it would be the last day of slavery.

Night came. The official men left the Sessions House. The Customs men went down to the dock to check Captain Throop's passenger lists and cargo. The Sheriff's men hung menacingly about the wharf.

At the salt-box house, the Judge -- leader of the night before -- opened the trap door, and offered the men a hand to pull them up. From the front windows, the ladies of the household watched for the signal from Captain Throop's steamer. Standing on the bridge of the ONTARIO, Captain Throop, an expert banjo player who had learned how to play from the Negroes he had carried to freedom, started plunking out Southern tunes. This drew the Southerners to the far end of the wharf. Playing the numbers they called out, the Captain completely diverted their attention while the Judge, after seeing the signal, led his men quickly out of the house, across the street through the cellar of the warehouse and into the woodpiles that extended from one end of the wharf to the other. To the casual observer, this steamer fuel seemed to have been piled in a haphazard way. But to Captain Throop, the Judge and the other members of the underground, it formed an intricate passageway that led from the warehouse at the beginning of the wharf to the very end of the dock where the ONTARIO was docked. Swiftly, the fugitives moved through the woodpile. The Judge, meanwhile, walked in full sight along the edge of the dock to where the steamer was snubbed. As the Judge approached, the Captain hallooed to him; and the Southern men passed their greetings. The Judge, looking up at Captain Throop, said, "Captain Throop, what do you carry?"

To this, the Captain replied, "My boat runs for passengers."

The Judge replied, "Have you sufficient fuel for the voyage?"

These words were the code to indicate that Negroes were in the woodpile. The Judge, turning to the Sheriff's men, indicated a good card game was in the offing and would they like to come along. With this and with the assurance from the Captain that no slaves were aboard, the Judge led the Sheriff's men back along the wharf to the shore. Quickly the Negroes moved from the woodpile, down the plank and into the hold of the vessel. On the bridge above, Captain Throop stroked Jeppa, who rested his head on his paws on the railing. With the last man aboard, the Captain yelled through his speaking horn, "Cast off!" As the boat left the pier, Throop smiled. The "Nigger in the woodpile" trick had worked again. Below deck one Negro prayerfully said, "Oh Lord! I'm free! That little boat that brought me here is going back to get my brothers -- back and forth, Oh Lord, back and forth to freedom. It's God's waters that flows both ways to get us and bring us to freedom."

Fanciful and imaginative, you say. Well, perhaps, but of such stories are folk tales made. If you go to Pultneyville today, they say you can still see the creek that sometimes flows in both directions. You can still see the salt-box house with the brick front addition. Inside, the trap doors are still there. (I know, I saw them.) The Lawrence and Throop houses live in quiet dignity; and in the window of Captain Throop's cobblestone house, a lifelike Jeppa, 85 years dead, still looks out of the window as though waiting for his master to return. On a stone cairn near Salmon Creek and the old wharf, the names of the captains and their boats that called Pultneyville their home port are forever inscribed. And in the homes that grace the lovely streets, gracious and dignified ladies remember these stories and the stories of other people now long gone. In their memories, the past life of Pultneyville still lives; and proud they are that "Nigger in the woodpile" meant freedom for so many African-Americans.

THE STORY BEHIND A FOLK HERO

Folk tales, by their very nature, come from the people. Usually they are simple in character and content. Since they deal with elemental vices and virtues, they are readily understood and easily loved. Most of the stories have their foundation in truth. In the telling and retelling, in the writing and rewriting, the original fact, however, is often embellished beyond recognition.

Folk heroes come in assorted shapes, sizes, places and deeds. By their very nature they come from the imagination of people. Stories and songs of their incredible acts have brightened the loneliness of the Wisconsin woods, the river water of the Ohio and Mississippi Rivers, the rolling countryside of America's midwest and the frontier trails of the far west. Each section has claimed its favorite: the woodsman Paul Bunyan or the keelman, Mike Fink. These are the superman variety. The rural areas preferred the milder Johnny Appleseed. The West exaggerated real characters, like Bowie, Boone and Crockett, into frontier heroes. Since the stories about them deal with elemental vices and virtues, they are readily understood and easily loved.

Almost every section of the United States has its characteristic tale about a folk hero. The Buffalo waterfront and Lake Erie are no exception. The hero there was a wheelman who guided a burning ship to shore and sacrificed his life. His story

312

caught on. In many a waterfront saloon and on the deck of many a laker, his story was told over and over again. He became a symbol of the courage and strength of all Lake Erie sailors.

It is believed that the original incident upon which the story is based was the burning of the steamship ERIE off Silver Creek on August 9, 1841. A little after eight o'clock in the evening that night, the ERIE, four hours out of Buffalo and eight miles offshore opposite Silver Creek, pushed ahead toward Dunkirk in a slightly rough sea that had started to abate with a falling wind. The ship's records listed 300 people aboard. Many were Dutch emigrants. With supper over some of the passengers walked along the promenade deck. Off-duty crew members relaxed in their quarters. The Captain had the ERIE on time and on course and he was pleased. At that moment, everything seemed shipshape.

Then suddenly, without warning, the boat was afire. There seemed no beginning; no spreading. Just all at once everything was burning. In moments there was almost no escape. In the hours that followed 250 people died horribly, some of them nobly, and one, according to the Captain's testimony, very heroically. His name was Luther Fuller. He was the helmsman. What he did that tragic night marked him for lasting fame.

The first of the stories following is based upon the numerous newspaper accounts which printed inquest testimony of some of those who were saved. The second story entitled "Helmsman of Lake Erie" might have been written by an Englishman -- at least one writer thinks it could have been Charles Dickens. It was probably this account which helped spread the fame of the young wheelman.

Here then is the story of how Luther Fuller, a wheelsman on the ERIE, became the John Maynard of story, song and poem; a hero worthy of Horatio Alger, the Great Lakes and the world:

It could have been just an ordinary day -- that is, of course, if any day could be ordinary on the Buffalo waterfront during the 1840's. In those days most of Europe seemed to be pouring through the Erie Canal and onto the emigrant steamers headed west for the wild frontier beyond. Several of the vessels, closely nuzzled together in the Buffalo Harbor, had a head of steam ready for the trip up the Lakes. Into their holds, dock walloppers rolled household goods, hardware, dry-goods and package freight. The loaders bawled out orders to hurry it up. Passengers, scurrying in and around the high piled freight, crowded onto the gangplank. At the moment -- the moment being four o'clock -- most of the raucous confusion centered on the steamboat ERIE, which was nearly ready to leave.

Boat runners went about their business with their customary gusto; pulling, pushing, punching, persuading. Over a hundred Dutch emigrants walked down Commercial Street toward the ERIE. Dressed in the traditional garb of their country, they made a colorful and picturesque parade as they boarded the vessel for what they hoped would be their promised land. Each clutched a carpet bag as if his or her life depended on it. In a sense it did. Most of them were carrying their life's earnings in specie in their bag as a grubstake in the new land. With wide-eyed wonder they jabbered among themselves. Occasionally an expletive "Mein Gott," "Be Jabbers," "Gott in Himmel," would crackle out above the normal harbor noises.

Close behind the emigrants, six painters followed with their paint pots, brushes and turpentine. They were employees of W. C. Miller's steamboat painting company of Buffalo on their way to Erie, Pennsylvania, to repaint and decorate the steamer JAMES MADISON. Standing a head above the crowd and just to the side of the painters was a clean shaven youth of seventeen years, dressed in the uniform of a United States Military Academy cadet. He seemed to be trying hard to look older than he actually was.

At the railing of the boat stood a group of ladies, dressed in the latest fashions, waving and calling to the people below. Some of them scattered coins to the Canal Street urchins who were tapping out dance rhythms on the dock boards. The band, gaily decked in brightly colored uniforms, played some of the lively tunes of the day. Standing apart from this group of ladies was Maria Jones. Her dress and manner told a story also. Her lineage was strictly Canal Street. To the initiated, that meant only one thing. Having served her apprenticeship there, she was now on her way west to open her own establishment at a western lake port.

The 300 passengers and crew represented a cross section of society. Rich and poor, moral and immoral, banker and laborer, theist and atheist. All came from different parts of the world; all were bound for different parts of the world. All were filled with hopes and plans for the future. Now, for a short time, they would all be riding the same boat, going in the same direction and sharing similar experiences.

Aboard the ship, meanwhile, the crew busied themselves with their respective duties. The chief and second mate checked the freight as it was stowed in the hold. In the engine room, fires were being stoked. At the tiller stood Luther Fuller. Carefully he checked the wheel and rudder. Few men had a steadier hand on the wheel than Fuller. About 28 years old, he seemed to have been bred to the water. The Captain had great faith in him.

Outside the wheelhouse stood Captain T. J. Titus, surveying and supervising the work below. Captain Titus was about 33 years old. For most of his life he had been associated with shipping on the Great Lakes. Starting out as an able-bodied seaman at sixteen, he soon worked his way up to a vessel command; first on the schooners, UNITED STATES and AURORA, and then on the steamboats, OHIO and SANDUSKY. Since the ERIE was first built and launched at Erie, Pennsylvania, he had been its master.

This was her fourth season. Titus loved his ship. She was a magnificent vessel of over 500 tons with a very strong draft -- the equal of any on the Lakes.

When everything was in order, Titus picked up his trumpet and shouted to the hands to cast off. The whole boat shuddered as the steam breathed life into the hull. Slowly the paddle wheels began to turn. They churned up the water. Luther Fuller headed her bow for the open lake. By his side stood Andy Blila, call boy, watching his every move. Someday he hoped to be a wheelsman like Fuller. Right now no job in the whole world seemed so important, and to Andy no one did it so well as Fuller.

When the boat was safely away from the dock, Captain Titus entered his cabin and took out his log. Under the day and date of Monday, August 9, 1841, he noted that the ERIE had left port at 4:10, headed for Dunkirk. He also noted that a fresh wind from the south and west had roughed up the lake. After completing his entry, Titus returned to the deck. The ship had already passed the light which marked the entrance to the harbor. Passengers, however, were still lingering on the promenade deck; some were still hanging over the rails waving to the people on the dock. The faint strains of the band rose above the low rumble of the engines.

Titus liked a happy ship. He was very proud of the ERIE. Everything seemed to shine brightly. The metal sparkled. The wood bore the high polish of new varnish. In fact, the boat had just recently been repainted inside and out. It had the pleasant smell of newness. As Titus looked about at the passengers, everyone seemed in a gay mood. Already many had begun to get acquainted. In the ladies' cabin there was talk of the latest fashions. The painters sitting fore told each other the latest bawdy jokes, roared with laughter, and speculated on what women would be available in Erie. The cadet, standing in the bow and looking forward toward Cleveland, was thinking how fine it would be to be home for a while. The Captain walked along the rail to the stern of the ship, passed the time of day with Fuller, and watched Buffalo fade in the distance. Another voyage seemed safely under way. Fuller had managed to squeeze the ERIE out of the crowded harbor without scratching a paddle wheel fender. It promised to be just another ordinary trip.

After Titus had satisfied himself that everything was in order, he returned to his cabin to prepare for dinner which was usually served at five-thirty. Dinner the first night out often set the tone for the entire trip. He wanted to make sure the first meal was happy and congenial. In the wheelhouse, Luther Fuller continued to hold a true course west by southwest as ordered. Below in the hold, the engineers fired for full speed ahead. One of the firemen on an inspection detail spotted several demijohns of turpentine atop a ledge which covered the boilers. Realizing the danger, he quickly removed them to a safer spot on the promenade deck. In the meantime, however, one of the painters returned and noticing that someone had moved their bottles of turpentine picked them up and put them back where they had been placed originally. He was, of course, unaware of the danger.

With supper over, the guests walked leisurely along the promenade deck. Occasionally lights could be seen on the south shore. Straight ahead was inky blackness. Captain Titus also strolled along the deck and stopped not far from the pilot's house. It was now a little after eight o'clock.

The Captain had been pleased with the dinner. He calculated that his ship was just about opposite Silver Creek, about eight miles from shore. While the wind had begun to subside slightly, the lake was still rough.

Suddenly, there was a sound like an exploding bottle. It was audible only to those in the immediate vicinity of the demijohns. A puff of smoke like a cloud of coal dust followed the sound. Those who heard sucked in their breath in terror. Before anyone could say anything, a red, lurid flame reached out, firing everything about it. In those few awful moments the whole boat heard the most feared word aboard ship, "Fire."

Captain Titus saw the fire coming out of the escape pipe before he heard the yell. Skylights started cracking from the intense heat. The space between the decks was already filled with a dense red flame. Smoke poured out of the hold. Titus, acting almost instinctively, quickly turned to the bow of the ship and said to the wheelsman, "Fuller, put the wheel hard to the starboard, remain at your post and keep the boat headed for the shore."

Panic had already seized the passengers. By now the entire hold was afire. The new paint and varnish fed the flames. Desperate men pulled up boards from the deck and threw them into the water. They then jumped into the water hoping to grab hold of the board for support. In their frenzy few were able to catch hold when they came to the surface. From the cabins came the screams of those trapped inside. A sheet of flame blocked any hope of getting to the cabins from the outside. The sickeningly sweet smell of burning flesh mingled with the smell of freshly painted wood. Out on the water the screams of the drowning pierced the darkness. Curses were mixed with prayers. Most seemed to prefer drowning to burning. That was the tragic choice opened to them.

Still seeing what he could do, Titus tried to get the engineer to stop the engines in the hope that that would slacken speed and would lessen the fanning of the flames. The intense heat made it impossible to unhook the gear. He yelled to Fuller to continue to hold fast to his course. Already flames had spread to the wheelhouse.

When Titus attempted to get to the ladies' cabin, the falling beams and flames drove him back. Inside were the life preservers which now would save no lives. He then ran forward to help with

316

the launching of a lifeboat. No sooner did they manage to get it in the water than twenty people swamped it. Those tossed into the water struggled to stay afloat. Their arms flayed desperately at the air and water. Fear froze their faces. One by one they would grow quiet and slip beneath the water. Once again the spot would grow calm.

From the promenade deck, attempts were made to lower the last boat. As hands hoisted it over the side, about twenty people appeared from nowhere. As soon as the boat hit the water, they were over the sides. Like the others, the boat tipped over. Within twenty minutes they were all drowned. Four men who had been swimming about grabbed hold of the keel. Titus looked around the deck. He could see no one. The boat was still headed for shore. Apparently Fuller was still at his post but it was so completely cut off by flames and smoke that it was impossible to see. When there seemed to be nothing more he could do, Titus jumped into the water. With an assist from a Negro swimming near the overturned boat, the Captain was able to grab a part of the keel.

All about him he could hear the screams of those who were drowning. He looked at the boat. It was still heading for shore. All the upper works had burned away. The hull was a dull red flame. It painted pictures of red devils dancing on the black waters. As the wind whipped the flames, it sounded to Titus like the roar of a hurricane. At the stern of the vessel, several people tried to climb down the tiller chains to the rudder. The chain was almost red hot. As they grabbed hold, the heat burned their hands. Then, with a scream of terror, they would fall into the water. The flesh from their hands hung in shreds from the chain links. Titus noticed one man who seemed, despite the pain, to be making it down. Squinting his eyes to get better distance, Captain Titus noticed that it was the young cadet. Hand over hand he lowered himself down the chain. The pain must have been almost unbearable. Finally he made it to the rudder. He straddled the rudder and dipped his hands, burned raw by the hot chain, into water to relieve the pain. By soaking his coat in the water and wetting the area in front of him he was able to fight back the flames. He seemed older now than his 17 years.

By now it was harder to distinguish anything on the boat. Titus noticed several clinging by their fingertips to the deck edge. Afraid to drop and yet, as the flames ate closer, finding it impossible to continue to hang on. One by one the flames cut them down. The most tragic scenes of all were those of parents trying desperately and frantically to save their children. The end was always the same. It would be but a matter of moments when all would go down.

Near the bulkhead the Captain watched in horrified fascination as a person, surrounded by fire and holding a piece of cloth in his hand, appeared to bathe his face to relieve the pain. All the while he was screaming for help. Then the flames hid him from view.

After two hours in the water, Titus noticed a two-stacked boat racing toward them. When it was over, only fifty people were rescued. Two hundred and fifty people lost their lives. Maria Jones would never open her house. The ladies would never again bother about fashions. The girls in Erie would have to forego the pleasures of the six painters who had turned a gay boat into a funeral pyre. The immigrants would never reach the prairie land of the American West.

What of the wheelsman whom Titus told to hold his course until they reached the shore? In the inquest following the tragedy, Captain Titus paid a hero's tribute to Luther Fuller, the wheelsman. "He remained at the wheel and never left it until he was burned to death." And then Titus added, "He was always a resolute man."

It could have been just another day and just another trip and Fuller could have remained just another sailor. But this is the stuff folk heroes are made of.

Among canawlers and sailors, Fuller's fame spread. In many a waterfront saloon and on the deck of many a laker his story was told over and over again. He became the symbol of the courage and strength of all Lake Erie sailors.

By 1845 his story was common property. An English traveler and writer on tour through the lakes apparently heard the story and wrote it down. In September of that year it appeared in the Buffalo Commercial Advertiser and the following month in the Western Literary Messenger under the title "Helmsman of Lake Erie." One authority believes the author was Charles Dickens who toured the lakes in 1845.

Several alterations were made and much embellishment added to the original story. The writer rechristened the ERIE the JERSEY and anglicized Lake terminology. He aged Fuller considerably, renamed him John Maynard and endowed him with all the virtues.

THE HELMSMAN OF LAKE ERIE

Old John Maynard was at the wheel -- a bluff, weather-beaten sailor tanned by many a wintry tempest. He had truly learned to be contented with his situation. None could ever say that they had heard him repine at his hard labor and scanty pay. He had, in the worst of times, a cheerful word and a kind look for those with whom he was thrown. Cast, often enough, into bad company, he tried, at least, and generally succeeded, to say something for its good. He was known, from one end of Lake Erie to the other, by the name of "honest John Maynard" and the secret of his honesty to his neighbors was his love of God.

"Dick Fletcher, what's all that smoke I see coming out from the hold?"

"It's from the engine room, sir, I guess," said the man.

"Down with you, then, and let me know."

The sailor began descending the ladder by which you go to the hold; but scarcely had he disappeared beneath the deck, when up he came again with much greater speed.

"The hold's on fire, sir," he said to the captain, who by this time was standing close to him.

The captain rushed down and found the account too true. Some sparks had fallen on a bundle of tow; no one had seen the accident, and now not only much of the luggage, but the sides of the vessel were in smouldering flame.

All hands, passengers as well as sailors, were called together and two lines were made, one on each side of the hold. Buckets of water were passed and repassed; they were filled from the lake, they flew along a line of ready hands, were dashed hissing on the burning mass and then passed on the other side to be refilled.

For some minutes it seemed as if the flames were subdued.

In the meantime, the women on board were clustering round John Maynard, the only man unemployed who was capable of answering their questions.

"How far is it to land?"

"How long shall we be getting in?"

The helmsman answered as well as he could. There was no boat; it had been left at Buffalo to be mended; they might be seven miles from shore; they would probably be in forty minutes; he could not tell how far the fire had reached. "And to speak the truth," he added, "we are all in great danger, and I think if there was a little less talking, and a little more praying, it would be better for us, and none the worse for the boat."

"How's her head?" shouted the captain.

"West-sou'west, sir," answered Maynard.

"Keep her south by west," cried the captain. "Must go on shore anywhere."

It happened that a draft of wind drove back the flames, which soon began to blaze up more furiously against the saloon and the partition betwixt it and the hold was soon on fire. Then long wreaths of smoke began to find its way through the skylight, and the captain seeing this, ordered all the women forward. The engineer put on his utmost steam, the American flag was run up, and reversed, in token of distress; water was slung over the sails to make them hold the wind. And still John Maynard stood by the wheel, tho' now he was cut off, by a sheet of smoke and flames, from the ship's crew.

Greater and greater grew the heat, the engineers filed from the engine room; the passengers were clustering round the vessel's bow. The sailors were sawing planks on which to lash the women, the boldest were throwing off their coats and waistcoats, preparing for one long struggle for life. And still the coast grew plainer and plainer. The paddles, as yet, worked well. They could not be more than a mile from the shore and boats were even now starting to their assistance.

"John Maynard," cried the captain.

"Aye, aye, sir," said John.

"Can you hold on five minutes longer?"

And he did try but the flames came nearer and nearer; a sheet of smoke would sometimes almost suffocate him and his hair was singed. His blood seemed on fire with the great heat. Crouching as far back as he could, he held the wheel firmly with his left hand, 'til the flesh shrivelled and the muscles cracked in the flame. Then he stretched for his right, and bore the agony without a scream or a groan. It was enough for him that he heard the cheer of the sailors to the approaching boats; the cry of the captain, "The women first, and then every man for himself, and God for us all."

And they were the last sounds that he heard. How he perished was not known. Whether, dizzied by the smoke, he lost his footing in endeavoring to come forward and fell overboard or whether he was suffocated by the dense smoke, his comrades could not tell. At the moment the vessel struck, the boats were at her side; passengers, sailors and captain leaped into them, or swam for their lives. All, save he to whom they owed everything, escaped.

He had died the death of a Christian hero -- I had almost said of a martyr; his spirit was commended into his Father's hands, and his body sleeps in peace by the green side of Lake Erie.

Probably more than anything else, this account gave John Maynard to the world. In 1875 the story was turned into poetry. Authorship has been attributed to Horatio Alger, Jr., who made his fortune as a writer of dime novels and to Kate Weaver. The ERIE in this work receives its third and final name, the OCEAN QUEEN:

'Twas on Lake Erie's broad expanse
One Bright midsummer day,
The gallant steamer Ocean Queen
Swept proudly on her way.
Bright faces clustered on the deck
Or, leaning o'er the side,
Watched carelessly the feathery foam
That flecked the rippling tide.

Ah, who beneath that cloudless sky,
That smiling bends serene,
Could dream that danger awful vast,
Impended o'er the scene --

Could dream that ere an hour had sped
That frame of sturdy oak
Would sink beneath the lake's blue
Blackened with fire and smoke?

A seaman sought the captain's side,
A moment whispered low;
The captain's swarthy face grew pale;
He hurried down below.
Alas, too late!
Though quick, and sharp,
And clear his orders came,
No human efforts could avail
To quench th' insidious flame.

The bad news quickly reached the deck,
It sped from lip to lip,
And ghastly faces everywhere
Looked from the doomed ship.
"Is there no hope -- no chance of life?"
A hundred lips implore,
"But one," the captain made reply, --
"To run the ship on shore."

A sailor, whose heroic soul
That hour should yet reveal,
By name John Maynard, eastern born,
Stood calmly at the wheel.
"Head her southeast" the captain shouts,
Above the smothered roar --
"Head her southeast without delay
Make for the nearest shore!"

No terror pales the helmsman's cheek
Or clouds his dauntless eye,
As, in a sailor's measured tone,
His voice responds, "Ay! Ay!"
Three hundred souls, the steamer's freight,
Crowd forward wild with fear.
While at the stern the dreaded flames
Above the deck appear.

He grasped the wheel, and steadfastly
He steered the ship to land.
"John Maynard, can you still hold out?"
He heard the captain cry;
A voice from the stifling smoke
Faintly responds, "Ay! Ay!"

But half a mile! a hundred hands
Stretch eagerly to shore,
But half a mile! That distance sped
Peril shall all be o'er.
But half a mile! Yet stay, the flames
No longer slowly creep,
But gather round that helmsman bold,
With fierce impetuous sweep.

"John Maynard!" with an anxious voice
That captain cries once more,
"Stand by the wheel five minutes yet,
And we shall reach the shore."
Through flame and smoke that dauntless heart
Responded firmly still,
Unawed, though face to face with death,
"With God's good help I will!"

That flames approach with giant strides,
They scorch his hand and brow;
One arm disabled, seeks his side,
Ah! he is conquered now!
But no his teeth are firmly set,
He crushes down his pain,
His knee upon the stanchion pressed,
He guides the ship again.

One moment yet! one moment yet!
brave heart, thy task is o'er.
The pebbles grate beneath the keel,
The steamer touches shore.
Three hundred grateful voices rise
In praise to God that he
Hath saved them from the fearful fire,
And from the engulfing sea.

But where is he, that helmsman bold?
The captain saw him reel,
His nerveless hands released their task
He sank beside the wheel.
The wave received his lifeless corpse,
Blackened with smoke and fire.
God rest him! Never hero had
A nobler funeral pyre!

JOHN MAYNARD

Theodore Fontane

John Maynard!
"Who is John Maynard?"
"John Maynard was our Helmsman,
he stood until he gained the shore,
he saved us, he wears the crown,
he died for us, our love is his reward.
John Maynard!"

The "swallow" soars over Lake Erie,
spray foams around the bow like flakes of snow;
she flys from Detroit to Buffalo.
The hearts are free and happy,
and the passengers with children and wives,
in the twilight already they see the shore,
and chatting with John Maynard they ask:
"How much further, helmsman?"
He looks ahead and he looks at them:
"Another thirty minutes . . . half an hour."

All hearts are happy, all hearts are free.
When from the hold of the ship there comes the cry, "Fire!"
smoke billowed from cabin and hatchway,
smoke, then flames in full blaze,
and still twenty minutes to Buffalo.

And the passengers, all mixed-up,
huddle together on the bowsprit,
On the bowsprit up front there is still light and air,
but at the rudder it's settling thick,
and a lament is being wailed: "Where are we, where?"
And still fifteen minutes to Buffalo.

The draft increases, but the smoke cloud stays,
the captain peers to the helm,
he sees no more his helmsman,
but through the megaphone he asks:
"Still there, John Maynard?" "Yes, Sir, I am."
"To the shore: To the breakers!"   "I'm headed there."
And the passengers rejoice: "Hold out! Hallo!"
And still ten minutes to Buffalo.

"Still there, John Maynard?" And the answer comes
with dying voice: "Yes, Sir, I'm holding out!"
And into the breakers, regardless of rock and stone,
he drives the swallow directly into it.

This is the only way to be saved.
Rescue: the shore of Buffalo!
The ship burst. The fire smoulders out.
All are saved. Only one is missing!

All bells peal; their tones swell
from churches and chapels heavenward,
a ringing and sounding, otherwise the town is still.
Only one duty to be done today:
then thousand follow or more,
and no dry eye in the procession.
They lower the coffin into flowers,
with flowers they close the grave,
and in golden letters in marble,
the town writes its dedication:

"Here rests John Maynard. In smoke and fire,
he held the rudder tightly in his hand.
He saved us, he wears the crown,
he died for us, our love is his reward.
John Maynard"

In 1901, John Gough, temperance leader, turned the poem into a prose oration entitled "The Pilot," and used it as part of his vast repertoire on cross country tours. It had real punch. It eventually appeared in many school elocution books. School children memorized it. It soon reached overseas.

Some in the United States think John Hay, Lincoln's secretary, had this story in mind when he wrote "Jim Bludso." Leastwise, the Mississippi story bears a striking resemblance to the Maynard story.

JIM BLUDSO

The fire bust out as she cleared the bar,
And burnt a hole in the night,
And quick as a flash she turned, and made
For that willer-bank on the right.
There was runnin' and cursin', but Jim yelled out,
Over all the infernal roar,
"I'll hold her nozzle agin the bank,
Till the last galoot's ashore."

Through the hot, black breath of the burnin' boat
Jim Bludso's voice was heard,
And they all had trust in his cussedness,
And knowed he would keep his word.
And, sure's you're born, they all got off
Afore the smokestacks fell,
And Bludso's ghost went up alone
in the smoke of the Prairie Belle.

John Maynard, or Luther Fuller, might have rested in his fame if it had not been for a revelation made in 1912. Over the years, all the writers who wrote their accounts from the original stories in the newspapers or from other accounts which had themselves been based on the testimony of Captain Titus, assumed that Luther Fuller, or John Maynard as they called him, went down with his ship. This was one of the few points upon which all agreed.

On November 22, 1900, a man died in the Erie County Hospital, Erie, Pennsylvania. His name was James Rafferty. He was a common drunkard, a convicted counterfeiter and a pauper. Little notice would have been paid to his passing if the secretary of the Erie Historical Society had not, in 1912, revealed that Rafferty was actually Luther Fuller, the John Maynard of Lake Erie fame. According to him, Fuller had stayed with the ship until all had left and then when the rudder ropes had burned and it was useless for him to stay aboard, he cut away a part of the paddle wheel fender and floated ashore. He had been badly burned.

Credence was placed immediately in the secretary's story because he had been little Andy Blila, the call boy on the ERIE the night it burned. Fuller often came into his father's saloon, Blila claimed, to borrow a dime for a drink. So it was that the man who had been capable, at least once in his life, of rising to such great heights, died a convicted criminal and drunkard, not far from the water where he had played out his heroic deed. But whatever happened to James Rafferty, John Maynard would always remain the hero of Lake Erie.

NARROW ESCAPE FROM DROWNING

The following is a news item printed in the Buffalo
Commercial Advertiser on October 6, 1868:

Nellie Sheehan, an old Irish woman living on the bank of the
canal, and known as the "Queen of the Patch," visited some friends
on a canal boat lying near the Western Transportation Company
Warehouse, last evening. She tarried until after dark, and when she
started to go home, instead of taking the right path, walked into the
canal. Her outcry speedily brought assistance, and she was fished
out and taken, in a very limp condition, to Station No. 1, where Dr.
Johnson attended and brough her 'round. It was at Nellie's
domicile where Catherine Johnson, alias "One-Eyed Kate,"
murdered Bridgett McDermott and Nellie is an important witness in
the case.
Had Nellie lost her life, the verdict of the Coroner's jury
would doubtless have been one of death from canal water and
whiskey.

As historians know, folklore is not "hard copy history."
And yet, in collecting, retelling and recording tall tales of the Canal,
I have been amazed at how often historical research has uncovered
basic threads of truth in folklore stories.
The title "Canal Water and Whiskey" took its name from a
story of the same name which I heard from a 90-year-old Irish man
in the 1920s. I cannot recall at this late date whether he used the
phrase or whether the story suggested it to me.
Strange it is, therefore, that in doing research in 1992 on
Buffalo's Canal Street for a book soon to be published, this story
about Nellie Sheehan was uncovered. She almost lost her life by
drowning in the Canal. The perceptive reporter speculated that had
that occurred, it would have been a death by canal water and
whiskey.
Truth is often stranger than fiction or folklore.

THE EMPTY BOTTLE

This world is a bottle,
Our life is a dram;
When the bottle is empty
It ain't worth a damn.

APPENDIX A

MAP

Republic Steam Presses, Buffalo.

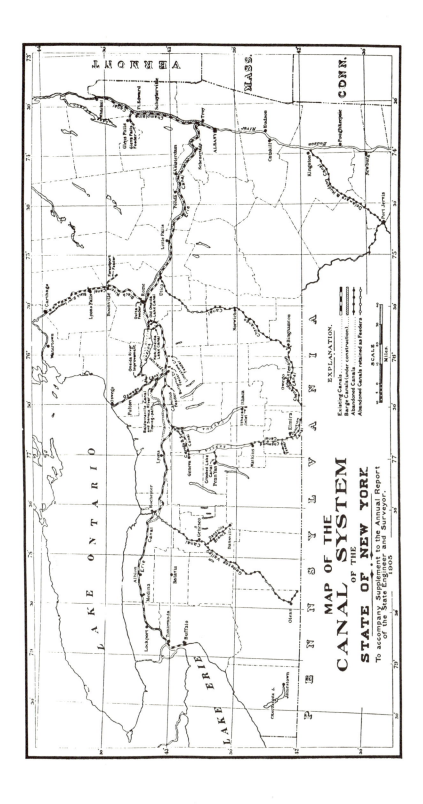

MAP OF THE
CANAL SYSTEM
OF THE
STATE OF NEW YORK

To accompany Supplement to the Annual Report
of the State Engineer and Surveyor.
1905

EXPLANATION.

Existing Canals.
Barge Canals (under construction).
Abandoned Canals.
Abandoned Canals retained as Feeders.

SCALE
Miles

APPENDIX B

CANAL GLOSSARY

Republic Steam Presses, Buffalo.

CANAL GLOSSARY

Berm The side of the canal opposite the towpath

Bowstable A stable for mules in the bow of the boats

Brainard barrow A wheelbarrow developed especially for construction of the canal. Named for Jeremiah Brainard, of Rome, who developed the roomy, well-balanced wheelbarrow

Bullhead boat A boat upon which the blunt, but rounded, bullhead was built flush against the cabin, forcing the helmsman to stand on the roof of the cabin when steering the boat

Canawl Irish pronunciation for canal

Canawlers Men who worked the Canal

Cleated bridge A slatted wood bridge used to help the mules on and off the canal boats

Clinton's Ditch The Erie Canal

Combine Another name for a lock; especially the locks at Lockport

(The) Deep Cut The cut west of Lockport which is nearly two miles long and required an excavation of 1,477,700 cu. yds. of material. It was once a great tourist attraction

Durham boat A long, clumsy boat which drew very little water. A modified scow, it had a small cabin in the stern and a stubby mast with a square sail to utilize when there was an easterly wind

Feeder A stream, brook or other source which provided water to maintain the proper level in the Canal

Fip Slang for a coin worth about 6 1/4 cents

Fog gang Workers who cleaned out the canal as an annual routine

Foofoo Erie Canal lingo for "foreigner"

Found Room and board

Freighter A canal boat which carried no passengers and whose only purpose was to haul freight

Hayburners	A contemptuous name given to mules by men who worked on steam-powered packets
Heelpath	The berm
Higgler	A peddlar, often a gypsy, who "higgled and haggled" to sell his wares
Hit the logs	To take the road (a comment on the state of "corduroy" roads, which were made out of logs)
Hoggee	(Also hoggie) A driver of a mule team (often a young boy)
Hoodledasher	Two or more cargo-less boats tied to a full-cargo boat so one team of mules could pull them all
Hurry-up boat	A repair boat with its own gang which repaired leaks, etc. . .
Jigger-boss	A boy hired by a captain to dole out half gills of whiskey to each workman sixteen times each day
Jularkey	A girlfriend
Linebarn	Where the mules and horses were kept along the towpath route so that fresh, rested animals were always available
Line-boat	Boats that carried both freight and passengers
Lock tender	(Also "Lock-keep") A person who opens and closes the locks
"(The) Lockport Five"	A group of five combines that lifted the Canal over the Niagara Escarpment at Lockport; considered one of the greatest engineering marvels of all time
Long-earred robins	Mules
Low bridge	A warning for those on top of the packet to duck their heads before passing under a bridge spanning the canal
Long Level	A 70-mile stretch of canal between Frankfort and Syracuse without any locks

"Look for a post!"	A canawler's cry referring to the stout snubbing posts located at intervals along the canal. They were used for tying up boats, etc. . .
Macaroni	A dandy
Marshmen	Robbers who hid out in the Montezuma Marshes
Miasma	Anything that caused illness (ague, swamp fever, etc. . .) along the canal
Mole	A dam-like stone barrier similar to a breakwater
Montezuma Marshes	A swamp located west of Syracuse near Waterloo; Today it is a wildlife refuge
Mudlarked	Grounded or stuck in the mud
Packet boat	A passenger boat with bunks and a diningroom
Pathmaster	An official in charge of keeping up roads and paths
"Pathmaster's Penance"	A muskrat, which was a constant hazard to the canal because its burrowing would weaken the canal walls
Pritties	Potatoes, boiled or baked (comes from Gaelic "praities")
Powder monkey	A mechanic who worked with blasting powder
Prog	Food
Red dog notes	Useless, worthless banknotes
Rhino	Ready money or cash
Runners	People who worked for the packet boat captains soliciting passengers and trade
Scalpers	Agents concerned with the assignments of cargoes
Seneca Chief	DeWitt Clinton's canal boat for the first trip down the canal in 1825
Setbacks	Small streams and creeks found in swampy areas through which the canal passed
Shanty boat	A flat hull boat on which a one room hovel was built to provide housing for the owner who often anchored in the setbacks for months at a time

Shunpike	A land detour around areas where the tollbooths were close together and the tolls were too high
(The) Sidecut	At Watervliet, where a lateral canal connected with the Hudson River
Simples	Herbs (used for medicine)
Skimmagig	Buttermilk
Spavined	Referring to a disease affecting mules and horses in which a leg bone becomes enlarged as a result of strain. A frequent expression among canawlers was the near-oath "Well, I'll be spavined"
Spill the nosebag	To tell a story
Steersman	The helmsman who guided the boats with the tiller
Stretching the blanket	To tell a fib
Terminus	The end of the canal (Albany and Buffalo)
Towpath	The path along which mules pulled the canal barges
Towrope news	Grapevine information; How gossip traveled along the Erie Canal
Trick	A tour of duty
"Walkin' passage"	Colloq. used to describe a hoggee's travels; since some boys signed on for a certain distance, they were literally "walking their passage" on the canal
Weighlock	Lock for weighing the boats and determining the tolls
Whiffletree	The pivoted crossbar to which the traces of harnesses of hauling horses or mules was attached

APPENDIX C
CANAL CHRONOLOGY

Republic Steam Presses, Buffalo.

AN ERIE CANAL CHRONOLOGY
1768 - 1828

1768   December 16 -- Governor Sir Henry Moore recommends improvement of the Mohawk river, but no action is taken by the General Assembly

1784   November -- Christopher Colles calls for removing obstructions to the navigation of the Mohawk River

1785   April 5 -- $125 is appropriated enabling Colles to essay removal of certain obstructions from the Mohawk River

1786   Jeffrey Smith introduces bill in the state Assembly for navigation of the Mohawk and Onondaga Rivers, "and, if practicable extending the same to Lake Erie"

1791   Governor George Clinton urges upon the Legislature the necessity of improving natural water channels

           A joint committee advocates opening water communication between the Mohawk River and Wood Creek

           Land Office commissioners survey between the Mohawk River at Fort Stanwix and Wood Creek to prepare estimates for a canal; Hardenburgh and Wright make survey

1792   Western Inland Lock Navigation Co. (Western Co.) is incorporated to open navigations from the Husdson River to Ontario and Seneca Lakes

           January 3 -- Commissioners report that the route from Albany to Seneca Lake could be improved by locks and canals for $200,000

           Surveys made by Western Co. from Schenectady to Wood Creek

1793   Work begun in April at Little Falls

           Wood Creek is cleared, straightened and improved as its length is shortened by approximately seven miles

1795   State Treasurer is instructed to subscribe for 200 shares of Western Co.'s stock at $20 each

1796   Western Co. is loaned $15,000 by NYS on mortgage security

           Western Co. canals are opened from Schenectady to Seneca Falls for boats up to sixteen tons

1796   Freight charges are reduced from $100 to $33 per ton

Little Falls locks are completed

William Weston makes examination and proposes plans for canal locks around Cohoes falls; Cost is estimated at $250,00

1797   Western Co. is authorized to borrow $250,00.00

October 3 -- Canal from the Mohawk River to Wood Creek is completed

1798   Niagara Canal Co. incorporated to construct a canal from Lake Erie to Lake Ontario. Specs: six miles long with fifty locks

Western Co. is allowed five more years to complete projects

1800   December 20 -- Governor Morris writes that ships may "be made to sail through the Hudson River to Lake Erie"

1802   Comptroller accepts Western Co. shares in payment of debts. Western Co. proposes to improve navigation of Wood Creek from Ft. Stanwix to Little Canada Creek. Specs: six miles, four locks and dams

1803   Governor Morris said to have urged the feasibility of "tapping Lake Erie and leading its water across country to the Hudson River"

Plan and profile surveys for improvement of Wood Creek to Ft. Stanwix to Little Canada Creek are completed by Benjamin Wright who also surveys the Mohawk River from Ft. Stanwix to Schenectady

1806   Western Co. is granted a seven year extension

1807   January 14 -- Jesse Hawley proposes the Erie Canal concept from Pittsburgh, PA and elaborates on it in a series of 14 articles published between October 27, 1807 and April, 1808 in the Ontario Messenger (Canandaigua, NY)

1808   February 4 -- Judge Joshua Forman offers a resolution in the Assembly for a canal joining the Hudson River and Lake Erie. A survey is ordered for a route between the river and the lake using Lake Ontario and other inland routes. James Geddes is appointed to make the survey

Western Co. surrenders its grant west of Oneida Lake and it is accepted by the State

1810   Commissioners are appointed to examine inland waters by a joint resolution made on March 13 and 15 Governor Morris, Stephen VanRensselaer, William North, DeWitt Clinton, Thomas Eddy, Peter B. Porter and Simon DeWitt are appointed as the first commissioners. Porter offers a resolution in Congress urging the appropriation of public funds to finance the construction of roads and canals in NYS

State appropriates $3,000

1811   Nine commissioners are appointed to consider the matter of improving internal navigation

February -- The commission reports the following: Lake Erie to the Hudson River, 310 miles with a 525-foot drop; estimated cost, $5,000,000

Commission invites cooperation of the United States and the individual states, $15,000.00 is appropriated for their use

1812   Commissioners under Chapter 188-1811 borrow $5,000,000.00 and also purchase the Western Co.'s property

March 14 -- Western Co. demands $190,000.00 for its property

Massachusetts, Tennessee, Vermont and Ohio pledge aid; New Jersey, Michigan and Connecticuit don's favor plan

1814   Holland Land Co. conditionally offers to donate 100,632 acres of land in Cattaraugus County

Sections 3, 4 and 5 of Chapter 231-1812, which gave the commission power to raise $5,000,000.00, is repealed

Commssioners report engagement of William Weston as engineer for the proposed canal

1816   Hudson and Mohawk Lock Navigation Co. is incorporated; capital stock is $500,000.00

Five commissioners are appointed to provide communiction by canals and locks between the Hudson River and Lake Erie and Lake Erie and Lake Champlain

1817   Construction is authorized between the Mohawk and Seneca Rivers; contiguous lands to be taxed;

February 15 -- Commissioners are appointed pursuant to Chapter 237-1816 to present surveys and estimates for the canal

June 27 -- The first contract is let

July 4 -- Ground is broken at Rome. Fifty-eight miles of the canal are put under contract during the year, all at the summit level; About fifteen miles of the canal are completed in the first year

1818 $12,000.00 is appropriated for a harbor at Buffalo.

Completion of the canal is authorized from the Seneca River to Lake Erie and the middle division to the Hudson River; Canal laborers are exempted from military duty
The Holland Land Co.'s grant of 100,632 acres is accepted

Construction is curtailed due to epidemic among workers. Nearly 1,000 are disabled in the vicinity of the Cayuga marshes

The middle section of the canal (98 miles) is completed from Utica to the Seneca River, including the Salina side-cut

December 10 -- Between 2,000 and 3,000 men (with 500 teams and tools) are employed in constructing the canal

1820   May -- Navigation opened on middle section

July 1 -- Tolls first levied and collected

October 2 --Western Co's rights are purchased by the State for $91,616

Fifty one miles of the western division (nine miles filled with water) is half completed and work on the Eastern section begins

1821   Ontario Canal Co. is incorporated to build a canal from Canandaigua Lake to the Erie Canal

Canal competed from Utica to Little Falls

Fifty miles of the Western Section is competed

1822   Buffalo and Black Rock harbors are improved

Speed on the canal is limited to 4 mph

Canal is completed from Little Falls to Schenectady and from Rochester to Pittsford, ; 180 navigable miles

Collectors' fees are established

Genesee River feeder (with a lock at the head) and the feeder and aquaduct at Little Falls are completed

1823   Niagara Canal Co. is incorporated

$1,300,000 is appropriated for the canal fund

The aquaduct (802 feet long, 11 arches) over the Genesee River is completed; the Salina sidecut is connected with Onondaga Lake; feeder dam is built at Johnsville; and the canal is completed from Rochester to Brockport and Schenectady to Albany

October 8 -- First boats from the west and north pass through the canal into the Hudson at Albany

1824 $1,000,000 is appropriated for the canal fund

The canal is completed from Brockport to Lockport; 300 bridges are built across the canal between Utica and Albany and 80 between Utica and Little Falls; the Tonawanda feeder is completed; the Niagara River lift-lock is completed; and hydrostatic locks are built at Syracuse and Utica

DeWitt Clinton is removed from office of canal commissioner

1825 $270,965.78 is appropriated for canal fund

October 26 -- Entire canal is completed; Opening ceremonies all along the canal; Fleet leaves Buffalo for New York City

13,110 boats use canal during the season; 40,000 people pass through Utica in freight and packet boats during the season

Twelve counties and eighteen towns petition to ban use of canal on Sundays

Hydrostatic locks (for weighing canal boats) prove efficient

1826   Side-cut planned at Montezuma

Limestone Creek and Mohawk River feeders, with dams and locks are completed

The Canal Board is established

1827   Maps to be made of all existing canals

Canal commissioners meet and organize the law reducing the number of commissioners to two

1828   375-ft pier built at Black Rock harbor

A new lock is constructed at Lyons

Longest season (to date) is recorded: March 27 -- December 20

February 11 -- DeWitt Clinton dies

APPENDIX D

SELECTED SONGS
AND
SHEET MUSIC

Republic Steam Presses, Buffalo.

Meeting of the Waters

Let the day be for-ev- er re - mem-bered with pride, That be
held the proud Hud-son to Er-ie al-lied, Oh the last sand of time from his
glass shall de-scend, E'er a un - ion so fruit - ful of
glo-ry shall end, E'er a un-ion so fruit-ful of glo - ry shall end.

2. Yet, it's not that wealth now enriches the scene,
   Where the treasures of art, and of nature, convene;
   'Tis not that this union our coffers may fill,
   Oh! no -- it is something more exquisite still,
   Oh! no -- it is something more exquisite still.

3. 'Tis that genius has triumphed, and Science prevailed,
   Tho' prejudice fl outed and envy assailed,
   It is, that the vassals of Europe may see,
   The progress of mind in a land that is free,
   The progress of mind in a land that is free.

My Old Canal Mule

This world it is great you may get what you want, There is trou-ble and fun all de-pends on your jaunt, But - I love the lat-ter with laugh-ter and song, And - if you don't like it move peace-ful-ly on. I - have an old friend and we get a - long fine, He - works on the tow-path helps keep up the line, Oh, how he would bray if he could hoist his cail, but that he'll not do for he can't raise his tail.

Simon Slick

I know an old can-al -ler, His name is Sim-on
wink his eyes, He'd wag his tail, and greet you with a

Slick. He had a mule with dream-y eyes, Lord
smile. Then gent - ly tel - a - graph his legs, and

how that mule could kick. He'd mile.
send you half a

Whoa! mule - Whoa! I'm done with you for-ev-er. You

ain't no good, you nev-er was and you nev -er will be

nei-ther. You're gon -na die and take a trip to the

hot place down be - low . Old Sa - tan sees you

com - ing He'll shout Whoa there mu - le Whoa.

Never Take a Hindshoe From a Mule

A sto-ry has come down from old Ma - thu - sam, I
learned it when I was a boy in school. You'll
make a great mis-take and don't for - get - it. If you
both-er round the hind parts of a mule So
nev-er tick-le a mule when he's re - pos - ing. If
you dis-turb his slum-bers you're a fool, If
you don't want to vis-it the un - der - tak - er,
Nev-er take the hind -shoe from a mule.

Black Rock Pork

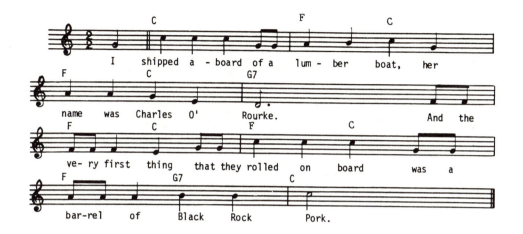

I shipped a-board of a lum-ber boat, her name was Charles O' Rourke. And the ve-ry first thing that they rolled on board was a bar-rel of Black Rock Pork.

2. They fried a chunk for breakfast,
   And a chunk for luncheon, too.
   It didn't taste so goody-good,
   And it was hard to chew.

3. From Buffalo to old New York,
   They fed it to dear old me.
   They boiled the barrel and the rest of the pork,
   And we had it all for tea.

Towpath Circus

One day on the tow-path I was scared for a bil-ly goat aimed right
at my rear, but I jumped quick up - on a mule, He looked at me just
like a fool, But soon he fol-lowed me with his bleat, I knew e-nough to
keep my seat, So qui- et, yes, just like a bird, Twas bet-ter seen but not heard.
what fun that old can-al, 'Twas some-thing new each mile,
my par-ents oft would laugh, when I met a frisk - y calf.

The Er-i-e

We were for-ty nine miles from Al - ban - y for - get it I nev - er shall. What a ter-ri-ble storm we had that night on the Er - i - e Can - al Oh! the Er - i - e was a ris - ing, and the gin was a get-ting low. And I scarc- ly think we'll get a drink 'til we get to Buf- fa - lo - o - o, 'til we get to Buf- fa - lo.

Low Bridge

I've got a mule, and her name is Sal, Fif-teen miles on the
Er-ie can-al - , She's a good ol' worker and a good ol' pal,
Fif-teen miles on the Er-ie can-al -. We've hauled some barges in our day.
filled with lum-ber coal and hay, And we know ev'-ry inch of the way from
Al-ban-y - , to - Buf - a-lo - 0. Low bridge ev'-ry-bod-y down.
LOw bridge for we're com-in to a town. And you al-ways know your neighbor, you
al-ways know your pal, If you ev-er nav-i-gat-ed on the Er-ie can-al.

Oh! Dat Low Bridge

Its ma-ny miles to Buf-fa-lo. Oh, dat low bridge.

Bal-ky mule he trav-el slow. Oh, dat low bridge. Dars

gra-vel on de tow-path, Dars hor-nets in de sand. Oh,

pit-y poor can - al-lers, dats far a - way from land. Den

look out, dat low bridge. *(Look out, dat low bridge.)*

Look out, dat low bridge. *(Look out, dat low bridge.)* The

cap-tain cook and all de crew, Oh duck your head way down, The

fast-est boat in all de fleet, two sis-ters come to town.

The Raging Canal

Come lis-ten to my sto - ry ye lands-man one and all, I'll
sing to you the dan-gers of that rag -ing can - al. For
I am one of man - y who ex - pects a wat-ery grave, for
I've been at the mer - cy of the wind and of the wave.

2. I left Albany harbor about the break of day,
   And if I rightly remember 'twas the second day of may;
   We trusted to our driver, altho' he was but small,
   For he knew all the windings of that raging canal.

3. It seemed as if the Devil had his work in hand that night,
   For all our oil was gone, and our lamps they gave no light,
   The clouds began to gather and the rain began to fall,
   And I wished myself off of that raging canal.

CHAPTER NOTES

Republic Steam Presses, Buffalo.

OLD BEALES AND COFFEE BEANS

The following is the text of a presentation made by Julia Snow regarding the early days of Buffalo, in particular the gale storm which destroyed Bealsville. It was delivered May 9, 1908 to the Buffalo and Erie County Historic Society.

In those early days, as now, there were fierce gales blowing sometimes down Lake Erie and as the stone storm pier was not what it is at present, and there was no breakwater to check the force of the waves, they swept over the flats and low-lying land below Exchange Street and thereabouts. I remember two or three such gales, but not its date (probably October 18, 1844.) The wind had blown two days and two nights, and the waters had come over the "flats" to Michigan Street, and nearly to Seneca. The poor shanties, which studded that district, were blown down and many more were made homeless. With the third morning the gale subsided, and the rescue work went on. The drowned people were carried to the court house (this was a very pretty colonial building behind Lafayette Park, on the spot where the public library now stands.) There was much excitement about town. The rescued but homeless ones were brought to the "market" (a fair-sized brick building standing on Mohawk Street at the corner of Pearl) and were quartered in its basement. This ediface had also a strong room, called the "Watch House," for drunk and disorderly persons under arrest, and this being opposite the rear of our house, afforded many interesting points of observation. I was not allowed to see the drowned people (although some of my little mates were) but as compensation I was permitted to carry one of the baskets of comforts to the rescued party. One woman, aged nearly one hundred, had been pulled out of the window of a floating house and was wailing in a corner over what she had lost. And there were children of my own age, and people of all ages. I was very sorry for them, and it was long before I connected the disappearance of certain favorite garments -- notably my little blue silk hood -- with my mother's and sister's benevolence, to my own sincere regret. There were many great gales, but this was my first knowledge of the awful power of wind and water.

SAM, SAM, THE JUMPIN' MAN

From the day Father Hennepin first described Niagara Falls, people the world over have come to gaze on its wondrous beauty. Many who have looked upon this beauty have felt a hypnotic power drawing them ever closer to the waters. Standing near the edge of the brink where the waters break out of the rapids and drop in a mad torrent over the 150-foot cliff, they have felt the pull of this magic spell most strongly. Some who fix their eyes steadfastly on the water as it curves over the cap rock, have found the mysterious force almost irresistible. Some even find it necessary to turn their eyes away. A few have been known to walk into the rapids and be swept to death. Others seem to feel a desire to pit their puny strength against the colossal power of Niagara. That many of these attempts have been ludicrous makes them no less tragic, for Niagara does not always stand for such humiliation. Exhibitionists have walked over Niagara on tight cables, flown under its bridges in planes and even rolled over it in barrels and rubber balls. In fact, one man even tried to jump over the Falls. His name was Sam Patch.

> Toll for Sam Patch! Sam Patch, who jumps no more,...
> he scorned the common way
> That leads to fame, up heights of rough ascent,
> And having heard....
> That some great men had risen to falls, he went
> And jumped....

A century ago Sam Patch's name was synonymous with courage and daring; in fact, to jump was "to Sam Patch." He was known throughout the northeastern United States and southern Canada as the man who leapt from the heights of Niagara Falls into the flood of water below. Yet, today he is virtually forgotten -- one of America's more colorful characters has to struggle against the race horse "Dan Patch" for posthumous fame even in his native Rhode Island. Sam was one of the "Comic-heroes" of the mid-nineteenth century but is now generally remembered only by a few folklorists and social historians who tend to chuckle over his motto: "Some things can be done as well as others."

In the early 19th Century there developed in America a genre of humor about extravagant individuals, such as the frontiersman Davey Crockett or the riverboatman Mike Fink. These were exaggerated characters who seem to personify the wild boisterousness of Jacksonian America. Although of more limited fame, Sam Patch was one of these comic-heroic figures. His short career of daredevil exploits produced a legend which flared in the

1830s and '40s only to decline and virtually disappear after the Civil War. He, along with a host of other regional and lesser national characters, suffered eclipse as the nation's interest and attention shifted to heroes of the Wild West and industrialism.

Sam was born in 1807 and lived with his mother Abigail Patch in Pawtucket at 277 Main Street in a building later known as Jones' Schoolhouse. When he was twenty, he worked at Samuel Slater's cotton mill as a mule skinner. For the young men working at the mill, swimming and diving were the principal diversions; and Sam apparently was good at both. One day in 1827 he jumped from the top of Old Yellow Mill, a tall building at the falls in the Blackstone River. When praised for this feat, Sam, for the first of many times, reportedly observed: "Some things can be done as well as others." He came to hit upon what he considered a great truth: "If God can make cataracts, men can certainly jump over them and live." He proceeded to devote the rest of his life to demonstrating this truth -- and to the consumption of rum. However, the Pawtucket town fathers decided that such jumping was dangerous and possibly immoral, and so forbade it. As a result Sam left Pawtucket forever.

He turned up next in Paterson, New Jersey, on September 30, 1827, where he announced that he would jump from a newly completed bridge, a plunge of seventy feet. However, the police stopped him. Undaunted, Sam sprang from a rock overlooking the chasm after proclaiming that Timothy Crane the architect of the bridge had shown them a great feat and that he, Sam Patch, would show them another. Later he jumped from the bridge itself. As a result of these stunts, Sam's fame spread throughout the East and invitations to jump poured in. He went about jumping from yardarms, topmasts, waterfalls and bridges; and when business was slack, Sam would choose his own jumping spot and pass a hat. During these travels he acquired a trained black bear. Sometimes as an added attraction he would push the bear over a waterfall and jump in after him. The crowds enjoyed this immensely; the bear did not. Sam's next recorded jump was at Hoboken in August, 1828, when he jumped ninety feet into the Hudson River before 500 spectators.

In the fall of 1829 Sam was invited to jump over Niagara Falls by a group of hotel keepers from Buffalo and Canada who wanted some favorable publicity for the falls. The honeymoon trade had slackened after the autumn of 1826 as a result of rumors that William Morgan who had been abducted and vanished after betraying Masonic secrets, had been murdered and his body thrown over the falls. The promoters planned a great show to consist of an explosion of 10,000,000 tons of table rock, the descent of the falls by a schooner and Sam Patch's leap. However, the festival was not much of a success. The roar of the falls muffled the sound of the explosion; the schooner ran aground on Goat Island and so did not go over the falls; and Sam failed to appear. So as not to disappoint the crowd or endanger his reputation, Sam did jump -- 130 feet into the chasm -- the next afternoon, October 7, despite the rain and the fact that his platform had broken in half. Newspapers reported the event as "a wonderful prodigious jump, such as mortal man has never made before" and "the greatest feat of the kind ever effected by man." An eyewitness wrote:

> Sam ascended the ladder and remained on top about ten minutes, resting himself and adjusting his position for the leap, during which he was repeatedly cheered by the spectators. At length he rose -- every eye was bent intently on him -- he waved his hand, and kissed the star-spangled banner that floated gracefully o'er his head, and then precipitated himself like an arrow into the flood below! 'Twas a matchless and tremendous leap. He very soon reappeared and swam to the shore with great ease. . . all rushed foreward (who were below) to take the jumping hero by the hand; and the intrepid Sam spoke to the first, 'There's no mistake in Sam Patch!' and by the waving of handkerchiefs and the huzza of the company there was no mistake, for with one consent they exclaimed. 'This is the real Sam Patch.'

That some doubted Sam would actually perform was suggested by an incident which reportedly took place the night before this jump. Sam had been sitting quietly in the taproom of his hotel, drinking rum with his pet bear at his side when some Irishmen from Buffalo entered, angry at the mishaps of the day. One asked Sam: "And will you be jumping tomorrow, slight man?"
Sam replied "Some things can be done as well as others."
The Irishman persisted: "And there's no hoax about it then. You'll lepp [sic]?"
Sam responded: "Of course, I will. There is no mistake in Sam Patch."
When Sam kept his word, the Irish bestowed upon him the honorific "Mr. Samuel O'Cataract, Esquire."
On October 12, 1829, Sam addressed a letter to the people of Western New York and Upper Canada announcing another jump over Niagara on the 17th because so few had been able to see him. He declared that he had jumped the first time to prove that "I was the TRUE SAM PATCH, and to show that some things can be done as well as others; which was denied before I made the jump." He made this second jump over Niagara and continued to jump frequently for the rest of the month. However, "The roar of Niagara had gotten into his head and some of its thunder into his mouth. He strutted. He waved his arms. Where he once sat quietly with his bear, he bellowed and banged on the bar." Gone was the quiet,

self-effacing man who said simply that "Some things can be done as well as others." Now he was Sam Patch, Conqueror of Niagara.

In November he went to Rochester. He was, as he said, "determined to astonish the natives of the West before returning to the Jarseys." Sam had stopped by the Genesee Falls while traveling to Niagara and had made soundings of the river and performed a practice jump. On November 6, he leapt publically at the Genesee Falls. The Anti-Masonic Enquirer, a Rochester newspaper exclaimed, "It was a frightful leap, but he performed it gracefully and fearlessly. It drew an immense concourse of people into the village. Great publicity preceded another jump scheduled for November 13th. The posters ironically declared that it was to be "Sam's last Jump." They read"

HIGHER YET
Sam's last Jump
"Some Things Can Be Done as Well as Others"
There is no mistake in
SAM PATCH!

A crowd of over 7,000 attended this last jump. An eyewitness reported that "the village was thronging with people from the country all anxious to see the amphibious jumper. . . ." Sam had already taken to wearing white tights but his costume at Rochester was unparalleled. He wore white pantaloons over his linsey-woolsey trousers, slippers on his feet, a big black silk sash around his waist, a woollen vest over his shirt and a knitted cap. On this occasion, too, he made the longest speech of his career. He boasted:

Napoleon was a great man and a great general. He conquered armies and he conquered nations, but he couldn't jump the Genesee Falls. Wellington was a great man and great soldier. He conquered armies and he conquered nations and he conquered Napoleon, but he couldn't jump the Genesee Falls. That was left for me to do and I can do it and will.

But, then, Sam had forebodings --his last request was that if anything should happen to him a collection be taken up for his mother.

The Manufacturers' and Farmers' Journal, the most important Providence and Pawtucket newspaper at the time reported the event:

Sam made his last jump from a scaffold erected on the brink of the falls, . . . The staging was elevated twenty-five feet. He sprung [sic] fearlessly from it, and descended one-third

365

of the distance as handsomely as he ever did. He then evidently began to droop, his arms were extended and his legs separated; and in this condition he struck the water and sunk [sic] forever! It was a fearful leap and fearfully has it terminated.... He had drunk freely in the morning.

Thus Sam died on Friday the thirteenth, November, 1829, at the age of twenty-two.

Sam's body was found the following Saint Patrick's Day in the river about six miles below Rochester when a farmer broke the ice to water his cows. It was known to be Sam by the black sash around his waist. He was buried in Charlotte Cemetery in Rochester. The identifying marker read, "Here lies Sam Patch, Such is Fame." It has since been removed and in 1948 the citizens of Rochester, mainly through the efforts of a high school student, placed a granite marker and plaque over Sam's resting place. Sam's next leap was to have been from London Bridge. He had already made arrangements with the captain of a ship sailing to Liverpool to go with him and jump from the yardarm every fair day for the amusement of the passengers.

What sort of man Sam was is difficult to ascertain. Indeed, some still debate the question. Richard Dorsen, an American folklorist said that he exemplified the folk hero of Jacksonian America. Recently, however, Gerald Parsons argues that Sam was reckless, mad, an "egomaniac" and "a young crackpot" whose slogans and posters "were marked by a kind of feebleminded extravagance that is found nowadays mostly on the signboards of certain pathetic creatures that we see strolling big city sidewalks." He denied that Sam Patch was a folk hero at all, but that his death was seen in his time to be senseless.

Hubert Wisely disputed Parsons' conclusions saying that Parsons hadn't done the proper research -- Sam was considered by the natives of upstate New York as "a foolhardy but courageous man who pushed his luck too far." He pointed out too that the Penn Central Railroad (now Conrail) used to stop at the Genesee River so that passengers could see the spot from which Sam jumped. Wisely concluded: "Actual hero or not, Sam Patch is certainly an authentic folk character and probably more of a 'hero' to the 'folk' than to sophisticates of his own day or today."

In any event, Dorson maintains that while different people in his own day called Sam "an ignorant loafer," "an intrepid, debonair acrobat" and a "devoted son." Whatever his actual traits they speedily disappeared before the onset of myth. In the 1830s and 1840s numerous poems, ballads, tales and plays were written about him. Some even refused to believe he had died. Reports of him turned up in a number of places afterward, including a letter supposedly from Patch saying, "You must know that I performed my last jump by proxy, and died by proxy." Some claimed he had hidden in the rocks below; and the tall tales asserted that he had jumped clear through the earth and came up swimming in the South Pacific.

The immediate reactions to his death were somber and even moralizing. The Anti-Masonic Enquirer declared that Sam had been "reckless," and the jump had been a "daring and useless exposure of human life." A local literary magazine "The Gem," said, "Thus has Sam Patch, who had rashly, but till now uninjured, sported with the law of nature, given us an example that vain and mortal man may not trifle with bounds prescribed by an Omniscient God."

Nathaniel Hawthorne reacted characteristically when he wrote:

How stern a moral lesson may be drawn from the story of poor Sam Patch. . . . Was the leaper of cataracts more mad or foolish than other men who throw away life, or spend it in pursuit of empty fame, and seldom so triumphantly as he?

Elsewhere, the comments contained praise. The National Gazette (Philadelphia) proclaimed that the country "could have better spared a better man." The U.S. Gazette (Philadelphia) suggested that the keeper of the Temple of Fame clear a place for Sam Patch and let the panegyric take note that Sam's "ambition was without bloodshed and his patriotism was pure for he fell in his country's falls."

The Manufacturers' and Farmers' Journal printed the following elegy:

"ATTENTION GIVE"

Good people, all, attention give.
And list with mournful brow,
If you have any tears to shed,
Prepare to shed them now.
Sam Patch is dead, that famous man;
We'll ne'er see him more.
He used to wear and old felt hat
With rim torn all before.
His jacket was of iron grey,
His heart was full of glee
They say he's killed by jumping off
The falls of Genesee.
Full six score feet they say he jumped
And struck upon his side.
He sunk beneath the roaring flood
And thus Sam Patch he died.

Yet, the comic character of Sam's fame led to irrepressible editorial punning about his death -- such phrasing as divers time, a

367

drop too much, untimely bier, and this sad fall described Sam's last leap. His fatal plunge eventually evoked laughter, as this poem of the 1840s suggests:

> Poor Samuel Patch -- a man once world renouned
> Much loved the water, and by it was drowned.
> He sought for fame, and as he reached to pluck it,
> He lost his ballast, and then kicked the bucket.

The extent of Sam's living reputation is difficult to learn. He had traveled all over the East and as far west as upstate New York. Contemporary Rhode Island newspapers, at least, referred to him familiarly as "Sam Patch, the jumper." After his death, newspapers and the stage made much better known .

Robert Sands wrote a biography of Sam in nineteen Byronic stanzas classifying him far above Leander, Sappho, Icarus, Helle and Empedocles. Seba Smith, creator of Jack Downing, wrote a ballad about Sam. E. H. Thompson wrote two New York plays: *Sam Patch or the Daring Yankee* and *Sam Patch in France.* According to the Annals of the New York Stage, the plays were performed from 1837 to 1849 with Danforth Marble, a famous Yankee portraiturist, as Sam Patch. The plays were one act farces in which Sam did daring deeds, fell in love and, in the end, leapt over Niagara Falls in a "union of courage and virtue proving some things can be done was well as others." The handbills announced: "Mr. Marble will leap from the extreme height of the theatre, a feat never attempted by anyone but himself and prove that 'cold water won't drown love.'" This cost Marble many minor bruises and a stand-in broke his leg and dislocated his hip by repeating Sam's Genesee mistake and landing on his side.

Dorson maintains that few people in the 1830s and 40s could have escaped all the Patch literature. Dan Marble performed as far west as Ohio where "hardy western applause greeted his jumping" and according to Marble's biographer, the Sam Patch pieces set everybody in a jumping fever. The boys in the street *jumped*, the old folks *jumped*, clerks *jumped* counters and the rustics *jumped* fences! The supernumeraries *jumped*, actors and actresses *jumped*. The mania for "doing Sam Patch" was general. . . .

German immigrants at Rochester built a beergarden next to the falls (a fitting memorial for Sam) and wrote poetry to "Der Sampatsch." One such poem begins:

> In the Bierhaus garden I linger
> By the Falls of Genesee
> From the rock that's in the middle
> Leaps Der Sampatsch, bold and free.

Sam's fame persisted for some time. Later in the century, about 1870, a picture book called The Wonderful Leaps of Sam Patch was published for children. In the colorful biography Sam began his career by leaping from his mother's lap. The verses were all in dastardly rhymes. It began:

> Come and hear the story told
> Of the feats of Sam the Bold
> All the heroes ever seen --
> Heroes fat and heroes lean;
> Heroes short and heroes tall!
> Heroes heavy and heroes light
> Heroes black and heroes white
> Up from General Thumb, the plucky
> To the giant of Kentucky,
> Were not fit to hold a match
> To our hero, Sammy Patch!

Sam's name popped up in other places. William Dean Howells showed a familiarity with Sam in *Their Wedding Journey*. A young husband defended Sam's name: "It's just as good a name as Leander to my thinking and it was immortalized in support of a great idea -- the feasibility of all things. . . . William Carlos Williams, too, devoted several pages of his poem *Patterson* to Sam.

Sam Patch was a typical American comic-hero. Daniel Boorstin sees the comic-hero resulting from the ambiguity and incongruity of American life. America was a half-known country with uncertain boundaries and dubious landforms. Sam lived at a time when the Great Plains were called the "Great American Desert" and thought to be fit only for Indians and buffalo and when people believed the Great Salt Lake was part of the Pacific Ocean. The American style of talking and advertising was half truth, half fiction. The heroes of the age ranged from a mythologized George Washington to comic supermen like Davy Crockett. There was a lack of clarity; the laughable and the admirable, the wonderful and the ridiculous were never far apart.

Sam's era was the age of Andrew Jackson -- a period of national movement, growth and expansions. John Ward argues that a strong impulse of the age was "to restrain philosophising." Humility and prudence played no part. It was a philosophy of action in which thought was subordinate. Henry Nash Smith has pointed out that major themes in American literature throughout the 19th Century emphasized action-fighting like Daniel Boone, James Fenimore Cooper's "Leatherstocking," Davey Crockett and Kit Carson.   Richard Jofstadter has argued that politics, religion and education itself have strong traditions of antagonism to the life of the mind in America; and the Jacksonion period found the stream of anti-intellectualism in all three realms at a high point. The Presidential election in 1828 brought the tendency of the period into sharp relief with "John Quincy Adams who can write. And Andrew Jackson who can fight."

Elsewhere, a Jacksonian said: "Jackson made law, Adams quoted it." Jackson won easily; the man of action defeated the man of contemplation. The summit was hit in 1840 when Indian fighting, a log cabin and hard cider became qualifications for the Presidency. The impulse of the time was on doing rather than thinking. As Ward suggests, Jackson, the symbol of the period, was idealized for being a man of action and will. And Alexis de Tocqueville noted contemporaneously in the Democracy in America that "The Americans, then, have found no need of drawing philosophical methods out of books; they have found it in themselves."

Thus might the basic philosophy of the age might well be stated: "Some things can be done as well as others." Sam Patch simply iterated the philosophy and applied it to waterfalls.

Sam was a unique mixture of two traditions of humor in America. The oldest was the Yankee character which originated in colonial times with the "Brother Jonathan" anecdotes and continues even today in jokes about the Yankee farmer of few words. Sam was portrayed on stage as "The Daring Yankee" and was later described as "a square shouldered, thick-set boy whose rather broad face wore an expression of perpetual placidity which was pretty close to a dumb stare." One typical form of the changing Yankee tradition was this imperturbable demeanor and the laconic utterances of the character. Sam's two sentences "Some things can be done as well as others" and "There's no mistake in Sam Patch" generally comprised his entire speech. However, a shrewd, reserved Yankee would not have jumped over a waterfall. In this respect Sam was part of the Ring-Tailed Roarer tradition -- the boastful humor of the new American west of the 1830s. This was the humor of exaggerations and tall tales, of Davey Crockett, Mike Fink, Billy Earthquake and Pompey Smash. Typical was Davey Crockett's boast: "I'm . . . half-horse, half-alligator, a little touched with the snapping turtle; can wade the Mississippi, leap the Ohio, ride upon a streak of lightning and slip without a scratch down a honey locust; can whip my weight in wild-cats. . . hug a bear too close for comfort, and eat any man opposed to Jackson." The adoption of a showy costume and Sam Patch's speech before the leap at the Genesee, in which he compared himself favorably with Napoleon and the Duke of Wellington, are indicative of the Ring-Tailed Roarer side of Sam's character.

Today, however, except for an occasional newspaper reminiscence or a jubilee float in Rochester, Sam is generally forgotten. Dixon Wecter suggests in <u>The Hero in America</u>, "Hero worship flowers most freely in the youth of a race." Or perhaps Sam simply lacked the dimensions of a lasting hero. Wecter worships that comic-heroes like Pecos Bill and Mike Fink are juvenile -- they lack such characteristics as the unselfish service of a popularized Washington or Lincoln. Another factor in Wector's scheme counting against Sam as a continuing hero is his boasting ("No hero must announce that he is infallible. . . ." which Sam did.) Besides humility, Sam also lacked the preferred virtues of hard work, tenacity and informality while he had the unappreciated qualities of profundity and eloquence (all invested in one perfect sentence: "Some things can be done as well as others.") Sam's disesteem seemed to be like that which one writer said to be Paul Bunyan's downfall: ". . . nobody wants to respect him for what he is. People harbor a perpetual desire to start laughing as soon as his name is brought up." Also the very ambiguity of the land which spawned so many of the comic-heroes in the 1830s and 40s was replaced by certainty. The blank spaces in the map were filled-in and surveyed into neat squares. In addition, the Civil War intervened with a new type of hero which was far from comic.

Whatever the reasons, Sam Patch has been forgotten. His life and philosophy have been lost to the popular culture. Sadly, today so few are familiar with Sam's simple philosophy; but its essence lives on: "Some things can be done as well as others."

Chapter Sources

"To Tell The Tale"   Rapp, Marvin A. <u>Canal Water and Whiskey</u> (New York: Twayne Publishers, Inc., 1965)

Bottoming Out   Rapp, 1965

More Bottoming Out   Rapp, 1991

I. The Dream

"Vision of Columbus"   Barlow, Joel (1787)

Heno and the Buffalo Creek   Rapp. (1965 -- Originally titled "As Crooked as the Crick)

How the Canal Was Born   Rapp

Canal Passed by One Vote   Condon, George E. <u>Stars in the Water</u> (Garden City; New York: Double Day & Co., Inc. 1974)

"Federal Son of a Bitch"   Toomey, Jean. <u>Knickerbocker News Union-Star</u> (New York: May 16, 1976)

"Why Grin?"   Merrill, Arch. <u>The Towpath</u> (Rochester: Gannett & Co., 1945)

II. The Digging

"Free as Air"   Rapp. (1965 -- Giles, The Rev. Charles. The Convention of Drunkards. New York, 1840)

Irish Diggers and Whiskey Jiggers   Rapp. (1965 -- Moore, Walter Burritt Public Service of the State of New York Vol.1. Boston: Jones, Osgood & Co. 1883)

"Paddy's Song"   Condon

"Diggin' a Ditch"   Waggoner, Madeline S. The Long Haul West (New York: GP Putnam, 1958)

"Montezuma Mud"   Waggoner

Canal Feeders   Waggoner

Dig a Complete Canal   Rapp. (1965)

Canawl Water and Whiskey   Rapp, Marvin A. New York Folklore Quarterly (NYFQ) Vol. XI No. 4 (Winter, 1955)

" 'Tis Done"   Woodworth, Samuel. (c. 1825; reprinted from Condon)

"Meeting of the Waters"   Hullfish, William. Canallers' Songbook (York, PA: American Canal and Transportation Center, 1984) Written in 1825.

"Master Dixon"   Poet unknown. (Published in Poets and Poetry of Buffalo; James W. Johnson, ed. Matthews Northrup Works, Buffalo, 1904)

The Erie Canal: How Man Made a Miracle   Rapp

"Oh! Rock!   Niagara Democrat (Lockport, NY: Nov. 1, 1843

Canaler vs. Laker   Atkins, Barton . Modern Antiquities (Buffalo: Courier & Co., 1898)

Fish Story   Condon

III. Working on the Towpath

"Canawler, Canawler"   Wyld, Lionel D. Low Bridge (Syracuse: Syracuse University Press, 1962)

Conversation With Team Driver   Scothold, Earl. "Rome and the Canal," Rome, NY: A Centennial History 1870-1970 (Rome, NY: Rome Historical Society Museum, 1970)

Hoggie on the Towpath   Canal Museum Archives, Syracuse

Mule Driver   Syracuse Sunday Herald-American, interview with Raymond Crean (June 13, 1976)

Hoggies and Swamp Ghosts WPA Guide to New York State (Springwater, NY: 1937)

The Erie's Paul Bunyan   "American Folklore & Legends" Reader's Digest, Jane Polley, ed. (Pleasantville, NY: Reader's Digest Association, 1978)

Agnes the Mule   Logan, Nancy. "Look for a Post" (Captain Link, "Spike Galloway's Saloon") NYFQ Vol. XII, No. 4 (Winter, 1956)

"My Old Canal Mule"   Hullfish

Horace the Mule   Canal Museum Archives, Syracuse

"Simon Slick"   Hullfish

Makin' Mules   Broder, Mitch. Rochester Democrat and Chronicle (Rochester, October 19, 1986)

Never Take a Hindshoe From a Mule   Hullfish. (Originally from the show *The Mulligan Guard.*)

A Life Saving Canal Horse   Scientific American Vol. LIII, No. 18; October 31, 1885)

The Rattlesnake Hunter   Winner, Julia Hull. NYFQ Vol. XIV, No. 4 (Winter, 1958)

Rattlesnakes   Centennial History of Rochester (1932)

Rochester Rattlesnakes   Centennial History of Rochester
(1932)
Snakes and Irish Mud   Logan

Big Drought   Logan

Entertainment at the Sidecut   Thompson, Harold. <u>Body, Boots</u>
<u>and</u> <u>Britches</u> (Philadelphia: J.P. Lippincott and Co., 1940)

Canal Sturgeon   Logan

Privy   Logan

9 Million Stone   Highbee, Elizabeth. "They
Remember the Erie Canal" <u>NYFQ</u> Vol. XI, No. 2 (Summer,
1956)

The Day the Bottom Fell Out of the Canal   Brewster, Arthur J.
 <u>Life Was Never Dull</u>

"Fingy" Connors and the Scoopers   McCarthy, Max. "Irish War
on the Waterfront" <u>The</u> <u>Buffalo News</u> (Buffalo: November 4,
1990)

The Arcole Foundry and the Cotton Factory   "Come and Take Me"
<u>The Old Corporal</u> Vol I, No. 1 (Buffalo: October 29, 1849)

"Black Rock Pork"   Thompson

Black Rock Turkey   Merrill

"Hash is Fried"   Bartley, J. "Alhambro Varieties"

IV. Whores, Wastrels and Waterfront Guerrillas

Barbary Coast of the East   Thompson

The Old Corporal   The Old Corporal   Vol. I, No. 1
(Buffalo: October 29, 1849)

Taverns and Trapdoors   Rapp (1965)

"Hole in the Wall"   Buffalo Express (February 5, 1859)

The Drunkard Man   Utica Herald (August, 1854)

Old Beales and Coffee Beans Rapp (1965)

Tall Tale Teller   Rapp (1965)

Hay on the Sun   Rapp (1965)

"The Cholera Cometh"   Adams, Samuel Hopkins.
Grandfather Stories (New York: Random House, 1955)

"If Mr. A"   Adams

Waterfront Pirates: Dublin, Mugger and the Cotton Hook Man
Rapp. (1965 -- Buffalo Times: October 11, 1913)

Burnt Bread and Broom Handles   Rapp. (1965 -- Adapted from
Jack London's The Road. New York: Macmillan and Co., 1907)

V. Canal Entertainment

"Buffalo Gals"   Rapp. (1965 -- Attributed to Edward
Christy; Sung by "Christy's Minstrels," Canal Street, Buffalo)

Peg-Leg Harrison   Matthews, Sylvester J. Memories of
Early Days in Buffalo (Buffalo: Buffalo Historical Society
Publications Vol. XVII)

Millstone Minuet   Atkins

"Towpath Circus"   Hullfish

Pigs and Players   Thompson

Cockfighting   Buffalo Courier-Express, Sunday
Magazine (October 19, 1980)

Koonin'   Buffalo Express (August 3, 1870)

Kitty on a Pedestal   Rapp (1965)

Sam, Sam the Jumpin' Man   Rapp (1965)

VI. Water, Wine and Whiskey

Water, Water Everywhere   Rapp. (1965 -- Nichols, Thomas. <u>Forty Years of American Life</u>. New York: Johnson Reprint Corp.)

Fresh Water and Free Wine   Rapp (1965)

Drinking Water   Lender, Mark Edward and James Kirby Martin. <u>Drinking in America</u> (New York: The Free Press, 1982)

I'd Rather Drink Buttermilk   <u>Buffalo Express</u> (July 29, 1847)

Mixing an Erie Canal Cocktail   Adapted from Lender & Martin, <u>Drinking in America</u>

Recipe for Whiskey   Adapted from Lender & Martin, <u>Drinking in America</u>

Drink   Mather, Increase. <u>Wo To Drunkards</u> (1673 -- Reprinted in <u>Drinking in America)</u>

"The American Toast"   Rapp. (1965 -- Rothman's East Norwich Inn, East Norwich, Long Island, 1732)

Five Reasons For Drinking   "Beers' Calendar" (1825)

Temperance-Intemperance   Lender & Martin

Skeleton in the Closet: LeGrand Marvin   Hollister, Frank. <u>Early Characters of Buffalo</u> (Buffalo: Buffalo Historical Society Publications, 1913)

Drinking and Thinking   <u>Buffalo Express</u> (Buffalo: May 26, 1847)

"Convention of Drunkards"   Giles, The Rev. Charles. <u>The Triumph of Truth</u> (New York, 1840)

Penn Yan   McIntosh, W.H. <u>History of Ontario County, New York</u> (Philadelphia: Lippincott, 1876)

Smelling of the Bar Rag   Thompson

"Temperance Rhyme"   Lender & Martin

How the Teetotalers Got Their Name   Lender & Martin

Teetotaler's Oath	Adams
Temperance to Dry	Lender & Martin
"To a Poor Old Bum"	Thompson
Loafer Jim	Buffalo Express (October 24, 1846)
Deacon Wormwood and the Drunk	Hollister
Description of Whiskey	Lender & Martin
"The Er-i-e"	Hullfish
Tavern Tippling	Canal Museum Archives
Tavern in a Tree Trunk	New York State Heritage, Vol. 6, No. 6 (July/August 1990)
"Liquor and Longevity"	Rapp (1965)
Tale of the Pickled Porkers	Rapp (1965)
"Ode to a Drunkard"	Rapp
"Come, Come Away, Ho"	Marvin, LeGrand. The Benefits of Rum
The Case of the Stiff Canawler	Rapp. NYFQ Vol. XII, No. 3 (Fall, 1956)

VII. Life on the Raging Canal

Commending My Soul to God   Lewis, Mrs. Gilbert. New England Pioneers   (Rochester: Rochester Historical Society, Vol. VIII, 1929)

Leaves Wife in Syracuse   Waggoner

Passing the Lock   Buffalo Patriot and Commercial Advertiser (September 13, 1837)

"Low Bridge, Everybody Down"   Hullfish. (Thomas Allen, 1905)

Bridges Low   Woodrock, Thomas   Fifteen Miles on the Erie Canal (1836)

"Oh! Dat Low Bridge"   Hullfish. (Written for a vaudeville show, *The Grip*, in the 1880s. Music by David Brigham, lyrics by Edward Harrigan)

Corns Cured   Haydon, Roger. Upstate Travels (Syracuse: Syracuse University Press, 1982)

To Bed Aboard a Canal Boat Dunbar, Seymour. History of Travel in America (New York: Tudor Publishing Co, 1937)

Fat Man in a Berth   Gerstaeker, Frederick. Wild Sports of the Far West (Boston: Crosby, Nicholson & Co., 1859)

Like a "Working" Barrel of Beer   Buffalo Express (October 24, 1846)

Agriculture   Haddock, DeWitt C. Utica Daily Press (August 6, 1897)

Game to the Last   Adapted from the Buffalo Express (January 23, 1846)

Frog in Stone   Merrill

The Empeyville Frog   Littler, Joan. NYFQ Vol. XI, No. 2 (Summer, 1958)

Mark Twain in Buffalo   Paine, Albert. Mark Twain's Letters (New York and London: Harper and Row, 1924)

"Let the Storm Come Down" Thompson

A Storm on the Canal   Buffalo Express (1846)

The Raging Canal   Graham, Lloyd. The Niagara
Country (New York: Duell, Sloan & Pierce, 1949)

"The Raging Canawl"   Hullfish (Steven Foster, 1949)

"The Aged Pilot Man"   Twain, Mark. (S.L. Clemens;
Roughing It New York: Harper & Bros., 1924)

VII. Here, There and Everywhere

The Irishman and the Falls   Rapp

God Made Niagara Falls   Paine

Garden of Eden   Twain, Mark. "Adam's Diary"
The Niagara Book (Buffalo: Underhill and Nicholas, 1893)

The Tailor and the Falls   Edwards, C.R. A Story of Niagara
(Buffalo: Breed, Lent and Co., 1870)

Cave of the Winds and a Breath of Whiskey   Power, Tyrone.
Impressions of America During the Years 1833-1834 (London:
Richard Bentley, 1836)

At Niagara Falls   Edwards

Holy Water and Whiskey   Edwards

A Whiskey Smuggler   Edwards

The Ghost of Lock Herkimer Rapp

Whiskey and the Ghost   WPA Guide to New York

Swamp Water and Gallinippers   Condon

Bunions, Blisters and Bootlikker High, Norma. "Folklife Across
the Frontier" NYFQ   Vol. XII, No. 4 (Winter, 1956)

The Devil Wore a Cane and a Crutch Rapp. NYFQ Vol. XIII,
No. 2 (Summer, 1957)

Adirondack Stories   Rapp

The Buckskin Rifleman   Atwell, Charles and Marvin A.
Rapp. American Rifleman NRA (c.1941)

The Deer of Panther Lake   Atwell & Rapp

Waterways of New York   Bottoming Out (the official
publication of the Canal Historical Society of New York State)
Vol. III, No. 1 (October 1958)

IX. Mayhem, Murder, Mystery and Mischief

The Philosophy of Crime   Buffalo Express (November 13, 1869)

Irish Sense of Humor   Thompson

Chippy Connolly   Thompson

You Eat It   Reader's Digest, "American Folklore and Legends" Jane Polley, ed. (1978)

Bucko Ben and Sleepy Frank   Schisino, Gerald. The National Hotel, Cuylerville, NY

Murder a Day   Rapp (1965)

Man on a Mule   Burkin, Ernst O. (Stratford, NY) Letter to Martha Brooks (Schenectady, NY) October 12, 1965

The Man Without a Sleeve   Rapp (1965)

Epitaph   "The Glory Hole" NYFQ Vol. XVI, No. 2 (Summer, 1960)

Of Sand and Time   Rapp (1965)

"I Discovered America"   Siemsen, Harry. NYFQ Vol. XX, No. 1 (Spring, 1964)

Black Becomes the Bride's Ghost   Rapp (1965)

Whiskey Cargo and John Wilkes Booth   Rapp (1965)

Freedom in the Woodpile   Rapp. NYFQ Vol. XIV, No. 1 (Spring, 1958)

The Story Behind a Folk Hero   Rapp

Helmsman of Lake Erie   Rapp (1965)

"John Maynard"   Attributed to Horatio Alger

"John Maynard"   Fontane, Theodor

Jim Bludso   Hay, John

Narrow Escape From Drowning   <u>Buffalo Commercial Advertiser</u>
(October 6, 1868)

The Empty Bottle   Daca's New Door Bookstore, New
York City

INDEX

Republic Steam Presses, Buffulo.